THE COLLECTED LETTERS OF
KATHERINE MANSFIELD

VOLUME TWO

1918–1919

Passport photograph of Katherine Mansfield, August 1919.

THE COLLECTED
LETTERS OF

KATHERINE
MANSFIELD

EDITED BY

VINCENT O'SULLIVAN

WITH

MARGARET SCOTT

VOLUME TWO

1918–1919

CLARENDON PRESS · OXFORD
1987

Oxford University Press, Walton Street, Oxford OX2 6DP
Oxford New York Toronto
Delhi Bombay Calcutta Madras Karachi
Petaling Jaya Singapore Hong Kong Tokyo
Nairobi Dar es Salaam Cape Town
Melbourne Auckland
and associated companies in
Beirut Berlin Ibadan Nicosia

Oxford is a trade mark of Oxford University Press

Published in the United States
by Oxford University Press, New York

British Library Cataloguing in Publication Data
Mansfield, Katherine
The collected letters of Katherine Mansfield.
Vol. 2: 1918–1919
1. Mansfield, Katherine—Bibliography
2. Novelists, New Zealand—20th century—Bibliography
I. Title   II. O'Sullivan, Vincent, 1937–
III. Scott, Margaret, 1928–
823   PR6025.A572/
ISBN 0–19–812614–X

Library of Congress Cataloging in Publication Data
(Revised for vol. 2)
Mansfield, Katherine, 1888–1923.
The collected letters of Katherine Mansfield.
Vol. 2– :Oxford [Oxfordshire]: Clarendon Press;
New York: Oxford University Press.
Includes bibliographical references and indexes.
Contents: v. 1. 1903–1917—v. 2. 1918–1919.
1. Mansfield, Katherine, 1888–1923—Correspondence.
2. Authors, New Zealand—20th century—Correspondence.
I. O'Sullivan, Vincent.   II. Scott, Margaret, 1928– .
III. Title.
PR9639.3.M258Z48   1984   823'.912   83–12189
ISBN 0–19–812613–1 (v. 1)

Set by Hope Services, Abingdon, Oxon.
Printed in Great Britain
at the University Printing House, Oxford
by David Stanford
Printer to the University

CONTENTS

INTRODUCTION

When Katherine Mansfield left England early in January 1918 she was sure that her illness was a temporary inconvenience, and that a few months of Mediterranean climate would restore her health. Her usual excitement at again being on the road was enough to carry her through a trying journey without her good humour being too impaired. The unheated carriages, an absence of porters, unruly soldiery, and a pain in her chest like a 'flat-iron' could be sustained well enough with the prospect of Bandol at the end. It was there after all that she had been happiest with Murry, and done some of her best writing. So she could pass the trip off lightly to her friend the Scottish painter J. D. Fergusson: 'I would not do it again for all the oranges and lemons and lovely girls dans tout ce pays.' But she told him what did bother her. 'I thought last night it is a bad thing during this war to be apart from the one or two people who do count in one's life. After all we are not solitary palm trees in deserts – thank God – we are groups of two or three with a spring of sweet water between us and a piece of grassy shade' (15 January 1918). And the fact of the matter was that the winter journey had set her back considerably. Within a couple of weeks she would admit it to Murry – 'I have been *bloody ill*' (20 January 1918).

In those extracts Mansfield touches on two of the factors that will dominate this second volume of her letters, written from a few months into her twenty-ninth year until just before her thirty-first birthday. These were her sense of isolation, soon to be exacerbated by the rages that went with her consumption; and the War, which lay so strongly on her thinking that even when peace was declared she saw its effects as enduring scars.

The delight Mansfield always took in returning to France buoyed her through the first weeks. 'There was simply one word that flew over the place like a flag. BEAU . . . "I' fait vraiment beau" ' (24 January 1918). Her letters share her pleasure in simply watching southern life. But then there is the inevitable swerve as remembered characters from her last visit disappoint, as men pester her, as old acquaintances bore, and her cough persists. And it is Murry who must carry the weight of deferred hopes. 'Youre my country', she tells him, 'my people – my whole life is bound up in yours' (26 January 1918). Thus resumes that established routine where love between the two of them is proportionate to how successfully everyone else is held at bay. Because there is this insistence that nothing else really matters, there is a quickness to turn minor mishaps, a late letter, a delayed reply, into occasions of reprimand or grief. The pendulum of her feelings effectively cuts down other friendships, which are construed only as threats. Before Ida Baker arrives in Bandol she is commended as having already 'been an angel to me', but also condemned as 'a ghoul' (24 January 1918). Lady Ottoline Morrell sends a concerned letter, and as Mansfield 'reads between the lines' she decides 'We must not make her an enemy – but oh she is *corrupt* – *corrupt*'. While the unfortunate French, blessed with a country that is 'the very most exquisite enchanting place', do not even merit a capital letter as she pours her Anglo-Saxon contempt. 'I am very sincere when I say I *hate* the french . . . . As *animals* they are interesting monkeys but they have no heart – no heart at all' (27 January 1918).

It is almost as though any kind of warmth or honesty in life must be confined to Murry and herself. Yet again in a vein familiar from the first volume of her letters, 'My grown up self sees us like two little children who have been turned out into the garden' (28 January 1918). Murry in return fed these notions of precious exclusiveness, her insistence that 'this grown up world everywhere *dont* fit me' (6 February 1918). Very soon she would dream and write down her story 'Sun and Moon', drawing from that same privileged perspective, but the magic circle in fact collapsing as reality stakes its claim. But there is a far more mature voice, telling another story. Mansfield's Francophobia, her memories of Francis Carco, and the opportunity fiction presented for coldly operating on her own feelings towards Murry, each contributed something as she began work on *Je ne parle pas français*. So much already in the letters flares out in that account of French cynicism and betrayal, the too cautious Englishman and the deserted woman. Mansfield herself said she had no idea where it came from, but Murry frankly told her she had 'begun to drag the depths of your *consciousness* . . . . You are looking into yourself'.[1]

The letters written at the same time as that story set out the corrosive angers that for the time being fill her mind. There is Ida Baker, devoted and obedient, true, but also 'revolting' and 'hysterical' (12 February 1918). And there is the confrontation of armies a few hundred miles from where she wrote: 'its never out of my mind – & everything is poisoned by it. Its *here in* me the whole time, eating me away' (3 February 1918).

Mansfield felt the War and her illness were inseparable, and knew how writing could be affected by both. 'I have a horror of the way this war creeps into writing . . . oozes in – trickles in' (13 February 1918). While the consuming nature of her disease seems to provoke those frequent images of eating and devouring, of threatening animals

---

[1] 8 February 1918, *The Letters of John Middleton Murry to Katherine Mansfield*, ed. C. A. Hankin (1983), 115.

and disturbing insects, that emerge in her fiction and notebooks and correspondence. There is an increasing sense that either barriers are being erected between herself and the world she wants, or external threat is drawing closer. She tells Murry 'You cant imagine how I feel that I walk alone in a sort of black glittering case like a beetle'. At the same time, 'My night terrors here are rather complicated by packs & packs of growling, roaring, ravening, prowl and prowl around dogs.' To add to the menagerie 'there is a great black bird flying over me and I am so frightened he'll settle – so terrified. I dont know exactly what *kind* he is' (3 February 1918).

The link between this state of mind and the condition of her lungs became apparent with her first haemorrhage. She hurried to assure Murry that the bleeding was not serious, and 'absolutely easily curable' (19 February 1918). But she herself faced the possibilities from the start. On the same day she wrote in a notebook the thoughts that immediately came into her mind. She wanted more than anything else to be with Murry. And she acknowledged the fear that she might die before she had written much more. '*That's what matters. How unbearable it would be to die, leave "scraps", "bits"* . . . *nothing real finished*' (*Journal* 1954, 129).

Here then is Mansfield saying what she will repeat dozens of times in the next few years: that yes, of course she is ill, there is no denying that. But no, they would not accept it for what it might seem to others. Boge and Wig, those *enfants du Paradis*, would charm threat away with their '*absolute faith* and *hope* and *love*'. It was a matter of having to stand by that certainty, or conceding that something outside themselves held the winning hand. For the moment, though, in Bandol, 'to be on alien shores with L.M. a very shady medicine man and a crimson lake hanky is about as near Hell as I want to be' (20 February 1918).

With a serious illness and war standing between her and everything she hankered after nearly a thousand miles away in England, it hardly surprises that Mansfield tended to see her life as a clear-cut contest between what she wanted and what increasingly malign circumstances permitted her. A similar and rather schematic clarity struck her as explaining the obvious division in her stories. On the one side she saw the feeling of 'real joy' which lay behind her working on *The Aloe* when she was in Bandol two years before. On the other, what she believed prompted her now, that 'cry against corruption' as she explained to Murry her '*extremely* deep sense of hopelessness – of everything doomed to disaster' (3 February 1918). What it was that distressed her, and yet drove her to write, was her intense feeling of possibilities withering, a more and more commanding sense of stupidity and waste. The associations that massed around the words 'home' and 'work' were the strongest supports available to her.

The journey back from Bandol to London in April, for all the discomfort of the three weeks she spent under bombardment in a besieged Paris, had at its promised end the marriage that Mansfield looked forward to far more than she would reveal to any of her friends. It was to be the seal to that familiar and serious game of 'little mates' (18 January 1918). It would mean that her increasing hope 'faire un enfant' was within sight. The protective certainty that she looked for in her living with Murry, but felt only intermittently, now seemed the logical consequence to their legal commitment to each other. There was also the social fact of being Mrs Murry. For ten years she had carried the name of 'Kathleen Bowden' on her passport, a reminder of escapade and mistake. She had to face her family with what they thought was a quasi-bohemian lover, while her sisters married well. To be a mistress when friends like Virginia Woolf and Anne Drey were wives was something that mattered to Mansfield. And as she told Murry even after they were married, 'my whole soul waits for the time when you and I shall be withdrawn from everybody'. Yet there is a foreboding that surfaces through whatever hopes she mustered, a kind of cruising fear that 'A very dark obscure thing seems to . . . *threaten* these desires' (8 June 1918).

Something of that fear was domesticated, so to speak, with Murry's own behaviour on the day of their wedding. She reminded him a month later, when circumstances again compelled them to live apart, 'Our marriage – You cannot imagine what that was to have meant to me . . . . It was to have shone – apart from all else in my life – And it really was only part of the nightmare, after all. You never once held me in your arms & called me your wife. In fact the whole affair was like my silly birthday. I had to keep on making you remember it' (27 May 1918).

So the pattern keeps on. What Mansfield, in that same letter, called her 'terrible – exhausting – utterly INTENSE love' at times bewildered her husband with its quick, exquisitely-pointed alterations, its accusations and subsequent regrets. While she spent so much time alone, refining on that closed-circuit of apprehension and hope, Murry was extraordinarily conscientious in his work at the War Office and frequently exhausted. He was in charge of his section of Intelligence, and his efforts were recognized with an OBE. In the evenings he worked at reviewing French fiction for *The Times Literary Supplement* and political journalism for the *Nation*. He also wrote to his wife every day. He was as dependent on her fluctuations of mood, on her approval and warmth, as Mansfield was on his. As he tells her after she has set out his failings, 'It's comic how with one letter I am left shivering & naked . . . . You say it all so beautifully that you must have meant it as it was written.'[2] She is then swung by 'hideous remorse & regret' (27 May 1918) in what so frequently is a painful correspondence. Yet Mansfield's vivacity, for all that, is the constant note of her letters, her *élan* as she records the life that surrounds her. There are the same dashes of mood, sympathy, insight, that distinguish her stories. There is that same febrile acuteness, the sense that to grasp at so much so quickly is not quite separable from a deep temperamental reluctance to expect that anything endures. The bright seductions of detail are the other side to her pressing consciousness of time. 'As I write the willows fly streaming in the sun – & someone is playing the piano – oh! so wonderfully – seeking out, gently, tenderly, with light, whimsical fingers *something* . . . . Isn't it awful to feel full of life and love and work and joy & to think one will have to turn up one's toes & be still one day –' (to Brett, 7 June 1919).

Occasionally there were people like Mrs Honey, the old woman who looked after her in Cornwall, who reminded Mansfield that life could be simple and straightforwardly honest. More often her 'innermost "credo"' was that life is 'loathesomely ugly'. How that phrase goes back to the teenage girl so under the spell of Oscar Wilde, in those days when she believed that Life, like Art, could be shaped to what one wished. Yet as she explained to Lady Ottoline, there were also the intimations of 'something at the back of it all' which, if understood, 'would make *everything* . . . indescribably beautiful'. It was there only in 'glimpses, divine warnings – signs' (16 July 1918).

Even after the Armistice the vast corruption of the War continued to possess her. Her distaste for fashionable jingoism during the hostilities had led her to refuse the re-issue of *In a German Pension*. Those early stories with their simplistic dislike of Germans she did not want turned to the ends of propaganda. In peacetime, she objected quite as much to the rampage of victory, writing to Lady Ottoline in the week of celebrations over the Peace Treaty how 'These preparations for Festivity are too odious . . . . When I read of the preparations that are being made in all the workhouses throughout the land – when I think of all these toothless old jaws guzzling for the day – and then of all that beautiful youth feeding the fields of France . . . . I keep seeing all these horrors, bathing in them again & again (God knows I don't want to) and then my mind fills with the wretched little picture I have of my brother's grave – What is the meaning of it all?' (*c.* 13 July 1919).

By the time Mansfield wrote that her strongest bid for domesticity was well under way. But the pleasure she took in her new house in late

---

[2] 24 May 1918, *The Letters of John Middleton Murry to Katherine Mansfield*, 152.

August 1918, in decorating its rooms and handling its servants, in the business of actually running a *home*, was tempered at its beginning by her mother's recent death in Wellington. Annie Burnell Beauchamp was fifty-four. Mansfield's own illness over the past year seems to have given her a fresh appreciation of her delicate mother. What she remembered now was not the maternal coolness that survives in several of her family stories, but the gaiety, the '*high courage*' she would now like to show herself. 'She *lived* every moment of Life more fully and completely than anyone Ive ever known' (to Brett, 14 August 1918). Although the example could scarcely be sustained when it came to husbands. In the business of supporting one's ailing wife, Middleton Murry was no Harold Beauchamp, nor did he pretend to be. Money continued as something that he guarded cautiously, to the extent of concealing from Mansfield how much he actually earned. Each kept separate accounts, each meticulously paid his or her share. But in 1919, between Murry's £800 as editor of the *Athenaeum*, her own allowance of £300 a year, and whatever each made from journalism and stories, there was a middle-class comfort at 2 Portland Villas.

The house was put in order in other ways as well. Mansfield had resumed the friendships with Koteliansky, Beatrice and Gordon Campbell, and Mark Gertler, that had fallen away in the previous two years. With Koteliansky especially, real closeness was renewed. For a time Virginia Woolf became considerably more than an acquaintance. Bloomsbury called in the figures of E. M. Forster and Desmond MacCarthy; T. S. Eliot and Aldous Huxley were more or less friends; Bertrand Russell came back. The malicious turning against Lady Ottoline at Bandol had been replaced by affection. Dorothy Brett joined Anne Drey as Mansfield's most intimate female friends. Ida Baker, who lived in, continued in that ambiguous role that demanded her variously as confidante, companion–servant, 'slave'. D. H. Lawrence, even more vacillating in his friendships than Mansfield, was again on good terms for a time. It was Virginia Woolf who guessed early on at the darker currents that flowed through Portland Villas in those months when Mansfield was too ill to leave the house. When she visited in November 1918 she noted her friend's physical debility, her husky voice, the 'childlikeness somewhere which has been much disfigured, but still exists', and the suspicions she harboured of those who were closest to her. 'Murry & the Monster [LM] watch & wait on her, till she hates them both; she trusts no one; she finds no "reality".'[3]

Once Murry took over the *Athenaeum* early in 1919 it did seem at last that a full literary life was available to them both. The paper focused

[3] *The Diary of Virginia Woolf*, ed. Anne Olivier Bell, I (1977), 216.

attention on Murry in a way he had always wanted, and he rose to the editorial demands. His weekly was soon read as the most intelligent in the country, its pages open to the finest writers of the day. 'To front experience on behalf of mankind: that was Murry's ideal; and it was as much an ethical ideal as an aesthetic.'[4]

As in the days of *Rhythm* half a dozen years before, Mansfield enjoyed her association with the magazine. Although she was not a prolific writer, her recent stories were innovative enough to maintain her confidence even after *Prelude* was published to murmurs of dissatisfaction among acquaintances and silence from reviewers. The *Athenaeum* now offered her new channels. She began with Koteliansky to translate Chekhov's letters, and expected they might move on to the fiction. She revealed a gift for reviewing that may not have shown a consistent critical stance, but she was amusing, perceptive, and just. It now seems more than odd that Murry would ask Sydney Waterlow to write on the centenary of George Eliot when his wife had been discussing the same subject with Virginia Woolf for *her* essay in *The Times Literary Supplement*; or that he himself reviewed new translations of Chekhov while 'K. M.'s' column often enough was squandered on ephemeral novels. But there is no evidence this irked her. She welcomed both the chance to try her hand at a different kind of writing, and the opportunities for entertaining that the paper brought with it. Each helped to enliven the months when she was not well enough to think of moving far from her room.

Mansfield had consulted several doctors in 1918, as though she were casting about for alternative advice. The decision to stick it out in Hampstead during the winter of 1918–19, rather than face either France again alone or the public care of a sanatorium, was made with the help of Victor Sorapure, the doctor who set her to looking beyond the physical symptoms of her disease. From now on there will be the growing sense that she needs to face her difficulties in some 'spiritual' way. She is vague about this, and knows that she is vague. For it is attunement she is after rather than anything so grand as enlightenment. And it is from now on too that one begins to see how Murry will continue at the centre of her affections, but whatever it is she is seeking, she knows it will not be found through him. The dreams of 'the Heron', of their life together in the country with the child she frequently had hoped for in 1918, no longer work the same enchantment a year later. Perhaps their living together in what they could consider their first permanent home had made it clear that difficulties between them were going to continue. The 'simple eager passionate boy' she spoke of to Dorothy Brett (26 July 1918) was not quite compatible with the husband she now had.

[4] F. A. Lea, *The Life of John Middleton Murry* (1959), 70.

There was another factor in the change one detects in Mansfield in 1919. It was Sorapure who told her that what for years she had thought of as her 'rheumatism' was a venereal disease, and that her chances of having a child were slight. She seems not to have told this to Murry, but much of that play element between them, their way of anticipating the future by reverting to the manœuvres of childhood, must have taken a hefty knock. There is probably that new knowledge behind her last notebook entry for 1918, and a grim acceptance of how things now stood.[5] She takes up an image that she had used before and that later would be at the centre of one of her best-known stories. '*Fly*: Oh, the times she had walked upside down on the ceiling, run up glittering panes, floated on a lake of light, flashed through a shining beam! . . . And God looked upon the fly fallen into the jug of milk and saw that it was good. And the smallest Cherubims and Seraphims of all who delight in misfortune struck their silver harps & shrilled: How is the fly fallen fallen' (*Journal* 1954, 153).

When Mansfield leaves England at the end of this volume, it is in a very different frame of mind from that in which she made the other journey at its beginning. She knows that her illness is serious enough for her to make an informal will before she leaves – 'just in case I should pop off suddenly' (9 September 1919). She accepts that life as an invalid is pretty much what lies ahead of her. As she had already told Anne Drey, her friend since their carefree days in Paris, 'What wouldn't I give for one of our *laughs*, ma chère. As it is, things aren't funny any more' (13 August 1919). Brett had been informed how 'I was always acting a part in my old palmy days & now Ive thrown the palm away' (10 June 1919). Although to Lady Ottoline she admitted 'oh! I do not want to be resigned' (12 June 1919). Before she set out for the Italian Riviera with Murry and Ida Baker in attendance, Mansfield jotted in one of her notebooks a sentence she may recently have read. Its balance of realism and hope in any case preserves something of the mood in which she left. 'It is pleasant to plant cuttings of futurity if only one in ten takes root' (*Journal* 1954, 179).

Vincent O'Sullivan

[5] See Antony Alpers, *The Life of Katherine Mansfield* (1980), 289.

ACKNOWLEDGEMENTS

The editors are obliged to the various institutions and private owners, listed on the following page under 'Manuscript Sources', who have allowed the use of original letters or transcriptions of letters in their possession.

All unpublished material by Katherine Mansfield and John Middleton Murry is copyright by the respective Estates of Katherine Mansfield and of John Middleton Murry, and is quoted here by permission of the copyright owners. We are grateful to the Murry family for their support of this edition, and to Messrs Constable and Co. for allowing quotations from C. A. Hankin's selection, *The Letters of John Middleton Murry to Katherine Mansfield* (1983). Published material (such as the text of the *Journal of Katherine Mansfield*) has been corrected against the manuscripts.

As well as those whose help over several years has been noted in Volume I, there are several individuals who have given particular assistance with this volume. First among these is Mansfield's biographer and the editor of *The Collected Stories of Katherine Mansfield* (Oxford University Press, Auckland, 1984), Professor Antony Alpers. The editors also thank Elizabeth Caffin for her knowledge of Paris; Dr Michael Freyne, of the University of New South Wales; Alexia Galt for her skills as a research librarian; the eminent bibliographer Miss B. J. Kirkpatrick; Mrs Roma Woodnutt of the Society of Authors; and Jacqueline Simms for her sustaining expertise as editor on behalf of Oxford University Press.

Margaret Scott was assisted in her work by a grant from the Department of Internal Affairs and the Alex Harvey Industries Award. Vincent O'Sullivan is grateful to Professor Bruce Bennett of the Australian Studies Centre at the University of Western Australia, and to Dr Syd Harrex of the Centre for Research into New Literatures in English at Flinders University, Adelaide, who so kindly allowed him to spend part of his time on this volume during periods at those institutions.

In this volume, as in Volume I, the transcriptions of the letters were made by Margaret Scott. Vincent O'Sullivan is responsible for the annotations, dating, and other editorial aspects of the edition.

The reader is referred to the Editorial Note in Volume I for details of editorial policy; and also for a Chronology of Mansfield's life (1888–1923).

V.O'S
M.S.

Adelaide
November 1985

LIST OF ABBREVIATIONS AND MANUSCRIPT SOURCES

KM = Katherine Mansfield

The following abbreviations and short forms are used in the description and provenance given at the foot of each letter:

MS	autograph original
TS	typescript original
draft	autograph draft
MSC	handwritten copy of original
PC	photocopy
TC	typed copy

MANUSCRIPT SOURCES

Institutions

ATL	Alexander Turnbull Library, Wellington
Berg	The Henry W. and Albert A. Berg Collection, New York Public Library, Astor, Lenox and Tilden Foundations
BL	British Library
Dartmouth	Dartmouth College Library, Hanover, New Hampshire
Newberry	The Newberry Library, Chicago
Stanford	Stanford University, Stanford, California
Sussex	University of Sussex, Brighton
Texas	The Humanities Research Center, University of Texas at Austin

Private owners

Alpers	Professor Antony Alpers
Onuma	Mr K. Onuma
Strachey	The Strachey Trust, London

SOURCES OF PREVIOUS PUBLICATION
and short forms used in the annotation

Adam 300	*Adam International Review*, No. 300 (1963–5)
Adam 370–375	*Adam International Review*, Nos. 370–375 (1972–3)
Alpers 1953	Antony Alpers, *Katherine Mansfield, a Biography* (New York, 1953)
Alpers 1980	Antony Alpers, *The Life of Katherine Mansfield* (1980)
BTW	John Middleton Murry, *Between Two Worlds, an Autobiography* (1935)
CLKM I	*The Collected Letters of Katherine Mansfield*, ed. Vincent O'Sullivan and Margaret Scott, vol. 1 (Oxford, 1984)
Clarke	Isabel C. Clarke, *Katherine Mansfield* (Wellington, 1944)
Dickinson	John W. Dickinson, 'Katherine Mansfield and S. S. Koteliansky: Some Unpublished Letters', *Revue de littérature comparée*, no. 45 (1971), 79–99
DVW	*The Diary of Virginia Woolf*, ed. Anne Olivier Bell, vol. I (1977); ed. Anne Olivier Bell, assisted by Andrew McNeillie, vol. V (1984)

Exhibition	*Katherine Mansfield: An Exhibition*, Humanities Research Center, University of Texas (Austin, Texas, 1973)
Glenavy	Beatrice [Campbell], Lady Glenavy, *Today We Will Only Gossip* (1964)
Journal 1954	*Journal of Katherine Mansfield*, Definitive Edition, ed. John Middleton Murry (1954)
LDHL	*The Letters of D. H. Lawrence*, ed. James T. Boulton and Andrew Robertson, vol. III (1984)
LJMM	*Katherine Mansfield's Letters to John Middleton Murry, 1913–1922*, ed. John Middleton Murry (1951)
LKM	*The Letters of Katherine Mansfield*, 2 vols., ed. John Middleton Murry (1928)
LVW	*The Letters of Virginia Woolf*, ed. Nigel Nicolson and Joanne Trautmann, vol. I (1975)
MLM	Ida Baker, *Katherine Mansfield: The Memories of LM* (1971)
Morris	Margaret Morris, *The Art of J. D. Fergusson: A Biased Biography* (1974)
Murry	*The Letters of John Middleton Murry to Katherine Mansfield*, ed. C. A. Hankin (1983)
Stories	*The Stories of Katherine. Mansfield*, Definitive Edition, ed. Antony Alpers (1984)

The place of publication is London unless otherwise noted.

I
FRANCE – BANDOL AND PARIS: 1918

On the advice of her doctor, Katherine Mansfield left England on 7 January 1918. Although she did not know it then, tuberculosis was established in her left lung. Her plan was to spend some time in Bandol, where she and John Middleton Murry had been happy together for several months two years before, and to return home in the spring, when they would marry. Murry was not able to leave his Intelligence work with the War Office, and Ida Baker ('L.M.') also was engaged in essential war work. KM was obliged to travel alone, and later Murry was convinced that but for the rigours of her journey, she may well have recovered. During the next few months she wrote her long story *Je ne parle pas français*, suffered her first haemorrhage on 19 February, and grew more unhappy as her expectations of Bandol went unfulfilled. Ida Baker's going out to join her earlier that month in fact provided her with a full-time servant, but KM's irritation with her friend developed into a detestation whose basis, as she knew, was her own physical condition.

When she left the South of France on 21 March, KM expected to be in London within a few days. But in Paris she found the city more directly involved in military action than she expected. On the day after she arrived the Germans began their bombardment from the new 'super Kanon' they had set up in the Forest of Crèpy near Laon, air raids on the city were frequent, and the movement of foreign civilians was subject to strict control. The physical and mental stress of these three weeks' obligatory stay in Paris was apparent when she arrived in London on 11 April. As Murry remembered it, 'She was haggard and frightened. The hardships she had suffered had given phthisis a secure hold upon her.' (*LJMM*, 246.)

To J. M. Murry, [8 January 1918]

[Le Havre]

Dear Ribni[1] –

This is for you but you must let him see it too. It is *just* what I feel like[2] – Ici il fait si beau – & there were —— Oh Ill tell him all in his letter –

Ta maman

My hotel here was *10.50*!!![3] et les deux lits restent vierges.

MS (picture postcard) ATL.

[1] KM's Japanese doll, named after Colonel Ribnikov in Aleksandr Kuprin's short story. See *CLKM* I, 348, n. 1.
[2] The postcard was of a sailing ship, 'Trois-Mâts au plus près'.
[3] The exchange rate was 27 francs to the pound.

To J. M. Murry, [9 January 1918]

Paris. | 5.30. P.M. | Wednesday.

My precious darling.

I shall not be able to write you a 'proper' letter until I arrive in Bandol. It is so difficult to get calm and I have spent an immense day rushing after my luggage and to Cooks (who wouldn't 'arrange' my affairs for me) and to the P.L.M.[1] However it is all done now and I am in a cafe near the station, with my grande malle registrée, my little uns at le consigne, writing to you before I go to <that> Duval[2] where we went to get some dinner before the train goes.

Everything on the whole has gone wonderfully. Its not a nice journey now a days & it was immensely complicated this time by the blizzards. We left South Hampton at about 9 oclock & did not arrive at Havre until after *10* next morning. We anchored for hours outside Havre in a snow storm & lay tossing & pitching & rolling – – You wont believe me when I say that I enjoyed it. I did. For one thing I had a splendid supper when I got on board – a *whack* of cold lean beef & pigheels, bread, butter ad lib, tea, and plenty of good bread – Then I took a nip of brandy & went right to bed – in a little cabin – very clean and warm – with an excellent stewardess in attendance. The upper berth was a generals widow (more of her later) except for her imitation of a cat with a fish bone in its throat I was divinely comfortable & slept & woke slept & woke but did not move until we reached Havre. Then I tumbled up on deck to find everything white with snow – I shall tell you nothing in detail now for I mean to write it all. It was too wonderful to miss. We had to spend the day in Havre so I took a bedroom at a hotel had breakfast & washed & went to sleep, until late lunch. The food in France is simply wonderful. *Bread* that makes one hungry to look at, butter, sugar, meat, 7 kinds of cheese for lunch & 7 hors d oeuvres. Then we started for Paris at 5 to arrive at 9.20. The carriage was packed, *un*heated with a broken window & the snow drifting in. This was very vile. But a red cross old party took me in charge & rubbed me and cossetted me & finally made me eat a dinner which cost 6 francs but saved me as we did not arrive until 2 A.M. Then a plunge into the pitch dark and snow as all the entrances to the Terminus[3] were shut except the one in the street. God! how thankful I was that I had reserved a room. Crowds were turned away, but I staggered up a palatial staircase, through ballrooms, reception rooms, *hollows* glittering with chandeliers to a yellow & blue brocade bedroom which seemed to be worth £50 to me. I slept like a top and got up early and (L'Heure! Liberte! *La* Presse!) saw about all my affairs. It is snowing hard. The streets are all ice and water – and so slippery qu'on marche comme un poulet malade. All the same I am unreasonably deeply happy. I thought I would be disenchanted with France this time, but for the first time I seem to recognise my love for it and to understand *why*. It is because, whatever happens, I never feel *indifferent*. I feel that indifference is really foreign to my nature and that to live in a state of it is to live in the only Hell I really appreciate. There is too, dispassionately speaking, a wonderful spirit here – so much humour, life, gaiety, sorrow, one cannot see it all & not think with amazement of the strange cement like state of England. Yes, they do feel the war, but with a difference.

But this, too, I must write about seriously.

My treasure this is not a letter. It is a kind of intake of breath before I really begin to tell you all. Ah, how I love you here! The spring of my joy is that we belong to each other and that you and I are lovers and wedded to each other –

You are mine and I am yours for ever. I cant "get over" that. It simply fills my being with a kind of rich joy which I know I shall *express* marvellously marvellously for you & through you.

Ribni – our little John the Baptist. Kiss him for me –

As for you – you are my own – and I am forever yours

Tig

MS ATL. *LKM* I. 91–3; *LJMM*, 111–13.

[1] The office of the Paris–Lyon–Méditerranée Railway, at the Gare de Lyon.
[2] Duval, one of a large chain of restaurants.
[3] The Terminus Hotel at the Gare St Lazare.

To J. M. Murry, [11 January 1918]

Hotel Beau Rivage | Bandol
Friday

My dearest Bogey,
   My enthusiastic letter from Paris has been in my mind ever since. *And*
mocked me. I took it to post; it was dark by then, piercing cold and so
wet underfoot that ones feet felt like 2 walking toads. After a great deal
of bother I got established in the train (no pillows to be had now-a-
days) and then the fun began. I liked my fellow passengers – but God!
how stiff one got and my feet hurt and the flat iron became hot enough
to burn the buttoned back against which I leaned. There was no
restaurant car on the train – no chance of getting anything hot – a
blinding snowstorm until we reached Valence. I must confess the
country was exquisite at sunrise – exquisite but we did not arrive at
Marseilles until *one* o'clock. Good! As I got out a pimp getting *in* to
hold a seat for some super pimp gave me such a blow on the chest that
it is blue today. I thought "this is Marseilles sans doute". Feeling very
tired and hungry I carried my luggage 3 miles to the consigne &
finding that the train left for Bandol at 3.30. decided to have a snack
at the Buffet just outside – that place under a glass verandah. It was
rather full so I sat down opposite an elderly lady who eyed me so
strangely that I asked if "cette place est prise." "Non Madame" said
she, insolent beyond everything, "mais il y a des autres tables n'est ce
pas. Je prefere beaucoup que vous ne venez pas ici. D'abord – j'ai deja
fini mon dejeuner, et c'est tres degoutant de vous voir commencer car
j'ai l'estomac delicat, et puis – – " and then she raised her eyebrows &
left it at that. You can judge what I ate after that – and what I
thought. At 1.30 I went to get my bagage registered – waited for one
hour in a queue for my ticket & then was told I could not have one
until my passport was viséd. I had that done, waited again, carried
my luggage to the platform finally at 3 o clock juste, and waited there
in a crowd until four. Then a train came in at another platform & the
people swarmed in just like apes climbing into bushes – & I had just
thrown my rugs into it when it was stated that it was only for
permissionaires & did not stop before Toulon. Good again! I
staggered out, & got into *another* train on *another* platform, asked 3
people if it was the right one who did not know – & sat down in the
corner – completely dished. There were 8 serbian officers in the
compartment with me & their 2 dogs. Never shall I say another word
against Serbians. They looked like Maidens Dreams – excessively
handsome & well cared for – graceful, young, dashing with fine teeth
& eyes. But that did not matter. What *did* was that after shunting for
2 hours – five yards forward five back – there was a free fight at the

station between a mob of soldiers & the civilians. The soldiers demanded the train – & that les civils should evacuate it. Not with good temper, but furious – very ugly, & VILE. They banged on the windows, wrenched open the doors & threw out the people & their luggage after them. They came to our carriage swarmed in – told the officers they too must go and one caught hold of me as though I were a sort of packet of rugs – I never said a word for I was far too tired and vague to care about anything except I was determined not to *cry* – but one of the officers then let out – threw out the soldiers – said I was his wife & had been travelling with him five days – & when the chef militaire de la gare came, said the same – threw HIM out – banged the door, took off their dogs leads & held the door shut. The others then pressed against the connecting door between the carriages & there we remained in a state of siege until seven o clock when the train started. You should have heard the squalling and banging. They pinned the curtains together and I hid behind them until we were under way. By this time it was pitch dark & I knew I should never find the station as a terrific mistral was blowing & you could not hear the stations cried – but as we came to each stop they pulled the window down and shouted in their curious clipped french to know which it was. Ah, but they were very nice chaps – splendid chaps – I'll not forget them. We reached Bandol at 9. I felt that my grande malle was gone for ever but I seized the other 2 & dashed across the line. I could not have walked here but happily the boy from the Hotel des Bains was at the station & though he said "qu'il n'etait pas bon avec le patron" he brought me.

When I arrived the hall was rather cold and smoky – a strange woman came out wiping her mouth with a serviette . . I realised in a flash that the hotel had changed hands. She said she had received *no* letter but there were plenty of rooms – and proceeded to lead me to them – My own was taken – I chose finally the one next door which had 2 beds on the condition that she removed one – Also it was the cheapest 12 francs a day – The others have had de l'eau courant put into them and cost 13. The big stoves were not lighted in the passages . . I asked for hot water and a hot water bottle. Had some soup, wrapped up to the eyes & simply fell into bed after finishing the brandy in my flask. For I felt that the whole affair wanted thoroughly sleeping over and not thinking about . . .

In the morning when I opened the persiennes it was so lovely outside, I stayed in bed until lunch. Ma grande malle really did turn up. Then I got up, and after lunch went into the town. The Maynards [Meynets][1] are gone for the present. The tabac woman did not know me & had no tobacco. Nobody remembered me at all – I bought writing things and a few bull eyes – about a penny for two, they were, and suddenly I met Maam Gamel. She, too did not recognise me until I had explained who I was – Then she was very kind – "Ah! Ah! Ah! vous êtes beaucoup changée vous avez été *ben* malade, n'est ce pas. Vous n'avez plus votre air de p'tite gosse vous s*aa*vez!" I went with her to the shop, which is just the same & saw the old mother who was most tender about you. I bought a tiny pot of cherry jam, and came home – to find my room not yet done –

You can see, love I am depressed. I feel faible still after cet voyage, but I shall get better and I shall arrange things here as soon as I have la force necessaire. The place is even to my blind eyes as lovely as ever, glittering with light, with the deep hyacinth blue sea, the wonderful flashing palms and the mountains, violet in the shadow, and jade green in the sun. The mimosa outside my window is in bud – Don't worry about me. Having got over that journey and that Paris thaw I shall never fall by the way – & when my room is ready I shall *work*. That I do feel, and that is what matters Bogey. I am not even very sad. It has been a bit of a bang though, hasn't it? and Ill tell you exactly what I feel like. I feel like a fly who has been dropped into the milk jug & fished out again but is still too milky & drowned to start cleaning up yet. Letters will take a long time, perhaps 6 or 8 days – so do not worry if you do not hear. And take care of yourself & LOVE ME. As I LOVE YOU. Ah, this is not the day to start writing about that, for my bosom begins to ache & my arms fly out to embrace you. I want you. I am lonely & very fainting by the way but only for now – you know. Always your own woman

Tig

This is one of the truthful letters we promised each other my precious one . .

MS ATL. *LKM* I. 93–7; *LJMM*, 113–16.

---

¹ Acquaintances from KM's stay in Bandol two years before (see *CLKM* I, 201–52), as was Ma'am Gamel.

To J. M. Murry, [12 January 1918]

[Hôtel Beau Rivage, Bandol]
Saturday

Bogey,
    You are to write as often as you can at first – see? Because letters take so long, so long, et je suis malade. I have just got up and am sitting wrapped up in all my clothes & my wooly cover & your geranium jacket over & the Kashmir shawl over that & Ottolines pink

one round my legs & the rug folded on the floor – The fire is alight but it will not burn unless I keep the iron shade right down!! The old old story. It is bitterly cold – and a deep strange grey light over the sea & sky. I have got up because I <u>must</u> work & I cant in bed. If I am going to languish in Foreign Parts all alone I must have a great deal of work done – or it will be no use.

Please Bogey write me warm letters – tellement il fait froid. Ah, do let everything be lovely 'chez vous'; that would be the greatest joy I could have. That *you* are well and comfortable and that you think of me and work in the evenings.

You cant get any cigarettes here; nothing but cigars. There is a 'crise' in tobacco, too. This hotel is so quiet. There are only four uglies in it. I wonder they keep it open. I shall write to Madame Geffroi[1] tomorrow.

If L.M. was here she could blow up that fire.

My little precious. My love, my child playfellow. Didn't we wave to each other a long time that day?

Say you want me back in April. Tell me I *must* come back then.

Your
Wig.

MS ATL. *LKM* I. 97; *LJMM*, 116.

---

[1] Another acquaintance from KM's earlier stay. Régine Geoffroi was married to a doctor who was now Mayor of Carpentras.

To J. M. Murry, [13 January 1918]

[Hôtel Beau Rivage, Bandol]
le dimanche

My precious

I got so cold yesterday that I decided, willy-nilly, to take a small walk and try and 'warm up' before the evening. So I made myself into a bundle, and started off. First I went to the Mairie to be registered. The old secretary was there at one desk in his braided cap; the drum stood in a corner. He was very solemnly engaged in cutting a spanish beauty's picture off a card & gumming the same on to the back of a pocket book, breathing like a grampus. The Mayor did not (as usual) want to have anything to do with my passport. However I persuaded him that it really *was* necessary & when he did make up his mind he went very thoroughly into the affair. Result. I am written in the books as Kadreen Bovden, fille d'Arnold Beauchamp et Anne Dysa de Nouvelle Zelande etc etc. I could not make him get anything more accurate so I just let him go on – Then I saw that the Meynets blind was up & went in. M[onsieur] only was there. He sat on a stool stitching a long red leather boot more + eyed than ever. Didn't remember me. Madame is away but he expects her back. "Marie est allée à Marseilles il y a deux mois, et puis – elle n'est pas revenue! Voilà!" Did I want a villa? And he began to press villas de quatre pièces on me, but I felt a bit sick and went off. I then decided to go & see Maam Allègre. The afternoon was very cold and grey & just going dusky. The sea was high and made a loud noise. When I passed the vineyard where the two little boys used to work I realised quite suddenly, that I was suffering – terribly terribly, and was quite faint with this emotion. Then came at <all> last the road with Gravier 2 K. written on the post. And then came our little home in sight. I went on though I don't know how, pushed open the Allègres swinging gate, walked over those crunching round stones – – The outer door of our villa was open.[1] When I reached the stone verandah, and looked again upon the almond tree, the little garden, the round stone table, the seat scooped out of stone, the steps leading down to the cave, and then looked up at our pink house, with the swags of shells painted over the windows & the strange blue-grey shutters I thought I had never, in my happiest memories, realised all its beauty. I could not get any answer from the Allègres, but I felt certain I heard someone moving in our villa, so finally I knocked on our door – You remember how hard it was to open – It tugged open & there stood Maam Allegre in the same little black shawl, lean and grey as ever –

"Vous desirez Madame", said she. I just managed to say "bonjour Madame. Vous m'avez oubliée?" And then she cried Ah! Ah I know your voice – Come in come in Madame. I am just airing the villa. Come in to the little salon. Comment ça va? Et votre mari? etc etc etc. I crossed the hall; she opened one half of the persiennes and we sat on either side of the table, she in your place, I with my back to the fire in mine and had a long talk. She remembers us well. Many times her husband & she have talked of us and wished to have us back again. Her husband always wondered what had happened to us – we were like deux enfants said she and it was a happiness to them to know that we were there. Her son is wounded, and is on the swiss frontier in a post office. They went all the way to Paris to see him. I asked her what has happened to the flowers – for there is not a single flower, not a jonquil, not a geranium, not a rose not an orange – and she promised they would all be here "plus tar' plus tar'. Cest la faute du mauvais *temps*, vous saavez!" But oh, as we sat there, talking & I felt myself smile and answer & stroke my muff & discuss the meat shortage & the horrid bread and the high prices & *cette guerre* I felt that somewhere, upstairs, you & I lay like the little Babies in the Tower, smothered under pillows & she and I were keeping watch like any two old crones! I could hardly look at the room. When I saw my photograph that you had left, on the wall I nearly broke down – and finally I came away & leaned a long time on the wall at the bottom of our little road looking at the violet sea that beat up, high and loud against those strange dark clots of seaweed – – As I came down your beautiful narrow steps – it began to rain. Big soft, reluctant drops fell on my hands & face – The light was flashing through the dusk from the lighthouse and a swarm of black soldiers was kicking something about on the sand among the palm trees – a dead dog perhaps or a little tied up kitten –

It is so quiet today. I remember sundays like this, here. Not a hint of sun. A leaden sky – a sea like oil – I almost think I may reasonably expect a letter from you tomorrow. I had a very bad night, coughing and sweating so that I had to keep sponging my face & kept thinking "it *must* be five o clock" and finding it was only a quarter past one. Oh, these long, long, lonely nights when one is ill! They are unforgettable! But after breakfast this morning I slept until eleven oclock. I heard all the noises in the corridor but still I *was* fast asleep.

Good God! I have just remembered – It was only last Sunday that I came to you – & we were so happy & you cut my bread & butter & we kissed each other ——

Be still! Be still!

This will all pass & I shall get better, our spring will come – & it will be warm & you will write to me & we shall be together again – Lord I believe –

Your child
Wig.

MS ATL. *LKM* I. 97–9; *LJMM*, 117–19.

---

[1] The Allègres were the owners of the Villa Pauline, which KM and Murry had rented from January to the end of March 1916.

To J. M. Murry, [14 January 1918]

[Hôtel Beau Rivage, Bandol]
Monday 15th

Read this first.

Boge

The Lord took Pity on me today & sent me a letter from you. As it was only written on Wednesday I thought that very good. I had been told letters took 8 days at least! I read it from beginning to end & then from end to beginning, upside down and then diagonally. I ate it, breathed it, & finally, fell out of bed, opened the shutters & saw that the day was blue & the sun shining. So your Wig put on her clothes & went for a walk round by the Golf Hotel. It was very exquisite, cold in the shadows, but warm in the light. I still have an appaling cold, cough, and flatiron, but your letter was the best medecine, poultice, plaster, elixir, draught, I could have had. Bless you for it.

A word more about this place. There is a destroyer anchored here, close to the Quai & Sheds etc erected for the sailors. Who spend their time ½ in the urinals ½ flirting with the girls. Quantities of black soldiers everywhere – I saw that woman whose husband was in Salonique yesterday – She is quite changed, very made up but pale & impudent – and horrid. I realised yesterday she is a type for negroes – You remember the lovely geraniums in this garden. They are little scrubby bushes now with broken bottles & bits of lead piping chucked among them. These hotel people are no good. A widowed mother & two Bragian daughters. And now there are only 2 people <except> here beside me. However I cant leave. Je n'ai ni la force ni l'assurance. It may improve. Certainly the weather has. I shall be back now, when you get this, in 14 weeks. Then I am going to somehow or other faire un enfant – so that when you ever should want to rush away from me je ne serai pas seule – My precious darling. Try & get inside the buses while the cold lasts.

Wig.

MS ATL. *LKM* I. 100; *LJMM*, 119.

To J. D. Fergusson,[1] 15 January 1918

My official name and address.
Madame Bowden | Hôtel Beau Rivage | Bandol | (Var.)
15.1.1918.

Dear Fergusson,

Take the word of a 'sincere well wisher' and never attempt this journey during the War. When Murry and I came down here two years ago it was nothing of an ordeal, but this time . . . Well, a hundred Bill Nobles crying Jesus Christ isn't your sofa pillows would not be enough. I would not do it again for all the oranges and lemons and lovely girls dans tout ce pays. I would say: 'No! Leave me on the dear old Fulham Road,[2] let me hail the bus that none stop, go to the butcher who hasn't any meat, and get home to find the fire is out and the milkman hasn't come and doesn't intend coming . . .'

Just to mention one or two details. The train was not heated. There was no restaurant car. The windows of the corridor were broken and the floor was like a creek with melted snow. The cabinets did not open. There were no pillows for hire. We were hours late.

The French do not suffer as we do on these occasions. For one thing I think they obtain great relief by the *continual* expression of their feelings, by moaning, groaning, lashing themselves into their rugs, quietening their stomachs with various fluids out of bottles, and charming the long hours away with recitations of various internal diseases from which they and their friends have suffered . . .

We arrived at Marseilles to find no porters, of course. I was just *staggering* out when a pimp in white canvas shoes bent on reserving a place for a super pimp bounced up and gave me a blow on the chest which is still a very fine flat ripolion purple.[3] 'This, thought I, is Johnnie's Marseilles'. And it was the harmonising motif of my stay there. You know the kind of thing. Waiting in a Q for one hour for a ticket and then being told I must have my passport viséd first, and finding myself after that at the end of the tail again, without even the excuse of the little woman in front of me who got on famously by tapping each man on the shoulder and saying 'Pardon Monsieur j'attends un Bébé'. Even her ticket seemed to be punched ten times faster in consequence and the porter simply whisked her luggage away. It's quite an idea pour la prochaine fois.

When I did pass the barriers it was to discover that the train for Bandol was due to arrive at all four platforms and there was a terrific crowd on each. Every time a train came in it was thronged by people and even then not an official knew whether it was the right one or not. After two hours of this the real train did arrive, on the furthest platform of course. You picture me running on the railway lines with my rugs, suitcase, umbrella, muff, handbag, etc. and finally chucking them and myself into a 1ère where I sat for the next ten minutes in a corner saying to muff 'Fool! do not cry. You can't begin crying like a baby at this stage'. However, there was suddenly an immense uproar and a body of soldiers rushed the train, commandeered it and began throwing out the civilians bag and baggage. They were not at all a 'I-tiddley-i-ty take me back to Blighty'[4] crowd either. They were bad tempered and very ugly. Happily I was in a carriage with 8 Serbian officers and they put up a fight. It was very unpleasant – the soldiers swarming at the windows, tugging at the doors – and threatening to throw you out. But these good chaps lashed the doors up with leather straps, pinned the curtains together and barricaded the door into the passage. They won, and I got here in the middle of the night, walked into a dark, smoky, wet-feeling hall, saw a strange woman come forward wiping her lips with a serviette and realised in a flash that the hotel had changed hands. If you will just add to all this 1 raging chill and fever which I caught on the journey I think you will agree that it's not a bad total . . . That was on Thursday. ·

Today is Tuesday. I have not even unpacked yet – it is cold. Wood costs 2.50 le panier and this hotel is much more expensive. But I shall have to stay here until I am well. At present I spend my time getting in and out of bed – and although there is a bud or two outside the windows and a lilac-coloured sea I feel what the charwomen call 'very *low*'. At night especially, my thoughts go by with black plumes on their heads and silver tassels on their tails and I sit up making up my mind not to look at my watch again for at least five minutes. However all this will pass. To Hell with it.

I thought last night it is a bad thing during this war to be apart from the one or two people who do count in one's life. After all we are not solitary palm trees in deserts – thank God – we are groups of two or three with a spring of sweet water between us and a piece of grassy shade. At this time, to go away alone to another country is a thoroughly bad idea. (This of course is the precisely useful moment for me to make this discovery).

Are you working? You know quite well what I thought of those pictures, don't you. I knew in a way they would be *like that* but that did not make them any less of a revelation. They are unforgettable.

Write me a card when you feel inclined to, just to give me a hail from your ship. Goodbye for now.

Yours ever,
Mansfield.

MS lacking. Morris, 121–4.

¹ John Duncan Fergusson (1874–1961), Scottish painter, a friend of Murry's; see *CLKM* I, 125, n. 1. He was closely associated with Anne Estelle Rice (Drey) when KM first met him in 1913, but now lived with Margaret Morris (1891–1980), the *danseuse* and choreographer. After Koteliansky, he was KM's closest male friend.
² Redcliffe Road was off the Fulham Road. Fergusson lived at no. 14.
³ Ripolin was the brand name for an enamel paint commonly used in house decoration.
⁴ 'Take me back to dear old Blighty', a song written by Jack Godfrey in 1916.

To J. M. Murry, [16 January 1918]

[Hôtel Beau Rivage, Bandol]
· Wednesday.

My own,

I had a very gay letter from Marie today including one from Mr. Kay¹ to her which says that 'heaps' of letters are waiting for me at the Bank. Well, he's got my address by now so I hope they are on their way . . Dont forget my papers – will you? Of course I simply devour, believe and eat up every word of the Paris Daily Mail in the meantime. Its latest scare is that The Germans are going to try marching on Calais again & that the channel passage will be cut off for aye.

It is a very grey misty day. After that one fine one it has relapsed into winter again. A plaintive wind howls in the corridors – I shall light my fire this afternoon and sit tight. Oh dear! a panier of wood only lasts me 2 days try as I may to economise.

The post here is much better than I had been led to believe. One hardly dares to say so, in case it snows again or more troops pour into Italy, but Marie's letter was only posted on the 12th and today is the 15th or 16th Im not sure.

I still feel far from as well as I did when we went to Harvey Nicholls[2] together. I lie in bed all the morning until 12 and go to bed again as soon as dinner is over. The *interval* I spend in going for a very small walk and in working: I have begun thank God to work a bit. But my back hurts horribly and I cough an awful lot. However I did not compose a single farewell telegram last night in bed so that is *one up*.

Our butcheress isn't there any more. The pig faced woman is and an old man. The patisserie where the girl was always eating is closed, sadly with big official notices plastered on the windows. The shop with the funny smell where we bought our charbon de pierre is now the Municipal Food Depot. I went round by the golf hotel yesterday & just as I got to that place where it says you are responsible for your own degats & frais the sheep with their little lambs passed by. God! What a woeful company. The sheep with just a saddle of dirty wool on their backs, their bellies shaven, many of them with swollen feet, limping pitifully – the lambs tottering past – but *they* were pretty – there was one ginger one that managed to give a hop or two. Behind them went a shepherd who was half a dog, I think. But he whistled to them in a way I had forgotten.[3]

There are 2 submarines in the bay & a black steamer with a big white cross on her bows. The officers take their meals here – Their talk and grouping etc is pure Maupassant – *not* Tchekov at all – not deep enough or *good* enough. No, Maupassant is for France.

I read Wordsworths sonnet beginning

Great men have been among us; hands that penned . . .[4]

Look it up & read it. I agree with every word. There is a change of front, if you like! Whenever I am here I seem to turn to William Wordsworth.

My precious Boge. Your real Wig lies on Ribni's bosom so clasp her there. This old sort of penwoman with a croak and a sad eye is not really me. Still not a cigarette to be had in all the land. "It is sad." Please try and send me a book, a Dickens would do. I have read Barnaby Rudge twice – What about Our Mutual Friend. Is that good? I never read it.

This letter goes like one of those sheep I saw. But by the time it reaches you you must feel that I LOVE LOVE LOVE you amen, and that I am for ever your own

Wig

Tell me you are taking care of yourself for me.

MS (with enclosures) ATL. *LKM* I. 100–2; *LJMM*, 120–1.

¹ Alexander Kay, manager of the London branch of the Bank of New Zealand.

² Harvey Nichols, the store in Knightsbridge where KM and Murry had gone on 28 December to change the dressing-gown given her by her sister Chaddie (Marie).

³ KM enclosed three postcards with this letter. One of them was of the Bandol railway station, with 'do you remember?' written on the back; on the second, a view of the Bandol market place, she wrote 'and darling, do you remember us here with our "sheep"?'. The third card was a drawing of a young girl with a poodle doll sitting on a Union Jack, with the printed words 'Never mind, Fifi, The English Will Look After Us!' On the back KM wrote 'Bien tendrement Tig.' (ATL.)

Murry replied on 20 Jan: 'Oh, that old marché of which you sent me the picture and the neat little station with the stupid train! To think that the place where we were so happy, where we entered on the phase of our perfect love, should have become morne and desolate. Those wounded mangy sheep!' (Murry, 109.)

⁴ From Sonnet XV in Wordsworth's *Poems Dedicated to National Independence and Liberty*, 1807.

To J. M. Murry, [17 January 1918]

[Bandol]

IS ALL WELL ANXIOUS BOWDEN¹

Telegram ATL

¹ Murry wrote back, on the evening of 18 Jan, blaming himself for not sending a letter between Wednesday and Sunday the previous week: 'Somehow, during that first week it didn't seem to me that you had really gone away. It was only on Monday that I realised it – and then I knew that this affair of two letters a week was all nonsense, utter nonsense, that we had to write to each other every day.' (ATL.)

To Annie Burnell Beauchamp, 18 January 1918

Hotel Beau Rivage | Bandol (Var.)
January 18ᵗʰ 1918

My precious little Ma,

Although I have not yet received the home letters of which Mr Kay makes such prodigal mention in the enclosed note I *did* get this morning your budget to Chaddie & Belle which arrived by the same mail. And, much like you and Jeanne, upon receipt of the Bath Tablets I sat up in bed and very nearly ate them. Who writes such a witty, pointed admirable letter as you? After the war, my dear, when we are all on our lean beam ends you will have to regather them from your children, and publish them as a kind of second 'Rosary' and wait for the guineas to come spinning up the Wadestown Hill . . .[1] But they always leave me with the regret that we are so peppered about the earth. What talks we could have, if we were all together. How we could sharpen our friendly claws upon each other. Chaddie and I are always saying "if only the little Ma were here to join the joke."

(Just an aside before I go on to a full retailing of my past and present adventures. You mention Jack, love, as though he were a kind of flower in a bath chair or as though he walked abroad clad in complete jaegers with one or two abdominal and cholera belts over his patent weskit and a respirator soaked in creosote for final trimming. Do please believe this is NOT so. He is NOT consumptive. I cannot go so far as to say that he is twin brother to Belles quondam admirer in the tiger skin – the Sydney dentist – wasn't he? But otherwise he is full of fire and though he is a *lean* bone he is a very *sound* one. Talking about lean bones. Farewell to my portliness. For I, who weighed 10 stone 3 at the age of fifteen now weigh 8 stone 6. At this rate I will be a midget tooth pick at fifty.)

Well dear (as the precious brother used to say) I have had some very strenuous times since last I wrote. My studio is a thing of the past, I have spent three days with Chaddie at her Club[2] and finally have come all this way. I much regretted giving up the studio, but its day was over. While its contents were moved to Jacks flat I went down to Garsington and was very much spoilt and coddled by my good friends there – coming away with, for final 'goo' the most exquisite spanish shawl which Ottoline's father, the Duke of Portland had given her. I said to Chaddie when we had both admired it until we were full fed: "Of course I shall have to give it to Mother when I see her again, but she must then lend it to me for state occasions and christenings." It is a heavy black silk crepe (here I see Papa begin to ask if it has any *gussets* and if not would not a tuck or two be advisable) embroidered very thickly with flowers and fruits and birds in the most lively yet delicate colours imaginable. Even your indian daughter with her nine packing cases full of silk carpets and brass instruments was taken aback by it. To continue. I then puffed up to London and spent three days with Chaddie as her guest at the Club. You can well imagine how much I enjoyed this. She had engaged a very snug room for me with instructions as to fires which were most "reckless and bold", and we saw of course more of each other than we have for months and had great talks. Jack came in to dinner and I of course spent most of my time with him. Chaddie has promised to keep a sisterly eye upon him while I am away: I know she will. At the last moment the French Authorities refused to allow ([*after blots in the text*] *not* my fault. It is *war* blotting paper) Ida to come. This was rather a blow, but if she did come it would have meant her giving up the factory finally, for nobody is allowed *out* of England for less than four months and of course she could not have expected such extended leave. However on Jack's suggestion and as I assured them I was well enough to go alone I took first class all the way, booked a room in Paris at a good hotel and a sleeping car on the train to Marseilles. He provided me further with such luxuries and comforts that I felt like a foreign princess 'en voyage' – even down to a good John Pound travelling bag, a little *electric torch* and a flask (the last named was a perfect boon). In fact he behaved as though money flowed, not that he was extravagant, but he did do me very proud indeed and I hate to think what a hole my wing-bother has made in his savings. However as he is perfectly cheerful about it and is hard at saving again I suppose I must not bother. I had, on the whole, a wonderfully comfortable journey as far as Paris but after that it was pretty warlike! France is, I realised then, very different to England at present. Her railway system and organisation simply does not exist – really. The trains are hours late, often unheated, with broken windows and unimaginably *filthy* carriages – and this is endured so without protest that I presume it to be an accustomed state of affairs. I, also, in my final train got into a very nasty fight between a body of soldiers who rushed the train and the civilians whom the soldiers attempted to turn out. This was not in at all the good old english spirit, but very violent and ugly. I hope I never see the like again or at any rate that I am not *in* it. However, thanks to some serbian officers who were in my carriage, I managed to stick it – and finally steamed out of Marseilles station leaving a howling mob and *no regrets* behind me. Since then I have been going slow and getting back my puff. Staying in bed till midday and going back to that very uncongenial spot at eight oclock in the evening. But by the time this reaches you I shall be a tower of strength again and thinking of spreading my wings for Blighty again, I fondly hope.

It is a great pity, things being as they are that you and I are not neighbours. We might build a kind of neutral ward, a very fair and gay place with two beds and suitable trimmings, so that when we were seized with the desire to put up our toes we could do it in company and cosiness. I sadly miss a partner in my present condition and have cursed the michaelmas daisies on the wall paper far more roundly than they are worth.

By the way, my dear, *re*, again, your letter to Belle and Chaddie this talk of woolen jackets really does begin to make my mouth water. If you *can* toss them off <their> your knitting pegs like positive pancakes – why cant your poor little K have one? It *is* mean; Im older than Jeanne.

This dear little port is greatly changed since we were here before. The people look yellow and thin. Their gaiety has gone and the only ones left full of fat and go are the coal black nigger soldiers in full french uniform who strut up and down *bulls eyeing* the girls. I have a horror of black men even though Deepa [Great-uncle Henry Herron Beauchamp] declared them my weakness, and the sight of these particular ones, in their spruce european clothes gives me an unpleasant turn. If I were queen they would never be allowed to escape from their cotton fields and coconuts. Well, darling I will stop here and wait to see if tomorrow's post brings me my letters so that I can comment on them. I wish I had not become such a very great baby about *missing Jack*. As far as my practical side is concerned, for all your references to me as a kind of mild "dotty", I feel extraordinarily more practical and capable and settled since I knew him, but as regards my *loving* side I seem to have turned into a sort of child and can't feel really happy without "my little mate". Don't laugh or be cross. Im sure you understand really, because if the truth were known I believe you understand every one of us in a way that nobody else does. But you *do* know what I mean don't you dear? I miss quite absurd things, like just having him under my eye and hearing all that has happened to him during the day, down to what he had for lunch etc – and then telling him in detail all that has happened to me, and enjoying to the full that confidential "give and take" which people who love each other enjoy and yet can't explain. I try to tell you this, because I always want to *confide* in you, and to feel that you know me through and through. See? If you don't like it make a curl-paper of the page, my dear and say no more.

[No signature]

MS Newberry.

[1] KM's parents now lived at 'The Grange' in Wadestown, overlooking the city and the harbour.
[2] The Empress Club in Dover Street.

To J. M. Murry, [18 and 19 January 1918] .

[Hôtel Beau Rivage, Bandol]
Friday

My precious darling Bogey

I jumped out of bed this morning as though a bull had brought me your telegram on his horn, tied and buttoned myself and blew off to the Post Office to wire Geoffroi to wait till he heard from me.[1] Whether I was in time or not, I don't know. My spirit faints with horror that I wasn't. If that little chest of drawers does turn up I expect he will carve me in a dozen bits & have done with me for ever. And THE EXPENSE! No, now I shall never never tell you the truth again, for you become violent. I should not write like this if something extraordinary hadn't happened. Last night I didn't feel very much better. I climbed into bed & fell asleep & had a marvellous dream about you. You came rolling at me in your way – & you said in the 'boy' voice that always overcomes me 'Wig I've grown a beard.' And you had. I never saw such a nice one. I held up a finger at you & (we were in a big hall full of people –) I suddenly felt that every single soul there loved us – loved us with their whole hearts. I was wearing my spanish shawlet & you were in your corduroys – very much so. You took me by the hand & we looked at each other and I thought the tears came rolling out of our eyes & we began to laugh. Ah, that sweet laughter! I woke and quite forgot my foreign bed – I found myself for the first time since I left you – laughing – & though when I realised it was a dream the laughter fled – never the less – it has made the pain so much less .. Today, for instance it is dark and very windy and cold, but 2 letters came from you & then my dream & I am clasping you – close – close to my breast – my beloved – & kissing the top of your darling head & calling you some of my hundreds & thousands of names for you . . . Love me. Love me as I love you – When the cloud has lifted from both of us we shall be like 2 little rays of light dancing over the daisy fields. I had better get well alone. Dont send Lesley. I can stand it & if I do get worse I will tell G[eoffroi] I have written him all about myself now & asked his advice from afar so that is best. I really am better than I was. I sleep more & the pain is a different one. I believe I have turned *another* of those corners just managed to turn it, you know, as though I were leaning to ride a bicycle round it. I heard from L.M. today too. She sounded very gay and 'sitting on the floory.' Boge, your letter was only writ on Monday & today is Friday. God I thank thee for thy merciful Posts.

Oh, my love –

. . . . "I would not wish
Any companion in the world but you;

Nor can imagination form a shape,
Besides yourself, to like of."[2]

Shakespeare knew our love – what it was like. Yes, love, I took away my copy. I looked up that out of The Winters Tale, the end of Camillo's speech.[3] It is extraordinarily 19th century.

It is safe for me to send M.S. registré to you or should I keep it? I'd *like* to send it so it would be typed & you could read it. Please remember to tell me.

We must get rid de Madame, votre femme de menage[4] when I come back. I shall start from here *the 1st week in April* at latest. And meanwhile the wind moans, the sky is purple and the sea boils up . . 4.15. It is already nearly dark. My bluff old watch that you bought me ticks away & away. I often feel inclined to <drop> dip him in things like jugs of water & cups of coffee, but I don't, darling. You shall have him when I come back. *When I come back when I come back* that is all my heart says. It doesn't see *this* or hear *this*. It is fast asleep in my bosom except when I write to you – Oh – I can just see far away a most lovely poem coming out of that – not that exactly. Love as a sleeping baby, and when she bends over him and whispers his fathers name to him, he stirs & stretches & opens his eyes & laughs – but she must let him sleep – must hush him and let him sleep. I see it – This is just a lift of the idea that I give you. Perhaps I can write it in prose. Now I am going to shut the shutters & work. I shall post this tomorrow –

Saturday 5.20. I had just got that far when Victorine poked in her head "c'est une dame qui vous demande en bas" and suddenly I heard steps & there was Madame Geoffroi. "Ma chère amie, j'avais idee que vous êtes paralisée!" She took me into her arms & I wept & she wept & I wept all over the collar of her impossible coat & she wept. Then I tried to explain how I had wired & *she* that your telegram had come the evening before. She had been travelling to get to me since <u>8</u> that morning – & was worn out. It was a *bit awful*. We both went on explaining & chère amieing each other until I thought I'd simply fall down like Slatkowsky[5] – & finally she understood & she said she would write you that I had très bonne mine & was pas plus fatiguée parceque le pauvre enfant – votre mari droit etre a la folie etc. etc. etc. She said her husband *never* practised and at any rate he is the mayor now. Voilà. & kept saying I must eat & put on wool & eat abundantly & wants me to go to Carpentras in March until I leave for England – At last the gong went for dinner & we dined together & then she came back to my room & sat till <u>11.30</u> talking about le Swinburne, Mistral, D'Aubanel, le Keats, la silence qui a pris pour sa maison la maison d'Henri Fabre.[6] Finally she left me & I simply groaned into bed. At *8.15* my dear – figurez-vous she was in my room dressed, ready pour aller envoyer la telegramme à le pauvre M Bowden – Good! We did that. Afterwards she sat & talked of literature with me until *lunch*. Then I took her to the 1.15 train which did not arrive until 5 moins quart. It poured with rain – it was bitterly cold and cheerless – & she poor creature will not be home until tomorrow. Avignon 2 heures le matin. God! What a pilgrimage of love on her side; & how I bore the conversations I have no idea. I simply died with them & rose again – died & rose again & I am sure there is not a poem unturned in the whole of the Provencale literature after that. She is gone, confident that she will reassure you & my left lung aches & aches so as I write that I must ask Jeanne if she knows of a doctor here just to tell me *what* this ache can be. It is like an appaling *burn*. Sometimes if I lift my arm over my head it seems to give it relief. *What* is it?

The Times & The Nation came today, thank you, my love.

25 to seven. Saturday. I love you so I love you so. The wind howls, the shutters squeak & this cold, deserted hotel seems to be on an island – far far away . . . . But I love you so I love you so. I am absolutely all yours for ever.

My precious, please don't ever send me a *penny* of extra money. That is very straight dinkum. Save it. Put it away. We shall want all our pocketsful for later. I shall save all I can & faire des economies as far as I can. *Trust me*.

And again I implore you take care of yourself. Dont sit in wet feet – eat – keep warm – sleep. Think of how I adore you – of how I cant bear a hair of your head should be harmed. Youre all perfection to me – but guard yourself – cherish yourself

for your little wife Tig.

MS ATL. *LJMM*, 121–4.

[1] Murry had written directly to the Geoffrois, although KM herself found the couple tiresome. Murry told KM on 15 Jan, 'I shall feel better if I know that she would look after you.' (Murry, 103.)

[2] *The Tempest*, III. i. 54–7.

[3] Murry told KM on 13 Jan about dining with her cousin Sydney Waterlow and the Cambridge don, Goldsworthy Lowes Dickinson, 'We had a good evening together: which chiefly consisted in guessing quotations.' (Murry, 98.) He had been 'completely knocked out' by the lines from Camillo's speech about Leontes' and Polixenes' friendship in *The Winter's Tale*, I. ii. 26–9, 'that they have seem'd to be together, though absent; shook hands, as over a vast; and embrac'd as it were from the ends of opposed winds'.

[4] Mrs Hardwick, the landlady who seems rather to have bullied Murry. The week before she had forced him to dismiss 'Ma Parker' as his char.

[5] Murry notes (*LJMM*, 123), '[R.S.] Slatkowsky was the proprietor of the Russian Law Bureau, where Koteliansky worked. He was a comic quasi-legendary figure in our circle.'

[6] Frédéric Mistral (1830–1914), poet and leader of a movement for reviving Provençal language and literature; Théodore Aubanal (1829–86), who wrote poetry in Provençal; Jean-Henri Fabre (1823–1915), poet, naturalist, and teacher in Avignon.

To Ottoline Morrell, 18 January [1918]

my official name and address ⎰ Madame Bowden, Hotel Beau
⎱   Rivage | Bandol | (Var)

January 18th

My dearest Ottoline,

My note from Paris has mocked me ever since I threw it so gaily into the letterbox by the Gare de Lyon. That action was indeed the end of the movement – the end of the allegro – the end of anything inclining ever so faintly towards the major. No, no, never come to France while this bloody war is on. It is tolerable as far as Paris but after that it is the most infernal weariness and discomfort and exasperation. Unendurable! The trains are not heated, they are hours upon hours late, one can obtain nothing to eat or what is much more, nothing hot to drink – they are packed to overflowing; the very lavatories refuse to work.

In such a case I crawled to Marseilles, and caught the most plaguey chill, stiff neck, sore throat, streaming cold that ever I had. Staggering out of the train, carrying my luggage, a pimp in white canvas shoes, eager to reserve a place for a super pimp, swung up the steps and dealt me such a blow on the chest that I am still blue with it. This thought I is joliment Marseilles, and it was indeed very typical, in a *mild* way, of the hours I spent there. Finally when I had *thrown* myself into the 2 hours late Bandol train there was a fight between the soldiers and civilians. The soldiers rushed the train, commandeered it and threw the civilians out, bag & baggage on to the platform. Not in any high-tiddly-i-ty take me back to Blighty spirit but in a very nasty temper indeed – in fact as ugly a crowd as I ever wish to see. They crawled into and over the carriages like apes, banged on the windows, wrenched open the doors – This seemed to me the comble. But I had happily got into a carriage with 8 serbian officers $\pm$ their two dogs and *they* put up a fight against the soldiers. They took off their dogs leather leads and held up the doors, barricaded the entrance to the next carriage and generally behaved as though their eight mothers had born and bred them in the most expensive, rare and exclusive cinema de luxe. Finally after complications innumerable, in the midst of which I became, for the railway officials a serbian, too, and the wife of one of them, they gained the day. It only needed that I should arrive here to find I was *not* expected, that the hotel had changed hands, was far more expensive and was *not* heated.

No, I lay down my weapons after that.

Since then I have been getting into bed and out of bed and doing very little else, in no gay fashion, dearest. As soon as I have recovered from this cursed chill Ill write again. But at present my jaundiced eye would as lief gaze on the Fulham Road as on this lilac sea and budding mimosa. As the night wears on I grow more and more despondent, and my thoughts walk by with long black plumes on their heads while I sit up in bed with your pink quilt round my shoulders & think it must be at least *4* o'clock & find it is just a quarter to *2* !

. My lovely gay shawl lies upon a chair & I gaze at it feeling rather like David Copperfield's Dora,[1] and wondering *when* I shall wear it again.

But I suppose all this will pass. Its just another little hell that must be gone through . . I simply long for a letter from you. Forgive a dull dog who loves you truly and take pity on *your* Katherine.

MS Texas. *LKM* I. 102–3.

[1] Lady Ottoline had given her a shawl for Christmas. KM is comparing herself with the invalid first wife of David in Dickens' *David Copperfield* (1850).

To J. M. Murry, [19 January 1918]

[Bandol]

MUCH BETTER SEEN MADAME GEOFFROI DONT WORRY

BOWDEN

Telegram ATL.

To Annie Burnell Beauchamp, 20 January [1918]

[Hôtel Beau Rivage, Bandol]
Sunday afternoon
January 20th
3.15

Book II

My precious Mummy,

Three letters from you two pounds from Papa and a note and two handkerchiefs from Jeanne enriched my morning's mail. I am writing separately to Father and Jeanne, so now I will reply to yours. I have just sent Belle a note and the receipt – rather a copy of it for the brown bread that you sent me. Alas! I cannot make it over the gas jet here, but as soon as I get back I will bake a loaf. My dear! The illustration of the *jam tart* in your letter made my mouth water; especially did my eyes pop at the button of sugar on the top. I hope you will not have

lost your cunning when we meet again. I am afraid you took my
mention of sausages and stout, a meal partaken of in company with
my dear sister & Jack, too much to heart, and have a dreadful fancy
that I live almost exclusively upon these highly seasoned comestibles.
Nothing could be further from the truth. I am just as simple in my
tastes as you. A cup of *good* old fashioned tea, bread and butter – jam –
and eggs plain or in any disguise satisfies me *at* any time and *for* any
time. Having inherited from my mother a *light* and *courageous* hand I
own that I am tempted to flights higher than these – and love
sometimes to go a trifle mad dog in the kitchen, but on the whole
nobody could be fonder of simple home made fare than Jack and I.

I had, exclusive of my home budget today, eleven letters on my
breakfast tray, including one from my good little doctor in reply to a
note I had sent him thanking him for his care of me. I agree with you
about doctors. Unless one wants a check action and a spring balance
put in or to be jewelled in two holes they are *not* very helpful, and I
shall always give them as wide a berth as I can. But this little man of
mine was very modern and professional and cheery. It is rather a
comfort to feel he is there in case one requires glueing or darning
together. I am so glad that our Christmas presents arrived and
eagerly look forward to your photograph. I shall have as good a one as
I can taken in April for you – I don't mean life-size by that or with
mother-of-pearl eyes but a good postcard. Chaddie's are perfectly
excellent and the image of her present self.

Mummy I shall have to wait until I get back to Paris before I can
send you a sachet. I will try and get you a 'special' one there. Your
love of sweet perfumes is another gift that you showered on me. I can
never have enough of fine sweet smells such as sachets and powders
and soaps. In fact the customs officials on my way here came across so
many small coloured sweet smelling bags in my yellow trunk that they
became quite suspicious and I was half afraid they would borrow the
bayonet from the sentry at the door, slit them open and have us all
wading in lavender verbena and rose. I don't think it is a vice or even a
vanity, but backed up by old Dean Swift I think "It is a virtue in a
woman to be exquisite and discreet in her person and of a delicate
perfume".[1] Do you remember that bottle of Indian Hay in your corner
drawer at 75 [Tinakori Road] ? I think you got it in Sydney.

This little village smells of nothing but shellfish, jonquils, a whiff or
two of goat and burning charcoal and bluegum wood. Which isn't a
bad mixture but difficult to capture for you and not to be relished far
from its native soil.

I feel so much better today. For the first time for weeks I felt really
hungry for lunch. The party at the next table to me are a trifle
hypnotising. A mother with her two little boys. The mother is very

thin, dresses in woolen jackets tied with ribbons and trimmed with swansdown, with short sleeves (the provincial french lady's idea of a sports coat) One little boy whose back is turned to me seems a dear little fellow, but the bébé, who sits next to Mamma, and cannot be more than five, is a terror. I am always catching him making the most dreadful faces at me or gazing at me through his wine glass, as though I were a ship on the horizon and could only be seen with artificial aid or else he slaps a slice of bread on his head, puffs out his cheeks and rolls his eyes at me. *And* his manners! Whenever there is fish he seizes his prey by the head and tail and devours it as though he were playing a finny mouth-organ – as to fowl or cutlet bones he is almost a professional performer upon those and ripe to give a concert on either instrument at the Queens Hall.

You can imagine how anxiously we are waiting for yours and Father's answers to the letter we sent about getting married! I know you believe in happiness, and that you think it is one's duty to be happy. If I could only tell you how happy I shall be to have my darling Jack for a husband. We are both great believers in the *power* of happiness and I know that our friends love to be with us because they feel we are happy and have enough and to spare to give to them, too.

Just four o'clock. I wonder what time you have Sunday tea, and if the kettle would be on if I were to turn up now. Its a great comfort to feel that dear old V. [Vera] will be with you so soon. I am longing to write to her; but I hope to hear from her and she will tell me where she may be caught with a letter. I wonder what Mack's plans are? I was so delighted to hear from Jeanne. She is the sister whom I know least but from her letters to Chaddie I get many a glimpse.

Poor little Godmother.[2] Would you convey to her my loving remembrances and most sincere sympathy. I hope she does build on her section so that you and she may walk in each others parlours.

Well, Mother dear I must bring this letter to a close, light my fire and make myself at least a glass of hot water. As old Minnie would say "Mrs Beauchamp might whistle for a cup of tea here."

My devoted love to you. I cannot thank you for all the riches that your letters heaped on my heart, but you know how warmly it beat for you under them – don't you dear?

Ever your devoted little child,

Kass

MS Newberry.

---

[1] A recollection of Jonathan Swift's *A Letter to a Very Young Lady on her Marriage* (1727), where he advises 'a suitable Addition of Care in the Cleanliness and Sweetness of their Persons'.

[2] Laura Kate Bright, a close friend of Annie Beauchamp's. After her husband committed suicide, she lived next door to the Beauchamps' new home in Wadestown, and in January 1920 became Harold's second wife.

To J. M. Murry, [20 January 1918]

[Hôtel Beau Rivage, Bandol]
Sunday

My Own Precious
I LOVE YOU.
I AM EVER SO MUCH BETTER
I AM COMING BACK IN APRIL.
BE HAPPY MY DEAR LOVE
ONLY WRITE TWICE A WEEK
OR YOU WILL BE 2 TIRED.
MY MONEY IS QUITE SATISFACTORY[1]

There is the bulletin. Oh Bogey I wɪsʜ that I had not told you the truth, for your two sad letters today, the one when my awful remark about malade jumped up & down the typewriter & the other wrung my heart this morning. It is quite true. I have been *bloody ill* but these last 2 days I feel ever such a great deal better & quite a different child. Chiefly because I know that I am not going to get worse & that we shall be together again. I really *did*, at one or two times, think I would 'peg out' here, never having had a heron or a heronette and that simply horrified me.[2] But now though the local pain is still there everything else in me is against it & not for it – I feel *hungry* and I keep making plans. i.e. I shall bring him, in my old biscuit tin, ½ a pound of mountain butter, a little pot of cherry jam, a tiny handful of sweet dried figs. & in my box Ill pack 4 of the biggest pine cones I can find.

Its the 20th of January today. By the 20th of April we shall be married[3] & sitting among our children I expect in some flowery field making daisy & buttercup chains. *If* I don't break off into a thousand pieces for love of you before then. My mother sent us great and little blessings today – to 'you & Jack'. She has a feeling that 'a happy future is unfolding for you both', though of course our letters havent arrived yet. She told me a way to make bread which sounds very easy for our farm. She says after the war she is going to do the cooking in their house & Father is going to do all the washing. Father bought the entire library with that house which sounds a pearl.[4] He has just finished reading Robinson Crusoe.

My Grandma Beauchamp is dead.[5] She had a stroke & died.

Aunt Li[6] has never recovered from her stroke.

'Bees'[7] husband has hanged himself in an outhouse.

As Mother says we seem to be all on strike or on string out here.

I had a nice letter from Ainger[8] today, asking me to tell him how I got on & I had a letter from Belle & Chaddie. In fact I had 11 letters. But they might all have gone down that wind. Yours were the only ones I really coveted – devoured –

Oh my cherished one – I wish I could somehow tell you *here* and *now* that I feel inclined to lie on my back & play with Ribni.[9] If we were together wed make some coffee & a bright fire & sit and talk curled up in one round. Next month I shall go to Marseilles for 2 days to see Cooks & to get some books. To see Cooks about all that one has to do to get back so as I can be ready.

It is dark and very windy today. The sea is all teeth and fury. It rained all night. But I would not be surprised if the sun came out next week. I feel I have lifted up my head again and all my petals have spread out ready to catch a ray. But I wish I had a pigeon to send this letter more quickly.

Its Sunday and some strangers came here for lunch – we had bouille baisse. I wondered what you had.

Yes, I am not one but *two* – I am *you* as well as myself. You are another part of me just as I am a part of you.

Goodbye for now, my bogey.

Yours ever
Wig.

MS ATL. *LJMM*, 124–5.

---

[1] Murry's letters continued to castigate himself for not writing more frequently, and expressed concern about KM's finances. On 15 Jan he had told her 'I've been working hard at articles for the *Times* & the *Nation* so that we shall soon be swimming in funds again' (Murry, 103), and on 18 Jan 'don't be afraid to let them swindle you so long as they will make you warm. Just tell me how much you want'. (ATL.)

[2] The 'Heron' embodied KM's desire for a small country cottage of their own, where she and Murry would support themselves as writers and live off the land.

[3] KM's divorce from George Bowden was heard in London on 17 October 1917, the decree *nisi* becoming absolute at the end of April 1918.

[4] Harold Beauchamp bought 'The Grange' in Wadestown from Lady Kelburn (later Lady Glasgow). As he recorded in his *Reminiscences and Recollections* (1937), 96, the house had been built in the 1860s 'on a design intended to reproduce many of the features of an English mansion'.

[5] Mary Elizabeth Stanley, b. Preston, Lancashire, in 1836, had married Arthur Beauchamp in Australia in 1854, and died at Picton on 24 November 1917. KM's father was the third of her ten children. She is the grandmother in KM's story 'The Voyage', written in 1921.

[6] Liza Trapp, KM's maternal aunt.

[7] Bee: her mother's friend, Laura Bright.

[8] William Ainger, the New Zealand doctor who had treated KM before she left London.

[9] References to the doll are frequent in Murry's letters. He had written on 15 Jan, 'If only I could send Ribni even to you just to make your heart warm.' (Murry, 102.)

To J. M. Murry, [21 January 1918]

[Hôtel Beau Rivage, Bandol]
Monday

My own Boge,

I am only going to write you a note today just to say that I still feel better. The weather is 1000 times rougher. Never, not even on shipboard or in my own little country or anywhere have I heard such wind. And in the night, when one lay quiet in bed & listened God knows how many Ancient Mariners cried in it or how many lost souls whirled past. I thought then what an agony it must be to be wife to a fisherman. How could a poor soul comfort herself & to whom could she pray when such a wind & such a sea fought against her . . . I thought too, it must have been just such a storm when Shelley died.¹ This morning at red dawn a destroyer & a submarine tried to put out to sea, but they were obliged to return. I despised them for that & thought no english sails would not have mastered it. But you know, for all my big talk, I never believe the frenchies can sail a boat, or throw a ball, or do anything at all which is a patch upon the English . . . If you could see this sea today heaving and smoking like a herd of monsters run mad . .

Last night my little maid brought me a present of rose buds. Two green jars full of them & some yellow *soleil d'or* beside. She had been for a walk in the country she said & a friend had made her a present. She came to the door with them – so pretty – wearing a black woolen cap and her cheeks were red – Shortly after the Madame came to ask if I would like some hot wine at night for my cough. "Je ne savais pas que vous avez été si fatiguée". Well, though it is a bit tard for remedy as I am such a much better girl I said Yes to the wine – & it was a rare fine posset. 3rd The submarine captain, having heard me try to get tobacco presented me with a whole packet of maryland – not cigarettes but tobacco – so I feel people have been unusually caring.

My precious heart, as I write the sun forced his head through a positive monks hood of a cloud & blesses you & me upon this page . . I thought this morning – in February I shall be able to say when I come back the month after next. And too February is a very tiny little month so that after it is gone & March has blown in there will only be a few weeks before April – Does this comfort you as it does me? I shall be awfully well – and all hung with presents for you with 2 candles that cant be put out – in my eyes – Youll have to discover me like a Christmas tree. Then we will wave & wave as the train carries us towards each other & then we'll be in each others arms. I fully expect Rib to be with you in your green overcoat cut down very small with a feltie on –

Does this letter make you feel that you are the most loved & cherished Bogey in all the world. If it dont – its none of mine – but it must. Now I am going to the post – then to have lunch then to come up here – light my fire & write.

I am always your own
Wig.

TAKE CARE OF YOURSELF –[2]

MS ATL. *LKM* I. 103–4; *LJMM*, 126–7.

---

[1] Percy Bysshe Shelley was drowned in a storm while sailing near Spezia, 30 June 1822.

[2] At the end of this letter (*LJMM*, 127) Murry included a sentence KM wrote on a telegram she received from him: 'The old man with the dog just brought it. I think *he* thinks I feed on telegrams – like silkworms on mulberry leaves.'

To J. M. Murry, [22 January 1918]

(Hôtel Beau Rivage, Bandol]
Tuesday

My love,

I cannot write to you as I wish until I know that this cruel barb that I plucked out of my bosom only to drive into yours has been withdrawn. Oh, that I should have hurt you so. No, I never will cry out again.[1] The bears can eat me first. Ill *never never* forgive myself. I will just tell you, so that you may know how I am taking care of myself: I stay in bed every day until lunch. Then I dress by a fire. If it is fine I go for a small walk in the afternoon then I come back to my fire. After dinner at about 8.30. I go to bed. The food here has got much better since the submarines have taken to lunching & dining here. It is now very good & they have begun giving me portions so big that I think they suspect me of at least twins sous mon coeur. I set sail across tureens of nourishing soup stagger over soft mountains of pommes purées and melt in marmalades. So you see how well I am looking after MYSELF. Now tell me about you. My love, my dear heart, my own. If you knew how all my being turns towards you, and is always anxious and wondering a little. I was always thinking when I first came here – we have never had a *real life together,* for only now are we grown enough in each others sight to understand what that means & how it can be enjoyed. It *must* it *shall* be ours.

But tell me when you answer this letter if you still feel hungry, if the Good Intent[2] is still satisfactory & what you have for lunch. Do you get milk enough? These things are most important as you know.

Unless you want me before I shall now stay here until the first week in April as I said yesterday, then my ship will point for home – Great

God! What is any country or richness in the world to me where thou art not – Until then I shall work & become a very strong girl, write to you, husband our money, and if I know that you are content, that you, my life, do not worry but can work & be at peace in the evenings – & perhaps get from my love a refreshment that will make your vile office a little more endurable then I will be as happy as I can be – lacking you.

For quite seriously I adore you.

I have decided to risk the post with my work. I shall always send it registered & always keep a copy but I want you to have it as it comes off my pen –

This Bogey is whispered, very privately. Rib can hear because he's ours. We shall have an english Heron even if its only one stout room looking out upon nibbled downs and sheep – I am as firm in that as you.

When I have heard from you in answer to my wire I'll write very fully.

Do you write twice a week, but as I don't spend any money on cigarettes (oh we are babies) I can afford to write once a day. Ive the time & until you tire of – just my fond embrace even – just taking off your ring, kissing your finger and putting it on again – I will write every day –

The wind still blows a hurricane here. In the night the rain joined it but now the sun beats in the air like a kite. It is like living on a ship. The hotel is all bolted and barred up – the big doors closed & a strange twilight in the hall. People go about in shawls and coats. If a window is opened the seas of the air rush in & fill it. Two great palm trees have snapped like corks & many a glittering plume trails in the dust. They say it never has been known before. I have begun to like it – Were I to feel that you, my life were put out of worry I should enjoy it –

Yours yours for ever – every part of me
Wig.

MS ATL. *LKM* I. 105; *LJMM*, 127–8.

---

[1] Murry had written on 15 Jan 'Oh, I wish that you had never, never gone. Everything seems so terribly to have changed', and 'the thought that I cannot look after you at all, even in my clumsy way, torments me'. (Murry, 102, 103.)

[2] A restaurant on the Chelsea Embankment where Murry frequently dined.

To J. M. Murry, [23 January 1918]

[Hôtel Beau Rivage, Bandol]
Wednesday.

My dear life,

Here is your letter of Friday night under my hand – the one in which Rib rolled over and laughed. I have an idea that our children will use us just so. They will adore us but our love will make them *laugh at us*, in just his careless, infinitely confident way. Oh, dont let us ever forget Ribni. He must be always with us and our babies must only be allowed to sit next to him & perhaps stroke down his fringe with their tiny brown hands.

Last night, when I had finished capturing all I could of this wind, and rain and cold, it ceased,and this morning the sun came out. There is still a stiff breeze but its warm in the sun and indescribably lovely. Every mortal thing looks to be sheathed in a glittering beauty. It began, for me with your letter. There was a pulse in your letter that set my heart beating. I got up at about eleven and went out to buy myself une canne avec une frique. The disagreeable shop has become aimable. I bought a small stout one for 1.25. and then walked up the road behind the front past Ma'am Gamels, to the top of the hill and a little way further. The sky over the sea was like an immense canterbury bell, darkly transparently blue. Towards me came walking an old woman in a pleated black dress with a broad straw hat tied under her chin with a linen band and she carried a pack of jonquils. Then there came a butterfly, my little sister, weak in the wing, and staggering a little but *basking*. The cats lay on the windowsills. In a field against the sea a man and a woman were digging; the olive trees blew silver and the sea, very wild still, embraced the shore as though it loved it. As I came back I saw an old man sitting in a corner of a field, some wine & bread in a basket by him. He had a pair of breeches over his knees that he was carefully darning. They looked awfully forlorn as though he had just given them a beating.

But how can all this have happened in a night? Yesterday – midwinter. I walked to the post wearing your wadded coat, my woolen one, my great blue one over all & was perished. I staggered home, and decided that I must ask you to send me an anchor, a small one, shaped like a crab perhaps, with whiskers, that I could draw behind me on a string, to keep me from blowing (a) into the sea or (b) over le grand cerveau – and here's today come to mock me. On a vraiment chaud. By the way, my precious, my wadded coat has been and is a perfect treasure. It keeps out the draughts like nothing else. I wear it every day & sit up in bed in it and enfin – it is just what I ideally wanted.

Oh, the washer girl came today while I was in bed. You remember her? How fine she was, always so gauffré with frills over her hands & gold rings in her ears, and very expressive sparkling eyes. Now, poor wench, shes so changed. There cant have been a soul in bandol with pyjame de laine 2.50 the washing since you left. She has shed all her brightness, jusqu'a ses pieds, which were covered in lovely red kid slippers. I hope it will *monte* again. She charged me 3.50 but it was not a 'swin' really.

I must tell you my little maid is becoming more and more friendly. She looks like the girl you read of who spreads the linen to dry in the orchard while the young boy up the ladder fills her apron with red pears. She was saying yesterday that she did not like the hotel to be so empty. We sit together, said she, there's nothing to do . . "Alors, nous nous regardons – nous causons – mais, c'est triste, vous savez, ce n'est pas si gai que la service!" What do they talk about & where do they sit? I began to wonder . . .

I am thankful that the studio is let and off our hands.[1] *No* don't send the £5. Put it in the bank. Ill cry when I am empty but being very well trained not before. I am doing all I can to live without spending, to wear my old clothes & shoes – We shall feast and array ourselves when we are together, and "fleet the time carelessly as they did in the golden world".[2]

My adored one. Now that you know I am so much better you will tell me all about yourself & you will take care of yourself.

> "And this is not a boon
> 'Tis as I should entreat you – wear your gloves
> Or feed on nourishing dishes, or keep you warm
> Or sue to you to do a peculiar profit
> To your own person."[3]

Warmly, warmly, passionately eternally I love you.

[*Across top*]   Wig.

Please can you send me my old mended shoes. I do need them so and L.M says she gave them to you . . . If its not a bother.

MS ATL. *LKM* I. 105–7; *LJMM*, 128–30.

[1] Murry wrote on 19 Jan that 141A Church Street was let, and that 'I have only to pay the £4 rent from Dec. 25 to Jan. 18'. (Murry, 107.)

[2] *As You Like It*, I. i. 124.

[3] *Othello*, III. iii. 78–81.

To J. D. Fergusson, [24 January 1918]

[Hôtel Beau Rivage, Bandol]
Thursday.

My dear Fergusson,

Don't cry déja! at the sight of my handwriting and don't be afraid that I shall keep on knocking at your door in this importunate way. I won't. Only – I can't let my last letter to you remain unanswered, on my side. Make a curl paper of it or use it 'to stop a hole to keep the wind away'. Thanks for yours.

This is an extraordinary country, very well described by an old type I saw today who was picking yellow and white jonquils in his proprieté. I remarked that it was winter before yesterday – 'Eh ben – que ce que vous voulez – c'est le facon de not' pays. Un jour nous sommes en plein hiver – lendemain on voyait les boutons et – puis – toute a la fois' and he raised up and stretched out his arms over the flowery field. That is just what has happened. The day before yesterday this whole place, swaddled up to the eyebrows, was rocking, tossing in the arms of the coldest, most biting unsympathetic nurse you could imagine. But yesterday there came a dawn when the sky and the sea were like silk, and the miracle happened – the sun came out. Toute à la fois the women who had looked like lean boiled fowls became beautiful and fat and rosy. Windows and doors flew open and the houses began to breathe and move. Cats, en escargot, appeared on the window sills. Girls appeared in the doorways plaiting wreaths of yellow immortelles, plus every green and blue pitcher went off to the fountain. Old hags in black pleated dresses, with broad black hats tied under the chin with a linen band hobbled in from the country with a load of jonquils on their backs or a pack of olive twigs, and old men swung off *into* the country, each with a pot of manure on a creaking barrow. There was simply one word that flew over the place like a flag – BEAU. 'I' fait beau. I' fait beau. I' fait vraiment beau'.

I went for a walk in the afternoon round by the sea coast. My God, Fergusson, to feel the sun again on one's breast and belly, to realise again that one had five toes on each foot and each toe has a separate voice with which to praise the Lord, and to know that the cheek that was turned to the sea *burned* as it used to when you were a kid! Then I turned inland. The lanes are bordered thick with wild candytuft and small marigolds; the almond trees are half in bud, half in bloom. All along the way there are little handfuls of earth thrown up, like handfuls of coffee, where the ants are busy. And everywhere you could hear the people working in the fields – you could see them digging on those flat terraces – bending down and raising up again, ample and leisurely, as though they were the children of this kingdom and so had

nothing to fear. It was nearing sunset as I came home and each round bright flower was turned to the sun – a cup of light – a sun of its own, and all the olive trees seemed to be hung with bright sparkles. Yes, this is a good place to be in. One word more and then you can throw me out of the window. Here's another thing that struck me as so 'typical' of these people. As I walked back along the main street I saw an old woman on the sea front. She was sitting on a little iron chair which she had planted there, about *one inch* from the deep sea water. And there she sat – *with her back towards the sea* doing a bit of crochet. This struck me mildly as 'most unwise' as my sister would say, as, had she coughed, sneezed or taken a false stitch, over she would have to go. However, it was no affair of mine. But another old 'un who was washing outside her door caught sight of this. Down fell the wet clothes. 'Marthe' she shrieked. 'Que?' said a voice. 'V'en vite'. And when Marthe saw she began to laugh and clap her hands. The windows became full of heads. 'Allez allez! Tu as vu Ma'am Gamel – la bas? Ah, mon Dieu tu as vu ca?' They came running to the doors to laugh more and all this time old Ma'am Gamel, who must have been stone deaf, sat on, doing her crochet, paying no attention at all.
'Allez allez! elle va tomber.'
'Non elle ne tombe pas!'
'Si! elle tombe!'
'Ah si j'avais un orange maintenant par exemple!'
Every one of them was simply longing to see the Comble – to see la vieille topple over – I could hear their laughter if she did – and I can imagine the way they would have leaned against one another, quite helpless, pointing to her old black hat and little bit of crochet floating out to sea!

Well, I'll stop. I have a vase of roses and buds before me on the table. I had a good *look* at them last night and your rose picture was vivid before me – I saw it in every curve of these beauties – the blouse like a great petal, the round brooch, the rings of hair like shavings of light. I thought how supremely you had 'brought it off'.

This hotel is quite deserted. I have a room at the end of a huge, dark, greenish, sousmarin corridor which might be miles away from anybody. I have begun to work – yesterday – and shall keep at it all I know . . .

I wish I could send you steaks and butter and la richesse de la terre. But its no go.

There's nobody to speak to here. Just occasionally I have a word or two with the lad or with you – but that ends it. And it's quite enough.

Here's to Art – God bless us all.
Mansfield.

Look here – don't even like to write.

MS lacking. Morris, 124–6.

To J. M. Murry, [24 January 1918]

[Hôtel Beau Rivage, Bandol]
Thursday.

Dearest of all,

I did not have a letter from you today. Perhaps you have already heard from me about the 'twice a week' idea. Of course my fond heart said: 'has there been an air raid?' But then I heard at length from Johnny & he would have told me – It was Sunday coming between.

Yesterday I took your letter with me and we walked our old familiar way – along by the coast & then inland – Well, I supposed we looked as though we were walking – but God God – my spirits never kept worse time with my toes . . . A sea like quilted silk – the lavender bushes growing among the rocks all in new leaf. Such air as you and I have drunk together and a whole flock of little winds to shake every perfumed bud and flower. The almond trees if one stands close & looks up are thick with white and red buds; the lanes have a thick border of white and yellow – wild candy tuft and small marigolds. The mimosa is coming out over the gate to our house[1] – which is still sealed up – still as remote – *more* beautiful *more* desirable than ever. This place is so full of our love that every little walk I take is a passionate pilgrimage – There is the villa allons-y – here is the field where we saw all the anemones – here the wall where the lizard lay basking – One could hear everywhere the voices of people in the fields – one could see, through the blue, fresh painted gates women bending to the earth and rising up again – with the old leisurely grace. They passed me, the dark people we know so well with their loads of little olive branches – *or* a squeaking barrow of manure – and as I came home I went by the Villa Pauline, and saw over the wall the geraniums in leaf & bud. (Ah, I did of course go in, & while you put the kettle on I took out the flowery cups, put our honey biscuits in a dish & we sat down, faint and warm and smiling we knew not why). These incredible people who avant hier were wrapped in every inch of fur or wool they could find were yesterday dabbling their legs in the water down on the shore . . . .

I had a lie down when I came home & then I worked – When it grew dusky I opened the windows to close the shutters. The moon was up. The sky over the sea faint rose – & there was a strange bright glister on the palm trees. After dinner in the hotel library I found a copy of Martin Eden[2] (which Orage always thought a famous good book) and a large shabby tome – Tissot – Litterature Francaise.[3] But I couldn't stomach the former. No, a little Shakespeare makes ones nose too fine for such a rank smeller as Jack London. The other is *rare* meat. It is examples of french literature from the 9th century to the end of the 18th. And it is followed by a *Revue* of the state of the whole world at that time – each country taken separate – very excellent amusement. And too, there are hundreds of the little engravings and fantastical letters that we love. I shall guard this in my room & bury Jack London again. I heard from Geoffroi yesterday <u>&</u> she included *une* poème. I send you both. By my passport I shall not be permitted to stay at Carpentras you know, but Ill tell her that, later. It would kill me – After the war with you to fly to I will – but alone to sustain that parfaitement, Madame – justement – mais bien sûr, for more than half an hour would turn me into a parrot for life.

When we do have a house here I think Ill try & get this maid to come. She's just *our* style, but I wish she would not give me a fresh bouquet more than once a day – Five vases of flowers are enough. The last is feathery mimosa. My own, I write to you thus and tell you all because you *must* share it. This is the news which comes from your country which I am visiting on your behalf just as much as mine. For the present, my love, you are the King in his counting house counting out his money & I am the Queen in her parlour eating bread & honey – Ah God, that there *wasnt* a door between us. All my joy here is half yours. It is my love for you which puts all the sweet breath into this. As I write, as I think of you I feel that I am love. Nothing else – Oh, I could weep like a child because there are so many flowers and my lap is so small & all must be carried home to you.

Farewell, my heart.

Your
Wig.

MS ATL. *LKM* I. 107–9; *LJMM*, 130–2.

[1] Murry noted (*LJMM*, 131): 'Not the Villa Pauline, but a small and beautiful cottage in an olive yard, about a mile away.'

[2] Jack London's autobiographical novel *Martin Eden* was published in 1909.

[3] Pierre-François Tissot, *Leçons et modèles de littérature française ancienne et moderne*, 2 vols (1835, 1836).

To J. M. Murry, [24 and 25 January 1918]

[Hôtel Beau Rivage, Bandol]
Thursday 24th

Dear Love

I *must* add this to today's letter. I have chuckled over it for hours – As I went out this afternoon I met the widow hurrying up from the town, très pandaresque and all aflower with smiles. Justement she had come to look for me. One demanded me at the Mairie, & the Mayor waited. I said I had better get my passeport first & she agreed. I told her I was already registered, but she said they were very strict now. She had NO idea (mark that!) what I was wanted for but enfin – voilà! Off I went. In that office of theirs the Mayor, his deputy & old Drum waited for me. The Mayor wore white shoes with blue strings & his cap back to front & a bout of cigarette in his mouth mais il etait tres serieux. You are Madame the lady to whom these papers refer? (The papers I had filled for the hotel). Yes, Monsieur. Bien! Will you follow me Madame to the Salon du Conseil? Tres volontiers, Monsieur. My spirits mounted with every step of the stairs. *He* is lame & had to get up them like a pigeon – you know – both feet on one step before he could reach to the next – Came a black door heavily gilded, hugely labelled SALON DU CONSEIL. This was unlocked & I had a glimpse of such a chambre sich as my irreverent British eye has never twinkled on before. A black paper with gold stamping – a huge table covered with heavy black cloth, fringed with gold. A few trunks of dead men, coloured, on brackets round the wall & one of those portraits with a striped glass over so that if you looked at it from your side it was La Liberté but if you looked at it from his it was – je ne sais pas – There were also an immense number of bundles covered in black cloth – dead mayors I think. We sat down on a couple of velvet chairs with gold fleur de lys so heavily stamped on their seats that if you had any chance vous pouvez montrer a votre ami une derrière mais vraiment chic – & he produced a perfect mass of papers. Connaissez-vous Madame, un certain *M. Parquerre*? Non, Monsieur. You are not expecting a gentleman to follow you to France? No, Monsieur. Then of course "I saw it all". It was *Baker*. He had heard from the British Consulate at Marseilles that a lady had tombéd gravement malade at Bandol – Was there such a lady? Her friend *M. Parquerre* prayed for permission etc. This was I think the first official document he had ever received from the B.C. He could not get over it – its importance – the whole affair. Well I explained. We had a lot of chat. Then said he – but do you want the lady? I can arrange it. C'est vite fait. That is so like the Midi. And I said *no* without hesitating – just like that. Are you surprised? Dabord none of us have the money unless the affair is urgent. (2). I feel she ought to stay at her factory. She is simply bound up in it really & would be wretched here. What could she do? But the money aspect is the important one n'est-ce pas? I did right, didn't I? I hope she will understand. *Also* this is strictly confidential it is *far* better she should not come. She has been an angel to me but in the new life she has not a great part – & she realises that. It would be very painful. I left the Mayor – his deputy & old Drum preparing the answer to this document – trying pens –

slapping the rubber stamp on the backs of their hands to see if it would work etc.

BUT: there was one unpleasant fly. He says le crise de chemins de fer will last – will grow worse with the spring – & at times the railway will be, as now, absolutely closed to civilian traffic – so he warned me if I want to get home to choose a moment well in advance. How awful it would be if I got stuck here Boge? Wouldn't it?

Goodbye for now, my soul. Oh, my MARK that. The Mayor said the widow had read the paper & knew all about it.

Friday 25th Not a word before I have greeted anew your poem in the Nation.[1] It is supremely beautiful – an achievement that "traces on your brow their secret mark" for ever. In a word Bogey it is *first chop*. Oh, my boy do you *know* how lovely it is – how far away and clear – how it rings across the water even to the shores of that other country. Great God! To think that this lovely voice still sings in England – that you're alive, twenty-eight years old – and that youre to be – who could doubt it for one instant after this poem – the Great Poet of our time. I sit here smiling but the tears press on my eyelids. I whisper "Oh my *wonder*". After the war is over we must cover our pennies in silver paper if they are not light enough & you must forget everything *except this – this treasure that is yours.*

My own – The letters were late arriving. Your Saturday letter came today & you had not yet heard that the weather has changed – I had no fire at all yesterday & today I have pulled down the iron screen. So paniers of wood *are* not any more for the present. You did not send the money – did you? I received a Lit. Sup. the Daily News & the Nation. I read your poem – all the others are to be browsed on plus tar'. I heard from L.M. rather melancholy. I must write to her. No, love, it is much better that I remain alone, now. I am really (except for one local funny 'spot' of pain about which I wrote Ainger yesterday) such a well girl – I hardly cough. They go on giving me wine at night & with my café au lait a jug of milk that must be a *whole goat* & two fishes in place of anybody else's *one* – and the weather is if possible lovelier than ever. I sat on a warm stone this morning until my neck got burnt. The two windows of my room are wide open. It is much warmer incomparably more exquisite than I have ever known it here. The sea is so clear (and every shade, blue & green & violet) that one can see, like a map outspread beneath you a whole new uncharted country with little lakes & forests and bays. The coast is pink like the flesh of a

peach is pink & everybody is out fishing, you know,

hanging over the end of the boat & spearing the fish – – –

I had today a portrait of mother sent me. I want you to see it. But I must wait. Whether its like or not like there is all that I knew or imagined of her in it & it seems to me that if you saw it youd agree with me that its rare to see a more *fascinating* woman. I am very glad to have it to show to you. Dear love, I shall be so relieved when you know that its warm here – & you do know now that I am coming back first week in April – don't you? Just reassure me – They are mending & tarring the boats outside my window – you can hear the little hammers & a whiff or two of tar breaks across the mimosa. La Ciotat – Marie-Réjane – the boats we know.

Another week has nearly gone – Six more days & it is gone. Then comes little February (& cant you see little February, waiting and please I can't stay very *long*) & then March – but I shall be making my preparations in March & then – I shall be in your arms again. You must not think I am a nuisance – will you? But dearest, you will tell me – won't you when you have a cold. If you hurt a finger or a toe – do not sleep well – feel shiny in the head. True, it is a kind of anguish to know these things but it is a thousand times greater *not* to know. When I don't know I imagine every possible thing – at certain hours –

Dont you think when this is over we must agree never to part again? I shall never come so far without you again (unless its you that flee me.) It is unbearable to love in our divine, childish way and to be out of hail.

(And do you ever think of getting married?)

Now goodbye until tomorrow. Yes, I think we were well out of the studio, & the other flat. I cant bear that you should have to spend the money you earn so painfully.

Oh, if there is a God he must simply devote his time to watching over you until I come back –

> Your
> Wig.

MS ATL. *LKM* I. 109–11; *LJMM*, 132–5.

¹ 'To my dead friends', the *Nation*, 19 January 1918.

To J. M. Murry, [26 January 1918]

> [Hôtel Beau Rivage, Bandol]
> Saturday.

My precious,

I seem to positively *eat* writing paper, but heres a bit of my old studio days at last. Today I had from you the letter with the £5. i.e. a Monday letter – and your *Sunday* one and the 2 Dickens. So yesterdays

& todays posts seem to have got very mixed. About the £5. Well, by now you'll have my letters asking you not to send me money till I say. I'll cash it, of course & hoard it. As a matter of fact if my Kay money don't come on the very very first I shall not have any left. So thank you my heart.

You have a cold. Oh Bogey, take care of it; and tell me if it is better. I hope you have not been too gay over the warm weather & run to the office without your coat. *Be sure to let me know when you answer this letter how it is.*

Our letters crossed again about Lesley. I heard from her today & I too felt callous cool, and retired into my shell. She *is* a ghoul in a way. She does blossom out and become a brick only when the other person is more or less delivered up to her. That's what I cant stomach. Thats why I dont want her here. As long as I am to be massaged shes an angel, for then c'est elle qui mange; if I am not in the humour out pours Mr. Webb[1] and I and why dont men etc etc. Shes all hungry fury then beating against my shores & trying to break down my defences. That's why I used to get so furious at the studio for there she ate me before my eyes & I really *revolted*.

Of *course* I did see and read what was inside the envelope. Do you imagine I dont always turn the envelopes upside down & breathe into them & shut one eye & stare up at them & shake them, always thinking one of your eyelashes or perhaps a tiny twinkle out of your eye may still be there – Oh Boge, I like the Wordsworth story:[2] it makes my heart warm to him.

It is a different kind of day today, il y a un peu de vent. But with the bright sun it makes the sea an incredible almost violet colour. I went for a walk yesterday & got lost – you know how one can. I couldn't find either the path to the shore or the main road inland – And it kept getting on for sunset & the shadows great appeared before I was found. You should see the *swerves* I take past the dogs. They really are Bragian upstarts and their bold eyes & lifted lips terrify me. I thought what if I had a bulldog of my own. Would that help? But then I would always be frightened that it would wait until we got to a lonely bit & then turn on me. No, the only thing would be a very awful imitation dog, one that I could make smoke come out of its eyes & fire out of its mouth when it passed one of these mongrels. Look out for one for me.

As I sit here I want you – I want you. I want to be at home with you – anywhere – Youre my country – my people – my whole life is bound up in yours. Come awfully close to me & let us hold each other tight a minute.

Ah Love Love when I come back – we shall be so happy – the very cups & saucers will have wings & you will cut me the only piece of bread & jam in the world & I will pour you out a cup of *my* tea.

Why arent you here *now* NOW. But I am coming Bogey – and I am all yours amen.

Tig.

MS ATL. *LKM* I. 111–12; *LJMM*, 136–7.

¹ An acquaintance of Ida Baker's.
² Murry wrote on 20 Jan that his brother 'told me a story about Wordsworth – where he can have got it from, I don't know. It's stupid, but characteristic, and it makes me love the old fellow rather. One day Wordsworth was dining with a friend. Some rather aged, yellowish peas were served. The friend in order to turn it off said to W. "Forgive me, but I forgot to send these peas to Kensington". "To Kensington", says W. "Why pray?" "Because that is the way to Turnham Green". W. thought this an extremely good joke, resolved to remember it, and to let it fly on the first opportunity. It came very soon. He was dining with a friend whose peas were also rather passé. He turned to the lady of the house. "Madam, I'm afraid you forgot to send these peas to Kensington". "To Kensington, Mr. W., why pray?" "Because that is the way to make them green". And he roared with laughter.' (Murry, 108.)

To J. M. Murry, [27 January 1918]

[Hôtel Beau Rivage, Bandol]

French blotting paper dont blot, curse it!
Sunday. Pas de courier pour moi.
Si! (See page 4)¹
Darling

Letter paper – except by the box at 7.25 has run out of Bandol & so I am forced to use this 'papier de commerce'. I am just up – its ten past eleven. What are you doing I wonder? It is also the last Sunday in January which does bring me nearer you – and is therefore blesséd. It has been a dead quiet golden morning, & I lay in bed feeling as quiet as the day – thinking. I decided to tell you as far as I could – *how* and of *what* . . . Something like this.

Why don't I get up now and sit at the table and write before lunch? No, I cant. I am too tired. I have over done it these last perfect days & walked too far and been out too long. For when I come back at 4 o'clock in the afternoon with three absolutely undisturbed hours before me I get into my room – lie on the bed – 'collapse' – and then get up light my fire sit down at the table leaning on anything I can find – leaning on my *pen* most of all & though I do write – it is only a matter of 'will' – to break through – its a sham and a pretence so far. I am so tired I can only just brush my fringe & get down to dinner & up here again to bed – Ah, how devilish it is! I am so tired I cant think of *anything* – and really can barely read. Still, my lass, this wont last.

Dont walk so far or so fast – Its months since you really have walked & your legs are bound to turn backwards. But if only I had the stickleback to lie on. These little chairs are for mean french behinds & they make me ache. However none of this is serious. Twill pass. Ill go on *grinding* until suddenly I throw away the stone & begin to really create something. Its no use being fiendish . . Are you sure this is not hypochondria? You are not getting idle here? Supposing you had a string kit & 10 little children – Oh, Id sit in public houses and on steps. No, its a feeling of confounded physical weakness – preparatory to great physical strength Im sure. Its the change & then I get so fearfully excited and that exhausts me. Keep your head. Youll be alright in a week – – – –

After this consoling homily I put my legs out of bed & dropped after them & got into the basin for a bath – But it is true. I have written 2 *patrias* (they are the pink cahiers) full here – and whenever I reread the stuff I cant believe its mine. Tame, diffuse – "missed it"[2] – Dont blame me. I shall perk <you> up – dearest. And I shall go slower till my legs get more WIRY! I know what I want to do as soon as I can do it. I have no doubts or false alarms at all.

My own Boge –

You know what I feel just this moment? Rather dashed because I have been such an enfant gate & now the old post has nothing for me. Its these trains again. Even if I had the money I could not travel about here, you know. It is impossible nowadays. Yesterday I saw a train come in here all boarded up, all the carriages locked, full of soldiers & those who wished to get out & "go to the base" as Marie calls it had to fling themselves through the windows & back again. A few poor civilians who were at the station were well jeered at by these braves.

. . . .

I left off there and went down to lunch. I stood on the terrace a moment in the sun wondering why french dogs & cats are so very unsympathetic & suddenly there at the end of the palm avenue sparkled the brightest jewel – the postman. Yes, a letter from you & a paper. I sat down & read your letter on one of those old brown chairs. My hearts dearest, dont suspect I wouldn't write because you had missed. Of course I wouldnt. What – to *you*? No, Ill reserve those tricks for the rest of mankind – *you* wont know them in me. What a curse this food problem is (see I am answering your letter.) When I come back we must cook meat & make dripping, & I swear your bregglechicks[3] wont be insipid. Ill arrange something fine. You *must* be fed in the morning. Yes, the tinge of depression did come through just as I know a tinge of fatigue & depression is in this letter & I cant get it out. Your letter though has brought you – oh so close to me – Every letter of yours is like a wave that brings you a ripple nearer – you in your boat – to me – Bogey I want you *terribly* . . . Of course I will keep your poem. I had already cut it out & put it in my letter case –

This *country*, quâ country is really ideally beautiful. It is the very most exquisite enchanting place – Yet I am very sincere when I say I *hate* the french, once I escape from a purely superficial interest in them – As *animals* they are interesting monkeys but they have no heart – no heart at all.

I heard from H[er] L[adyship] today – very insincere – But she mentioned your poem & said what a fine poet you were. I read between the lines almost a *shocked surprise* that you were so fine – We must not make her an enemy – but oh shes *corrupt – corrupt*.[4]

When I am HOME and we are living together perhaps you wont feel so depressed. I will be there & in the evenings well sit at the table with the lamp between us and work & then well make something hot to drink & have a small talk and a smoke and do a little planning. You know we are going to be quite different. We are going to be simply absorbed in each other – While this awful war goes on you must just fling yourself at me – & feel I am always there at the end of the day – and the beginning to make it a little bit lovely for you if I can. I am there to see about things & look after you – In the day Ill work like billy-o but I shall have time to do everything for us. You must believe that utterly because its true. Just till April darling look after yourself for me & then give me the keys & don't you bother.

Goodbye for now my blessed one – I live for you – you have all my love.

Your
Wig.

If your cold gets $\begin{cases} \text{worse} \\ \text{bad} \end{cases}$ see *Ainger* & ask about injections. Hes so sensible & we trust him.

MS ATL. *LKM* I. 112–14; *LJMM*, 137–40.

---

[1] KM's fourth page, on which she announces the lunchtime arrival of the postman.

[2] Alpers 1980, 266, suggests that KM is referring here to 'Love-Lies-Bleeding', a fragment Murry included in *The Scrapbook of Katherine Mansfield* (1939), 65–73.

[3] A KM word for breakfast.

[4] A harking-back to Murry's letter of 13 Jan, when he enclosed a note from Ottoline asking him to dine, and remarked that he was 'rather – in fact, very – hostile to H.L. nowadays'. (Murry, 99.)

To J. M. Murry, [27 and 28 January 1918]

[Hôtel Beau Rivage, Bandol]
Sunday night.

My love and my darling –

It is ten minutes past eight. I must tell you how much I love you at ten minutes past eight on a Sunday evening January 27th 1918. I have been in doors all day (except for posting your letter) and I feel greatly rested. Juliette has come back from a new excursion into the country with blue irises (do you remember how beautifully they grew in that little house with the trellis tower round by the rocks) and all sorts and kinds of sweet smelling jonquils . . . The room is very warm. I have a handful of fire – and the few little flames dance on the log & cant make up their minds to attack it – There goes a train. Now it is quiet again except for my watch. I look at the minute hand and I think what a spectacle I shall make of myself when I am really coming home to you. How I shall sit in the railway carriage, and put the old watch on my lap & pretend to cover it with a book – but not read or see – but just whip it up with my longing gaze, and simply make it go faster.

My love for you tonight is so deep and tender that it seems to be outside myself as well. I am fast shut up like a little lake in the embrace of some big mountains. If you were to climb up the mountains you would see me down below, deep & shining – and quite fathomless, my dear. You might drop your heart into me & youd never hear it touch bottom. I love you – I love you – Goodnight.

Oh Bogey – what it is to love like this!
Monday.
Your *Wednesday* & Thursday letters came together this morning – darling. In the Thursday one you said you had not had mine. Bogey I write EVERY day & post always at about the same time. I shall continue to write every day until I am home so if you do not get my letters they are stolen or strayed. I will never disappoint you – I will try an article for Richmond[1] as soon as I can. How many words does he want? Thank God you do feel that you want to write every day. I shut my teeth hard when I said twice a week & ever since then I have kept 'wondering'. For the day does not begin for me until the post has come. Will he be late? Or perhaps early? Is this Juliette with the letter – or no? Underneath everything that I do or think there is just this *attente*.

I have not been out yet today. I am going now & your letter shall go with me & be posted on my way home. Tell me about Sullivans friend.[2] I have an idea that all his friends are rather *small beer*. Boge have you read Our Mutual Friend – Some of it is really *damned good*. The satire in it is first chop – all the Veneering business par exemple –

could not be better. I never read it before & am enjoying it immensely – & Ma Wilfer[3] is after my own heart. I have a huge capacity for seeing 'funny' people you know and laughing & Dickens does fill it at times quite amazingly.

As I write to you I am always wanting to fly off down little side paths & to stop suddenly and to lean down and peer at all kinds of odd things. My grown up self sees us like two little children who have been turned out into the garden. There we are hand in hand, while my G.U.S. looks on through the window. And she sees us stop – & touch the gummy bark of the trees, or lean over a flower & try to blow it open by breathing very close – or pick up a pebble and give it a rub & then hold it up to the sun & see if there is any gold in it – As I write I feel so much nearer my writing self – my 'Pauline' writing self than I have since I came. I suppose because what I said about the children had a "little atom bit" of Kezia[4] in it.

I have enjoyed the Daily News very much. A course of the Paris Daily Mail makes me grey with anxiety. I see us *all* in the trenches for ever and the Germans victorious. But the D.N. really seems to smell Peace. It has been reading the Nation *re* Austria.[5]

Now my own I must go out for my small run. Will it be Thursday when you get this letter? I hope Chaddie will not be a bother. I am glad you are seeing her because of my family you know – its politic. But I wish I were there to help. I have written her today.

Here is a flower for you and a spidery bit for our Rib.

Oh – 'by the way' I wont go to Marseilles till the end of *March*. Its not a necessary expense & we cant afford it. What I ought to do – is write to Cooks there & get all particulars about the journey & then wait here for my April money which will see me home & start off then. Is that right

→ Please answer this.

Dont go to the Corner House more than you can help. I am so afraid the food is not good. Please spend pennies on yourself. If it is too late for the Good Intent go to the Italian place where we had our little dinner. Oh, how I see the Japanese wallpaper – & you in your courderoys – I was so happy. I must go back there with you. Yes, dearest of all do remember even on the tops of buses that I *adore* you & that no man living is as loved as you & never will be.

Your Wig.

MS ATL. *LKM* I. 114–15; *LJMM*, 140–2.

---

[1] Bruce Richmond (1871–1964), editor of *The Times Literary Supplement* from its foundation in 1902 until 1938, had said he was willing to consider contributions from KM.

[2] Murry wrote on 24 Jan that 'Sullivan is bringing one of his Russian friends here on Saturday, one of these strange people who think our Dostoevsky is one of the words of profound wisdom' (ATL). J. W. N. Sullivan became a friend of Murry's after reading and admiring his *Dostoevsky: A Critical Study* (1916) and was now a colleague at the War Office (and see *CLKM* I, 347, n. 2).

[3] The Veneerings are social climbers, and Ma Wilfer a shrewish mother, in Dickens' *Our Mutual Friend* (1864–5).

[4] The child based on KM herself in several of her stories. KM's Bible, given her as a child, has underlined Job 42: 14, naming Kezia as the second of his daughters.

[5] Murry had written an unsigned article, 'The Open Sesame to Peace', in the *Nation*, 19 January.

To J. M. Murry, 29 [January 1918]

[Hôtel Beau Rivage, Bandol]
Tuesday 29th

My dear Bogey

I feel greatly upset this morning because I realise for at least the millionth time that my letters to you are NOT arriving.[1] I have taken great pains to write the address plainly on the envelopes – Are they safe when they arrive at the house? Do they lie in the hall, long?

This has been brought home to me by your letter of last Friday in which you enclose Geoffrois'. You say you never heard from me that she had been here. Well, of course I wrote. And then I really cannot imagine that a great many other letters have not been lost. Did you get one with a telegram & a flower in it? You see I have no *notion* which letters of mine have arrived so I am quite in the dark as to whether you know it is warm here now. Your letters appear to turn up here quite safely, but mine obviously dont. However I shall go on throwing them into the french dust heap – but with – I assure you beaucoup de chagrin.

I have indeed tried to make you a little happy by writing to you at length and as hearty as I could – But it is I suppose another of those innumerable mean dodges of which Life seems more or less composed that – it don't come off.

Well well – – I wish I wasn't such a baby. The sun shines. It is almost hot. But if the sun were a reliable post office I should much prefer it & would dispense with all its other devoirs.

Thank you dear Bogey for telling me you do manage to get food. I hope that continues. What about porridge when the bacon is quite unobtainable? Could Mrs H[ardwick] make it? That 5 minutes stuff isn't half bad and can you eat Quaker Oats? These things do warm you before you plunge into the early morning street & thats the time you catch cold, I think. I do hope your cold is better darling.

(This affair about the letters has given me such a *turn* that I cant get over it. It aches in my throat.)

I went for a walk yesterday, a little one. I can't take big ones yet. I do feel assez vaillant, but plenty of the assez. I got very much thinner those first days I was here and I haven't recovered my lost weight yet. Of course I shall. I could not be more comfortable than I am here now, and absolutely private and remote. My room feels miles away from the rest of the hotel and I sometimes feel that Juliette and I are on an island & I row to the mainland for my meals & row back again. I keep on with my fires.

Jag Boge. You have a cold in your poor head & I have a cold place a little iceberg suddenly knocking about in my heart where all was so warm and sunny. I will get it out before tomorrow – But looking out onto the blue sea the blue mountains and the boats with yellow sails I feel full of HATE – hate for this awkward hideous world, these terrifying grimacing people who can keep ones letters back –

I cant help it.

Wig
who
loves
you.

MS ATL. *LKM* I. 115–16; *LJMM*, 142–3.

---

[1] At this time the posts were taking from three days to a week between the South of France and England.

To J. M. Murry, [29 and 30 January 1918]

[Hôtel Beau Rivage, Bandol]
Tuesday Night,

My very dear

I sent you a changeling today & scarcely a letter. Since then so much seems to have happened. I went out & walked & it was lovely but I was tired, besides which I had my heart on a string & it kept catching in things. When I came home Juliette met me quite excited. She had managed to get une demi litre of methy. She heard that it had come to the Dépot & rushed off. That pleased me awfully for now I can make coffee in the afternoon – and that will make a huge difference to ones fatigue to having something between midi et 7 heures. It was an awful price 5 francs but as she had bought it I could not object – & even at that it will in the end come cheaper than coffee at so much a whack.

Also she had gone another of her excursions and returned with a cane armchair with a cushioned seat & back. This is so grateful that I feel like a cripple in a Dickens novel who has been given it after 65 years of doorstep. Then the brazen wash girl came, gave me my washing & lifted 50 centimes off me while she said it was "si bon dans ma chambre – tout était si joli" – that made me furious of course – and this has been a heavy day for expenses. But all the same my heart feels a little bit lighter. There is a sailing boat moored to the quai. It is called Les Trois Amis. All the same Boge I miss you TOO much you know. Something in me PINES.

Wednesday.

No letter and the post has been. Two Daily News. Pas de lettre? Pas de lettre! So I suppose theres another gone or perhaps Geoffrois composition exhausted my poor boy. They are very trying efforts; I made one yesterday & shuddered to re-read it. It is a very warm still day. Not a breath of wind and a warm haze over the opposite coast. In the yard they are beating carpets: the sound 'fits' somehow. The sous marin has just sneaked out of the bay. They are ugly brutes.

Darling I do in a way live here – I see a great deal, am very solitary and quiet. Lead the life I tell you of – never speaking to anybody except bonjour & bonsoir – and yet in a way it is all absolutely unreal: it is all a dream. My mind seems to do nothing but build & build & try & try that bridge that brings me home. I get into *panics* that I shant be allowed home; the offensive will stop it; France will run out of coal – No you would laugh at my fears. But life as it is at present, *is* too terrifying to be endured alone. To be cut off, like I am here and then to think of all that can prevent me being joined on. And then *air raids, colds* – about a million other things rattle their skeleton bones at me. I cant really and truly enjoy it you know. I am doing it for my health – et voilà – but though it is exceedingly lovely & those first days were enchanted days Id rather live above a public house in the Mile End Road and hear you – – I can't *help* it. My heart is never free from anxiety and never can be while I am away from you and a war is on. That is why even one day without a letter is sufficient to start me off like this. Do you feel the same? And I look out and think: if he were here this would be Paradise Paradise.

Tu sais, mon cheri, je t'aime *trop*.

Your girl
Wig.

MS ATL. *LJMM*, 143–4.

To J. M. Murry, [30 and 31 January 1918]

[Hôtel Beau Rivage, Bandol]
Late afternoon.

My dearest

I am not going to make a habit of writing to you deux fois par jour –
but just on these days when there is something "out of joint" I must –
I must.

I decided when I went out this afternoon to buy the little coffee pot
& the coffee. But first I walked in the direction of the Hotel des Bains.
Yes, it was beautiful, very – silver and gold light – old men painting
boats, old women winding wool or mending nets – young girls making
those gay wreaths of yellow flowers – and a strange sweet smell came
off the sea. But I was homesick. I went to the paper shop to exchange
a smile with someone – & bought for 3 sous le Paris Daily Mail *and* a
smile. A commercial traveller with a wooden leg was in the shop
taking orders. "Toujours pas de chocolat" said Madame. "Mon Dieu,
Madame, if my poor leg etait seulement de vrai menier, je serais
millionaire!"

Ha Ha! Very good. Very typical. Very french. But I am faint with
homesickness. Although it is so goldy warm the tips of my fingers &
my feet and lips and inside my mouth – all are dead cold. And so I
walk along until I come to the public wash place and there are the
women slipping about in the water in their clattering sabots, holding
up those bright coloured things, laughing, shouting. & not far away
from them a travelling tinker with his fat woman sits on the ground
beside his mule and cart. He has a little fire to heat his solder pan & a
ring of old pots round him. It makes a good 'ensemble' – the washer
women bawl after me "t'as remarqué les bas!" but I do not care at all
– I would not care if I had no stockings on at all. And here are those
villas built up the hillside. Here is the one whose garden is always full
of oranges & babies clothes on a line. Still is. Also there is a dark
woman in a wide hat holding a very tiny baby to her cheek & rocking
it. The road is all glare & my shoes make a noise on it as though it
were iron. I feel sick sick – as though I were bleeding to death. I sit
down on a milestone & take out the Daily Mail. I turn my back to the
shining sea & the fishers all out in their little boats spearing fish.

Air Raid in London. Between 9–10 and again at 12.30. Still in
Progress. Thats all – – He would have had his dinner and be on the
way home – Or if he escaped that one he was in bed – Today is
Wednesday. It happened on Monday.[1] It is no use wiring. A cart
comes up full of chunks of hay. An old man in a blue blouse with great
bushy eyebrows holds up his hand & cries "Il fait beau au soleil" and
I smile. When he passes I shut my eyes – This must be borne. This

must be lived through. Back back again along the bright burnished road and all the way composing useless telegrams: Heard Raid Is all well" and so on and so on . . Varied with letters to the B[ritish] C[onsul] in Marseilles saying urgent family affairs compel me to return at once. Will there be any difficulty?

‖ Shall I come back now and not wait? Answer this my own.

Thursday.

My dear love

The facteur has just been and brought me a letter from Kay but there is again not a *line* from you. It is not as though the english post were delayed then; there must be another reason. I do most earnestly IMPLORE you to wire if all is not well. You know what this suspense is like. It is quite dreadful. I cannot write any more until I hear again for I am too uneasy. *For Gods sake never spare me.* Always write at once or wire. You can think what I felt when that bloody postman came to my door & left me empty hearted – oh Jag!

Wig.

MS ATL. *LKM* I. 116–17; *LJMM*, 145–6.

¹ On the night of 28 January, in full moonlight, the Germans made their first attack of the year on London, killing 47 and injuring 109.

To J. M. Murry, 1 February [1918]

[Hôtel Beau Rivage, Bandol]
February 1st (Friday)

Dearest Bogey

This morning I got your Sunday night, Sunday morning pc & Monday night letter all together, and they all seemed to be knocked off by such a steam engine that I wonder they didn't arrive sooner. I could feel your hurry & haste post haste in every curl of your 'ys' and I felt that by the time the letters had touched the bottom of the post bag you were up to your reine claude eyes again.

However it is very reassuring after my Days of Panic + Homesickness to feel that its all going on and its silly to worry – The D[aily] M[ail] yesterday said it was the worst raid London had had, but perhaps that is my eye.

I have also with great joy received the papers: they'll be a feast.

I am rather diffident about telling you because so many sham wolves have gone over the bridge – that I am working & have been for two days. It looks to me the real thing. But one never knows. Ill keep quiet about it until it is finished.¹

Blast your old cold. How rotten that the fine days didn't cure it. What extraordinary weather you have been having. As for today, here, at a quarter to nine it was hot in the sun for I got up to pull the curtain over my dresses, thinking they would fade. The sea is like a silver lake and the exquisite haze hangs over the coast. You can hear the fishermen from far, far away, the plash of oars and their talk to one another. Where there were 20 flowers there seem 20 hundred everywhere – Everything is in such abundant bloom. We never knew this place so warm – One could walk about in a cotton dress & old men survey their villa gardens in cream alpaca jackets & swathed sun helmets!

My wing hurts me horribly this morning: I don't know why. And I don't care, really. As long as I can work – as long as I can work.

Good God! there's some reckless bird trying over a note or two! Hell be en cocotte within the hour. I simply loathe and abominate the french bourgeoisie. Let me put it on record again. There are a round dozen of them descended on this hotel and all, after a day or two, in each others pockets, arms round each other, sniggering, confiding internal complaints & "elle m'a dit" et "mon mari m'a dit" and the gentlemen with their "passez-mes*dames*" – god how I detest them. I must show it in some way. For they avoid me like poison, only breaking into the most *amused* laughter after I have passed (you know the style) and staring until their very eyes congeal while I take my food. It is the ugliness and cruelty which hurts so much, beneath all ones cool contemptuous manner. But I suppose a great part of the earth is peopled with these fry only as a rule we dont see them. I do feel though that the frenchies must be the lowest.

When you feel you can afford it would you send me Nicholas Nickleby? (I am not reading Dickens *idly*)

The quiet day! The air quivers & three tiny flies have just performed a very successful and highly intricate dance in my window space.

I bought such a nice little coffee pot. It will do for hot milk at home. It has a lid & is white with blue daisies on it – in fact its *charming* and only costs 65 centimes. I do hope Lesley has helped you to get really tidy. (No, darling the shoes never came.)

Give my love to your Mother when you see her again. Did you ever take her that french muslin blouse?

Goodbye for today –

I am your own
Wig.

MS ATL. *LKM* I. 117–19; *LJMM*, 147–8.

¹ KM had begun work on the opening section of *Je ne parle pas français*, which she posted to Murry a few days later.

To J. M. Murry, 1 February 1918

[Hôtel Beau Rivage, Bandol]
February 1st 1918

IMPORTANT

Dearest

I have made a resolution tonight. I mean to come back next month, *March*, as soon as Kay has sent me my money.[1] I can see, from all signs, that if I dont get back then I may not get back at all – the difficulties of transport will be so great. Tell nobody. Of course a wangle will be necessary for the authorities. But the King of the Nuts at Havre told me that if I had any "urgent family affairs" I could of course get back before "my time". ∴ do you send me after the 1st of the March a telegram saying *Mother worse come back soon as possible Bowden* and I shall have that to show.

I can stick this anxiety until then but no longer – *Dont send me any money*, of course. I have plenty. And tell me just, frankly, what you think of this. I have headed the page important so when you refer to it say you have got the important letter & then Ill know which one you mean. By that time I shall be as well as I ever shall be during the war & – & – Oh I must come. I cant stick it out for longer. But tell me very frankly "vos idees".

Your woman
. Wig.

If you can afford a wire before you answer this letter – just the word *agree* if you do agree – it would be Heaven.

Wiggie.

MS ATL. *LJMM*, 146–7.

[1] KM's allowance from her father, which was now £208 a year, was administered by Alexander Kay.

To J. M. Murry, 3 February 1918

[Hôtel Beau Rivage, Bandol]
Sunday morning.
February 3rd 1918. Sunday

Dearest,

It is early for me to be up, but I had such a longing for a cigarette, and as I sit here in my pyjamas smoking a very good one Ill begin your letter. There was nothing from you yesterday & the facteur hasn't been yet today – however – –

I really feel I *ought* to send you some boughs and songs, for never was there a place more suited, but to tell you the truth I am pretty well absorbed in what I am writing & walk the bloody countryside with a 2d <envelope> note book shutting out les amandiers. But I don't want to discuss it in case it dont come off . . . . .

Ive two 'kick offs' in the writing game. *One* is joy – real joy – the thing that made me write when we lived at Pauline, and that sort of writing I could only do in just that state of being in some perfectly blissful way *at peace*. Then something delicate and lovely seems to open before my eyes, like a flower without thought of a frost or a cold breath – knowing that all about it is warm and tender and 'steady'. And *that* I try, ever so humbly to express.

The other 'kick off' is my old original one, and (had I not known love) it would have been my all. Not hate or destruction (both are beneath contempt as real motives) but an *extremely* deep sense of hopelessness – of everything doomed to disaster – almost wilfully, stupidly – like the almond tree and 'pas de nougat pour le noël'[1] – There! as I took out a cigarette paper I got it exactly – *a cry against corruption* that is *absolutely* the nail on the head. Not a protest – a *cry*, and I mean corruption in the widest sense of the word, of course –

I am at present fully launched, right out in the deep sea with this second state. I may not be able to 'make my passage' – I may have to put back & have another try, thats why I don't want to talk about it – & have breath for so little more than a hail. But I must say the boat feels to be driving along the deep water as though it smelt port – (no darling, better say 'harbour' or youll think I am rushing into a public house)

After lunch.

My Boge,

I have just read your Tuesday note, written after *another* raid.[2] You sound awfully tired, darling and awfully disenchanted. You are overworking . . . its too plain. (Curse my old shoes. Keep them for me. dont worry about them any more.)[3]

Yes I agree with you – blow the old war. It is a toss up whether it dont get every one of us before its done. Except for the first warm days here when I really did seem to almost forget it its never out of my mind & everything is poisoned by it. Its *here in* me the whole time, eating me away – and I am simply terrified by it – Its at the root of my homesickness & anxiety & panic – I think. It took being alone here and unable to work to make me fully fully *accept* it. But now I don't think that even you would beat me. I have got the pull of you in a way because I am working but I solemnly assure [you] that every moment away from my work is MISERY. And the human contact – just the pass the time away chat distracts you – & that of course I dont have at all.

I miss it very much. Birds & flowers and dreaming seas dont do it. Being a biped – I must have a two legged person to *talk* to – You cant imagine how I feel that I walk alone in a sort of black glittering case like a beetle – – – –

Queer business . . .

By the way I dreamed the other night that Frieda [Lawrence] came to you & asked you for money. She "knew you had some", she bullied you into giving her £5. I woke terrified lest this might happen. Never let it. Your money is really earned with your blood. Never give it away. You need it; you must have it. PLEASE please!

I wonder what you will say to my 'important' letter & if you agree will they let me through? Can they keep me out of my own country? These are a couple of refrains which are pretty persistent. They say here that after March this railway will probably be closed till June . . .

My own precious I love you *eternally*

Your
Wig.

MS ATL. *LKM* I. 119–20; *LJMM*, 148–50.

---

¹ KM is remembering the song by Jean-Henri Fabre, 'Ils Sont Pires Que Le Chiendent', with its opening stanza: 'Il y a des olives à Toussaint, et pour Pâques il y a des oeufs, – pour Noël, du nougat, et des truffes s'il pleut. – Des ladres il y en a toujours, dans tous les terroirs: – ils lèvent en toute lune et montent en graine en tout coin.' *Poésies françaises et provençales de Jean-Henri Fabre*, ed. Pierre Julian (Paris 1925), 69.

² There was a less severe raid on the outskirts of London on the night of 29 January.

³ Murry was refused permission to send her shoes through the post.

To J. M. Murry, [3 and 4 February 1918]

[Hôtel Beau Rivage, Bandol]
Sunday Night

My precious

I dont dare to work any more tonight. I suffer so frightfully from insomnia here and from night terrors. That is why I asked for another Dickens; if I read him in bed he diverts my mind. My work excites me so tremendously that I almost feel *insane* at night and I have been at it with hardly a break all day. A great deal is copied and carefully addressed to you, in case any misfortune should happen to me. Cheerful! But there is a great black bird flying over me and I am so frightened he'll settle – so terrified. I dont know exactly what *kind* he is.

If I were not working here, with war and anxiety I should go mad, I think. My night terrors here are rather complicated by packs & packs of growling, roaring, ravening, prowl and prowl around dogs.

God! How tired I am! And Id love to curl up against you and sleep.

Goodnight, my blessed one. Dont forget me in your busy life.

Monday. February 4th.

Dearest

No letter from you today. I had one from Ida written on *Friday* – so the posts have got a real grudge against you & me . . I am posting you the first chapter of my new work today. I have been hard put to it to get it copied in time to send it off but I am SO EXCEEDINGLY anxious for your opinion.

It needs perhaps some explanation. The subject I mean lui qui parle is of course taken from – Carco & Gertler & God knows who. It has been more or less in my mind ever since I first felt strongly about the french. But I hope youll see (of course you will) that I am not writing with a sting. Im not, indeed!

I read the fair copy just now and couldn't think where the devil I had got the bloody thing from – I cant even now. Its a mystery. Theres so much much less taken from life than anybody would credit. The african laundress I had a bone of – but only a bone – Dick Harmon of course is partly is

Oh God – is it good? I am frightened. For I stand or fall by it. Its as far as I can get at present and I have gone for it, bitten deeper & deeper & deeper than ever I have before. Youll laugh a bit about the song. I could see Goodyear grin as he read that . . . . But what is it like! Tell me – dont spare me. Is it the long breathe as I feel to my soul it is – or is it a false alarm? Youll give me your *dead honest opinion* – wont you Bogey?

If this gets lost I break my pen ——

I am only at the moment a person who works comes up to read newspapers, AND to wait for postmen goes down again, drinks tea. Outside the window is the scenic railway – all complete & behind that pretty piece is the war –

Forgive an empty head. It rattled all night. I cant manage this sleeping business.

Goodbye for now my hearts treasure.

Yours yours only for ever

Wig.

MS ATL. *LKM* I. 120–2; *LJMM*, 150–1.

To J. M. Murry, 4 and 5 February 1918

[Hôtel Beau Rivage, Bandol]

Tuesday is different. Just cast a beamy on this & then climb down the ladder.

Monday night 4.2.1918

Oh Bogey

It would be Heaven if I were to get a letter from you tomorrow – not *too* tired a one and one that brought me 'near'. Heavens knows, my precious that aint a complaint, but I *am* so tired tonight that Id give anything for *you you you.*

I decided after I posted your letter & MSS today & had my walk to try & forget work for an hour or two so I have repacked & resorted my box, gone through all my possessions & generally behaved as though this were my last night on earth. Even to the extent of writing my address *c/o of you* to be communicated in case of need in french and english in my passport case.

Now all is fair . . . What a fool I am!

The worst of REAL insomnia is one spends a great part of the day wondering if one is going to bring it off the coming night. Can I stand another last night? Of course I suppose I can. But must I? Not to sleep, and to be alone is a very neat example of HELL. But what isn't? Ah, there you have me.

Tuesday 5.II.1918

My precious love

I never had such a direct answer to prayer. Two letters, *real* letters from you about our cottage and all that[1] – a Wednesday & a Thursday one. This of course has given me the salto mortale – & I am a changed child. Also, I did manage by eating myself to death at dinner & only reading early poetry afterwards & taking 10 grains of aspirin to get to sleep. So + and + and +.

God! What it is to count on letters so. Now about us living on very little after the war. You know I am as determined as you about that. You must take the saddle & bridle off dashing off & we must watch him *bolt away* for ever. We MUST live in some remote place & all our food must grow on trees & bushes. No cities, no people. And of course we must have a good servant. Ill not do housework again or cook even though I shall long to because I think I do it so well – Least I mean I wont *be* the cook again – nor will you sweep the stairs. As to clothes – Ill never need them any more. I had a red wine letter from Marie today *re* your dinner. Oh what a point it was! I am delighted you did it. She was quite swept away & described you in a thick brown suit orange hanky, wooly weskit hair just right length – – I sent the letter to Mummy today: I could see her "lapping it up". After we are married I want to know your mother differently. I *cant* before. I wonder if you understand that? . . . Oh my love my darling how these letters have refreshed me! How that glimpse of the cottage has "lightened my darkness".

(By the way I had better tell you: I am a MISER)

I have worked 2 hours already today: its midi. If you knew the time it does take to steep & steep myself as I have to before Im anyway near content. My own, I love you – Your letters are HEAVEN – and I fly about in them like a gold & silver

Wig.

MS ATL. *LKM* I. 122; *LJMM*, 151–3.

---

[1] Murry wrote on 30 Jan that 'after this war we'll have to take living on nothing, seriously . . . . We'll have a beautiful cottage somewhere and a great big garden, where we'll grow almost everything we eat. We'll have a child, perhaps two; we'll have a printing press if we can possibly afford it. And I shall try to sell my poetry: and you will sell your stories. But somehow we must be independent.' (ATL.)

To J. M. Murry, 6 February 1918

[Hôtel Beau Rivage, Bandol]
February 6th 1918

Wednesday. Yes a letter. A 'fog' letter.[1]
My own precious,

Four years ago today Goodyear gave me the Oxford Book of English Verse. I discovered that by chance this morning . . . Do you know how much this (the cheapest paper here) costs? One sou the page! Isn't that a revolting swin.

I knew the weather was awful with you. How vile. The only thing to remember is that it isn't and *cant be* November. Is that a consolation when one is in the foggy spot? Im afraid not . . . Dearest, can you send me your financial statement one day soon? You know you promised you would. I should feel greatly relieved to know just what you had in your wild thyme bank. And don't think it will make me ask for a ta ra ra because you know I am more of a miser than you. But I would greatly like to know. By the way I think cultur*al* (one of Lavrin's words & a great one of Kennedy's)[2] a vile un.

I passed our house again yesterday & it looked so heavenly fair with the white & red almond trees & the mimosa attending that I went into a field hard by where they were gathering the flowers & asked for information. A big dark girl, with a great sheaf of flowers on one arm & the other arm raised, keeping her face from the sun said: "Ah Madame c'est *une mauvaise maison*. Non elle n'est pas louée. Le proprietaire habite Marseilles. Mais, vous savez la maison est *ben* mauvaise; elle se casse toujours. On a fait des grandes reparations, il y a un an, mais personne est venu pour la prendre – Et main-ten-ant, elle est à moitié cassée encore. On dit de cette maison, qu'elle n'aime pas les gens." And then she bent over the flowery fields again . . .

On my way home from my walk yesterday I met *le pere de Marthe*. We shook hands. He was very nice, you remember in a patent leather cap – rather like a drawing by Gus Bofa.[3] Marthe is married and lives in Toulon.[4] Son mari est à Gibralte. Yes, he was the young man who used to walk with her in the garden on Sunday. I said "when you write please remember me to her." Said he: "J'ecris *tous les soirs*, Madame. Vous savez elle etait *ma seule fille*." This of course warmed my heart to an extraordinary degree & I wished Chaddie hadn't given me my furs so I could send them to Marthe etc. etc. I worked a good deal yesterday but I slept, too. It is fatal for me to work late at night – when I am alone. I never realise unless I stop how *screwed up* I am. Last night, petit enfant très sage, I made myself another little 'front'

out of material I bought here   you know the kind & it sent me

into a fast sleep. The widow here actually gave me 2 bunches of white hyacinths yesterday. What can it mean? They smell simply divine & then Juliette still makes a garden of my room – I have to put the flowers on the windowsill at night; ils sentent si forts. In the early morning when I wake & see the row of little pots so gentiment disposés I feel rather like the heroine of a german lyric poem. We must grow all varieties of jonquils.

I am still in a *state of work* you know, my precious – Dead quiet and spinning away. I feel rather today & felt it yesterday too, after your letters that I ought to stick it till April, that people will be so cross if I come in March, & that I ought to wait & then come *bang* in April – I wonder – If you think so well you will say so, I know.

Have you got your meat card?[5] Of course I think the meat cards will stop the war. Nothing will be done but *spot* counting – & people will go mad and butchers & pork butchers will walk about with bones in their hair, distracted. Talking of hair. Do you know those first days I was here I went a bit grey over both temples. Real grey hair – I know, I felt the very moment it came, but it is a blow to see it . . .

Another thing I hate the french bourgeoisie for is their absorbed interest in evacuation. What is constipating or what not? That is a real *criterion* . . At the end of this passage there is a W.C. Great Guns! they troop and flock there . . and not only that. They are all victims of the most amazing Flatulence imaginable. Air Raids over London dont hold a candle to 'em. This, I suppose is caused by their violent purges and remedies, but it seems to me very "unnecessary." – Also the people of the village have a habit of responding to their serious needs (I suppose by night) down on the shore round the palm trees. Perhaps its the sailors, but my english gorge rises & my english lip curls in contempt. The other day one palm tree had a placard nailed on it *Chiens Seulement*. Was that funny? It provided a haw haw for the day, here. But on my life, Id almost rather, like that english lady, not know whether my husband went to the lavatory or not, than be so unbuttoned. No, this world, you know, Bogey, this grown up world everywhere *dont* fit me.

You do, though – You fit me. Oh my darling boy what would life be without love? I don't think Id stick it out: Id jump over something. I adore you (that's your reflection in me)

Your own
Wig.

MS ATL. *LKM* I. 123–4; *LJMM*, 153–5.

¹ Murry's letter of 31 Jan was written on a night when fog prevented buses running.

² Janko Lavrin (b. 1887), a Yugoslav whom KM knew through her earlier association with the *New Age*, wrote extensively on European and Russian literature. Also through A. R. Orage's weekly she had met John MacFarland Kennedy (*c.* 1880–1918), linguist, exponent of Nietzsche, and for a time foreign editor of the *Daily Telegraph*. He had been her lover in 1911.

³ Gus Bofa, pseudonym of Gustave Blanchot (d. 1968), a Parisian comic artist who through the War published a satirical weekly, *La Baïonette*.

⁴ The 'Mdlle Marthe' KM described in her letter to Murry on 29 Dec 1915. (See *CLKM* I. 240.)

⁵ Strict meat rationing was to be introduced in Britain from 25 February.

To J. M. Murry, 7 February [1918]

[Hôtel Beau Rivage, Bandol]
Thursday February 7th

My precious one,

The Aged brought me your wire¹ last night. How it can have got here with such unspeakable rapidity I *cant* imagine but there it was. But dearest I dont <u>want</u> any money. I shall have Kays & that will be more than enough. If you havent sent it please dont. If you have Ill tell Kay not to send his, because I must not travel too rich. I don't know what to say about your wire. I want your letter so, with vos idées in it. I still, in my heart, feel just the same but I *could* and *would* stick it till April & chance getting a train back if you thought (having thought it over) this would be better. Please 'note that'.

Today I havent got a letter from you but a Westminster has come & a D.N. Thank you, love. I am still *at it*. Oh! when can I hear about that MSS and *what* are you going to say. Now Im up – now Im down, but I am awfully frightened. The rest of the round world can take a 99 year lease of all the houses in Putney – but – what do *you* think?

I must write to H.L. today or she will take great offence and I don't want to have her my enemy. Its too nauseous. But, to tell you the truth, its difficult, very to keep it up: the 'atmosphere' at Garsington (which is now explained . . . one knows where the smell comes from, so to speak: its her false relation with Philip) does offend me unspeakably.[2] I don't feel I *could* go back there. I am always underneath so acutely uneasy – not at my ease, I mean, and I do so hate dragging the Poets into such a pose. Im so tempted to say, coolly & for all: "pray keep *Keats* out [of] this." . . . . You know? She *is* bloody interesting – the fact that she doesn't know she's poisoned par exemple, but I have really got all I want from her (down to the shawlet!!) Still we mustnt let her 'turn', I suppose.

Bogey, I have such a passion, such a passion for life in the country – for peace, for you lying on your back in the sun looking up through wavy boughs – for you planting things that climb sticks – for me cutting things that have a sweet smell. Once the war is over this is ours *on the spot.* For we shall live so remote that the rent cant cost much – and then you become dreadfully idle with long curly hair like a pony that has been turned out to graze in a speckled field.

If I do come in March you will keep the secret wont you & not let people know? Ill just turn up . . . and of course this is all *tremendously* trains permitting. This place does seem to launch me – I am simply packed with ideas and ways of writing which are important ones as I see it . . But the more I think the more astounded I am at the immense division between you and me and – everybody else alive. All the 'writers' whose books I see reviewed – Did you ever! Gilly [Gilbert Cannan] and Hughie [Hugh Walpole] and Co.

Its lunch time and the bell has gone & judging from the smell of fish the lunch is about to play the Mahomets mountain trick on me. Ill to it.

Goodbye for now, my soul.

Your woman
Wig.

MS ATL. *LKM* I. 124–5; *LJMM*, 155–6.

[1] When Murry received her letter of 1 Feb, proposing that she return in March, he wired back 'Absolutely agree. Sending ten. Love. Murry.' (ATL.)

[2] KM seems to have taken a strongly disapproving stance when, the previous June, she heard of Philip Morrell's infidelity.

To J. M. Murry, 8 February [1918]

[Hôtel Beau Rivage, Bandol]
Friday. February 8th.

Tell Rib Im 'coming soon now'.

My dear Heart

A postcard and your Sunday & Monday letter today. Yes, the posts are MAD. But Bogey, we won't go flying off again when this is over –

will we. Otherwise Id buy a pigeon today & begin to train it. Oh, Oh, Oh, your letters! My Sails flap, Im at the mercy of the sea & the tide and all the winds great & small if there is not one aboard. They are simply *everything*. I cannot imagine how letters can do so much. Why when I read you cooked a herring like a genius do I simply roll over squeeze the pillow, *hug* it & smile to every toe. But I do. And as I write this I love you that you must feel the tips of your fingers beginning to tingle.

I can see your & Sullivans gloomy little snack. "Unless they would marry a gallows and beget young gibbets I never saw two men so prone"[1] . . But Bogey, isn't it miraculous how our minds *cross*. You are feeling the war again just as I am – and just at the same *time*.

Funny you should have seen Cannan too when only yesterday I mentioned the gilly flowers and the wally poles . . . .

(God! I am smoking the most infernal camel droppings: 60 centimes the packet of 40 grammes – but its all thats to be had). Its in the air today – I feel as though I were blowing back to you – on my way. Juliette is like a double stock – tufty strong, very sweet, very gay – Yesterday she helped me wash my hair – Every service she makes a kind of 'party' of. It was *fun* to heat and stagger in with two huge pots of water – to warm towels & keep them hot in folded newspapers – and the success of the operation was hers too. She rejoiced over ones dry hair and ran away singing down the corridor. She sings nearly always as she works & she has a friend Madeleine who pegs the linen on the line between the mimosa trees. When J is doing the rooms M. calls from the garden Juli *e tte*! And Juliette flies to the window Ah Ha! C'est toi, ma belle! What an enormous difference it makes to have her about rather than some poor foggy creature – or some bad tempered one. But she could never be transplanted – She rises & sets with the sun, I am sure. I worked away yesterday, but Im almost frightened – My Leg-wings are bearing so beautifully and make such spiral dives & looping loops . . . . But its all for you to see.

Here is [a] note from Eric.[2] Its like the little chap – Cant you feel theres a touch of him in it – and I like him for not pretending he has been in the thick of it. You must see him when he comes back. The pa man sent me a letter the other day – to say he was 60. *Very* bitter about Mack[3] – (to my wicked joy.) Oh, my own – my love, my life – you know I could pray to the Lord to make me wise and good and 'big' enough to serve this love of ours – Dont let me ever be little, God, or mean. Dont let me ever forget the wonder and the glory of *this*. All the poetry of the world *ours* and you a poet – and me a writer. Both of us not only equipped but more & more able to do what we will – Yes, we'll have the press[4] – & well cut down our expenses to the last potato & print our books.

Oh Bogey I have positively to pin this letter down it flies like a kite. Catch it. I cant hold it a minute longer.

Yours amen
Wig

MS ATL. *LKM* I. 125; *LJMM*, 156–8.

[1] *Cymbeline*, V. iv. 207.
[2] Eric Waters, KM's first cousin, the son of her maternal aunt Agnes, and the original of Rags in *Prelude*. He was serving in France as a second lieutenant in Signals Section, New Zealand Expeditionary Force.
[3] Vera's husband James Mackintosh Bell.
[4] Murry and his brother Arthur were planning to establish the Heron Press.

To J. M. Murry, 9 February [1918]

[Hôtel Beau Rivage, Bandol]
Saturday 9th

My own

The postman brought today a roll of papers from you but no letter. It will come tomorrow praps. I was just brushing my fringe when I heard a clumpety clump in the passage that my heart seemed to recognise long before I did. It began to dance and beat – Yes, it was the Aged with your ADORABLE telegram Sthry receivid mafnificent Murly.[1] I read and of course this bowled me over so much that the pins wont keep in my hair and my buttons pop like fuschia buds and my strings all squeak when they're pulled. Well the only response I *can* make is to send you the next chapter which Ill post as before on Monday. But oh dear oh dear! You have lighted such a candle! Great *beams* will come out of my eyes at lunch and play like search lights over the pomme de terres and terrify these insect children.

Now of course my only faint fear is:– "will he like the next chapter as much?" Well I must 'wait and see' – I must say when I wrote about the *tea* last night – thats a funny little typical bit – I came all over & nearly cried those sort of sweet tears that Ive only known since I loved you. I say Boge – havent I got a *bit of you*. Funny thing is I think youll always come walking into my stories (and now of course I see future generations finding you in all my books "The man she was in love with")

No, dear love. I must wait until Ive had lunch before I go on with this letter. I am too much of a 'gash baloon'[2] altogether. *1.15.* Well, I wish you had eaten my tournedos; it was such a good 'un. The great thing here is the meat which is superb. Oh, but now I am turned towards *home* everything is good. I eat you. I see you. And my heart (apart from my work) does nothing but store up things to give you – plans for our life – wherever it is. Shall we really, really next month curl up together on the divan & talk with Rib sitting in the fender playing on a minute comb and paper? Id die without you. "Hang there, like fruit, my soul, till the tree die!"[3] The tree *would* die –

I have just looked at the T.L.S., read your Sturge Moore review which touched me. The last sentence is perfect[4] & 'noted' that Mr. M. M. had an article of really high quality in the Quarterly.[5]

How *damned* depressing and hideously inadequate that Versailles conference has been –[6] But what I do feel is that handful cant stop the dyke from breaking now – (Is that true?) I mean there *is* – isn't there perfectly immense pressure upon it & L.G. [Lloyd George] & Co may put their hands in the hole (like the little boy in Great Deeds Done by Little People that Grandma used to read me on Sundays) but its no use. Oh, I *dont* know. When I think I am not coming home and that 'all is over' – when that mood gets me of course I don't believe it ever will end until we are all killed as surely as if we were in the trenches. Not that *love* and *you* falsify my feeling about it – make it less terrible but they do fortify gainst it. Yes that is too true!

Now I am waiting for a letter from you tomorrow – Sunday. The post will be late & hundreds and hundreds of imaginary Juliettes will come along the passage to my door before the real one comes. But I can bear *that* as long as the real one *does* come.

I am yours eternally
Wig

MS ATL. *LKM* I. 125–6; *LJMM*, 158–9.

[1] KM touched up the story. The telegram in fact read 'Story received magnificent Murly.' (ATL.)

[2] A phrase taken from Mrs Bates, the original charwoman of KM's later story 'Life of Ma Parker'. The words were also used in a letter to Anne Drey on 22 Dec 1917 (*CLKM* I, 353).

[3] *Cymbeline*, V. v, 263.

[4] 'Mr Sturge Moore's child poetry', *The Times Literary Supplement*, 31 January 1918. The last sentence, speaking of the poem 'Lullaby', read: 'Mr Sturge Moore would not have dared to make it so beautiful if the child had not gone to sleep.'

[5] KM means that she herself noted Murry's 'Charles Péguy' in the *Quarterly Review*, January 1918.

[6] The Supreme War Council met at Versailles to co-ordinate the war efforts of the Allies. The members were the Prime Ministers of the United Kingdom, France, Italy, a representative of the United States, and top-level military advisers. At their recent meeting, 28 January 1918, they decided that only the complete military defeat and unconditional surrender of the Central Powers was acceptable.

To J. M. Murry, 10 February [1918]

[Hôtel Beau Rivage, Bandol]
Sunday February 10th.

My darling precious

I am out of breath. (1) After your telegram yesterday I decided that I could contain this story no longer & wrote & wrote at it with it & finished it today for you.

(2) Your answer to my Important Letter came.

(3) A MOST MYSTERIOUS TELEGRAM which so horrifies and bewilders me that I dont dare to let myself think of it. I must wait. It says am coming Leave this afternoon Baker!!! Of course I thought *immediately* of you. Something had happened – she had come to tell me – Half of me can believe nothing else. Half of me refuses to countenance such a thing. God wouldn't let it happen & even if he did you would never leave it to that great monster to tell me – But Oh! I am so terribly worried really – Of course I shant know a moments rest till she comes. And I could bear anything to have happened to anybody else – only you *you*. Can she be the ghoul made for this. Bogey Bogey Bogey. I shall (if alls well) of course come back in March. This is *unbearable* this separation.

If I had not had this telegram I should have been feeling almost happier than ever before in my writing life – Yes happier than ever before because I know I have not shirked it and I have finally set my hand to something & finished it and it is an achievement of our most blessed love. But all the while I write this you must know there is this great mountain bearing towards me – What does it mean? What is she bringing?

I will write again the moment she comes – But God! until then I have this to copy & send you & I must keep quiet. I can after all do nothing – but wait & wait . . .

Your own true love

[*Across top*] Wig.

I write in this 'callous' sort of way because my heart *wont* believe it.

MS ATL. *LJMM*, 159–60.

To J. M. Murry, [10 and 11 February 1918]

Hullo Jag. [Hôtel Beau Rivage, Bandol]
Sunday still. & Monday after.

My own

I am just going to ignore this wire from L.M. until I hear further. If I really did give way to it it would do neither of us any good. and it

CANT be bad news. So there, and you must understand. £10 is *more* than enough. Ill get no money for March from Kay. *When I feel the hour has come I will wire how is MOTHER? and then you will reply mother worse operation necessary come soon possible. See?* [*In margin*: But it wont be before March.] Thats not mad. Is it? I have ample ample money. I shall take care of myself *because* of you *for* you, Ill wire from Marseilles & from Paris . . .

I have just put up in an envelope the rest of our story. Again this *fusion* of our minds.[1] You talk of love poetry – all I write or ever ever will write will be the fruit of our love – love prose – This time for instance as I went on and *on* I fed on our love.[2] Nightingales if you like brought me heavenly manna. Could I have done it without you? No, a million times. You can see us cant you sprouting on every page. Even Rib had a part. I dont want to exaggerate the importance of this story or to harp on it; but its a tribute to Love you understand and the very best I can do just now. Take it. Its yours. But what [I] felt so curiously as I wrote it was – ah! I am in a way *grown up* as a writer – a sort of authority – just as [I] felt about your poetry. Pray God you like it now you've got it all.

I *dreamed* a short story last night even down to its name which was *Sun & Moon.* It was very light. I dreamed it all – about children. I got up at 6.30 & made a note or two because I knew it would fade. Ill send it sometime this week. Its so nice.[3] I didn't dream that I read it. No I was in it part of it & it played round invisible me. But the hero is not more than 5. In my dream I saw a supper table with the eyes of 5. It was awfully queer – especially a plate of half melted icecream . . . but Ill send it to you. Nothing is any good to me – no thought – no beauty – no idea – unless I have given it to you and it has become the property of these wealthiest little proprietors in the whole world Wig & Bogey & Bogey & Wig. Assistant *Rib.* En cas d'absence *Rib.*

I have asked you to wire when you get this second packet my own because of the sousmarins. Bogey I have MOUNDS of money. I shall arrive (without my March allowance) with a great deal. So don't worry, please. and dearest darling precious love guard yourself for me – oh *keep safe for me.*

See I ignore this black foreboding telegram. I feel that is what you would have me to do until I know why she is so awfully coming. I will keep this letter open till tomorrows post has been.

Monday. But the bloody thing kept me awake all night. I didn't sleep an hour I suppose. Now with this morning comes your Wednesday letter and the 2 books, my heart. Did you read in my other letter I would not come till March? It seems to me my case is stronger with the authorities if I have been longer here – & the days will go by. Oh please please dont worry my own – and dont worry about my wire *till* you hear from me *as* arranged on page 1. I feel so calm about it now it is decided. All this of course is subject to 'all being well' & the mystery explained. What horrifies me further is I received from L.M. this morning 2 hysterical mad screams – "Oh my darling make the doctor let me come" "Oh my darling *eat*". If she comes with news of you that you're ill – you want me – something has happened then I shall understand. If she comes for any other reason Ive done with her – But what could her other reason be? I have asked her *not* to come on my account. Oh its a circle: I *must* keep calm. I wrote & finished the dream story yesterday – and dedicated it to Rib. I knew I would not write it at all if I didnt on the spot & it kept me 'quiet'. Otherwise apart from this black ghoulish thought all seems Ah so fair – I am coming. Ive done some work. I am turned towards home – We are going to live in a biscuit box – and be the two most charming biscuit crumbs together. No, Beaufort Mansions is tempting,[4] but London is not our home – we only have a sort of biscuit tin there. Our home is a cottage with a gold roof & silver windows.

I can expect HER tomorrow night. Not before. Well I must work & bide her coming.

Yours yours every day & hour & breath Id say I am more your own

Wig.

MS ATL. *LKM* I. 126–7; *LJMM*, 160–2.

[1] Murry had written on 7 Feb of 'the miraculous, unearthly feeling of complete communion'. (Murry, 112.)

[2] Murry wrote on 5 Feb: 'Do you know I never think of writing but one thing – and that is love poetry . . . . I feel that in you & me our love & our work are become the same thing, inextricably knit together.' (Murry, 110–11.)

[3] KM changed her mind enough over the next two years to try to prevent Murry using 'Sun and Moon' in the *Athenaeum*, where it appeared on 1 October 1920.

[4] Murry wrote on 6 Feb that there was a first-floor flat to let in Beaufort Mansions, Chelsea, where they had lived for a short time on their return from Paris in February 1914.

To J. M. Murry, 11 [and 12 February 1918]

[Hôtel Beau Rivage, Bandol]
Monday 11th, 8 p.m.

No L.M. tonight. I thought she might arrive by this evenings train. Every sound from outside is *her* – *she*. What the HELL *does* it mean. What *can* it mean!

I am mad to begin another *big* story, now that Sun and Moon is ready to send you but between me and the difficult and desirable country looms this misty peak. Perhaps your letter tomorrow will lift the veil . . Bogey if all is well with you, and yet its so strange. Like our

Rib I cannot believe that all is *not* well with you – even though my mind can find no other earthly excuse for her . . . I simply cant listen to my mind. No, my heart wont hear it. My heart is an enemy to it. But the suspense! I walked & walked it this afternoon after I had posted your letter & the MS recommandé. I was like a blind shepherd driving a flock of – I knew not what . . .

This note (so neat, isn't it – such little stitches!) is to say that I love you eight hours more than I did when I said it before.

Wig.

Tuesday. With All the Flags of Love Flying.
My precious,

Your Thursday letter & the page explaining L.M.[1] has come & your Friday letter about my story.

My heart was right. Rib was right again. This relief is boundless & yet I *knew* it. There was just this 'panic' like there always is. And my own lover, be calm. Don't feel the strain. See? I am very calm about coming back. I will manage it – beautifully. Don't be frightened. I feel so strong. (I want to write about your Friday letter bang off first but Ill just finish with L.M. first. Bogey I have done with her. I asked her not to come; said I didn't want her & then she wired me 'leaving' – That ends it. Shes a revolting hysterical ghoul. Shes never content except when she can eat me. My God!! But I shall keep great control. As she has come I of course must see her & she must be here, but I can't stop working for her. Till I get back I shall not alter my programme in the smallest particular for her. Shes done it; very well. She must suffer for her infernal hysteria. I don't think it will make it more difficult for me to get back, because it is not until March that I am coming & I may travel with her but I shall ignore *her* object in returning. Shed *like* me to be paralysed of course – or blind – preferably blind. However I shall keep cool & explain that I only can see her at meals & a walk in the afternoon. All the mornings I always keep my room. After lunch I write or read till 2. When I come in at five its my *great* time to write till dinner & after dinner I read. She must find some occupation. I *loathe* her so much for this and for the drivel and moaning of her letters to me here that I shall never soften. If I did bang would go my work again. *Finis.*

Now about your letter about the first chapter.[2] I read it & I wept for joy. How can you so marvellously understand – and so receive my love offering. Ah, it will take all of the longest life I can live to repay you. I *did* feel (I do) that this story is the real thing & that I did not once (as far as I know) shirk it. Please God Ill do much better for us – but I felt there I can lay down my pen now Ive made that and give it to Bogey. Yes I did feel that. But Christ! a devil about the size of a flea nips in my ear "suppose he's disappointed with the 2nd half?" . . . Ill send you Sun & Moon today, registré, *but of course* dont *wire* about *it*. And, unless the mountain arrives here & milks me of money I must tell you I have a surprise for you on that score, which will make you happy: *To tell you your fortune I do not pretend* it sounds like. You know that machine we stuck a penny in. Yes Im sure I shall be able to manage it. You know the programme? *Wait* for my wire *how is mother*. That is the signal. Then wire *mother worse operation necessary return soon as possible*.

I don't think there can be a big big battle before March because the grounds not hard enough. (That sounds like Rib speaking.) Now I know about this woman I am myself again. She will have to look after herself – but shes nicely finished my (really on the whole) odious friendship. My new story is signalled.[3] And I love you I adore you. To eat in a kitchen with you is my ultimate wishing ring.

Your own woman
Wig.

MS ATL. *LKM* I. 127; *LJMM*, 162–4.

[1] Murry claimed he sent Ida Baker to ensure KM's safe return, but he admitted also, 9 Feb, 'I had absolutely nothing at all to do with it, because she had firmly decided.' He then made clear on 11 Feb that he had not encouraged her until he learned that Ida intended paying for herself, and would not expect any assistance from him. (Murry, 116, 118.)

[2] When Murry received the first part of *Je ne parle pas français* he wrote back, 8 Feb, 'my sensation is like that which I had when I read Dostoevsky's *Letters from the Underworld*. He observed, 'Here you seem to have begun to drag the depths of your *consciousness* . . . . Ordinarily what you express & satisfy is your desire to write, because you are a born writer, and a writer born with a true vision of the world. Now you express & satisfy some other desire, perhaps because for a moment you doubt or have not got the other vision. The world is shut out. You are looking into yourself.' (Murry, 114, 115.)

[3] 'Bliss', which she worked on over the next two weeks.

To J. M. Murry, [12 and 13 February 1918]

[Hôtel Beau Rivage, Bandol]
Tuesday Night.

My Precious

At about six oclock *loud steps special knock* (that special knock!!) black velvet head to follow familiar voice May I come *in*? And she was here. She seems to have got here all right, completely hysterical about me. I debated as [to] whether to hold over my feelings & intentions or to be sincere & was (but not horribly not *hatefully*) sincere. Told her just what I thought & so on & established my relation with her. I *cant* like her; in fact I am so shut away that shes a perfect stranger – She brought me some squashed *babas* au rhum from Paris. Why did that make me almost angrier than anything. However all is *out* and she took it alright, and I have told her my program. I think now she *is* here she'd better stay till March & we will travel back together (if she can get back.) Dont think me a cold hearted fiend; I am not. But really she has persecuted me and if I didn't put up a fight she'd ruin our own life. Thats what she wants to do. "If there wasn't Jack" – that is what she says – and that I really CANNOT STAND from anybody. But dont lets talk about her. I am not going to think about her any more. We shall feed together & walk together. The rest she must manage. If a toss up between work and L.M. work wins & it *is* a toss up. What she cant stand is you and I – *us*. Youve taken away her prey – which is me. Im not exaggerating. Well you have. So there & now she knows it. Finito.

I lay down today under a pine tree & though I spent some time saying "the wells and the springs are poisoned" they were not really. I began to construct my new story. Until I get back to you & we are safe in each others arms there is only one thing to do & that is to *work work work*. God! how I want you! There are no words for this. Its just longing . . . But I cant help feeling the wind is in our favour, somehow and I am blowing home. Until I come I shall reste as tranquille as I can & try & get a great deal done. This is just for to let you know she is here. Thank you for the book, my love. No more books now please. I have plenty to last me. Goodnight. Ah when shall I *say* that and *seal* it.

Your Wig

Wednesday. No english post today my darling but I am not really worried only as usual – a great piece – the living piece of day falls out – especially as the postman came singing all [down] the corridor – knocked & handed me a letter from an old woman who crossed over from England with me & who is [in] Paris. Any letter that is not yours I have such a grudge against that I dont want to open it even – I mean when it comes unaccompanied by one of yours.

When you have got this far – break off, look at Rib and say she loves me most frightfully today – & Rib will screw up one eye at you & say I know. Its burning me from right over here.

I put all the unfinished MSS I had brought with me here in a row last night and sitting on my Peggy I reviewed them – & told them that none of them were really good enough – to march into the open (Ugh! No – I cant even in fun use these bloody comparisons. I have a horror of the way this war creeps into writing . . . oozes in – trickles in.)

Until I go from here I live in a sort of rainbow, wondering will it be brighter? – thats my hope & you are the little pot of gold. Its such a warm day today I sat in a basin of cold water and had a bath like a sparrow in a fountain. I *love* you I *love* you. There is a new sort of jonquil here that I must find out the name of. We must grow it. Its so lovely – and the green is very deep, the flower very starry. You see our future is so miraculous – so delicate – so heavenly – that how can one help trembling – & feeling terrified when this great blast roars between us and it. How can we possibly even try to pass it and escape it if we're not simply clinging to each other.

But I am coming.

Your Wig.

MS ATL. *LJMM*, 164–5.

To J. M. Murry, 14 [February 1918)

[Hôtel Beau Rivage, Bandol]
Thursday 14th

My own

I had 2 letters from you today – your last *Saturday* letter & your *Monday* letter. No Sunday letter at all. Your Saturday letter is the one in which you speak of my staying longer & taking a villa perhaps now L.M. is here. However long I stayed I <u>would</u> never do that. I can keep apart from her more or less here but any other form of life would be quite intolerable with her. As it is she go[es] on just like Mrs. Nickleby[1] and nearly makes me die with fury at meals. Still – schweig! I am as strong as I shall be ever *here*. I shall be careful *there*. *Unless you feel I ought to stay till April when I will without a word* or that it would be better Ill make a d. for it in March. If you think it would be better for me to stay till April *for one moment* of course I will. She of course would go back. As it is it is: "oh dear me I wonder what my little foreman is doing" etc. etc. etc. Do please never **again** reckon upon L.M. in my life. When I get back I part from her – & she pretty well knows it & if she were honest (impossible) desires it, too. But remember if you think I ought to stay till April, I stay – and risk the offensive[2] & the sousmarins without a murmur. Put 2 little lines to your answer to this like Ive made & Ill know that you *have* answered. Voila! My health wont improve by being here: its as good as it ever will be to her rage disgust and chagrin of course – oh you should have seen her face drop when she said: 'I thought you were very ill'. My blood turned ice with horror. If I do come in March I will come with her. Frankly that *is* a relief – to feel I would have someone to help me. I am not much good at this travelling alone. Now you have my honest answer . . .

I went a great old walk yesterday came in – screwed my head tight & thought myself nearly black in the face but got very little down. Trouble is I feel I have found an *approach* to a story now which I must apply to everything. Is that nonsense? I read what I wrote before that last & I feel: no this is all *once removed*: it wont do. And it wont. Ive got

to reconstruct everything. I hate to talk like this when you are so
fiendishly tied & bound but my heart, my own, I do feel so that I shall
be able to relieve the strain a bit when I come back – I shall? Shan't I?

Family News. A disgusting letter from Vera. Mack's vocabulary,
very vulgar 'swanky' 'muchly' 'the mater'. Mack wont let her go to
N. Z. as arranged by Papa. Because after the great strain of his time in
RUSSIA he is to have 6 months' PEACEFUL LEAVE in Canada.[3] What
price shares in Mack? As far as Papa is concerned! Hes dished finally.
He is coming to England first & bringing me maple sugar which
Chaddie is to hand over. Do see that we get it. You know how good
it is.

I have got a fit of the war very badly today darling: this is why this
letter reads so hurried & strange. You know I feel it like a black cloud
pulling over. And I feel you overwork *horribly*. But there! Take me into
your arms & I am well again.

Oh Bogey Bogey Bogey!

Your own Wig.

MS ATL. *LKM* I. 127–8; *LJMM*, 166–7.

---

¹ Ida Baker seems to have shared the ability of Nicholas Nickleby's mother to make a feast of
misfortune.
² As in other years in the War, a new German offensive was expected with the return of fine
weather in the spring.
³ KM's brother-in-law had served in France and Russia as a Major with the 73rd Royal
Highlanders of Canada.

To J. M. Murry, [14 February 1918]

[Hôtel Beau Rivage, Bandol]

My darling,

Please give your mother this little hanky with my fond love – will
you? If you think it is fine enough. *And* please give her this receipt
for brown bread – will you? It is *my* mother's and she says it is most
awfully good. It sounds to me rather funny because of the bran, but
mother says that is quite right and everybody who comes to our house
walks off, full of it, a kind of human pincushion. Of course I long to
'knock up a batch' as they say. But do ask your mother to try it. And
remember to give her the hanky – won't you – just to prove I
remember her & do think of her.

Your own
Wig.

Brown Bread. Mix 2 cups of white flour with one cup of bran and

3 teaspoonfuls of baking powder. Add *1* dessertspoonful of golden syrup. Mix to a soft dough with a little warm milk and water. Bake in a greased cake tin for 1½ hours.

MS ATL. *LJMM*, 167.

To J. M. Murry, 15 [February 1918]

[Hôtel Beau Rivage, Bandol]
Friday 15th

My dearest dear

No letter today – Oh dear! how I *did* want one, too. The papers came registered but I had not slept & I was most enormously in want of *you*. So I signed for the papers & though they are full of meat . . . . still – *you* know! Im dull today. My story has got a bone in its leg – a big one. I may & I do (except for meals & a walk) ignore the mountain but she do cast a considerable big shadow. You see there is no lesser word for it: I *hate* her for so much – her insincerity, more her falseness & you can realise that she pays me back in pretty heavy copper – when I *do* see her. Still, it cant be helped.

I haven't a puff in my sails today, Bogey – you never saw such a head as mine must be within . . . Nothing less than a letter from you will do . . . Its also because I didn't sleep, see – and couldn't find my place in the bed & looked for it all night – *lashed* about in a hundred beds I should think but no – didn't find my place to curl in.

Yesterday, behind the hills at the back, I struck 3 divine empty houses. They have been empty a long time & will be (till we take one). I cannot tell you *how* lovely they all are – or how exquisitely placed – with gardens, terraces. Ours had also a stone verandah & two particularly heavenly trees embracing in the front of it. In the cracks of the stone verandah little white hyacinths were all in flower – a sunny bank at the side was blue with violets – There was a bay tree that waited to be hung with a poem & the approach! the approach! The colour of the house was a warm pink yellow with a red roof – the

shape –  oh I cant make it but it was I

think flying with little loves. It *faces* the city beyond the hills – which yesterday was bathed in light. But all this – without *you* – its such mockery such mockery. I look – I see – I feel & then I say the *WAR* and it seems to disappear – to be taken off like a film & Im sitting in the dark.

My own forgive this very tame little girl of yours today. Her heart is – Ah you know her heart – but it is looking for a letter and all the rest of her is empty.

Your own
Wig.

MS ATL. *LKM* I. 128–9; *LJMM*, 167–8.

To J. M. Murry, [16 February 1918]

[Hôtel Beau Rivage, Bandol]
Saturday.

Dearest of all,

No letter again today: that is 3 whole days. Isn't it simply *too* cursed! The D.N. for Tuesday came but I simply <u>long</u> for a letter – and it wont come. I had a moment, just after the post when I wondered if you thought now L.M. was here it wasn't so necessary, but that was unworthy of me. You'd not think that.

Yesterday your dull girl went for a dull crawl, got back & in 2 Ts a terrific squall had sprung up, it was icy cold, raging wind – Shelley was drowned again – the wind went on all night. Now it has dropped & it is SNOWING. I am writing to you with a pair of pale lilac hands & cheeks to match.

Such a fight goes on with my old work, too – The Mountain *will* sit on it – Though I stick so faithful to my programme, meal times & walk times are quite enough to exasperate me and lash me into fury beyond measure. "Katie mine who is Wordsworth. Must I like him? Its no good looking cross because I love you my angel from the little tip of that cross eyebrow to the *all* of you. When am I going to brush your hair again?" I shut my teeth & say 'never' but I really *do* feel that if she could she'd EAT me. Still I shall use her as a walking stick to help me to get home on – because I am *not* any good at travelling alone. I always seem to slip between the cracks in the floor like a pin and people do bang into me so. *Steps* at my door . . .

They were the Aged with your wire. Wasn't that a bit of luck? It has just come at the right moment. Now I know that all is well and now Ill just go on expecting those old letters tomorrow. You must have got my babies ['Sun and Moon'] as well as the other! Thank you my darling heart for wiring so soon.

I was thinking in bed last night of being with you, in some little strange town, it was, and we suddenly touched hands. I thought then how the feeling of your hand is such a wonder to me such a comfort. It

FITS me so – and I thought: 'their hands were QUICK with love' – That just expresses it.

I am homesick today, Bogey. I saw Ma'am Gamel yesterday & told her Id want to take some butter back. They will let me bring a pound of that butter I suppose? I can see you undoing the parcel. I can see you – see you – I don't see anything *but* you. Nobody else exists for me. I cant write letters or 'keep up' with people. A note perhaps to Johnny[1] (because I feel he in a way knows about us) but everybody else – don't count.

I can never know real peace or rest away from you: I freely confess it. Because I leave my heart with you – and all my desires –

It is very cold & pale outside: and I cant help thinking about that Versailles business. Its at the back of my mind all the while I write.

Ah love, take care of yourself for

Your own little
Wig.

MS ATL. *LJMM*, 168–9.

[1] Murry had told her on 11 Feb how 'Johnny [J. D. Fergusson] came last night . . . . He said "Oh, she's a good woman is Mansfield."' (ATL.)

To J. M. Murry, [16 and 17 February 1918]

[Hôtel Beau Rivage, Bandol]
Saturday night.

My darling Heart

The Lord saw fit to remove The Shadow from me this afternoon & I began to write free again, and was just in it when Juliette brought me a letter – a miracle by an afternoon post! It was your *Monday* letter but you said on the envelope it was Tuesday (oh yes: I understand.) It was the letter about L.M. & the money. If you *had* paid for her I think Id have *had* to kill her. It would have been more than flesh could stand. I wont give a sou or spend a sou: I save. I am mean if you like, but I save like a miser & account for every penny – so that I shall have some to add to our pot-au-feu when I get back. YOU ARE NOT TO THINK FOR ONE SECOND THAT THERE WILL BE THE SAME OLD CORVÉE AFTER THE WAR.[1] Please God we'll get our press. I agree absolutely: think with you, feel with you – *understand.* My serious stories wont ever bring me anything but my 'child' stories ought to and my light ones, once I find a place. I am sure I shall always have enough from Father to keep US in a cottage with penny packets of seeds to feed us & our fires we shall gather and our water we'll get in a well[2] – All you have to think of is that it cannot <u>not</u> come true – its so utterly simple. We shall live on honey dew and milk of Paradise; we shall be happy and free immediately. There is not a moment to lose. Ah, my soul, if you doubt *this*; if you feel for one instant that the big stone could fall on your head[3] then love is not what I think it is. Consider. Lets be practical. In a real cottage, deep in the country £150 would keep us at first, apart from a penny you earn or I might. Bogey, what can I say? It makes me so unhappy when you doubt it – I want to wring my hands & run up & down – – We know each other and our wants and ways are plain to us. We shall always be 'little gentle folk' wherever we live. Weve got furniture, books, a lovely doll. Don't you want to be my mate & live with me in a tiny cottage & eat out of egg cups? How *can* you torture me by thinking anything else is possible. During this bloody war its true youre a prisoner. But how could I live knowing you were in prison for one day after the war? If you really think you will be & that we cant live on my money – then I shall die. For I wont live any other life – no I wont. We'd better both take poison. Oh how awful this is.

Of course you cant ask people. You cant hate them like ı do.[4] I would put them all on a toasting fork & let them frizzle if I could. But who wants to ask?

Bogey, you can do whatever you please but you are not to take a little hammer & bang at my heart because it will break. Its not a rag heart or a calico untearable one even – & when you gave it *knock knock knock* by doubting our future this afternoon it hurt terribly. Yes you are to unburden yourself but you are not [to] doubt the very stuff of our love which is our freedom to work. The press is bound to come. You havent a Bee in your bonnet or if you have keep it & well start a hive with it. Why am I not with you. I cannot keep away. Oh that bag you run up the suburban stairs with!![5] Goodnight, my tired Boy. I will finish this tomorrow but do remember all the heaven there is before you and your Wig.

Sunday. Your Tuesday letter about the herring is here. I wonder if you [we?] were always alike or if we've grown so? *Or* and thats true I suppose we are become one person – a new one. Because I somehow get almost overcome by your letters – which say to me so absolutely what I *feel* how I *reason* how I *think* . . . Of course your 9 letters put me to shame. I havent yet written to H.L. & each day I dislike her a bit more.

Chaddie wrote yesterday saying Mack was here. If she asks you to meet him say you don't feel you'd ever gone [get on] with him: he rubs you up. She'll understand. But *do* mention the maple sugar!!!

What a superb chap Wilson is. I think he's a bit unpopular over here. They prefer L[loyd] G[eorge]. Dang their eyes.[6] The sun is out today but its still very cold. I am writing in my pigglejams & blue

cape – & look as though these were my last words from house on fire –
espèce de tiptoe pour flightisme – you know, darling. I am sorry you
have to go to the Woolves.[7] I don't like them either. They are *smelly*.
But there you are! Oh, *please* please shut your eyes a moment – open
them – rush into *our* garden & see the first smoke coming out of *our*
chimney – rush in again & put the kettle on – & kneel on the floor by
me & have a warm up . . . Dear Love, weve got sort of through tickets
to this place. Its only the frightful journey getting there – but it IS
THERE.

Now I must get dressed. L.M. is getting so fat that she will be
comandeered when she gets back. She eats portions for 2 + ½lb. dates
at a time + slabs of chocolate + anything else between meals. I hate
fat people. I shall always be able to play on my bones. Goodbye,
dearest dear for now. Give me a little small hail. Ill come back with
every penny I can hoard.

Your own
Wig

[*Across top*]
READ THIS CAREFULLY TWICE THEN SHOW IT TO RIB.

MS ATL. *LJMM*, 170–2.

[1] Murry wrote on 11 Feb: 'I feel as though I had been working on my last reserve: that I'm
perfectly willing, no, even happy to do this, if it is going to help us to be independent after the
war; but if it isn't and if there's to be the same old *corvée*, then I can't face it.' (Murry, 118.)
[2] The same letter pointed out that it was difficult for either of them to make much money from
writing. Murry's novel *Still Life* had made £8-10-0, and cost £9 to have typed. 'And, though I
think you're not in quite such an awful case as me, I think its really the same. But you and I may
very well find between us 250 people willing to pay £2 a year each for 4 privately printed books of
ours every year, and out of that we could make £300 a year profit . . . . Think of that *tripe* of the
Woolves!' (Murry, 119.)
[3] Murry also said, in the same letter (119): 'If I haven't enough money to buy a press, then I
feel that the big stone will have been put on my head again.'
[4] And again (119): 'And I can't ask people any more. I hate them. Really, the blackness of my
hatred of people like O[ttoline] M[orrell] staggers even myself.'
[5] He had told KM as well that 'I am like a little man with a bag from the suburbs running up
an endless moving stair.' (Murry, 118.)
[6] KM saw Woodrow Wilson as exercising restraint on those other Allied leaders who
demanded the total defeat and humiliation of Germany.
[7] She was to hear in a later letter that the engagement with Leonard and Virginia Woolf was
cancelled.

To J. M. Murry, 18 [February 1918]

[Hôtel Beau Rivage, Bandol]
Monday 18th

My darling Heart

I have just read your *Wednesday* letter & it makes me feel that it is
high time you had that ½ bottil of champagne. We will – in April. Oh,

if you knew my feelings towards Watergate House[1] . . . and all it means. But Bogey, I do feel that L. G. had a bit of a downfall in the H. of C.[2] *and* the German offensive (expected 2 days ago) hasn't given a sign. And then of course there is that eagle of a Wilson – All these are little rays of gold light on the shutters – aren't they?

I am up early, copying MSS for you. When I get back Ill work as regular as you (tho' with what a difference) but I do seem to have broken through once & for all, somehow, <u>&</u> I think there may be, if you hold me up by my heels and rattle me some pennies in me. Don't you? At last? On my table are wild daffodils – Shakespeare daffodils. They are so lovely that each time I look up I give them to you again. We shall go expeditions in the spring and write down all the *signs* & take a bastick and a small trowel & bring back treasure. Isn't that lovely where Shelley speaks of the 'moonlight coloured may'[3] . . .

Its still (I think) very cold & I am in my wadded jacket with the pink 'un round my legs. But the sun is out & Ill go for a big walk this afternoon & *warm up*. I saw old Maam Gamel yesterday. She is a nice old dear. The way she speaks of you always makes me want to *hug* her. Yesterday she said I must pass by her before I go back as she would send you a little souvenir – and then she looked up at me and said her blue eyes twinkling – 'il a toujours ses beaux yeux – le jeune mari?' . . 'Allez! allez! on n'a pas honte?' called Thérèse who was measuring biscuits for L. M. I also saw (looking for a bit of pumice stone: bought a bit for 1 sou) the old woman from the droguerie. She's got a new cat – called Mine – un grand, un sauvage, un fou avec les moustaches which would make a man pleure d'envie – In fact she says he is presqu'un homme – il *crache* absolument comme un homme – et le soir il est toujours dans les rues.

I have just made myself a glass of boiling tea, very weak with saxin.[4] Its good. I drink it on and off all day. Do you remember that funny sort of scum that used to come on the water here? It still does. I have to take it off with the point of my paper knife. Its very funny (something about me) I was thinking in bed this morning I cant think how we should have got on if we were *not* going to be married in April. It seems impossible to me – I feel that it will make things so easy, all sorts of things, & the feeling will be quite quite different. Now do you feel that? Apart from thousands of other things I know I shall take the most childish delight in speaking of you as my husband after you really are – But perhaps that is too babyish even for you – I would even like to roar it at the Garsington tea table and see their look of horror at my dreadful Bragian boldness. "I *do* think that is going a little *too* far" . . . But God forbid I should find myself there.

Oh I love you so – I love you so! I said that out loud just now – and now the watch is ticking it.

Ive nothing else to say – Oh Bogey when that train slows down and we wave . . . .

Wig

MS ATL. *LKM* I. 129–30; *LJMM*, 172–3.

[1] Where Murry worked for MI7.
[2] On 12 February Lloyd George had lost his head in the House of Commons, and Opposition spokesmen were cheered repeatedly.
[3] 'And in the warm hedge grew lush eglantine, / Green cowbind and the moonlight-coloured may', from the second stanza of 'The Question'.
[4] Saxin, proprietary name for an artificial sweetener containing saccharin.

To J. M. Murry, 19 February [1918]

[Hôtel Beau Rivage, Bandol]
February 19th

(Your Thursday & Friday letters received)

Dearest

I want to tell you some things which are a bit awful – so hold me *hard*. I have not been so well these last few days. Today I saw a doctor. There happens by an extraordinary chance to be an english doctor here just now, & L. M. got him to come. Look here! I cant leave this place till April – its no earthly go. I cant & mustnt – see. Cant risk a draught or a chill & mustnt walk. Ive got a bit of a temperature & I am not so fat as I was when I came – & Bogey, this is NOT serious does NOT keep me in bed is absolutely easily curable, but I have been spitting a bit of blood.[1] See? Of course I'll tell you? But if you worry – unless you laugh like Rib does I can't tell you: you mustnt type it on the typewriter or anything like that my precious – my own – and after all Lawrence often used to – so did I think [Aunt] Belle Trinder. But while it goes on Ive got to be most enormously careful. See? Ive got this doctor & Ive got the Slave – so I am provided for, & determined to stick it out till April & not come back till the first week of *then*. Its agony to be parted from you but it would be imbecile to get the March winds as I am so parky – and everybody would be madly cross – & I couldn't stick in bed in 47. Id only be a worry. So here I stay & work – and try to bear it. Ive *ample* money for everything & my journey money fastened up with a pin and locked away.

I can do all this and everything as long as I know you are taking care of yourself and that you dont worry about me and do *feed* and dont overwork too dreadfully. I am afraid it must be done. Before [the] doctor came (you can imagine) I was so frightened. Now Im confiding . . . its not serious. But when I saw the bright arterial blood I nearly had a fit. But he says its absolutely curable – and if I sit in the sun till April Ill then come back & see a specialist and Papa will pay for that – He can look at my wings with his spyglass & decide. Of course this man says this coast is my eye because its not bracing. Still now I am here – here I must stay & he is looking after me & I am to have injections of strichnine & other stuff – I don't know what, and more food still. So its a good thing L. M. came (even though I feel in some mysterious way *she has done it*. Thats because I *loathe* her so – I do.) Still Ill use her as a slave. As I shall be here a whole month longer I can get a lot of work done & that may bring pennies. Oh, I can bear it – or anything as long as you are well. And tell me when [you] feel a boiled haddock – don't disguise anything because I wont disguise things from you. See how I tell you *bang out* because our love will stand it. My money is splendid – and I shall *work work work*. In April there can't be the same chance of a snowstorm or a wind that might make 'pas de nougat pour le noël'[2] for us both. I think it must be – And then, please God we'll be married, & see how lucky I am I can work! I had your letter about the 2nd part of Je ne parle pas & I feel you are disappointed . . . Is that true & if it is true please tell me why – This is a silly old letter all about my wings. Forgive it, my love, and answer it as soon as you can. Oh my own precious don't work too hard – & love me love me till April. Your own little

Wig.

MS ATL. *LJMM*, 173–4.

[1] On the same day KM recorded in a notebook: 'I woke up early this morning and when I opened the shutters the full round sun was just risen. I began to repeat that verse of Shakespeare's: "Lo here the gentle lark weary of rest" and bounded back into bed. The bound made me cough – I spat – it tasted strange – it was bright red blood. Since then I've gone on spitting each time I cough a little more. Oh, yes, of course I am frightened. But for two reasons only. I don't want to be ill, I means "seriously" away from Jack. Jack is the 1st thought. 2nd I don't want to find this is real consumption, perhaps it's going to gallop – who knows – and I shan't have my work written. *That's what matters.* How unbearable it would be to die, leave "scraps", "bits" . . . nothing real finished.

But I feel the first thing to do is to get back to Jack. Yes my right lung hurts me badly but it always does more or less. But *Jack & my work* they are all I think of (mixed with curious visionary longing for gardens in full flower). L. M. has gone for the doctor.' (*Journal* 1954, 129–30.)

The Shakespeare quotation is from *Venus and Adonis*, l. 853.

[2] See her reference to Fabre's poem, 3 Feb, n. 1.

To J. M. Murry, [19 February 1918]

[Bandol]

NO GO BEFORE APRIL DARLING WRITTEN. BOWDEN.

Telegram ATL.

To J. M. Murry, [20 February 1918]

[Hôtel Beau Rivage, Bandol]
Wednesday

My darling Precious

I feel Much better today and the haemorrhage is – hardly at all.
Can't work much, or think very sensibly but I am ever so much better
than I was. The worst of all this *is* this. I have such a longing for you. I
feel once *you* had me Id get well. Once we ate together the food would
go to the right spot. If I was in bed with you Id sleep – and this is a
sort of *deep deep* conviction. I cannot help it. I *pine* when I am away
from you just like ladies do in old songs and all my efforts seem to be
in vain. However, I am making very great ones to be a strong girl for
April. Oh I *do* want to be home so. The absence from you eats at my
heart. I didn't have a letter today but I didn't expect one really. I had
such recent ones yesterday – The D[aily] N[ews] came & said eat
pulses instead of meat. Hadn't you better buy a first rate porridge
saucepan & eat it with *grated maple sugar*? As I write that for some
reason I feel a sort of small twinkle in my eye. I SEE you –

Now that Ive denied March it seems a long long way to April –
Hurry it up, Bogey – Put paper wings on the weeks. Let us be together
again – quickly – quickly!! And then all will be well.

Since this little attack Ive had a queer thing has happened. I feel
that my love and longing for the external world – I mean the world of
nature has suddenly increased a million times – When I think of the
little flowers that grow in grass, and little streams and places where
we can lie & look up at the clouds – Oh I simply *ache* for them – for
them with you – Take you away and the answer to the sum is o. I feel
so awfully like a tiny girl whom someone has locked up in the dark
cupboard – even though its daytime – I don't want to bang at the door
or make a noise but I want you to come with a key youve made
yourself & let me out and then we should tiptoe away together into a
kinder place where everybody was more of our heart and size. You
mustn't think as I write this that I am dreadfully sad. Yes, I am but
you know at the back of it is *absolute faith* and *hope* and *love*. Ive only, to
be frank like we *are* had a bit of a fright – See? And Im still 'trembley'.
That just describes it.

Tomorrow my own I shall write a gayer letter – Oh – just to forget
me for a minute. Do you remember or have I mentioned how the fool
in King Lear says: " 'Twas her brother who, in pure kindness, *buttered*
his horse's *hay*"[1] I though that was a good phrage for nowadays – 'It is
hardly the moment to *butter* the *horse's* hay' – Isn't it? Pin it in the
Nation.

I hate to ask you to spend on me but now Im staying can I have another Dickens sometime? *Bleak House* or *Edwin Drood*? If you can get them in a 7d – do – If you feel you cant afford them I understand. Mrs Gaskell positively fascinated me. I think she's an extremely good writer – The 2nd story in the Cranford book – 'Moorland Cottage' is really a little masterpiece.[2] *We shall read it at home.*

Now I am quite cheerful again, and can leave you with a smile and a wave instead of almost turning away like I had to on page 3.[3] And, oh my own lover – you just go on looking after yourself for me & I will go on looking after myself for you. Eight more days & this month is over – and then there's only March – *Yours yours*

Wig.

MS ATL. *LKM* I. 130–1; *LJMM*, 175–6.

[1] *King Lear*, II. iv. 127.
[2] Elizabeth Gaskell's *The Moorland Cottage*, first published in 1850, and later sometimes included in the same volume with *Cranford* (1848) and other stories.
[3] The section above concluding 'into a kinder place where everybody was more of our heart and size'.

To J. M. Murry, [20 and 21 February 1918]

[Hôtel Beau Rivage, Bandol]

Wednesday Night.

Dearest and most Precious one

That doctor is coming tomorrow so Ill tell you what he says. He is a most awful fool, I am sure, but still I suppose he *is* a doctor & thats a comfort. One thing he says this south coast is no use for me: too relaxing and I ought to have sat on a mountain – Fatal to stay here later than March. Well thats perhaps true – I think it is for every time the wind blows I shuts up all my petals – Even if its only a breeze – – – I feel *chirpy* tonight. I don't care *what* happens what pain I have what I suffer as long as my handkerchiefs don't look as though I were in the pork butcher trade. That does knock your Wig *flat flat flat*. I feel as though the affair were out of my control then and that its a nightmare. Last night was like that for me – Then this afternoon when I sat reading Keats in the sun I coughed and it wasn't red and I felt inclined to wave the fact to the whole world. And when L. M. said she woke at 3 am this morning & felt very melancholy "perhaps one doesn't see things in their true perspective then" and would I mind if she tapped at my door then if I had a light and she just *told* me I said I don't care a *damn* what you feel if youre not ill. Youve no right to feel anything except "thank the Lord Im fat and strong". I really feel that about her – Oh I do *detest* her personality – and her powerful broody henniness – and her 'we' and 'our' . . . I even go so far as to feel that she has pecked her way into my wing to justify her coming, which *is* cruel I know.

No Bogey, to be in England, to see you – to see a good lung specialist – that's my affair and no other – But to be on alien shores with L. M. a very shady medicine man and a crimson lake hanky is about as near Hell as I want to be – – –

Thursday. "Pas de lettre encore. Rien que le journal". "Merci Juliette". Well, that often happens on this day – Perhaps Ill get 2 tomorrow & it may have been those bloody raids which I see have been on again[1] – Boge I feel ever so much better again today and *hungry*. I should like us to have a chicken en casserole and a salad & good coffee – Its a bit windy today so Ill take the air behind a screen of my daffodils – and not rush forth. Do you remember, or have I mentioned lately that poem of Shelleys *The Question*. It begins:

> "I dreamed that, as I wandered by the way
> Bare Winter suddenly was changed to Spring" . . .

I have learned it by heart since I am here; it is very exquisite, I think. Shelley and Keats I get more and more *attached* to. Nay, to all 'poetry'. I have such a passion for it and I feel such an understanding of it. Its a great part of my life.

I cant but feel a brute if I write about my own work too much while you must sit with folded wings . . .

But each new D[aily] N[ews] I get I feel that the days of the N[orthcliffe][2] press and the L.G. reign are numbered – There has been a big loud recognised crack . . .

Once the war is over all our woes are over for ever I think. Then comes in the sweet of the year[3] for you and me.

You wont worry about your girl – will you? Truly she is better again and today the crimson lake is back in the paint box & there's not a sign of it.

If you only knew how I love you at this moment you'd give a great jump for joy . . .

Later. Ive just had lunch. They give me *pounds* of fish now. I had one today with lovely violet bones: I wish Id kept one for you – Goodbye my own for now. A letter must come tomorrow mustnt it – and keep your big umbrella over your *darling* head when the bombs come. April! April!

Your own
Wig

MS ATL. *LKM* I. 131–2; *LJMM*, 176–8.

¹ 27 persons were killed and 41 injured in air attacks on London on the nights of 18 and 19 February, although press releases claimed the air defences of London were 'constantly improving. The work of gunners and airmen seems to have been the best known.' (The *New York Times*, 19 Feb.)

² Alfred Charles Harmsworth, Viscount Northcliffe (1865–1922), the enterprising journalist who founded the *Daily Mail* and the *Daily Mirror*, and became proprietor of *The Times*. He exercised enormous influence through his pro-War sympathies, and his papers' support of Lloyd George's policies.

³ 'sweet o' the year' is from Autolycus' song in *The Winter's Tale* (IV. ii. 3), and in KM's next letter she quotes Perdita's words to Florizel: '[daffodils that] come before the swallow dares' (IV. iii. 119), harking back to the earlier exchange with Murry, see 18 and 19 Jan, n. 3.

To J. M. Murry, [22 February 1918]

[Hôtel Beau Rivage, Bandol]
Friday

My Life

A Horn of Plenty! Your Sunday letter & postcard and your Monday letter. Oh, *how* I have devoured them. The Monday one, which was written with smiling twirley letters made me a bit sad; it was in answer to mine saying *March* was definite and now alas! our plans are altered and I cant come before the swallow dares. But oh! knowing this – all the same let us try and be happy – We *must* try & be happy looking forward to April.

I feel marvellously better today. NO temperature – *vegetarian* – and on the mend again, flying down the road to you – But Bogey I have more than my share of alarums and tuckets – don't you think? Great big black things lie in wait for me under the trees and stretch their shadows across the road to trip me – Youll have to keep shouting 'Look out Wig!' when we walk together again. The doctor has been and says – if I use all his remedies Ill be a well girl. (I think he is such a *ponce* – oh I could write you reams about him but I'll *tell* you). However his remedies are sound I think – injections of some stuff called goneol and another called Kaikakilokicaiettus as far as I can make out¹ – *and* a tonic *and* fish to eat – whole fishes – fish ad lib. If I am torpedoed on the way home I expect I shall burst into fins and a mermaid tail as I enter the water & so swim to shore – Je t'aime je t'aime! The Ghoul is of course doing all her possible. Its good shes here after all – I don't see her more than I can avoid, & I dont let her *touch* me . . . I will send you some more work as soon as I can copy it – But I am a bit *slow* just now – just for a day or two. Oh if only you were working² . . . But dearest dear – how I shall make it all easy for you as soon as this war is over. All youve got to do then is to say – its *my* turn and Ill fly –

That was a nice letter from Sullivan. He is a good chap; I am glad you see him. I wonder if you escaped H.L? She has become to me now a sort of *witch* – I cant write to her – When I put my pen on the paper it begins to tremble and make crosses & won't go further – – I see you lunching with Brett much as you would lunch with a mushroom . . .

Theres a bit of wind today: its a ¼ to 12. Im just up. L.M. I believe ranges the mountains all the mornings – She comes back & I meet her at lunch – rosy, with bright eyes and an Appetite which makes the hotel *tremble*, and after having devoured the tablecloth glasses & spoons says what I miss are the puddings. Dont you *ever* care for currant duff, *my dearie or* – & then follows about 100 puddings as fast as they can tear – She keeps them all flying in the air, like a conjuror & still like a conjuror – eats em – What a strange type she is – but good to travel back with – Yes, good for that.

You can feel from this letter that I am loving you today & that I am a very much stronger girl & inclined to tickle Rib – *Dont overwork my darling.* Remember I shall come back with a penny in my hand for our store. Im taking every care of myself for you. Please never post your letters while the guns are going. I hope the little boy upstairs is better – poor little chap![3]
Bogey Bogey, je te baise je t'adore –

Wig

MS ATL. *LKM* I. 132–3; *LJMM*, 178–9.

[1] Gonal was a name for capsules of sandalwood oil, but it is likely that KM misheard her doctor. The second remedy she clearly invented.
[2] At his poetry, she means, rather than his work at MI7.
[3] A boy in the rooms above Murry's, whose pleurisy had turned to congestion of the lungs.

To Ottoline Morrell, [22 February 1918]

[Hôtel Beau Rivage,] Bandol. (Var)
Dearest Ottoline

I have taken this tiny piece of paper in the slender hope that I may still be able to hide behind it and try (ah! try) to explain my inexplicable silence without falling into too dread a panick at sight of your stern looks of anger and dismay.

Would to God I were *not* this fickle, faithless, intolerable, devilishly uncomfortable creature whom you must, a thousand times, have whistled down the wind! But Lady? Pity her – Alas – poor soul! Katherine is curst!

All goes well. She makes merry. She delights in sweet talk and laughter. She runs in the fields with her darling companions filling their wicker arks and hers with a thousand pretties – She hugs the 'black but beautiful' fire with her dearest and is not last in gossip of those who are not there – And then, quite suddenly, without a wing shadow of warning, without even the little moment in which to tie up the door knocker with a white kid glove or a chaste crepe bow she is shut up in her dark house, and the blinds are pulled down, and even the postman who hangs upon the doorbell might hang there like fruit, my soul, till the door rot[1] – she could not answer him.

The real, tragic part of the affair is that what happens to her while she is so wickedly *out* yet dreadfully *in* she cannot tell or explain. And though her enemies may see her at those times dressed in a little snake wesket and supping off toads livers with friends wild and slee, she dares sometimes to dream that her friends (can she *hope* for friends – accursèd one!) will perhaps be kinder, and even beckon her to her stool by the chimney corner – and even hand her the custard cup of Hot Purl or Dogs Nose[2] that was her share aforetime – – –

A curse on my pen! It twing-twangs away but my heart is heavy. Why aren't I true as steel – firm as rock? I am – I am – but in my way Ottoline – in my way. And yes I agree. It is no end of a rum way –
– –

I wish you were *here*. Dark England is so far and this room smells spicy and sweet from the carnations – pink and red and wonderful yellow. The hyacinths in a big jar are put on the window sill for the night for my little maid says they give you not only sore throats but *dreams* as well! It is very quiet. I can just hear the sea breathe – a fine warm night after a hot day.

Spring, this year, is so beautiful that watching it unfold one is filled with a sort of anguish. Why – oh Lord why! I have spent days just walking about or sitting on a stone in the sun and listening to the bees in the almond trees and the wild pear bushes and coming home in the evening with rosemary on my fingers and wild thyme in my toes – tired out with the loveliness of the world.

It has made the War so awfully real – and not only the war – Ah Ottoline – it has made me realise so deeply and finally the *corruption* of the world – I have such a horror of present day men and women that I mean never to go among them again. They are thieves, spies, janglours all – and the only possible life is remote – remote – with books – with *all* the poets and a large garden full of flowers and fruits – *And* a cow (kept for *butter only*!)

What have you been reading lately? Shelley? Have you read 'The Question' lately?

I dreamed that as I wandered by the way
Bare winter suddenly was changed to spring.

Oh, do read – this moment – its so marvellous. Why aren't I talking to you instead of writing. I shall come back to dark England soon – Its a trouble you know to have *two* Souths of France, as I have. But a sweet trouble – and Id not be without it.

No, there is nobody to talk to – I have written a great deal – I think the Woolfs must have eaten the Aloe root and branch or made jam of it[3] –

Goodnight dearest
Katherine.

MS Texas. *LKM* I. 157–8.

---

[1] 'Hang there like fruit, my soul, till the tree die!' *Cymbeline*, V. v. 263.

[2] Both names for a mixture of warm beer and gin, supposedly beneficial as a morning drink.

[3] *Prelude*, the story shaped from the longer version *The Aloe*, was not published by the Hogarth Press until July.

To J. M. Murry, [23 February 1918]

[Hôtel Beau Rivage, Bandol]
Saturday

My life

The papers came today in a bundle – I am very glad of them but no letter came. It will be here tomorrow. I have a sort of doubt in my bosom today as to whether I should have told you about my last attack or not – I have such a perfect horror – (if you *knew* how strong) of worrying you – of adding to your burden. And yet we must be truthful to each other in all things and at all costs. That, too, I believe. *Im much better*: its as though the last affair had never been again now – and Im going slow & eating and trying to collect flesh at least – Im not a bit an ill girl – just a very slightly 'faible' one – but that Ill always be till we're free and at rest. How *can* one be otherwise in the midst of all these horrors? War and anxiety and you imprisoned there and us parted – Its stuff for an L.M. to fatten on but not Bogeys and Wigs.

Yesterday the woman at the paper shop gave me a bouquet of violets – here are some. And Juliette has filled my vases with yellow goldy wallflowers – God! how I love flowers –

After all my own precious – my coming back is only delayed by a little more than three weeks. Thats what I cling to for consolation. Then I SHALL come back for I cant stop here any longer. Even the Doctor says not to stay here after March – so I must come. Hooray! Will my Rib be at the window? What a throwing about he will get. Does he ever walk up you? Never? Do you ever read who made him on his tummy. Never. Attend un tout p'tit p'tit p'tit beau moment as they [say] here and he'll know all these joys again. I'll have to get food cards – won't I? Id better wait till we have thrown this old name away and then it will be easier I am going to get Belle to give us a fat fowl a week: I think it is a good idea. It would make such a difference. On Monday P.G. Ill post more manuscript to you, darling. Would the Nation publish Sun and Moon?[1] If they publish that rubbish by Stephens[2] I think they might. Have you read any reviews of Yeats' book? And did you see the pompous ass' remarks on Keats?[3] There was a good story agin him (tho' he didnt know it) in a quote I saw. He dreamed once '*in meditations*' (! ?) that his head was circled with a flaming sun. Went to sleep & dreamed of a woman whose hair was afire, woke up, lighted a candle and by & bye discovered 'by the odour' that he'd set his own hair ablaze.[4] This *he* calls sort of prophetic. I think its wondrous apt. Its just as far as he & his crew can get – to set their hair afire – to set their lank forlorn locks afrizzle – God knows theres nothing else about them that a cart load of sparks could put a light to. So he can jolly well shut up about Keats. If you should ever have the chance, dearest Bogey pull his nose for me as well as Conrads. But oh! how *ignorant* these reviewers are how far away & barred out from all they write – There was a review of Coleridge in the Times[5] – so bad so ill-informed – – But then of course I feel I have rather a corner in Coleridge and his circle. In fact you and I are the only two people who can write and think and whose opinion is worth while – The sea is breaking restless and high on the coast opposite – so are these waves and waves of love breaking over you –

Your Wig.

MS ATL. *LKM* I. 133–4; *LJMM*, 179–81.

[1] Apparently not. (But see p. 67, n. 3 above.)

[2] On 26 January the *Nation* had published 'Desire', a story by the Irish writer James Stephens.

[3] KM read in the *Nation*, 16 February, an unsigned review of W. B. Yeats's recently published *Per Amica Silentia Lunae*. She refers to the lines in 'Ego Dominus Tuus' that say of Keats:

> I see a schoolboy when I think of him,
> With face and nose pressed to a sweet-shop window.
> For certainly he sank into his grave
> His senses and his heart unsatisfied,
> And made – being poor, ailing and ignorant,
> Shut out from all the luxury of the world,
> The coarse-bred son of a livery-stable keeper –
> Luxuriant song.

Yeats makes similar observations in prose in Section III of 'Anima Hominis'.

[4] An anecdote recounted in Section XI of 'Anima Mundi', the second part of *Per Amica Silentia Lunae*.

⁵ Under the heading 'Coleridge as Critic', a review of *The Table Talk and Omniana of Samuel Taylor Coleridge, with a note on Coleridge by Coventry Patmore, The Times Literary Supplement*, 7 February 1918.

To J. M. Murry, [23 February 1918]

[Hôtel Beau Rivage, Bandol]
Saturday Night.

Dearest Bogey

I wish I knew where you were, what you are thinking and doing. It is just 9 oclock. I have been sitting by the fire. L. M. came in after dinner for a few minutes with her knitting but now she's gone to bed – thank God! It is impossible to describe to you my curious hatred and antagonism to her. Gross, trivial, dead to all that is alive for me, ignorant and *false*. I spoke about the war to her tonight – about the meaning of it and like a fool told her how it was at the back of my mind all the time – was a sort of sea, rising and falling – never never still . . . And then I said how *sick* this new offensive made me feel – and so on. Said she, (knitting a grubby vest) "Roger has got four teeth. Does that interest you? It *is* interesting, my Katie." "And the gardener says that little black kitten is the *child* of the grey *lady* cat". I felt exactly as Lawrence must have felt with Frieda – exactly. You remember the feeling Lawrence had (before he was so mad) that Frieda wanted to destroy him; I have oh – just that!!! We must go off at the station and she must go her ways and we must not meet for a long time. Don't soften to her: don't feel grateful. Shes *so* happy to feel that she was right after all about coming . . . Until I am rid of her I shall always see myself in a kind of desert & she hovering above on broad, untiring wing – ready to descend the moment I stumble over a grain of sand . . . Enough about her. I *had* to get rid of that.

Yes, I was sitting this afternoon round by the Golf hotel, watching the waves. They reared very high and loud and as they fell – came those bright 'golden windows' that you and I so loved to see – and I realised again that they were *nothing* to me – that the sound of them was like a bombardment and all their roaring only said 'danger! danger!' God! how I want you tonight. We would fold up close in each others arms and perhaps talk softly or not at all – but I would feel your heart beat in my bosom & I'd rest . . .

All over the hotel (it is full now) I can hear people going to bed, talking, pouring out water, dropping their boots on the red tiled corridors. A little dog yelps and the bells ring and the tired maid runs up and down. What am I doing among these people? Je me demande – *Or* 'I fondly ask'.[1] But its only for four weeks more or at most five. If

I leave here the last week in March – – – I shall not write any more until the morning. As the night deepens it drags my courage down with it and Ive no right to cry to you then. If a *letter* comes tomorrow – – – Goodnight, my love. We are aliens and strangers in this world and when we are alone we are very lonely. Goodnight my soul.

[*No signature*]

PLEASE READ TOTHER FIRST
LETTRE MINEURE.

It makes me nearly *laugh* today because I am *so* in love & confident.

MS ATL. *LJMM*, 181–2.

---

¹ ‘“Doth God exact day-labour, light deny'd?”/I fondly ask.’ John Milton, Sonnet ‘On His Blindness’.

To J. M. Murry, [24 February 1918]

[Hôtel Beau Rivage, Bandol]
Sunday.

My dearest love

I have written II on the other letter because it was one – is one – oh youll see why. I needn't explain.

Today there came 2 letters from you; one contained Fathers, one said my wire had come. I simply fix my eyes upon April. March has *got* to be weathered – *got* to be borne. It only has four Sundays – There are only five Sundays more before Im home – I *wont* think of March. Only your disappointment my darling Heart – that I hate – I have never known children so positively *chivvied* as you and me. We cant go on for a minute by ourselves without something happening – But once we are together we wont let the chance occur – not till you positively run away from me – & then Rib and I and two babies hanging out of one window will call call so loudly that youll come back for shame.

Now about the Pa man's letter – Ill be frank. It amazed me. I thought it very possible hed have an attack of *gravel* or *stone* & write about ‘Duty’ – or ‘as a practical man of affairs’ or ‘one cannot live on mulberry leaves like a silk worm’ or something like that. Also, knowing how extraordinarily shy and reserved he is and how horribly difficult it is for him not to shut up like an oyster I consider the letter an amazing tribute to yours. For one thing he put *on Tour* on the top (which is a family joke) and the preface had a twinkle in its eye – & I thought he put that bit about worldly considerations & my allowance very well. Yes, darling, knowing the Pa man it is extremely satisfactory. I wish you *would* reply – Just a word when you are in the mood – saying how relieved we are – & that you read his Bank speeches,[1] praps and if you could make a very small little joke – just a sort of preliminary hop – it would chauffe him. Hes *far* shyer than you are even. I think Mother will write for sure – I have had no letters yet from them. Kay is steaming them at the Bank I suppose.

God! the afternoon is so fair! Your letter about *our* work – the fusion of *our* work simply dropped into my heart and opened there like a rose and every breath I draw its fragrance is upon me. Five more Sundays & then Im <u>home</u> – Next week Ill write four more. Like that it don't seem so long. Especially as I think Ill cheat a Sunday at the last moment & come back at a gallop. Five more walks in your corduroys & then if youll have me you will carry me in your pocket & we'll try and look in a curiosity window at a teapot & we'll come back very slowly and put the kettle on and take off our hats and lift our arms and drop into each others bosom. I am bringing back a small flower basket. I think it would do so well for sanitches don't you – Ill put a pound of butter in it. I must bring figs, too. They are delicious & very cheap – one franc a pound – What about *dates*? Can you get them? Shall I bring some? It will be nearly March when you write.

Im still better so that old ugly one has gone back to his lair after a final growl.[2] I must write to Geoffroi & say this hotel is full (which is true). She *is* a jingo but all the French I know or hear of – are – What they cant stomach is *paix sans victoire*. Who wrote Washington & Versailles in the Nation[3] & wasn't Earps poem ridiculous.[4] It was like a dead earwig.

Mais, tu sais, je t'aime *trop*.

Your loving, longing, faithful, hoping – *hoping*
Wig.

MS ATL. *LJMM*, 182–3.

[1] With his reply to Murry's letter about his and KM's impending marriage, Harold Beauchamp must have sent a copy of his Report on Proceedings as Chairman of Directors of the Bank of New Zealand, delivered in Wellington on 7 December 1917. The report offered his views on European affairs, as well as summarizing local economic conditions.

[2] KM is comparing her recently spitting blood with details in Alphonse Daudet's 'La Chèvre de M. Seguin', which she had translated for the *New Age*, 6 September 1917. In the story a goat 'all spotted with blood' is finally devoured by a wolf.

[3] 'Washington or Versailles', the unsigned leading article in the *Nation*, 16 February.

[4] 'Summer' by T. W. Earp, a young American whom KM had met at Garsington, and who had founded with Aldous Huxley in 1917 the short-lived undergraduate magazine, the *Palatine Review*.

To J. M. Murry, [25 February 1918]

[Hôtel Beau Rivage, Bandol]
Monday.

My own precious

The D[aily] N[ews] and the French Book came today but no letter.
I shall hear tomorrow. I wish it wasnt always such a disappointment,
but it *is*. You know the feeling . . .

Isn't this nice paper? A biggish block of it costs 65. I shall bring you
one. Theres fresh nougat here, too. I must put a great lump of it in my
box for you. You see where *all* my thoughts turn to. Yesterday par
exemple, it was as warm as summer. I sat on a bank under an olive
tree, and fell adreaming . . . Now I came back as a surprise & just sent
you a wire to the office – *Look here she's back Rib* and then I lighted the
lamp and arranged the flowers & your presents were on the table –
And at last your step – Your key in the door. 'Wig! Bogey!' *Or* I came
again as a surprise & phoned you from the station. 'Is that you Jack –
Ive just arrived.' I sat there, thinking like this until I nearly wept for
joy. It seemed *too good to be true*. Will it *really* happen Bogey – really &
truly?

I managed to send Sullivan a sort of Broken Meat note yesterday &
I have tried to put off the Geoffroi. She & L. M. would drive me quite
dotty. As it is L. M. has pretty nearly finished me. I mean not quite
seriously but I live in a state of the most *acute exasperation* and black
rage. Yes its just like Lawrence & Frieda. I try to put up a fight
against her but its like trying to sing against the loudest thunderstorm
in the world – She would, if I lived with her send me out of my mind –
just like Lawrence *is*.

Oh Bogey Im so subdued today. I expected N.Z. letters & got none
– and its very windy and cold – & my work is *thick* absolutely *thick* for
the moment. Under it all – is: will the offensive prevent me coming
back? Will the channel be closed? You know this mood. Your letter
tomorrow will start the wheels going round again & Ill be a gay girl
and write more. But I dont seem to have seen anything to tell you of –
I feel in a sort of *quiet daze* of *anxiety*. I tell you so you will understand
the tone of this letter. *All is well really*. But Id like to call out your name
very loudly until you answer – & I begin to run. Take care of yourself
for your

Wig.

MS ATL. *LKM* I. 134–5; *LJMM*, 183–4.

To J. M. Murry, [26 February 1918]

[Hôtel Beau Rivage, Bandol]
Tuesday.

My darling Heart

I have a *Gorgeous Letter* from you written on Thursday (Chummie's birthday). You remember the one – It was about Love and War . . . and our future and 'not by a long chalk'[1] – Thats given it to you I expect. But oh, it has done me so much *good* real solid *good* – just as if Id been with you and we had broken bread together and this *ache* were past. But when I read about Bertie being carried shoulder high I felt quite *sick*. For such a silly, incredibly stupid thing.[2] How humiliated he ought to feel. It would be for me, like if I was a burglar & was caught after having burgled the potato knife. I expect if he goes to Prison hell get immensely fat in there, in fact hes so blown already that I shudder –

Mother has written to you. It may or may not be a nice letter. She said, in hers to me that she had lain down and recited silently to herself a polished oration but since then "my brains have gone and I cant find them – What will Jack think you spring from?" I wish her letter to you would come – Jeanne sent you this note and the Pa man wrote delightfully to me. Ill send you his tomorrow. I like especially what he says about always having longed for a remote existence in the country – but 'man proposes woman disposes'. That is so like him.

Last night after a full moon and a sea like velvet a huge thunder storm burst over the town. Rain, bright lightning, loud wind. I was sitting up in bed writing for thank God! Ive managed to stave off the werewolf a bit and the storm was wonderful. I had forgotten what it sounded like. But just in the middle, while the rain drummed I saw you lying asleep – all your youthful slender body that I love so, your black, round head, your hands and feet – and I *longed* to clasp you – & to curl up in my place which is there.

Trust L. M. for knocking then – a low, ominous knock. I think she hoped I had been struck by lightning – (I always feel her dream is to bury me here & bring back a few bulbs from Katies grave to plant in a window box for you). She asked if she might lie on the floor (you know these *tile floors*) till it was over as it was so very agitating –

Boge we must have plenty of gilly-flowers in our garden – They smell so sweet.

How shall we spend the day?
With what delights
Shorten the nights?

> When from this tumult we are got secure,
> Where mirth with all her freedom goes
> Yet shall no finger lose
> Where every word is thought and every thought is pure;
> There from the tree
> We'll cherries pluck,
> and pick the strawberry . . .³

Dont you like that – darling mine?

I shant go out today because it rains. Ill read Le P'tit this afternoon & Nausicaa⁴ and write you about them tomorrow, and Ill make no END of an effort to finish this story called *Bliss*. I hope youll like it. Its different again – I was thinking last night that I must not let L. M. obsess me – After all she is a trial but I must get over her. Dosty would have. She adds to the struggle, yes, but the struggle is always there – I mean if one dont feel very strong & so on. But they have nearly all had to fight against *just this*. So must and so will I. I hope I have <been br> not been a coward in my last letter or two. At any rate my loins are girded up no end today – and I spent the morning in bed full steam ahead. Queer the effect people have on one. Juliette is a positive help to writing. She is so independent and so full in herself – I want to say 'fulfilled' but its a dangerous word⁵ – I love to feel she is near and to meet her. She *rests* one positively. Shell make some man tremendously happy one day – Yes, shes really important to me. As to all the other *swine* with which the hotel is full – – well they are swine.

> Unhappy! Shall we never more
> That sweet militia restore
> When gardens only had their towers
> And all the garrisons were flowers;
> When roses only arms might bear
> And men did rosy garlands wear?⁶

I *keep* (as you see) wanting to quote poetry today – When I get back I shall be like a sort of little private automatic machine in the home. You wind me up & a poem will come – Ive learned so many here while I lie awake –

Now, darling I must write to Kay & get my next month's money – *at once. Money is splendid*, and I am keeping it fast. I have more than enough for every need.

I shall make Rib a wedding dress of blue jersey, sailor knot – full blue trousers & praps a very tiny *whistle* on a cord – if I can find one.

What about your food cards? And ought I to apply for 1st week in April and onwards?

I adore you, Bogey and I am

Wig

MS ATL. *LKM* I. 135–7; *LJMM*, 184–6.

[1] Murry wrote on 21 Feb, 'I don't work anything like so hard as I used, & don't intend to. The secret of it all is that because I don't see anybody & don't want to, I just tumble everything out of my bag on to your lap; and somedays it happens to be bits of string & used up blotting paper. But the bag ain't me, no, not by a long chalk.' (Murry, 125.)

[2] In the same letter, Murry said, 'Would you believe it, but at a *Herald* meeting the other night they carried Bertie Russell shoulder-high because he'd been prosecuted for writing an incredibly stupid attack on America?' In the *Tribunal*, no. 90, 3 January 1918, Russell had written an article called 'The German Peace Offer' which included this sentence on the build-up of American troops in Europe, and the prospects of the coming year: 'The American garrison which will by that time be occupying England and France, whether or not they prove efficient against the Germans, will no doubt be capable of intimidating strikers, an occupation the American Army is accustomed to at home.' Russell was charged with prejudicing relations with the United States, and sentenced to six months imprisonment. There was an appeal on 12 May, and the conditions of his serving his sentence in Brixton Prison were relaxed.

[3] From a poem by Thomas Randolph, as she explains on 8 Mar.

[4] Murry had reviewed Jean Ajalbert's *Raffin Su-Su* in *The Times Literary Supplement* on 21 February, and the same day sent on the book, saying 'I only want you to read "Le P'tit" & perhaps "Nausicaa". Tell me what you think: I want to know.' (Murry, 126.)

[5] Murry explained (*LJMM*, 186): 'I.e. because so much used by D. H. Lawrence in a special sense – sexually "fulfilled".'

[6] Andrew Marvell, 'Upon Appleton House', XLII, 329–34.

To J. M. Murry, [27 February 1918]

[Hôtel Beau Rivage, Bandol]

Wednesday.

My own darling

Your Saturday letter has come. The one about the Eye and about my wings. Now I am being an absolute old *coddler* for your sake and doing *everything* and feeling ever such a great deal better SO do you the same. Please see a specialist about your eye if its not better. We are the most awful pair Ive ever heard of. We'll have to pin notices in our hats & on our chests saying what we've got & then get a couple of walking sticks and tin mugs if this goes on . . .

But though I write so lightly I am really worried about your darling eye. Can you knock off for a day or two and just rest it. Oh dear – you oughtnt to look at anything smaller than a cow . . . But you know the *great necessity*: *don't* neglect it. See Ainger & get him to tell you who to go to. He *is* a decent chap. And what about a week end with the Waterlows? Could you stand it? It would be a rest perhaps. I don't mention Garsington because its 2 vile.

Bogey March is nearly here and then Ill begin to count the days. Ill make you out a list of them too and cross one off each night. *Dont* strain your other eye if you tie up the one – Now Bogey that really would be silly – wouldn't it? Now I won't say any more about it in case it has gone or you'll get cross.

I feel simply spanking today: it must be 'La Faute des Poissons' – Ill live on fishes when I get back and all will be well . . .

Don't forgive L. M. I cant bear to hear you say you do even – My feeling at present is that Ill never see her again after I get back. I *do* manage to work in spite of her, but if I did not I think I'd really go *insane* with exasperation. She *is* Frieda II . . .

I have read Le P'tit. Its *very* good, very well done – I think its got one fault or perhaps I am too ready to be offended by this. I think the physical part of le p'tits feeling for Lama is unnecessarily accentuated. I think if Id written it I wouldn't have put it in at all – not on his side – On hers – yes – but never once on his. Am I wrong do you think? Yes of course I agree its well done – that part – but I would have left it *more mysterious* – Lama must do all she does & le P'tit must say: 'Si tu savais comme je t'aime!' But 'lorsqu'un spontané baiser dans l'affolement furieuse de l'instinct chez le jeune homme . . .' That I don't like.

But the 'way' it is done the 'method' – I *do* very much. 'Nausicaa' has got something very charming, too. If he wasn't a frenchman hed be a *most* interesting chap. But I do find the french language, style, attack, point of view, hard to stomach at present. Its all *tainted*. It all seems to me to lead to dishonesty – Dishonesty Made Easy – made superbly easy! All these *half* words – these words which have never really been born – and seen the light – like 'me trouble' – [?'bagne'] – 'tiède' – 'blottant', 'inexprimable' (these are bad examples but you know the kinds I mean & the phrases & whole paragraphs that go with them) – They wont – at the last moment – *do* at all. Some of them are charming – and one is loathe to do without them – but they are like certain plants – once they are in your garden they spread & spread & spread – and make a show, perhaps, but they are *weeds*. No, I get up hungry from the french language. I have too great an appetite for the real thing to be put off with pretty little kickshaws – and I am offended intellectually that 'les gens' think they can so take me in. Its the result of Shakespeare – I think. The english language is damned difficult but its also damned rich and so clear and bright that you can search out search out the darkest places with it. Also its *heavenly* simple and true. Do you remember where Paulina says:

"I an old turtle
Will wing me to some withered bough

And there – my mate that's never to be found again
Lament till I am lost!"[1]

You cant beat that. I *adore* the english language – and that's a fact.

"Your eyes be musical your dewy feet
Have freshly trod the lawns for timeless hours
Oh young & lovely dead."[2]

There's a man who can 'use' it! This is all very badly put – But do you agree?

Having got so far I am so seized with the wonder of the english tongue – of english poetry – and I am so overcome by the idea that you are a poet and that we are going to live for poetry – for writing – that my heart has begun dancing away as if it never will stop – & I can see our cottage and our garden & you leaning against the door & me walking up the path and now you say – all those seeds we planted are *well up*. Come and see! And we go and see – Oh – Id die if this wasnt all before us. But it *is*. (We must have a garden table under a tree with a bench round it).

Now Ill stop for today.

Darling, darling Heart – it is really on its way you know – I can *smell* the land even if we cant see it yet.

And how I love you! Ah – youll never know –

Wig.

MS ATL. *LKM* I. 137–8; *LJMM*, 187–9.

---

[1] *The Winter's Tale* again, V. iii. 132–5.
[2] From Murry's own recent poem, 'To My Dead Friends', the *Nation*, 19 January 1918.

To J. M. Murry, [28 February 1918]

[Hôtel Beau Rivage, Bandol]
Thursday.

(Ill pay back these wires because its not fair but they do make such a galumptious moment!)

My darling Heart

Its three oclock; Ive just finished this new story *Bliss* and am sending it to you. But though my God! I *have* enjoyed writing it I am an absolute rag for the rest of the day and you must forgive no letter at all. I will write at length tomorrow. Oh, tell me what you think of our new story *(thats quite sincere.) Please try and like it and I am now free to start another. One extraordinary thing has happened to me since I came over here! Once I start them they haunt me, pursue me and plague me until they are finished and as good as I can do.

You will again 'recognise' some of the people. *Eddie* of course is a fish out of the Garsington pond (which gives me joy) and Harry is touched with W. L. G. Miss Fulton is 'my own invention' – oh you'll see for yourself.[1]

No letter today. Thats because of England's Sunday post. Ill get one tomorrow.

I walked to a little valley yesterday that I longed to show you. I sat on a warm stone there: all the almond flowers are gone but the trees are in new leaf and they were full of loving mating birds – quarrelling, you know about whether to turn the stair carpet under or to cut it off straight. And the trees were playing ball with a little breeze, tossing it to each other –

I sat a long time on my stone, then scratched your initials with a pin and came away – *loving* you. I am really spankingly well again and have absolutely NO NEED of any money. So dont you talk about it, but keep it tied up tight but use it for your darling eye. You can feel how I am wheeling this old letter along in a creaking barrow. My head is *gone*. Ill send a long one (letter not head).
I love you beyond all measure and for ever and ever I am your own girl.

Wig.

MS ATL. *LKM* I. 138–9; *LJMM*, 189.

---

[1] Characters in her story 'Bliss'. The novelist W. L. George had introduced Murry to KM in December 1911.

To J. M. Murry, 1 March [1918]

[Hôtel Beau Rivage, Bandol]
MARCH 1st

(I am delighted with the books & papers thank you my own).
My darling Heart my dear Jack Murry

Your Saturday, Sunday and Monday letters all came together today and I *feel* that you are ill and you have said not a word about your eye. Yes, of course you must write to me when the world hangs like a large cloud over your head. I can bear it; I do the same (And yet I feel that if I were true to myself Id have it from you but I oughtnt to come to you on my own account.) Still as you know, I do.

My faith, my hope my star is that this is our last month apart – that on April 1st I shall be on a strong wing back to you & well just catch each other in each others arms – and all will be well – with Rib playing on the flute a composition of his own called *Welcome-Home-No-More-Away*. Now I am going to be jet frank about myself for a minute.

I am simply 1000 times better and stronger – can *walk eat sleep* am not so thin – guaranteed to twinkle all over at the sight of a Bogey. Simply *bursting with love*. You will be so beautifully taken care of next month. Not fussed over – don't be frightened – but there will be always little surprises happening – and oh God, I write like a child – I feel like a child. We are the only pair who are walking hand in hand. But that is not quite true for I met another yesterday trundling along, not saying anything, neither much bigger than Ribni and he (who had been sent to buy bread) was having a small nibble off a loaf nearly as big as him on the way. (At the back of my mind I am worried about your eye – *Please* tell me *exactly* about it.)

Yes, dearest love, nearly all the world is vile and we are the wrong size for it. But why do you say you were hanging saucepans for the Heron 2 weeks ago? As though the Heron was not any more?[1] *That* gave me such a shock that I am going to wire you today just to say it is.

I am so glad that Arthur sees you. Hes a very good lad & hes going to be a great deal in our lives. Wont he be nice to our children?

Oh Jag Bog my precious own – clip me tight. I must hug you – warm you – put my hands on your breast – see you look down and smile at me and call me a worm. It is so sweet to be called a worm –

I feel very strongly that Mother has come bang over to our side and loves us. She keeps saying to me *your Jack*. Her heart was very warm when she wrote – didn't you think – and when she said her second to you wouldn't be so cramped for conversation – as though there you were in that little book of hers where she makes notes –
Must write to children
Must write poor old Lizzie Fleg
Must write K's Jack.
She always has small notebooks like that and a very professional absurd way of crossing out the used ones – you know – by ✓ and ⌇⌇⌇ and \\\\\ which all have different meanings.

Look here – if I love you any more the top bit of my hair will blow off with a pop like a champagne cork. Ill be home in 4 weeks – 4 weeks – only four more Fridays! And then the fun we'll have. Say to Rib please from me:– *Rib what larks*! and see him blow out his sleeve & bang it with the other hand as though it were a paper bag!

·Kiss your darling little Mother for me. Im going to start a new story today[2] – If you knew all the poems I have learnt to recite to you in bed – when we wake early!

Its a calm calm day – I am going out. Do you know I believe my last attack was coming on ever since I came here & now its over its sort of *cleared the air*. Here is a gilly flower for you – There are the goats passing: I hear the bells and that lovely fluty whistle.

Oh, tell me about yourself *always always* and about your eye – and if you feel strong or weak (it sounds, love like coffee.)

And until I see you *God* keep you. He must. He must keep us for each other for we really are lovely in our way and look at the fair place we are going to make –
All all – every bit of my heart is yours for ever

Wig.

MS ATL. *LJMM*, 190–1.

---

[1] Murry had written on 25 Feb, 'I've been writing my article (which now seems to have become regular weekly) for the *Nation*. Three weeks ago, when I felt I was hammering out bricks and saucepans for the Heron, it went all right, with a kind of zest even. Three more guineas, good. But now, my Wig, my heart's too frightened to breathe. The sky is on top of my head.' (Murry, 129–30.)

[2] It is not possible to say what story KM had in mind here, or in the later reference to her 'new story' on 7 Mar. No other work was completed in Bandol after 'Bliss'.

To J. M. Murry, [1 March 1918]

[Bandol]

MARCH FIRST HAY FOR HERON HOME APRIL DARLING BOWDEN

Telegram ATL. *LJMM*, 191.

To J. M. Murry, [2 March 1918]

[Hôtel Beau Rivage, Bandol]
Saturday.

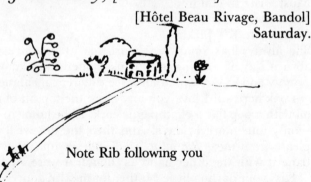

Note Rib following you

My dearest Life ⟋
I sent that wire yesterday but when the Mayor asked me to translate '*hay for heron*' I was rather up a tree! So I said 'tout va très

très bien' that was true – wasn't it but if the wire *is* stopped what a roundabout I and the censor would sit in before I explained!

It is so Bitterly Cold today that no amount of clothes food or fire can stop spider webs of ice flying all over ones skin. Juliette says I am like a little cat & I feel like one because I am always by my own fire or as I go along the corridor purring round any stove that is lighted there. And there was pas de poste aujourd'hui. (What I want is my wire to arrive on Saturday pour vous chauffer un peu le dimanche mon amour cheri.) I didn't really expect any letters. Look here! Did you know you sent me *2* copies of Master Humphreys Clock? It was in the back of Edwin Drood as well as in the separate volume. I thought Id just tell you. What an old wind bag G. K. C.[1] is: his 'preface' to the Everyman book is simply disgraceful.

I must talk a bit about the Heron. We must find a place where it is warm and at the same time *bracing* – i.e. abrité and yet rather high. But to be absolutely frank I am beginning to change my mind about this place for the winter. I wont come here again. If it is calm its perfect but there is *nearly always* un peu de vent & that vent is like an iced knife. One would be much snugger in a thoroughly snug cottage with doors & windows that fit – a good fire – etc. *And* I don't want ever *to have two homes*. No-one can. If we have the money & the desire we shall always be able to cut off together for a bit irgendwohin, but one home with all the books – all the flowers is enough and cant be beat. Also we cant afford another arrangement I dont think.

If I talk about my own physical health – well I know I ought to be in the air a lot – Well, if we have a garden thats what I call being decently in the air to plant things & dig up things – not to hang pegged on a clothesline & being blown out like a forlorn pantalon. Also I want to range about with you BUT ALWAYS with our cottage to come back to & its thread of smoke to see from far away – *Thats* life thats the warm south – wherever it is.

My God! how we shall talk when I get back. Planning all this and saying "yes I think so, too!"

I don't think I *can* wait much longer for a garden – for fruit trees and for vegetables – The thought of knocking the lumps of earth off a freshly pulled carrot fills me with *emotion*. Je suis tout émue – as these crawly froggies say at the idea – And then – plums with the bloom on them – in a basket – and you & I making jam – & your Mother coming to stay with us – and – and – everything – with you – like the cupid on top of the wedding cake – giving the whole thing its meaning. (How is my precious darlings eye?) Please when saying youve got this letter say your *Heron* letter & Ill know.

L. M. has made me perfectly *sick* today. Shes skittish "dearie Im very proud – I remembered the word for candle – *bougie*. Thats right isn't it? Im not really very stupid you know. Its only when I am with you because you are so many million miles ahead of all the rest of mankind" – and so on – I *squirm* – try & hold my tongue – & then *bang* and again I shoot her dead – & up she comes again –

Ive begun my new story. Its nice.

Du reste – je t'adore – and Im eagerly looking – staring towards the land – towards you. You must picture your girl all wrapped up, always rushing up on deck to see if that is a cloud or a piece of coast or a gray feltie in the distance. For that is all she does till April first.

Your Wig.

MS ATL. *LKM* I. 139–41; *LJMM*, 191–3.

---

¹ G. K. Chesterton wrote an Introduction to Charles Dickens' *Edwin Drood* (1870) for the Everyman edition of 1915. *Master Humphrey's Clock* (1840) was in the same volume.

To J. M. Murry, [3 March 1918]

[Hôtel Beau Rivage, Bandol]

Sunday morning. (*3* more Sundays only.)

My precious darling

Another jour glacé – so cold, indeed that the country might be under deep deep snow. Its very quiet and through the white curtains the sea shows white as milk. I am still in my bye for I have just had mon petit déjeuner. It *was* good. I made it boiling in my tommy cooker. I really think that Maman must have gone to see a fire-eater or been frightened by one before I was born – why else should I always demand of my boissons that they be in a 'perfeck bladge' before I drink em . . . And now I am waiting for the courier. Alas! the same light quick steps wont carry it to me any more – for Juliette is gone. She came into my room last evening, in an ugly stiff black dress without an apron. I noticed she had her boots on and that she was very thickly powdered.

She leaned against a chair looking at the floor & then suddenly she said, with a fling of her arm: 'Alors je pars – pour toujours . . . J'ai reçu des mauvaises nouvelles – une dépêche – mère gravement malade viens de suite. Alors! et ben – voila i'y rien à faire' – & then suddenly she took a deep sobbing breath: 'J'ai bien de la peine!' I was so sorry that I wanted to put my arms round her. I could only hold her warm soft hand and say 'ah ma fille je regrette, je regrette de tout coeur.' She lives on the coast of Corsica. The idea of the journey of course *terrifies* her and then she was so happy – 'si bien-bien-bien-ici!' And the beau temps is just coming and she did not know how she could pack her things – for she came here 'avec toutes mes affaires enveloppées d'un grand mouchoir de maman', but she'd never saved and always spent 'il me faut acheter un grand *panier serieux* pour les emballer' – Of course she thinks she'll never come back here again – she's in the desperate state of mind that one would expect of her – and she wept when we said 'goodbye' – 'Qui vous donnerait les fleurs main-ten-ant, Madame – vous qui les aimez tant – c'était mon grand plaisir – mon grand plaisir!' I saw her in the hall before she left wearing a hideous hat and clasping her umbrella and panier serieux as though they had cried *To The Boats* already. I must not write any more about her, darling Heart, for after all she cant mean much to you. She *has* meant an enormous lot to me. I have really loved her – and her songs, her ways – her kneeling in front of the fire and gronding the bois vert – her rushes into the room with the big bouquets and her way of greeting one in the morning as though she loved the day and also the fact that she distinguished your letters from others. 'Ce n'est pas *la* lettre – malheur!' Goodbye Juliette, my charming double stock in flower. Ill never forget you. You were a real being. You had *des racines*.

(L. M. is s̈eaweed if Juliette is double stock.)

This morning it was Madeleine the laundrymaid, Juliettes friend, promoted, who brought mon déjeuner. Très *fière*, in consequence. With her fringe combed down into her big eyes – a dark red blouse and a scalloped apron – I could write about these 2 girls for ever I feel today – Yes, Ill write just a bit of a story about them – & spare you any more –

You remember writing me in your criticism of *je ne sais pas* that Dick Harmon seemed to have roots. It struck me then & the sound of it has gone on echoing in me.[1] It is really the one thing I ask of people and absolutely the one thing I cannot do without. I feel so immensely conscious of my own roots. You could pull and pull & pull at me – Ill not come out – You could cut off my flowers – others will grow – Now I feel that equally (it goes without saying my darling) of you – and *Johnny* has roots – Sullivan (I think) – Arthur, I am sure – Ottoline never – L. M. never. In fact I could divide up the people with or without them in a jiffy – and although one may be sometimes deceived – (sometimes they are so clever – the bad ones – they plant themselves and look so fair that those two little children we know so well stand hand in hand admiring and giving them drops of water out of the tin watering can –) they fade at the going down of the sun and the two little children are perfectly disgusted with them for being such cheats & they *hurl* them over the garden wall before going back to their house for the night.

Well well! The heap of dead ones that we have thrown over – but ah the ones that remain. All the English poets. I see Wordsworth, par exemple – so *honest* and *living* & *pure*.

(Heres the courier.)

Good God – Bogey – your Tuesday letter – and I read 'Wordsworth – so honest and so pure.'[2] And remember my letter yesterday about our little house and here is yours in answer – just the same – We *are one*. Well I suppose I ought to accept this – but oh, the sweet sweet shock that goes through my heart each time it happens!

Yes, you are quite right, my precious shipmate. I *do* laugh at your preparations for this voyage of ours – I laugh so quietly that not even a harebell could hear – I laugh with every drop of my blood – and two tears laugh on my eyelids. You see – I am doing *just the same*. How many times have I lighted the lamp, wrapped up in my shawlet – sat down on the floor at your knees & said Boge – you read first – How many times has Cinnamon & Angelica been published by us – have we leaned over each others shoulders looking at it – have you said in a rough soft voice 'it looks pretty good'. Now Ribni has begun walking all over the cushions with a walking stick & a broad hat on pretending he is fetching in our cow – What an *imp he* is.

Why Ive just remembered I did a drawing of our house yesterday.

Oh – our divine future – The mists of morning are still upon it but underneath it sparkles – ready – waiting just for the sunrise – and then we shall catch hold and *run* & run into its garden & I will put the key in the door & you will turn it but being small ones we'll walk in together –

I must get up darling Heart and make myself a pretty girl for Sunday. I feel *simply immensely well today*, skipping and hopping never never stopping[3] – dont cough at all – dont know how to – madly hungry and my hair in the most lovely little curls of bacon out of sheer crispness.

And its March 3rd and the next month Mrs J. Middleton Murry will arrive – which *ought* to excite you –

How is your EYE?

You know you feel how I love you – How I am this moment as you read running into your arms & having a small lift up while I *hug* my darling Bogey until he cant breathe – Yes, underneath of course I am serious – but oh God! what a joyful thing it is to have a true love! I have given myself to you for keeps for ever.

Wig.

MS ATL. *LKM* I. 149–51; *LJMM*, 193–6.

[1] Murry's letter of 8 Feb, speaking of Raoul Duquette in *Je ne parle pas français*, observed that 'he's conscious of having no roots. He sees a person like Dick who has roots and he realises the difference. But what it is he hasn't got, he doesn't know.' (Murry, 115.)

² Murry had written on 28 Feb that he had been reading Wordsworth's *The Excursion*: 'It's all so honest, so desperately honest; and so *pure*.' (ATL.)
³ Words from 'Moonstruck', a song in the musical *Our Miss Gibbs* by Ivan Caryll and Lionel Monkton, 1909.

To J. M. Murry, 4 March [1918]

[Hôtel Beau Rivage, Bandol]
Monday March 4th

My own precious darling Bogey

I am writing to you – as yesterday – after my early breakfast & still tucked up – Immensely tucked today, just a fringe and 2 fingers showing because outside it is all white with SNOW. And icy cold within. These houses are not made for such rude times. There seem to be a thousand knifelike airs that draw upon each other and do battle even unto th'extremities of the floor.

Jag: Wiggie you are very silly.

Wig: My breakfast crumbs have gone to my brain. But it is very silly of the *Lion* to come in like this. I expected him to be a rough rude tumbling monster but not with a mane of icicles!

Bang at the door. Une dépêche Madame. Cinq sous for the Aged. I open it. Hurras for April Bonie Murry! What *is* that word? It may be Boge – it may be Love: it is a very funny one. And, my dear darling, how can this have arrived so soon? I only sent yours late on Friday afternoon.

God! God! How I love telegrams!

And now I see you handing it across the counter and counting out the pennies. But the telegraph form, feeling awfully gay, flies off while the girl hands you the change and begins to buzz and flap round the gas jet & against the window pane – UNTIL, finally you have to make a butterfly net out of a postman's bag on the end of your umbrellachik and climb onto the counter and on to that iron rail (a Lovely Fair holding your grey wooly ankles the while) and do the most awful terrifying balancing feats before you snare it. Then out you go, quite exhausted saying: ' I shant have time for any lunch now!' But at that moment Wig appears riding on a cloud with a little heavenly hotpot tied up in a celestial handkerchief . . . No, Bogey I must put this letter away to cool until the postman has been – –

Later but no calmer – a Wednesday and a Thursday letter came. Quick March is the best joke of the year, I think.¹ I shall never never forget it. Now about the Food cards. I am so glad you have got bacon because it means fat. I had already decided to try & persuade you to let us feed at home le soir while the war is on. Ill go out with a bastick and buy things and make scrumbuncktious little dinners for us. It will be 100 times as cheap and awfully good for I have gleaned many hints here – and essen *muss* der Mensch & I should always be black with fury if I gave up a cowpong and did not get what I thought *a fair cooked return*. The sugar of course I will save too for jam. Saxin just as good in coffee – That kitchen is so 'to hand' that we must make use of it while the war is on and save save save. See, Ill be mobilised too. I wont do it after the war but I will while the war is on. And Mrs H.[2] would be no good. We'd hate her ways you know because we are such a chic little couple and so dainty.

Were I to live long with L. M. I should eat *nothing*. While she was at the factory I could in a way understand but here she eats *all day* and has even gone so far as (in fact always does) two huge plates of soup as a kickoff for dinner. God I must not talk of her.

I am very shocked that such a pirate as you profess to be should not have seen my skull & crossbones! Ill bring you the dates & figs and butter if I can & pine cones.

(But these 2 letters of yours written with the most lovely pale blue ink are so sweet that I cant stop hovering over them. I read & reread them!) Oh, Ive got that coat collar changed. You know it *was* big & now its little & furry up to the chin. Great improvement. But I shant have the money surprise for you after all for the chemist + the Doctor have snapped it up. It was money Pa sent me for Xmas. Still, there it is & its good I had it to pay these ponces with. Ill have to leave here on the 26th I think for L.M. and I cant manage otherwise – However there is time enough to talk of that. Of course I told you not to tell people about the marriage & of course a light lager sent you popping off[3] – Its no matter: I like you for it. But what ye Gods – dont I like him for – love him – adore him.

Wig

MS ATL. *LKM* I. 141–2: *LJMM*, 196–7

[1] Murry wrote on 27 Feb, 'It seems but a little while ago when you were saying in your letter Soon "little February" will be here. And now little February has his hand on the latch saying goodbye. And then there'll be "Quick March".' (ATL.)

[2] Mrs Hardwick, Murry's landlady at 47 Redcliffe Road.

[3] Murry's note (*LJMM*, 197) explained 'I had told Sullivan of our impending marriage'. His letter of 28 Feb however admitted to his telling not Sullivan but E. H. W. Meyerstein, a friend since their membership of the intercollegiate Milton Society at Oxford (ATL).

To J. M. Murry, [4 March 1918]

[Bandol]

Mon loup chéri [Ribni]

Ta maman revient dans un petit petit moment. Soi sage. Baise ton père.

Ta petite Maman.

MS (postcard) ATL.

To J. M. Murry, [4 and 5 March 1918]

[Hôtel Beau Rivage, Bandol]
Monday Night.

Love, it is very late – the winds are howling the rain is pouring down, I have just read Wordsworths Poem to Duty *and* a description in a N. Z. letter of how to grow that neglected vegetable the kohl-rabi. I never heard a wilder fiercer night, but it cant quench my desire – my burning desire to grow this angenehme vegetable, with its fringe of outside leathery leaves and its heart which is shaped and formed and of the same size as the *heart* of a *turnip*. It is of a reddish purple colour & will grow where there have been carrots or peas. Of course I can see *our* kohl rabi – the most extraordinary looking thing & Wig & Jag staring at it.

Do you think it ought to look like that?

No. Do you?

No. I think its done it on purpose.

Shall I show it to somebody and ask?

No, theyll laugh.

And as they turn away the kohl rabi wags and flaps its outside leathery leaves at them . . .

Tuesday.

Thunderstorms all night & today torrents of rain and wind and iciness. It is impossible to keep warm – with fires, woolies, food or anything and one is a succession of shivers. The DRAUGHTS are really infernal. How I despise them for not being able to fit a window! or a door! And how my passion for *solidity* and *honesty* in all things grows. I feel the time has come when you and I have put everything to the test. *We* are alright: we are dead honest. Our house must be honest and solid like our work – everything we buy must be the same – everything we wear even – I cant stand anything false. Everything must ring like elizabethan english and like those gentlemen I always seem to be mentioning '*the Poets*'. There is a light upon them especially upon the elizabethans and our 'special' set – Keats, W.W., Coleridge

Shelley de Quincey, and Co. which I feel is the bright shining star which must hang in the sky above the Heron as we drive home – Those are the people with whom I want to live – those are the men I feel are our brothers & the queer thing is that I feel there is a great golden loop linking them to Shakespeare's time and that our Heron life will be a sort of Elizabethan existence as well. If you knew what a queer feeling I have about all this as I write – Is it just because I am so steeped in Shakespeare? I cant think of jam making even without:

> 'And if you come hether
> When Damsines I gether
> I will part them all you among'.[1]

And you know, if ever I read anything about *our* men you should see how arrogant I feel – and how inclined to say 'child child' – I positively feel that nobody has the right to mention them except you and me! And dreadfully inclined to say to the poor creature who makes a mild observation about *my* S[amuel] T[aylor] C[oleridge] "You really must not expect to understand!" Yes, Bogey, I am a funny woman – and a year or two at the Heron will make me a great deal funnier I expect. *Arthur* is very real to me, by the way and a part of our life. He is going to 'fit' isn't he? I want us to have him and to give him a rich true life right from the start with no false alarms.

Pas de courier – only a D[aily] N[ews]. Its lunchtime – I must get up. Tomorrow, D. V. Ill get your first of March letter. I hope nothing will happen to this letter while L. M. takes it to the post – that she wont in a fit of absentmindedness eat it. Thats a dash about the courier. I wanted to warm my hands and lips and heart at one of your adored letters. Oh, as well as every other sweet name that ever blossomed on the tree of love – my *friend.* I do long to see you again & talk BOOKS. For your worm is the greatest bookworm unturned. It grows on me – I always was a bit that way, but now – and with the Heron before us – Well – Do you feel the same? My Shakespeare is full [of] notes for my children to light on – likewise the Oxford Book. I feel they will like to find these remarks just as I would have.

Goodbye for now, dearest dear. I am writing you with a cold cold hand – all stiff.

I love you

Wig.

MS ATL. *LKM* I. 142–3; *LJMM*, 198–9.

---

[1] From Edmund Spenser's *Shepheards Calendar*, Fourth Eclogue, ll. 151–3.

To J. M. Murry, [6 March 1918]

[Hôtel Beau Rivage, Bandol]
Wednesday.

Dearest of All

I might have known that having written to you as I did yesterday
your next letter saying youve bought Ben Jonsons plays would arrive
today. That *you* should write about books & the Elizabethans & Keats
– that *you* should talk of the Heron as I did! You see we do seem to be
in some utterly mysterious fashion two manifestations of *the same being*.
We don't echo each other for our voices are raised at the same
moment. But it *is* damned queer that it should have reached such a
fine intensity – For Gods sake Buy Lamb. We'll love to have that
book[1] – My mouth waters at all those new treasures that I so soon will
fondle –

Oh Jag Jag – Geoffroi is here with her husband – and she is nearly
doing for me – I cant *think* or write – or escape. She *is* a dear and
generous and all that but a most APPALING bore and I havent the
physical strength for her. I feel as though all my blood goes dead pale
and with a slight grin. When she goes on Friday I shall spend
Saturday in bed *with the door locked*. I hate people: I loathe Geoffroi –
unlimited, tearing, worrying Geoffroi – saying the same things –
staring at me – If only I were bien portante I suppose I should not feel
like this at all – but as it is wave after wave of real sickness seems to
ebb through me & I dissolve with misery. She & my ghoul would have
me fixé if it lasted long. I cant say her nay. Nous sommes venus exprès
pour vous voir – & she brought me books & berlingots pour Monsieur
etc – – Its not the slightest use pretending I can stand people: I *cant*. I
hate L. M. so utterly and detest *her* so that shes torture enough but +
this grande femme, forte et belle – me parlant du midi – des poèmes
ravissantes d'*Albert Samain*[2] . . . et le Keats & M. who dogs me saying
what I ought to lick up pour me donner les belles joues roses. I said
faintly – clinging hold of a rosemary bush finally – and aching to cry
'La santé est une question de l'esprit tranquille chez moi, Monsieur et
pas de bouillon gras' – and the darling rosemary bush squeezed my
hand & left its fragrance there and said "I know, my dear!"

I am sorry dear love to make so loud a moan – but *you know – don't
you*. No escape till Friday. Alors en plein Enfer jusqu'à le vendredi
soir. Une lettre! Send me a letter & Ill wear it over my heart & try &
keep these big grown up mangeurs away – You should see L. M.
under their directions alimenting herself avec le potage. No, my gorge
rises –

Aid me ye powers. Oh, my poets. Make a ring round little me and
hide me. Oh I must find a daisy for an umbrella & sit under it but

then down would come L. M.'s shoe just for the pleasure of raising up cette plante si frêle si délicate – once again –

No, you must wear me next to your heart & never let anyone know Im there – Ill lie ever so lightly & only creep up & kiss you from time to time – Everybody is too big – too crude – too ugly – Goodbye darlingest heart. I dont want to seem depressed – but till Friday – till they go I wont be your gay Wig, only your adoring one.

She has asked me to send you these cards pour vous donner une impression quoique frêle etc. etc., in this treacle tongue. But the house is nice – isn't it?[3]

MS (with enclosures) ATL. *LKM* I. 143–4; *LJMM*, 199–201.

---

[1] Murry had written on 1 Mar that he intended buying two volumes of Charles Lamb's *Letters*.

[2] Albert Samain (1858–1900), French poet who helped found the *Mercure de France*.

[3] A photograph of the house of Jean-Henri Fabre, the Provençal writer and entomologist already mentioned.

To J. M. Murry, [7 March 1918]

 draw this when you answer this letter & Ill know which one it means; its a spring chicken.

[Hôtel Beau Rivage, Bandol]
Thursday. Quick March

My dear Love,

This is my little moment of quiet before I am thrown to the Three Bears again (Fancy *Southey* being the author of the Three Bears!)[1] I am in bed. Its ten oclock. The post hasn't come but at break of day the Aged brought me your telegram[2] – a particularly nice one & so with that smiling on my knee I feel almost as though I'd had a letter . . . Its a blue and white day, very fair and warm and calm. The sort of day that *fowls* enjoy – keeping up a soft far away cackle . . . you know the kind? Were I alone I should dive into my new story. Its so plain before me but I don't dare to. They'd see me: they'd look over the fence and call – No, darling new story, youll have to wait till Friday night –

Poor old Carpentrassienne [Mme Geoffroi]! If she knew how she offends me – how the sight of her binding up her baloon like bosom preparatory to la fête de la soupe makes me frisonne! If she mentions another book that shes going to make me eat when I go and stay with her I think I may – fly into bits! And this french language! Well, of course, she always did caricature it but in my clean, pink elizabethan ears it sounds the most absolute *drivel*! And poor old L. M.'s contributions. "en anglais mange les poudings c'est très bien."

Hours and hours and hours of it! Are you wondering where Wig has left her sense of humour? Oh darling, my sense of humour wont take his head from between his paws for it – wont wag his tail or twirk an ear.

It is a comfort that the bloody cold has gone again pour le moment. I hope it has in London, too. Here, today, it feels very quick March indeed – *we shall have to send our telegram all the same* you know. The man at Havre said: 'Of course if you have urgent family affairs which recall you to England before the time is up it can, doubtless, be arranged' – – I think he meant that I should do wisely to have *evidence*, like a telegram. So, unless you think the how is Mother telegram with its answer Mother worse operation necessary come soon possible, too extreme that will be the one we shall send. I think it is alright. Of course Ill be *most awfully frightened* till I am on English shore. And even then, dearest heart it will be no good for you to attempt to meet me because the trains are hours late – or perhaps nearly a day late & we'd both suffer *too* cruelly. You know what Id feel like thinking you were waiting and I couldn't get out and push the engine. No Ill have to (a) phone you at the office (b) go home by taxi if its not office hours – voilà!

My poetry book opened this morning upon 'The Wish' by old Father Abraham Cowley:[3]

> 'Ah, yet, ere I descend into the grave
> May I a small house and large garden have
> And a few friends, and many books, both true
> Both wise and both delightful too!
> . . . .
> Pride and ambition here
> Only in farfetched metaphors appear
> Here naught but winds can hurtful murmurs scatter
> And naught but Echo flatter.
>
> The gods, when they descended, hither
> From heaven did always choose their way:
> And therefore we may boldly say
> That 'tis the way, too, thither.'

5 P.M. Dearest darling. Two letters came – Saturday & Sunday heavenly ones full of rashers of bacon & fried eggs & casseroles. Oh I *love* what you write to me. I *long* to know if your & Johnnies eyes popped when you 'lifted the lid as the hedgehog did'[4] –

Ignorant Boy! Havent you ever heard 'Sing hay' for something – and then you have to sing 'ho' after –[5]

Sing hay! ⎫
Sing ho! ⎬ Isn't that familiar?

Well I sang *Hay* & waited for Boge to sing *ho?* But he stood with his hands behind his back & said 'I don't know what hay means'.

OFFAL is a filthy word: but I have read about it in the D. N. & it seems a useful idea – one can get kidney & *brains sweetbreads* liver – heart – all that without getting ones coupong snipped. (Can't you hear Gordon Campbell). Très utile. No, I don't think Ill write to that Food Depot[6] – Because it will be so vilely confusing when I change my name – again & Id have to register as Bowden etc. etc. *So* Ill bring 1 lb of butter to last me till Der Tag & Ill eat fish to your meat. You know I never eat bacon in the morning – Thats my best idea. Then we can start 2 square after the 18th.[7]

This gaiety is the result of absolute desperation. Ive such a headache that everything *pounds* even the flowers I look at – everything beats & drums. I feel all over absolutely *bled white* & it still goes on till tomorrow evening 8 p.m. Insufferable monsters!!! L. M. & she have just snapped up a whole half pound of biscuits (2 francs) bought by L. M. for me (I *said* a ¼!) "Oh I am so sorry Katie!!!" In consequence I never touched one & watched them dip the ½ lb in their tea. *Les sucreries de la guerre épouvantable.* My knees tremble — where my little belly was there is only a cave. If they were *not* going tomorrow I'd leave myself with a handbag. *Or* die & have L. M. plus the Gs at my pompes funèbres. 'C'était une femme telle-ment douce!!!' No, madness lies this way.[8] Ill stop, & try to get calm. Oh God! these monsters!!

On Saturday D.V. after a whole day alone I will be again at least a gasping Wig – not a Wig in utter despair.
DAMN PEOPLE!
STILL IN PRISON & being tortured by
P. G. ⎫
R. G. ⎬
L. M. ⎭

MS ATL. *LKM* I. 144–6; *LJMM*, 201–3.

---

[1] Robert Southey (1774–1843) did not invent the story, but gave it its popular form in the third volume of *The Doctor* (1837).

[2] On receiving her new story the day before, Murry had wired 'Your Bliss Mine. Boge Murry.' (ATL.)

[3] Abraham Cowley (1618–67), poet, essayist, scholar and Royalist during the Civil War. This, with the other poems KM quotes during this time, are from *The Oxford Book of English Verse*, ed. T. Quiller-Couch (1912).

[4] From a nursery rhyme KM was fond of quoting:

> Come button your boots with a Tiger's Tail
> And let down your golden hair

And live for a week on Bubble and Squeak
At the foot of the Winding Stair
And when you feel like a conger eel
Or as tough as an old split pea
Lift up the lid as the hedgehog did
And come and listen to me.

⁵ Murry had not fully understood her telegram on 1 Mar.

⁶ Murry explained on 2 Mar, 'Before you come back you must write a letter to the Food Office, Kensington Town Hall, telling them you want a food-card and a butter-card to be ready by the time of your arrival.' (ATL.)

⁷ The divorce case *Bowden v. Bowden* had been heard in London on 17 October 1917. KM presumed the decree *nisi* would become absolute six months later to the day, and she and Murry would marry immediately.

⁸ 'O, that way madness lies, let me shun that!' *King Lear*, III. iv. 21.

To J. M. Murry, [8 March 1918]

[Hôtel Beau Rivage, Bandol]
(Friday. My last day of Three in Hell and Hell in Three.)
My dearest dear

In bed. Breakfast over – the window open – the airs waving through & a great beam of sun shining on a double stock . . . . But Im blind till tomorrow: the Gs go by a train at 8 oclock tonight & tomorrow Ill be myself again. So Ill be really rid of two of my vampires at least & the third I can at least keep out of my room and not see except at meals. After these other two she seems a mild vulture, almost, but perhaps it is only that they subdue her & she has not had occasion to VENT the factory on me as she does otherwise. I feel horribly weak & frail and exhausted I must confess & if they stayed a day longer should take to my bed. But once the *great pressure* is gone I will perk up as you know, ever so quick again – But dont ever worry about not replying to the Geoffroi and don't feel under the least obligation towards her. Shes so blown that not even the ox could brake her belly – and shes a damned underbred female. All that she has done or wants to do for me is the purest fat conceit on her part – because I am english. You write pour le Times and we have been innocent enough to flatter her vanity – She said yesterday "Mais qu'est-ce que c'est, mon amie! Même quand vous n'êtes pas très bien portante, c'est seulement avec vous que j'ai le sens de la vie!" And I thought of L. M.'s "even if you are nervy Katie mine, it is only when I am with you I feel full of life", and H[er] L[adyship]'s "*so* strange – the divine sense of *inflation* that I have when I come near you." Oh Jag, if you are a little warrior in times of peace *do* keep me from harpies & ghouls!!!

I write those three remarks out of horror you understand because they do terrify me.

The lines of the poem I quoted alas! were not mine,[1] darling. They were writ by Thomas Randolph 1605–1635 and were part of an ode to Master Anthony Stafford to hasten him into the country.

> Come spur away,
> I have no patience for a longer stay
> But must go down
> And leave the chargeable noise of this great town;
> I will the country see . . .

And the verse ends with this line:

> *Tis time that we grow wise, when all the world grows mad.*

It is altogether, a most delightful poem: I wish I knew what else he had written. Theres another line charms me:

> *If I a poem leave, that poem is my son.*

I feel he is a man we both should have known – that he is, most decidedly, one of the *Heron Men*.

And did Sir Thomas Wyatt write a great many poems? He seems to me extraordinarily good! Do you know a poem of his: *Vixi Puellis Nuper Idoneus?*[2] My strike! Bogey, its a rare good 'un. (I don't know why I keep on saying '*poem*')

Oh, how I do thirst after the Heron and our life there. It must come quickly. We must indeed start LOOKING for it, spying it out, buying maps of England and so on and marking likely spots as soon as I get back. Sundays will be Heron days. You shall go slow, my very dear & sleep in the afternoons 'an you will – At any rate we'll lie in the sommier and smoke and plan our real real life – & that will – please God, rest my tired boy.

4.40 p.m. I have escaped for a moment after giving them tea as usual. (Oh here comes L.M.!!) Darling dearest no go. Free tomorrow. Here's R. G. as well. *Dead again.* Wants me to recite Keats Grecian Urn to her!!!? . . . en englais.

Well she goes tonight.

Your Wig

MS ATL. *LKM* I. 146–8; *LJMM*, 203–5.

---

[1] Murry asked if she had written the lines quoted in her letter on 26 Feb.

[2] Sir Thomas Wyatt (1503–42), lyric poet, translator, courtier. KM returns to this poem the following week, on 14–15 Mar (when see also n. 6).

To J. M. Murry, [9 March 1918]

[Hôtel Beau Rivage, Bandol]
Saturday.

Dearest Love

A cold wild day, almost dark with loud complaining winds – and no post. That's the devil! None yesterday, none today! I should at least have had your Monday. I am very disappointed . . .

However the Monsters have gone – A darling brown horse dragged them away at 8 oclock last night. For the last time I, shuddering, wrung M's little ½ lb. of swollen sausages – and Madame's voice rang out – 'J'ai eu entre mes mains *cinq mille* lettres de Mistral' & then they were gone & I crept up to my room, ordered a boiling coffee, locked the door & simply sat & smoked till midnight. Ill shut up about them now. I feel better *physically* already. Isn't it awful to mind things so?

Oh, why haven't I got a letter? I want one *now now* – this minute, not tomorrow!! And I believe its there and the post office just wont deliver it – to spite me. I believe that *quite seriously.*

'By the way' re President Wilson. M. Geoffroi says he is not at all liked in France. Why? . . . Its all very well for him to stand on a mountain and dire les belles choses. *He's* never suffered. He only came into this war because he saw that the allies were going to be beaten and realised that if they were Germany would attack America – with fleets & fleets of sousmarins puissants. America's entry & 'retard' were both on purely commercial grounds. Wilson held out to collect as much war profits as he could, came in, to avoid having those profits taken from him by Germany. *So the* men are L[loyd] G[eorge] and Clemenceau.¹ They *do* understand that you can never *traiter avec ces gens-là,* that we must go on – until – bien sûr, England & France bleed again – but equally bien sûr Germany is in the hands of whoever is left en Angleterre ou la France to do whatever they please with. Their pleasure, being of course, to make strings of sausages out of the whole country. 'Gôutez vous! Ce sont les Boches. Pas mauvais!'

Later.

I told you how vile the day was. Terrific wind & cold. I went down to lunch to find L. M. had asked the patronne for her dinner in a paper to eat it on the rocks as she explained to the patronne she preferred to do this so as not to be late and to keep me waiting!!! Its the sort of day when youd ask the fowls to come under cover to feed – & here's this fool done this & sits I suppose shivering on a rock eating dates – rather than RISK being late for lunch and 'upsetting' me . . . I could push her into the sea for this sort of idiocy. Now its raining – Not being made of stone I can't ignore the fact that she does these things – but nobody – not even you could not make me believe that she does them to torture me, to keep my attention engaged with her at all costs.

God! if you knew how sick to death I am of all this and how I long for home and peace. Ill not stick this much longer, Bogey dear & I shall very soon ask for news of Mother[2] – – – They will kill me between them all.

Tomorrow Ill have letters and Ill be a merry Wig again. Forgive this dull little toadstool.

(Found a word in Shakespeare I liked *WRITHLED* means wrinkled or furrowed – Hen. VI Act II Scene III.
'This weak and writhled shrimp!' And another word which interested me was *peise*. 'Lest leaden slumber peise me down tomorrow'.[3] French *'peser'* I suppose.)
Jag: But Wiggie I know all this. You are so dull today –
Wig: Yes I *am* Jag. Please forgive me, and love me for I do love you
Wig.

MS ATL. *LKM* I. 148–9; *LJMM*, 205–6.

---

[1] Georges Clemenceau (1841–1929), Premier of France 1906–9, and elected again to lead his country in 1917, took the same hard line as Lloyd George on 'total victory' over the Germans.
[2] That is, send their prearranged telegrams to justify KM's returning to England.
[3] *Richard III*, V. iii. 105.

To J. M. Murry, [11 March 1918]

[Hôtel Beau Rivage, Bandol]
Monday-in-love.

Bytwene Mershe and Averil
When spray beginneth to spring
The litel foul hath hire wyl
On hire lud to synge[1]

I can see her out of my window on a branch so fine that every time she sings it bends in delight. Oh, it is such a sweet sound. It is an early morning Heron bird and now you must wake up and leap and fly out of bed; there is a smell of coffee from downstairs and I run onto the landing and call: 'Mrs Buttercup will you please put the breakfast in the garden' and I come back to find you dressed already and a *staggering* beauty in corduroy trousers and a flannel shirt with a

Cremosin necktie![2] And then Arthur comes up from the field with a big bright celandine in his buttonhole and you say as we go down: 'My God! Theres a terrific lot to be done today' – but not as if you minded – While I pour out the coffee you cut up the bread and Arthur says: 'I say, Jack, couldn't you make a fine woodcut of the house from here with the sun on it like that.' And just at that moment Mrs Buttercup hangs a strip of carpet out of an upper window which gives it the finishing touch. We are going to drive over to a sale today in our funny little painted cart to see if we can buy some ducks and we have to call at the station on the way back for a parcel of paper . . .

Knock. C'est la blanchisseuse, Madame. Je suis très matinale. Il fait beau, n'est-ce pas?'

Well, its a good thing she did come. I might have gone on for ever, Bogey.

But dearest love was ever wine so potent as this Heron brew? A sip, and I am completely bowled over – 'Knocked out' as you say – and then, in addition, I think that in a fortnights time I shall be winging my way home and instead of writing to you – talking to you, looking at you – hearing you – holding you – well – then – my pen even begins to dance and says 'Lay me down and let me be until the post has come' –

My love, my own, your Wednesday letter is here. Ive just read it and if you remember what it was about youll understand that it has simply added fuel to the flame – It was all about the Heron – The most divine – Heaven kissing letter that any woman ever received. 'For what we *have* received (and are about to receive) may the Lord make us truly thankful' – as I used to say with my eyes shut when I was a tiny – Well, as you say, our life is built on it! It is the fortress and the hiding place of our love – the 'solid symbol' . . . Heavens! what would the world think if they looked through a little glass door into my head – and saw what sweete madnesse did afflict my brayne.[3] The miracle is of course that we are at the Heron already. We have found it – we are children of the Heron and no other home. Little exiles everywhere else – Funny you should have mentioned a cow. I was *worrying madly* over a nice name for a cow in bed last night. I wanted first to call it *Chaucer*: then I thought *Edmund Spenser* – and only after I had ranged up & down for a long time did I remember that a cow was *feminine*!! and would kick over the pail & give you a swish in the face & then stalk off if she were so insulted. Butter we must make with a stamp cut by ourselves. Oh, darling! I feel the whole world is homeless and 'makeless' except us – but wilfully so – How then can they ever understand?

Now I must get up. Kay has sent my money. All is well. *Keep* yourself – for me. Take care of yourself for 2 weeks more – and then – Wig and Bogey will fly into each others arms –

There is a certain little white pink striped with dark red called 'sops-in-wine'. *We must grow it*. I have also a feeling too deep for sound or foam for all kinds of *salads*.

[*no signature*]

MS ATL. *LKM* I. 151–2; *LJMM*, 207–8.

---

¹ The opening lines of 'Alison', an anonymous fourteenth-century poem in *The Oxford Book of English Verse* (ed. Quiller-Couch).
² Cremosin, an obsolete form of crimson, which KM took from her recent reading of Edmund Spenser – 'Upon her head a Cremosin coronet', *The Shepheards Calendar*, Fourth Eclogue, l. 59.
³ Another phrase taken from Spenser:

> . . . idle hopes, which still doe fly away,
> Like empty shaddowes, did afflict my brayne.
> *Prothalamion*, ll. 8–9

To J. M. Murry, 12 March [1918]

[Hôtel Beau Rivage, Bandol]
March 12th

My very dearest

L. M. has heard from Gwynne.¹ She is to come back as soon as possible; that being so and I, wishing to travel with her I wired you as arranged today. I shall not be able to tell *when* we start until I hear from Cooks as to what sort of chance we have of getting places in the Paris train – But of course Ill wire you as soon as anything definite occurs. I feel (as you may imagine) on the wing already – oh, ever so on the wing!! And so to the letters – as you say they are flying – Your Friday 8 and Thursday 7th letters came together this morning – And now – just having sent your telegram & been to the mairie with it & so on I feel very empty in the head and its hard to write. Ill calm down & be more fluent tomorrow but to have really despatched my pigeon! Pretty thrilling, Bogey! Dont let Rib answer. Hed say '*shes* all right' and do us in the eye – I hope Rib does post me a card. I rather see him tagging along the Redcliffe Road with a ladder to prop against the pillar box made of dead matches –

That sounded a vile raid² – So many houses were destroyed. But I do somehow feel that you will take care. You could not be so cruel as not to. I shall be *extremely* interested in your Rousseau.³ I feel you are pleased with your operation on him even though it had to be hurried –
– –

Oh – I *am* coming – yes – really coming, Bogey. There goes a train which isnt *the* train but is at all events one of the trains before – And I have ordered nougat (specialité d'Ollioules) for you & Arthur to be ready in quelques jours.

I had a Tragick letter from H[er] L[adyship] in reply to my *un*written ones. She sounds very 'sombre', and is ranging round to seek someone to devour. 'My passionate desire for *vivid life*. I have been up in London & saw Desmond [MacCarthy]'.(!) Sassoon has gone to the Holy Land[4] (With a hay down bough down.[5])

That reminds me of old Goodyear. Id like to see his fathers letter.[6] Send the sonnet. I wish you had time to write a sort of memoir, & see we get the book – wont you?

(By the way I am afraid the english colour *maroon* was a corruption of the french *marron*: Ive just thought of it.) However that is no reason why it should not be orange tawny – but english *maroon* – I had once a maroon sash I remember and it was not gay[7] –

Its such a vile day here – cold dark – the sea almost red – very sinister, with bursts of thunder. And dogs are barking in the wrong way & doors bang in the hotel & all that is pale looks too white – blanched – I must get the idiot to give me a handful of wet leaves or so to light my fire with. And then I must try not to pack & repack my trunk for the rest of the evening (in my head, I mean.) But you know the feeling. Think of it! No, I just cant. I wish the Channel wasn't between us: I am very frightened of being torpedoed. Id be sure to sink and oh, until I have been potted out and grown in a garden I don't want to be either drowned or otherwise finitoed. So wear something crossed over your heart – for a good omen. No, Boge I cant write today – my heart is wrapped up in that telegram. I feel almost serious, too – anxious, you know, and don't dare to *think* of my happiness if all does go well.

I am your own girl who loves you.

Wig.

MS ATL. *LKM* I. 153–4; *LJMM*, 208–9.

---

[1] The foreman at Ida Baker's factory, who required her back at work.

[2] On the night of 7 March two German planes reached metropolitan London, their bombs killing 17 persons, and injuring 46. It was the first air raid conducted when there was no moon, although the pilots were assisted by the aurora borealis.

[3] Murry was writing 'The Religion of Rousseau', a review of Pierre-Maurice Masson's *La Formation religieuse de Jean-Jacques Rousseau* for *The Times Literary Supplement*, 21 March 1918.

[4] Siegfried Sassoon, after his convalescence in Scotland, had returned to active service. On 6 Mar 1918 he wrote to Lady Ottoline from 'a huge base-camp on the Suez Canal', and said 'Some day soon I shall get on a train and go up to Jerusalem.' (Texas.) Lady Ottoline apparently knew already of his intentions, and passed them on to KM.

[5] From the refrain of the Warwickshire folk-song 'The Keeper', arranged by Cecil Sharp.

[6] Frederick Goodyear's father had written asking Murry if he had kept any of his son's letters suitable for a small private edition. See *CLKM* I, 250, n. 1.

[7] Murry wrote on 7 Mar: 'The rockets, called Maroons, have just gone for an air-raid. Now come the whistles. I think it's very exciting to call them maroons don't you? I wonder why. It's a

queer word, that. Marooning buccaneers on desert islands – and then there's some sort of colour called maroon. I don't know what it is, but I hope it's as beautiful as it sounds. It ought to be "your orange-tawny beard" that old Bill S. talks about somewhere.' (ATL.) The Shakespeare reference is to *A Midsummer Night's Dream*, I. ii. 96.

To J. M. Murry, [12 March 1918]

[Bandol]

HOW IS MOTHER[1] BOWDEN

Telegram ATL.

[1] The first of the agreed series of telegrams to persuade the authorities to permit KM's return.

To J. M. Murry, [13 March 1918]

[Hôtel Beau Rivage, Bandol]
Wednesday.

My dear Love

No post today. Well I am not surprised. It could not have gone on at that rate – I am writing to you, for the first time depuis mon arrivée in the garden in a summer house which is thatched with a pretty delicate thing rather like – not very like – a honeysuckle. L. M. sits by. As long as I am out of my room she always does. Elle est très forte très vaillante aujourd'hui & has nearly knocked me down. If I hadnt the telegram at the back of my mind I *should* be flat – *E.G.* "Of course I will come back to '47' with you in the taxi & unpack you even if Jack is there. You will be bound to want somebody to look after you *decently* after the journey." And if you saw her eyes rivetted on me while she says that 'decently' you'd know why I hate her. Thats a *bite* to her. She's drawn my furious blood & she knows it. Shes made me feel again *weak exhausted* with rage and so shes happy. I don't exaggerate. I grant I have an L. M. complex – but to hate anyone as I hate this *enemy* . . . of ours. Please darling love for my sake don't forget never to give her a loophole – And never never must she walk into the Heron –

There is such a sad widower here with four little boys – all in black, all the family in black – as though they were flies that had dropped into milk – There was a tiny girl too but she was not fished out soon again – and she died. They are so *silly* so *stupid*: thats what makes me sad to see them. Like a Dostoievsky 6th floor family to whom this has happened. The man cant quite make up his mind whether his little boys can walk or if they must be carried – so he does half and half – & sometimes during meals he feels one of them, & dashes up his eyes

rolling – dashes out of the salle à manger to get a coat or a black shawl
– – –

I read in my Daily Mail today that the double daffodils are in in
English gardens and red wallflowers. I have been to Gamels also
today and asked her to put in reserve for me 1 lb of butter – that
makes me feel presque là. The tulips are coming out here but I shant
dare to bring them because of the journey. Oh God! this pathetic
widower! One of the little boys has just begun to make a sort of weak,
sick bird piping and to jump up & down & he is *radiant*. He is sure
they are well already.

Dear & precious one – thats all for today. Tomorrow I shall hear
from Cooks I hope & then Ill feel more settled. You know I am
already 'on the wing', you know – and have been making up my
marvellous accounts – You know pages & pages where everything is
reduced & then turned back again – and the simplest sum seems to be
thousands.

Addio my darling love

Your
Wig.

MS ATL. *LKM* I. 154; *LJMM*, 209–10.

To J. M. Murry, [14 March 1918]

[Hôtel Beau Rivage, Bandol]
Thursday.

My Precious

I have just received your *Sunday* letter. It was very noble of you to
do as you did and so beautifully keep your promise about my story.
You're, of course, absolutely right about 'Wangle'.[1] He shall be
resprinkled mit leichtern Fingern, and Im with you about the
commas. What I *meant* (I hope it don't sound highfalutin) was,
Bertha, not being an artist, was yet artist manqué enough to realise
that those words and expressions were not & couldn't be hers – They
were, as it were *quoted* by her, borrowed with . . . an eyebrow . . . Yet
she'd none of her own . . . But this I agree is not permissible – I cant
grant all that in my dear reader. Its very exquisite of you to
understand so *nearly* –

You know (seriously) I don't feel as though I have really written
anything until you have passed your judgment – just as I should never
feel that I had had a child, even though it were there & screwing up its
fists at me until you had held it and said 'yes its a good kid.' Without
that I am just in a state of 'attente' – you understand.

I have, of course, kept all of your letters ever since my arrival here, knowing that they will be of use to us one day –

All that you write of the *Heron* and of our 'departure' is so true and clear to me that I can only look at you & smile & say 'yes Bogey'. You see – the Heron is the Miracle . . . I cant write about it today. Very soon we shall talk – for ever – and as we talk we shall become more and more at peace and wisdom from on High shall descend upon us –

I hope Lamb arrives in time[2] to go home with me as fellow traveller. (I will make a corner for him so that he shall come to no harm.) And I *dont want* the £5 dearest love. However, if you send it I shall just keep it. I heard from Cooks this morning. There is evidently great difficulty in getting places on the Marseilles–Paris rapide. But otherwise all seems more or less plain – I think I shall leave the middle of *next week.* Though I write that I don't feel it – Somehow a curious *numbness* is beginning in me about this journey – *or* a sort of feeling that it is all going to take place in the pitch dark – with no thought of place or time – Rib must be a little crusader & sit with his feet crossed 'for luck' all the while I cross the Channel. I am still terrified of that part of the journey[3] – I keep thinking myself into a little boat with a bundle or not a bundle on my lap and the cold sea water round us – & you & the Heron you & the Heron – all my solid earth and all my Heaven far away. But its silly of Wig. Its a gay sunny day and the tamarisk trees are *blowing* into leaf. Tomorrow I half expect an answer to my telegram – Did it surprise you awfully . . .

Goodbye shipmate
Wig.

MS ATL. Cited *BTW*, 472; *LJMM*, 211–12.

[1] Murry had written on 10 Mar to say that the name Eddie Wangle struck a false note in 'Bliss'; KM subsequently changed it to Eddie Warren. He queried as well her use of inverted commas in certain phrases of Bertha's (Murry, 135).

[2] The volumes Murry had posted. See n. 1 to following letter.

[3] Perhaps KM had in mind the sinking of the French State Railways steamer the *Sussex*, torpedoed near Dieppe on 25 March 1916 with the death of 50 civilian passengers.

To J. M. Murry, [14 and 15 March 1918]

[Hôtel Beau Rivage, Bandol]

This begins on Thursday – and continueth unto Fri-i-i-day –

   A

     A

      A

        MEN.

Dearest Love

I received your telegram this (Thursday) afternoon. I had also a letter from Cooks today saying that one must engage a place a week in advance for the *rapide*. So I am sending Ida to Marseilles tomorrow (Friday) to spy out the land and she will get the seats for as soon as possible. In the meantime I will wire you my delay. I must try *at all costs* to get across before Easter – that means however that I cant possibly leave here before the 20th at earliest, and it may be a day or two later. It will be as soon as I can. I shall have much more to go upon once L. M. has been to Cooks & if possible to the Consuls. Your telegram, of course, made me feel I must *rush* even tonight. I was amused because it had been *opened read* & translated by these people for it was still *wet* & they gathered in *force* to see me receive it, with their hands and eyes all ready to be lifted proper – You see your little Britain casting a moonlight beam upon it and saying, as she read: "Voulez vous me monter une thé simple à quatre heures, s'il vous plait!" They were very cool upon that – so was the tea – from a sort of 'ice to ice' principle, I suppose.

Saturday – no Friday. Charles [Lamb] came and a perfectly heavenly letter – which simply *bore* him on rosy wings to my bedside – Also the papers that bound him. I am going to make him a very thick coat with a velvet collar and ten buttons a side for the journey. For I cannot resist such a companion across France, Bogey dearest love. Your letter has made my coming *real again* – It keeps flashing in and out – now light, now dark, like a revolving lighthouse (not your letter – my coming.) Sometimes I do see – but sometimes theres naught but wavy dark. L.M. is gone, a great mistral is roaring. Its a *brutal* day & my room is only just done 4 p m and I spent the night hunting and halloing after a flea – I saw it once – a pox on it, sitting on the edge of my navel & looking into that organ through a telescope of its front legs as though it were an explorer on the crater of an extinct volcano. But when *I* hopped *it* hopped and beat me. Now it is still roaring in this room somewhere. It was a very wild savage specimen of a monster – the size of a large china tealeaf & tore mouthfuls out of me while I slept – I shall hang out a little sign tonight: *no butter no margarine no meat* – But Im not hopeful.

The Sunday Evening Telegram which was Lambs undervest, as it were, gave me a Great Shock. In this little time – & even with the P[aris] D[aily] M[ail] occasionally, I had almost forgotten that appalling abyss of vulgarity – which does exist – I had to ring for a bonne & have it took away. Did you read Lamb on Rousseau[1] Oh, oh, I *burn* to read your article.[2] Its going to be wonderful!! What idiot wrote that leader on Morris[3] I wonder – & there were *good bones*. And how shockingly ill the novels are reviewed.[4] The Stevenson 2nd thoughts was interesting[5] –

So you have got Thomas Wyatt. Well – I suppose that is quite natural. The poem I meant begins

> 'They flee from me who sometime did me seek
> With naked foot stalking within my chamber'

And what especially caught me was the second verse which I cant now read calmly.[6] Its marvellous I think. I could say why but I must take this to the post before the wind blows *too* loud and *too* cold –

And I am, dearest, on my way. Oh Bogey – just a moment before I shut this letter up & it is carried away from me. I love you – love you – love you – and you are all the secret of life for me.

Wig.

MS ATL. *LKM* I. 154–6; *LJMM*, 212–14.

[1] Charles Lamb (1775–1834), essayist and critic, wrote to Samuel Taylor Coleridge on 8 Nov 1796 of the pleasure he took in communications from his friend: 'I love them as I love the Confessions of Rousseau, and for the same reason; the same frankness, the same openness of heart, the same disclosure of all the most hidden and delicate affections of the mind.' The two volumes of Lamb's *Letters* which Murry sent KM would have been those edited by Alfred Ainger (1888, rev. ed. 1913).

[2] See 12 Mar 1918, n. 3.

[3] 'Waste or Creation?', ostensibly on William Morris, but also a patriotic call against waste in wartime, was the leading article in *The Times Literary Supplement*, 8 March 1918. Its author was A. Clutton-Brock, a prolific essayist on social and religious issues.

[4] As with all *The Times Literary Supplement* contributions the reviews of 'New Novels' were unsigned.

[5] 'R. L. Stevenson's Second Thoughts', an article on the manuscripts then for sale of sections I and II of *Virginibus Puerisque and Other Papers*, 1881.

[6] The second stanza, as KM read it in the *Oxford Book of English Verse*, under the title given the poem by the editor, Quiller-Couch, 'Vixi Puellis Nuper Idoneus . . . .' [Horace, *Odes* I, i.]:

> 'Thanked be fortune, it hath been otherwise
>   Twenty times better; but once especial –
> In thin array: after a pleasant guise, ·
>   When her loose gown did from her shoulders fall,
>   And she me caught in her arms long and small,
> And therewithal so sweetly did me kiss,
> And softly said, '*Dear heart, how like you this?*'

To J. M. Murry, [16 March 1918]

[Hôtel Beau Rivage, Bandol]
Saturday.

(No letter today).

Dear Love

I must tell you just how matters stand and you must help me please, if you can. L. M. saw the Consul at Marseilles yesterday. *She* can return without any trouble but my telegram re Mother will not do at all. It appears that everybody who came to the Riviera 'for fun' this year has been recalled by the same sort of thing and the french authorities will not allow it. It is absolutely insufficient. What I have to do is to *write* to the authorities at Bedford Square asking their permission to return before my time is up i.e. before the END of April. They, having looked into my reasons, communicate with the Consul at Marseilles and either grant me a permit or do not grant me one. The Consul at Marseilles says he has *no power over the matter at all*. So this you see will take a most confounded time and I have had to cancel my wire of yesterday by sending you another today – I am, as well, *extremely* anxious not to travel without L. M. as she'd be such a help to me on the journey.

My plans then are as follows: I shall endeavour to obtain from the english doctor here a chit to the effect that it is no longer advisable for me to remain on this coast and then, if I have to go to England it *is* necessary for me to have a companion. As L. M. is practically forced to return *now* that means Id have to be let through with her. This 'chit' he may or may not give me. I cant see him until tomorrow afternoon (such is the press of illness at Bandol) and then it depends very much in what mood the man is – He is so exceedingly shady and suspicious that he may have a lively fear of signing his name to anything; on the other hand he may do it just for that reason. If he *wont* Ill write to Bedford Square & state this same case and I thought I might also plead that I wish to remarry on the 7th of April & wish to return to make preparations. I cant *tell* whether that is wise or not. Id give anything for your advice on that point. Indeed I really think I will not mention this marriage until t'other has failed. If I can reinforce my plea with the chit I think there will be no difficulty, otherwise there will be . . . L. M. of course, will stay for the present and as long as anything is unsettled she will stay – Yes, I am now brought so low as to be thankful.

It is all very vile and unlooked for. This new 'strictness' has only been established during the last fortnight on account of all the false reasons people have given. I do not think I *could* wait here for another whole month – I mean – until May. The idea almost frightens me. I feel there is a plot to keep us apart – & then *our marriage – – –*

I suppose you can do nothing from your side – *influence* nobody – ask nobody? In case you can I give you the number of my passport 177256. You see dearest Bogey, I write in this *numb dumb* way, because at present I know nothing & the idea that the war can do *this* in addition to all it has done to us *strikes* me and lays me low for the moment. Ill get up again. Im only speaking 'spiritually' but at present, after I had packed & taken my tickets (*trans*ferable) I should cry if I wrote any more. I feel I cant *bear* this absence a great deal longer – & yet – – – they *will* torture me. If any change occurs I will wire you and do you wire me if you can think of anything I ought to do or anything that *can* be done. What about that friend of Pierre MacOrlan?[1] Any use?

I sit thinking & thinking. Curse this doctor – hes either the victim of a big bottle or a little 'un & not fit to be seen today – & hes the only person who can help – a little sot with poached eyes who bites his fingers.

No, we must comfort and sustain each other a *great deal*. Comfort me! Put your arms round me! Its raining here, too & the rain is all over my floor & its blowing & cold & I feel so *far* so *far* – and oh how my homesick heart *faints* for you & you only – Love me

Wig.

But harder to bear than anything is *your* disappointment. Thats what hurts – oh! like sin!

MS ATL. Cited *BTW*, 471; *LJMM*, 214–15.

---

[1] Pierre MacOrlan, pseudonym of Pierre Dumarchais (1883–1970), French author of humorous and exotic fiction, and an acquaintance of Murry's in Paris. As for his friend, Murry wrote back on 19 Mar, 'curse it – I have completely forgotten his name' (Murry, 140).

To J. M. Murry, [16 March 1918]

[Bandol]

NO SEATS RAPIDE BEFORE TWENTIETH EARLIEST LOVE

BOWDEN

Telegram ATL.

To J. M. Murry, [16 March 1918]

[Bandol]

STILL DIFFICULTY PASSPORT DATE RETURN UNCERTAIN KEEP WRITING
DON'T WORRY DARLING BOWDEN

Telegram ATL.

To J. M. Murry, [17 March 1918]

[Hôtel Beau Rivage, Bandol]
Black Sunday.

My Precious Love

Your wire this morning simply *smote* me in two[1] (½) of me was pain
for your watching at the window, you and our darling valiant cabin
boy, watching for the boat which isn't even *remotely* allowed to leave
the harbour yet by these *cursed* war officials. (½) of me was agony at the
thought of the letterless days I must endure before I write again. And
never never have I so wanted the support of letters! God, why didn't I
say that it might be a difficult process – that there was 'enfin' a *risk*.
But you knew there was, didn't you, my precious darling? And of
course you knew Id have taken *every possible precaution* that a letter of
yours should not be lost – but should be returned to me – I lay in bed
with that gay beflagged little telegram on my heart & felt *it could not be*.
Why, Bogey, must we have this new trial – & this new agony. Why is
it so dreadfully – difficult? And then there came the last letters I shall
get for a while, I suppose – and the one where you waited for my *wire*
from *Paris* & my telephone message?[2] Heart dearest! Its far away still
– Dont wait – dont wait so ardently. They wont let me out yet and
while I know you wait 'like that' my lamentable state in this prison is
like to kill me – I could *break through* & yet I cant . . . Just try & keep
calm and keep *confident* & know how I am fighting & then Ill get
strength from you. Otherwise I feel a sort of desperation and 'I cant
get out' startling feeling which wont help. I have delayed writing to
you today in the hope that the doctor would have been as he
promised. L. M. went to remind him this morning, but now its
5 oclock & there is no sign so I suppose he is 'hors de combat'. I paid
his bill a week or two ago (which he didn't acknowledge) and asked
him not to come again unless I sent for him & I am afraid he is faché.
I have not told you about him – & its not necessary to go into details
now but he's shady – and unreliable – to say the least. This being so, if
the storm has abated at all tomorrow I shall go to Marseilles
tomorrow & try & see a man there and get a chit from him. But you
understand this *all* takes time – *days* & *days* – even if I can bring it off.

So turn from the window & dont wait for me just yet. Only know that I am doing every single thing I can – and so is L. M. that every drop of blood I have is sick for home & that your letters – your adored – confident letters have made it seem almost impossible that I am *not* coming. Our telegram the consul at Marseilles merely laughed at. Its the telegram they *all* send when *they* wish to return. "It wont do – dear lady; its too old". You must apply through the London office – It may take 10 days for a reply – So, until I come – I shall be doing nothing – & thinking of nothing except of the ways and means. All we have to do is to try & keep calm & weather the storm & win through – Im strong enough if I feel your umbellalla is over me[3] – Oh, once I really *am* under it – never let me forth again –

I say nothing about Charles Lamb while *this is on*. But he has been an immense comfort – even though I read him in that mingled fever, dread, and dismayed impatience that one must feel in a tumbril, I should think. Now I must put my arms round you & kiss you & lean against you & do you kiss me. And then I must go again for a little. Its still a great wild storm here – rain & cold and wind – Tomorrow Ill have my try at Marseilles & wire you from there – These wires are not an extravagance – I feel you must have them. But do you try not to worry – & remember how hard I am trying to – to keep calm & not to allow myself to be overwhelmed –

Your small but fighting Wig

MS ATL. Cited *BTW*, 472; *LJMM*, 216–17.

[1] The wire Murry sent on 16 Mar read 'Not written since Wednesday waiting take care yourself darling hurrah watching at window. Rib Murry.' (ATL.)

[2] Murry wrote on 14 Mar 'I shall simply wait in anxiety till I have a wire from Paris . . . . I shan't have any quiet of soul until I hear your voice on the telephone.' (ATL.)

[3] Murry told KM on 12 Mar 'Come in under my wing – a rather bony one, but full of warmth and love. I'll be your bodyguard for ever.

> Come along Isabella
> Under my umbellella
> Don't be afraid
> There's a good maid
> Come along Isabella.'

(ATL.)

He noted (*LJMM*, 217) that this was 'a favourite rhyme of Katherine's'.

To J. M. Murry, [18 March 1918]

Marseilles Monday.
Café de Noailles

Dearest,

Everything seems changed – My whole life is *uprooted* and this calm of living in Bandol & even with the G[eoffroi]s and L. M. feels like *calm* compared to this violent battle. I arrived here, very late this evening, too late for the Consul or for Cooks: the train was 2 hours en retard. And so I got a room at the Hotel de Russie, had some food and here I am. I must bring you up to date with this Battle of the Wig. Last night after I wrote you I felt desperate & sent L. M. after Doctor Poached Eyes. Even though it really was rather late. He was at dinner – fatal time! but promised to turn up. Whereupon I set to – turned L. M. out of my room – dressed in my red frock & a black swanny round my neck, *made* up – drew chairs to the fire – & waited for this little toad. If you could have come in you would have been horribly shocked I think. I have not felt so cynical for years – I knew my man & I determined to get him by the only weapon I could – & that *he* could understand. He came, far more than 3 parts on – and I sat down & played the old game with him – listened – looked – smoked his cigarettes – and asked finally for a chit that would satisfy the consul. He gave me the chit but whether it will Ill not know till tomorrow. It could not be more urgent in its way – I dictated it & had to spell it <u>&</u> lean over him as he wrote <u>&</u> hear him say – what dirty hogs do say – I am sure he is here because he has killed some poor girl with a dirty buttonhook – He is a maniac on *venereal* diseases & *passion* – Ah, the filthy little brute! There I sat and smiled & let him talk. I was determined to get him for our purpose, any way that didn't involve letting him touch me. He could say what he liked: I laughed and spelled – and was so sweet and soft & so *obliged*. Even if this chit fails I think he can get me through in other ways – He has, for all this shadiness, a good deal of very useful influence in high quarters in Marseilles & Toulon – & its all at my disposal. So Ill use it.

Oh dear oh dear! I feel so strange. An old dead sad wretched self blows about – whirls about in my feverish brain – & I sit here in this cafe – drinking & looking at the mirrors & smoking and thinking how utterly corrupt life is – how hideous human beings are – how loathsome it was to catch this toad as I did – with *such* a weapon – I keep hearing him say, very thick 'any trouble is a pleasure for a lovely woman' & seeing my *soft smile* . . . I am very sick, Bogey.

Marseilles is so hot and loud – They scream the newspapers and all the shops seem full of caged birds – parrots & canaries – shrieking too – And old hags sell nuts & oranges – & I run up & down *on fire* –

Anything – anything to get home! – It all spins like a feverish dream. I am not *un*happy or happy. I am just as it were in the thick of a bombardment – writing you, here, from a *front* line trench. I do remember that the fruit trees on the way were all in flower & there were such big daisies in the grass & a little baby smiled at me in the train – But nothing matters until I have seen the Consul. I am staying tonight at the Hotel de Russie. It is clean and good. I have Elle & Lui to read[1] – But this is all a dream you see. I want to come home – to come home – Tomorrow Ill wire you after Ive seen the man. Under it –above it – through it I am yours – fighting & tired but yours for ever
                                                                                Wig.

MS ATL. *BTW*, 472–4; *LJMM*, 217–19.

---

[1] George Sand, *Elle et lui* (1859).

To J. M. Murry, 19 [March] 1918

CAFÉ DE FRANCE, | RUE CANNEBIÈRE, | 3 MARSEILLES
                                                    19ième. 1918.
                                                    Bulletin du Front:
I advanced to the consul and gained a local success, taking the trench as far as Paris. I expect to advance again under cover of *gas* on Saturday. The enemy is in great strength but the morale of the Wig is excellent. Please explain this to Ribni & make him salute.
Dearest of all
    Well as far as I know the 'wangle' has succeeded. At any rate I have leave to go as far as Paris & try my luck there – and I don't think – having got so far & pleading as I shall – they can withhold their consent to my going further – Especially as L. M. (lunatic attendant) has permission. The Consul here was *not* agreeable about the affair – but whether that was just a formality or not I don't know – I rather think it was. After having been there I went to the police – & had my passeport viséd again & then to Cooks to take the ticket. It is still a divine day, a sort of *anguishing* beauty of spring – wonder if you know what I mean. I mean something so definite – I have bought myself a bottil of genet fleuri (which I cant afford) so that I shall be a little perfumed bride (*if* I get back). I think I shall today. Oh, how much I could tell you. I have lived through lives & lives since I last wrote to you in calm – That night at the hotel – par exemple – but *that* I have written at four oclock this morning. Its pretty good I think – this city seems to me to be stranger & stranger. Does one always have fever here? And are these things here to be seen or are they all 'dreams' –

Birds on the trees – so big – so fat – flowers to sell, lovelier and more poisonous-looking than flowers could be, & the beggars – who are like the beggars of the 14 Century (Wig that is swank) and then the blacks & the women with white faces and pale pale gold hair & red dresses & little tiny feet – Women – who seem themselves to be a sort of *VICE*. L. M. has of course just been like an immense baby without a perambulator. I have carried her everywhere, paid for her, ordered for her, arranged for her bath – showed her the cabinet – & answered all the questions that my grandmother used to ask my father when *she* came from Picton to gay, wild, evil Wellington. I go back this evening, pack tomorrow & leave by the early Thursday train. In Paris on Friday – start for Havre Saturday (all being well) & I suppose at that rate England on Tuesday – or perhaps Monday. But that is still dark. At any rate the lighthouse throws a beam as far as Paris. Oh, my *lean* purse. Its *bones* – its *stringiness*. But all is well – I am so full of black coffee that if you see at the station a dark copper-coloured little Wig don't despise her – Now I must go back to the trenches & go over the top to the station – Goodbye – breathlessly with all my loving heart

Wig.

MS ATL. *LJMM*, 219–20.

To J. M. Murry, [20 March 1918]

[Hôtel Beau Rivage, Bandol]
Wednesday Night. Packed & sent to the station.
Darling Heart

Just in case I don't arrive as soon as I hope to Ill go on writing. Because I know what it feels like not to have letters (no earthly *vague* reproach intended). Much more because its a habit I can't break when I am away from you. Pray God its a habit I *shall* break very soon – I arrived back last night & your two wires were here – about the £5. As I had just been really wondering about money I was terribly glad. (All the same I shall have a bright penny for you, I hope.) I wired you then and ever since I seem to have been 'en voyage'. *Figs* I have for you & nougat du pays & chocolat for you & little brother & a big pine kernel and safran and carnations (these last a present). The nougat is the thrilling present. It is made at Ollioules of the very almond trees *here* & I feel that when you eat it your eyes will crinkle up. Shall I *really* give you this – really feel your arms round me – really be a child with my child playfellow? . . . Oh Jack – if I dare think my heart would break for joy. I have said goodbye to everybody like a good girl & they like me – in their way, I suppose – And all who knew you ask to be remembered to 'your jeune mari' – They always seem to think we were so very very young at the Villa Pauline – playing houses – going to bed under the table for a minute with the cloth pulled down for a blind – calling out 'morning' & getting up & eating each a most lovely fried marguerite daisy for breakfast – – –

I leave by that early train – If God loves us I shall be home on Sunday – and perhaps you will come to the station & wait for me with your casserole[1] in a hanky & sit on a bench there & eat it (the inside only) if the train is late – But no – it *blinds* me – I can't see so bright – not such heavenly brightness. And our Rib – our little tiny one – Will you tell him you are going off to bring me home? Oh Jack Jack Jack. My love, my darling Heart. I cant write – everything even in this room seems to move and breathe & have being because I love you and I am turned towards the only home I long for – God keep us for each other till Sunday   Amen

Wig.

MS ATL. *LJMM*, 220–1.

[1] Murry's letters frequently expatiated on his cooking.

To J. M. Murry, [20 March 1918]

[Bandol]

LEAVE MARSEILLES THURSDAY WILL WIRE PARIS IF SUCCESSFUL THERE HURRAH FIVER LOVE BOWDEN

Telegram ATL.

To J. M. Murry, [21 March 1918]

[Marseilles]

At the Cafe Noailles. Thursday. The train goes tonight at 7.5.
Darling Heart –

Tea, orange flower water, fever, a pain in my stomach, tablettes hypnotiques (ne pas dépasser huit tablettes dans les 24 heures) – sun, dust, a great coloured – a dreaming swaying baloon of baloons outside – yellow, red, orange, purple. (A little boy has just had one bought for him & he's terrified of it & he thinks it means to carry him away. Whats the good of being cross with him? But she *is* cross. She shakes him and drags him along.)

L. M. has lost all her luggage, but *all* & has had to buy it all over again with a rucksack to put it in. She can't think how it disappeared. 'Will you see about it at Cooks for me <u>&</u> write to the Hotel and explain?' Ive done that. But she is good otherwise – quieter now that she is en voyage – & she has bought oh such *good* figs . . .

I feel so bloody ill – such a bellyache & a backache and a headache – The tablettes hypnotiques cost 7.50. What do you think of that? But they are the same things that good old Dr Martin[1] gave Mother to give me when I was 13 and knew myself a woman for the first time. That being the case I bought them, just as Mother would have – and felt a *mysterious wellbeing* all through me as I swallowed one – I couldn't have gone off tonight if I hadn't bought 'em – I should have had to go to an hotel & lie there.

Cooks seemed to take a perfect joy in giving me the £5 & long *beams* of light came from my fingers as I took it and tucked it away. It is so *hot* so very *very hot*. One feels as though some fiend had seized one by the hair and peppered one all over with dust and sand. *Rotten sentence!*

I had an omelette for lunch 2 francs – and then thought some cauliflower – because it was only *20* and very harmless. So I had that & then some stewed fruit. God! The cauliflower was 2 francs instead! And you can buy whole ones at Bandol for 35 centimes. Can you see my face? And L. M. comforting me. '*Its not as if it is for every day but only for one day.*' Paris tomorrow & then the offensive at the Consuls. Shall I arrive before this letter & will Rib make fringe papers of it under my very eyes – what he will call les petits frissons. Or does it mean I am going to be torpedoed & thats why I keep on writing? Oh I *hope* not. I am very frightened of the journey in the sea because my wings are so sinkable – (Deux limonades – deux. That gives you the day.)

Oh darling, have you got my wire tonight & do you know I am on my way & are you holding thumbs? This place seems to me *infected*. I mean in the fire & brimstone way. It ought to be destroyed and all the people in it. It is a filthy place and the actor next to me who is holding out the promise of a part to a poor little woman *while* he eats her sweets & drinks her chocolat – on him I would let fall the biggest brimstone of all – Goodbye for now my own – God help us –

Yours yours for ever

Wig.

MS ATL. *LKM* I. 159–60; *LJMM*, 221–2.

---

[1] Albert Martin, an English physician and surgeon who was the Beauchamp family doctor during KM's childhood.

To J. M. Murry, [22 March 1918]

[Paris]

Dearest

They wont let me through until they have obtained permission from the office at 19 Bedford Square. That will take AT LEAST a week & having to stay in Paris a week it means I must notify the Commissaire of the Police of the quarter in which I intend to reside & he will give me permission to leave France in 8 to 10 days – not before – So I must really *count* on ten days here – What a *more* than B. curse. They were very decent at the office here but absolutely *immovable*. They would do nothing via Bedford Square except by letter & I am told to write as well & crave permission to return. Otherwise I must stay in France until May!! I am now going to Cooks to postpone all the remainder of my ticket. I am also going to wire you and to ask you to write to me at Cooks as I have not yet found a hotel. *Please John I don't need any money*. I will tell you if I do, but please dont send a farthing until I do ask. I have more than enough to last me here & get me over. And more would only be an awful curse.

The hotels we have known here are become deadly swindles. Cheapest room at Odessa without déjeuner 7.50. Cheapest room at de Loire 6 and *filthy*.[1] I have just been to the L'Univers[2] where they may have something tomorrow. L. M. will wait with me. I shall send her to Cooks every morning – for a telegram or a letter from you & I beg you to wire me here just to say *all is well*. I shall get a cheap room tomorrow & stay in it & work till I do get back. I have a great many formalities to arrange with the police – military permit office here etc. and at this moment my head is quite empty – after the journey and getting about – and the disappointment and fatigue of this looking for rooms. Also the fact that I have not heard from you for days is *dreadful dreadful*. I might be in China. I have made careful arrangements for all your Bandol letters – but God how I crave news! Please wire just a word, dearest. Oh God – it *is* a blow. Ten days more. This journey – it never never ends – I seem to have been trying to get back from that moment we stopped waving. Now I must dash off to Cooks. I will write again tonight – Bogey write soon & at length to your wandering child.

Wig.

MS ATL. Cited *BTW*, 474; *LJMM*, 222–3.

---

[1] The Odessa-Hôtel, 28 rue d'Odessa; Hôtel de la Loire, 57 boulevard du Montparnasse.
[2] The Hôtel de l'Univers at 9 rue Gay-Lussac was where KM and Murry first stayed in December 1913, during their brief attempt to survive as writers in Paris.

To J. M. Murry, [22 March 1918]

[Paris]

KEPT PARIS TEN DAYS ADDRESS COOKS DONT NEED MONEY FONDEST LOVE
BOWDEN

Telegram ATL.

To J. M. Murry, [22 March 1918]

My address. I will not change it. { *Select Hotel*
{ *Place de la Sorbonne*

[Paris]

Friday night

My precious darling,

At last I am *free* to write to you again, even with this horrible ten days delay between us. I mean – my spirit is free. You know, somehow, at the back of my mind I couldn't altogether believe that I *would* be home on Sunday. I saw you preparing, and yet I had to keep on writing you letters in case it didn't come off. Oh, I am so glad I did now, even though they were silly ones. They will keep you in touch and you will know what happens more or less while it is happening. It is not the worst that has happened. That would have been to be tied up in Bandol until May – I think, from the manner of the man at the Military Permit Office today, that there is no doubt the 19 Bedford Square people will grant me a permit – the only trouble is the time it takes and the horrible worry it entails here with the police. For Paris is guarded against strangers with hoops of steel – However all can be arranged. And having written and sent my doctor's chit to *no. 19* and gone to the Commissaire for permission to remain here and permission to depart as early as possible I must just see it through. This has been a *bad* day – looking for an hotel all day – with '*do* let us take a taxi Katie' and strange desires on L. M.'s part to go to Hotels at about £1000 a bed and £500 petit dejeuner. Finally, late this afternoon I was passing along the Boulevard St Michel & saw this – at the end – next door to the Sorbonne. It is very quiet – trees outside, you know, and an extremely pleasant chiming clock on the Sorbonne même. Also next door there is the best looking bookshop I have ever seen – the best set out – with exquisite printing on all the window cards and so on. The hotel seems just what is wanted. Six francs for my room with déjeuner – a big square room with 2 windows a writing table, waste paper basket – two armchairs, de l'eau courante, a low wooden bed with a head piece of two lions facing each other but separated for ever kept apart for eternity by a vase of *tender flowers*.

There is also a white clock with 3 towers. It stands at six. But this is a fine room to work in. Immediately I came in – I *felt* it and took it. The people are quiet and simple too and the maid is pretty. The two armchairs I have just observed are very like pug dogs, but that cant be helped. Very well until they let me come home I shall stay here and write. All the back of my mind is *numbed*. The fact that this *can* happen seems to me so dreadful & I feel we must never go apart again. Getting back is too difficult, Bogey, and oh so tiring and wearing. Now you & Rib are nearly in my arms. Now they tell me – no that is not the land you see. Those are clouds . . . Oh God. Better not think. And I *cant* write properly any more until I have heard from you. *One certain* thing is send NO money please. I have enough and more than enough. And oh dearest while I fight this through – take care of your darling self for me. It is very warm here – just as warm as Bandol & the chestnut trees are in leaf. It is like early May. If there are bad raids I will sit in the caves & try & hold a door over my head. Oh Bogey – I want a letter so much that my heart can hardly beat any longer without one. On Monday there ought to be a wire at Cooks for me. If you want to write me *here* I am sure it is quite safe. It would be a very lovely surprise to get a letter – I am just going to sit under my working umbrella now till I start off again. That is all & go on making notes about Charles Lamb & Georges Sand – & wandering in that shop next door to see if I can find a present for my love. Goodnight my soul – Oh Bogey – *do* hold me tight & *never* let me go again.

Wig.

My letters lately have been so hurried and written with such a feverish pen. I want to tell you how I love you – now – very gently. Kissing you, my soul – Oh, I long for you so: it is rather hard to bear these extra days. But Bogey – I love you so immensely tonight – – – –

MS ATL. *LKM* I. 160–1; *LJMM*, 223–5.

To J. M. Murry, [23 March 1918]

Select Hotel | 1 Place de la Sorbonne | Paris
Saturday.

Tel. 'Selecotel'

My precious darling

I am afraid I shall have to wait until Monday before I hear from you. Ive never been so long without news. It is simply horrible, but it can't be helped and I must just go on – trusting that they will finally let me through . . . I have written to Bedford Square, applied at the Police for permission to return & now there is nothing to do but wait. This place is in a queer frame of mind. I came out of the restaurant last night into plein noir. All the cafés shut – all the houses – couldn't understand it. Looked up & saw a very lovely aeroplane with blue lights – 'couleur d'espoir' said an old man pointing to it. And at the door of the hotel was met by the manager & made to descend to the caves. There had been an alerte. About 50 people came & there we stayed more than long enough. It was a cold place & I was tired. At eight this morning as I lay in bed – bang, whizz – off they went again. I washed & dressed & just had time to get downstairs before the cannons started. Well *that* alerte n'est pas encore fini. Its now *3.45*. Most of the shops are shut – all the post offices – the shops that are not quite have a hole in the shutters & you put your arms over your head & *dive* through – The *curse* is the post office as I have to register my letter to Bedford Square & now Ive lost a whole day. I have gone out, between the showers, to the police & fixed all *that* up, thank goodness – & now as soon as I can post this other – there will be rien de faire qu'attendre. C'est joliment assez!

I look out at the lovely hot day and think – I might have been at Havre by now! Does this letter tinkle far away? I feel it does. It ought not to but oh Bogey it is so very long since I have heard from you – & tu sais comme je suis un enfant gaté – *and* I hardly know where I am myself until I know that you know. I am not *found* until you have found me too & taken my hand & walked away with me – – If I had a letter. Yes, a letter. Thats what I *need so*. I am getting so very very impatient. Also I want to see a medicine man & ask if there is any divine reason why I have never seen Aunt Marthe *since that Sunday afternoon*[1] – I shant hope a bit till I have asked him. But I had to tell you: its on my mind, rather. This *waste* of life here – Why should the Lord treat us so: its not fair. Oh Bogey a letter a letter to revive a parched fainting little Wig.

MS ATL. *LKM* I. 161–2; *LJMM*, 225–6.

[1] 'Aunt Marthe' was KM's euphemism for menstruation. She is referring to the Sunday before she left for Bandol, back in January.

To J. M. Murry, [24 March 1918]

[Select Hôtel. 1 Place de la Sorbonne]
Paris. Mothers Birthday.
Sunday.

Bogey, my precious

What *is* the good of writing anything – except that I love you & I cant get through yet & I would be home by now if all had gone well &

here I am in this cruel town – waiting for the bonté of the Military! Theres nothing else to say – I want a letter or a telegram – *something* to break this silence. News of any kind from you. It is incredibly long since I have heard today – Has Rib forgotten me? Given me up? Oh Bogey I do my best but you know it is a most awful obstacle race – The only grain of comfort is that I am *here* & not là bas – for I *am* nearer – once they let me start it'll not take long. Please don't despair. Please keep on hoping for me: its awful, Boge.

And then, this battle and this bombardment of Paris. I don't know what the English papers say about it. All I care is that it holds up all communication with England – no telegrams get through & letters are delayed. I thought, this morning, I'd tell you a bit about it – but you don't want to know – There it just *is* – This afternoon I went to the Luxembourg Gardens. The spring this year seems to me *hateful* – cruel – cruel – like pigeons are cruel – all the leaves burst into claws. But praps its just me. And then the people in black, with made up eyes & red lips & black embroidered handkerchiefs. And then all the young men – still in light overcoats – wet brushed hair – stocks – pincé at the waist – boots with light uppers – still going – I feel that corruption and destruction are in the air & we just may survive. The world is *hideous* – & we are apart & I haven't heard of you *since your letter of Wednesday week* – Ah God! As soon as I hear again dearest love I will write differently. But at present I *am* not – I am fast asleep until my little knight wakes me – What are you doing *now*? We are so near – really – Paris – London its nothing & yet between us there are swords & swords –

Bogey, you must go on loving a great deal your wandering

Wig.

MS ATL. *LJMM*, 226–7.

To J. M. Murry, [25 March 1918]

Monday –
Café de la Source.
[35 Boulevard St Michel, Paris]

Darling

There is still no word from you at Cooks. I went first thing this morning & last thing this evening. Nothing. The rest of the day is just – nothing – too – in consequence – I am simply a sort of 'vide' until I get a letter & I feel at moments – just despair – as though I shall be kept here – and ages & ages will pass before I ever leave Paris – – – –

At one oclock this morning, I got up & wrapped up in shawlets &

went down to the cave & sitting there in a heap of coal on an old upturned box – listening to the bloody Poles & Russians – it all seemed a sort of endless dream – Oh so tiring – so utterly fatiguing. Ive caught a cold, too – and that makes the life in the caves so beastly – They are like tombs – I have nothing to say – nothing – nothing. L. M. is simply awful again. Again she is one of the Geoffroi family – poor creature & doing her best to kill me – but it cant be helped. Perhaps THEY *will* let me through. As long as I hear from you – I can bear it – but this silence. And 'writing' is rather difficult because of the bombardments – You see one *cant* stay out of the caves when they are near & they were yesterday to put it mildly – *extremely near* – I am sending L. M. to the consul tomorrow to ask again for me & plead my chill & this life in the tombs for a further excuse. You see all the posts & police affairs are held up. They told me at Cooks today perhaps you hadn't yet got my telegram – When they said that – well I felt in despair.

Far far away – I expect those 2 little children are standing at the door of the Heron trying on tiptoe to reach the knocker – But oh, my love, my life – it is so long since I have heard from you – I am weary – All I *can* do is to go on. I have not missed a day – You *at least* must have news, & perhaps tomorrow I shall have a letter too & the world will change. As it is I am nearly *starving* and all is dark because I haven't heard.

Jag Jag Jag –

I am your little
Wig.

MS ATL. *LJMM*, 227–8.

To J. M. Murry, [26 March 1918]

[? Café Mathieu, 27–29 Boulevard Ménilmontant, Paris]
Tuesday

Bogey

I have just been to Cooks & there is nothing again. Now I have come back by tram & I am sitting in the Café Mahieu – an *old spot* of mine. Its not really a *cold* day. Its cloudy & strange but I am bitterly cold, trembling with cold. This long silence really has begun to frighten me at last. The only consolation that I have is that please God – *you* hear from me. Its not a silence on both sides. God! how dreadful it is. Will it ever be broken again? I had moments yesterday when I almost gave up & I saw myself living here – for ages – till the end of the war, and never getting a letter – not a single letter or word again – I had moments when I felt that you & Rib were tired with the waiting & had not only turned from the window but given me up – I walk – walk – walk – and go into cafés & try & get coffee hot enough & go back to the hotel and stare at my room – in a sort of stupor of fatigue & anxiety. And each time I go out I seem to buy another newspaper – It is like 1914 over again.[1] L. M. has gone to the Consul today to tell him what a bad thing it is for me to stay here & live in these *caves*. It was my idea that she should go & tell him of my chill. I dont suppose it will help but at any rate it means we keep in touch with the office and are not forgotten.

As I write I can hear the patrol planes booming away – and out on the boulevard all the shops are being protected with strips of paper over the windows – in all sorts of patterns –

But this is *not* Paris: this is Hell & L. M. who walks about with me – stopping in front of all the shops & murmuring: 'I should like one day to see your little hands covered with *fine rings*' is a sort of fiend-guardian.

Well – well – now I must pin my faith – (it only needs the tiniest pin) on to tomorrow & hope for a letter or a wire or a *sign* then. If it *dont* come I suppose I shall go on till the next day – and so on – – – – for ever –

I must say *darling* before I finish this letter – *darling darling* – You havent forgotten have you – to keep the door open just a crack & just a speck of light burning for your child who has such an awfully long walk home –

Wig

MS ATL. *LJMM*, 228–9.

[1] When KM stayed on in Paris and Murry returned to London at the beginning of 1914. (See *CLKM* I. 131–9.)

To J. M. Murry, [26 March 1918]

[Select Hôtel, 1 Place de la Sorbonne, Paris]
Tuesday Night.

Dearest

I have just sat down to a tea – as that seems the best value & the hottest – It is most infernally cold – impossible to keep even moderately warm & the charbon question leaves (as Charles Lamb would say) the hotels cold! As I am nearer tomorrow & ∴ nearer the possibility of a letter or a telegram I feel a little bit more cheerful – But the *waste* of this – this appalling cold – this rushing from bed into the tombs – but why do I put those silly things first? They don't really count. But I feel the things that *do* count you accept & know as I do – the *silence* into which I am fallen as though I had fallen into a lake – something without source or outlet – the *waste* of life – of our love and energy – the cruel 'trick' that Life has played on us again – just when we timidly hoped – and timidly stretched out our longing hands to each other. Well – I suppose it has some sort of meaning (I dont suppose any such thing. I wish to God I could stop my suffering with those endless comfits that L. M. can suck.) But I cant. Its the devil – – –

I have been to Cooks again this evening. I thought thered be a telegram & the idiot took out a wire handed it across and then said – 'thats not the name, is it?' No, it was not the name – After this I felt very inclined to sit down on the pavement & put a shawl over my head & *stay there*. L. M. returned from the Consul. She had seen him, but he says there is nothing to be done until we obtain the permission from Bedford Square – and as those letters were practically thrown into the Cannons mouth God knows if they will ever get there –

I am *sure* that Rib understands & waits. You do, too, don't you? If you knew how I hate Life at this moment and all these parisian dogs and their b—ches. What a set! How vile they are – Oh who will come & take me away? Nobody – Not even a telegram. I am so tired of this anxiety – plus lack of sleep that I am beginning to get a sort of *dulled feeling* – and I don't think I shall mind anything soon – What the Hell is the good of putting up a fight? Why should *we* who are good & loving & wise be treated so?

My soul is full of hate – but if you were to come all the clouds would roll up & the sun would come out & shine on the far far away Heron windows.

Goodbye my darling – Your Wig.

MS ATL. *LJMM*, 229–30.

To J. M. Murry, [27 March 1918]

[Paris]
Wednesday. *BYRHH*

Dearest Jag

This is a funny little café where I am come to write you my forlorn forlorn letter. I have been to Cooks – Rien de rien encore – so out comes my little flag, so small now that it can hardly be seen & I must pin it on to tomorrow – This is just a hail, my darling, far away, silent one – just to prove that I *do* faithfully, faithfully, come up to the top of the hill every single morning & look into the direction of the empty sea and wave – as long as I can – just in the hope that *one* of these days Ill see a speck there and it will turn out to be a boat –

Its very cold & foggy – There is such a pretty girl in this café a girl you would admire & the man & woman who keep it, too, are *your sort.* There are also some red carnations, a white dog & a yellow basket covered in a red & white fringed cloth. It would be very beautiful if I were in the least alive. But I am not – Goodbye darling Boy. Ill write tomorrow. Tomorrow the telegram at least ought to be there – But who knows? – –

I am always for ever your own Wig who loves you *utterly.*

MS ATL. *LJMM*, 230.

To J. M. Murry, [28 March 1918]

[Paris]

THREE LETTERS RECEIVED PROFOUND RELIEF NEED NO MONEY WRITTEN IMPOSSIBLE LEAVE BEFORE TUESDAY FONDEST LOVE YOU AND RIB BOWDEN

Telegram ATL.

To J. M. Murry, [28 March 1918]

[Select Hôtel, 1 Place de la Sorbonne, Paris]
Thursday.

Darling Heart

Three letters came from you today. 2 Saturdays & 1 Sunday; one of the letters had £3 in it. I have received no wire at all. This is the first news. Upon getting it I wired you, rather at length: because my letters have been depressed and I wanted to get near you if I could a bit quickly. But they say at the 'poste' there are at least 48 hours delay for telegrams in England – so God knows when this will arrive. *I do not want any money at all.* Please keep this secret. Mother sent me some money to make myself a lovely girl the day I was married, but she said I was not even to tell Chaddie, as it was her 'secret funds'. This money I am spending and it will see me and the mountain through. That is provided we are allowed to leave France – One cant say anything for certain with this battle raging and the whole infernal upset – here and everywhere. I have lost confidence for some ghastly reason. I go on, do all there is to do, make all possible efforts, but my heart dont pay any heed. *Its gone quite dead.* I feel I suffered and hoped & tried to pull through unendurably before the moment. Now the snail simply cant put out its horns again for the moment. It will of course – mais – – – And topping it all this long *inevitable* wait for letters – – – And this great half-idiot woman at my heels always with "Katie what shall we do now?" . . . God what Hell one does live through!

The Military Permit people although they will not let me through without having heard from Bedford Square are not the Great Brick. Its the police.

Any person who stays longer than 48 hours in Paris must obtain a permit to leave France – This sauf conduit takes from 8 to 10 days to obtain – & is, even then, uncertain – as to one day or another. Have you had any dealings with the French police? They are like the russian police rather in D[ostoevsky]'s books. I dont want to discuss them here – I went again to the office yesterday, but they laughed in my face at the idea of my getting a permit sooner. In fact my anxiety seemed to amuse & delight them so much – and the fact that I was *une anglaise* in a predicament that I did my case no good, I fear.

I hope Sydneys man helps; it sounded a good idea.[1] I was infinitely relieved to have letters from you after so very very long, dearest – and the lovely little poem – But I cant help it. To be sincere, j'ai très fatiguee aujourd'hui. Nothing serious – only I am *tired out* and everything seems so far away – As though you were in London & I were passing Cape Horn.

You wont send me any money – will you? I have 300 francs. That is enough to pay both our bills, HER food etc. – all the extra booking expenses. Ive worked it all out.

Here is an easter card for Rib. *He* mustnt be a sad one: hes my brave little boy who looks through his telescope every morning & comes down & blows in it & shakes it out as though it were a trumpet & says: 'I think I can see something . . .'

Goodbye darling –
Wig.

If you were not there I'd really die, you know. I only live, I think, *with you*. Without you Id give up.

MS ATL. *LJMM*, 231–2.

[1] Murry wrote on 20 Mar that he had seen Sydney Waterlow at the Foreign Office, who 'promised that he would write this very day to the head of the English Section of the French Military Permit Office to say how advisable it was that you should be allowed to return' (ATL).

To J. M. Murry, [29 March 1918)

In case this letter is opened or detained I append my name and
address.   Bowden
                          Select Hotel | 1 Place de la Sorbonne | Paris.
                                                                  Friday
rec. (a wire at this address *and* a letter, written on Monday night.)

My own darling,
    Not very good news today – in fact as damnable as can be – I don't
know why I am dropping into L.M.'s 'preparations for a shock' –
They dont suit you and me – Cooks told me this morning that all
civilian travelling is cancelled for 8 days at least *and* that no letters will
either go to or come from England. This latter fact I shall ignore. I
don't believe it. The former gave me a *new blow.* I had just pinned that
unfortunate, quivering, frightened little faith of mine on to Tuesday
and Bogeys holiday week – and all this agony over – Now I must undo
it again. You will have your holiday without me. (Ah try & make it
one – my own – Try & let us forget just a tiny bit our present misery &
read and rest.) There is no explanation given of this new order and my
faith [in] it is un peu vague! "Eight days for the moment, Madame".
    I went to the Military Permit office this afternoon to ask for further
news, but found it was *closed.* Nobody there except one rather fishy
eyed frenchman and a notice stating that the service was suspended.
This gave me a most unpleasant feeling, – and as I came out *bang* –
"What a burst" as Matthew Arnold so dreadfully says of the
Nightingale[1] – the big gun had started again! All this upon one of
those heavenly blue and white and tender green afternoons – Those
afternoons that almost make you weep. I stood at a corner, thinking
this out & trying to 'get over it' enough to walk home – & in a blue
pool of sky a tiny cloud came to the edge to drink – a "little lamb who
made thee" cloud.[2] And at the same moment a lobster in a bowler hat
rushed at me and shouted – "Ne vous attendez pas Madame. Rentrez!
C'est le canon qui a commencé encore" and then he waved his arms
and cried '*L'obus*'[3] – – – What does it all mean? What does everything
mean?
    Well one must just go on. Your letters my precious are *healing* me.
Each letter seems to be another sort of divine protection against this
bitter life. When I was without them I suffered so that I grew almost
numb. Now all the tenderness comes back & I can breathe & look up
and whisper "Oh Bogey, my darling" and weep – – –
    I cannot go on if you are not there. It all becomes then the
nightmare that it is. You must know – you do – what this further

disappointment is to me. We have to bear it and go on – I suppose. But oh, do not let us ever again leave each other. It has been too bad a time and I am still very terrified.

I cant stay in the cave while the bombardment goes on, but in case of air attacks of course I shall. My cold is much better. I wired you this afternoon about my April allowance from Kay. You see – it is due & I thought he being a banker could wire it across or get it over somehow. I dont want any other moneys. You know also, what it is like for me to feel that I seem to eat up your money as fast as you make [it] – your *divine sacred* Heron money. But that will not always be so. I will explain when I get home – if dear love I get home.

Do remember every single moment how I love you. How I long for you – How hard it is for me to be here and in danger of being, I feel – swept by a great broom further & further away from *all* my world *all* my life – *all* my heaven – which is you. If my letters ever seem cold or dull it is because I am tired or frightened. Those are the only reasons.

I simply live for you and in you and our future. I still believe we shall be together again & all this will be over – but whatever does happen my own darling – youre my whole life – amen – Keep on writing until I let you know. Lets risk the ugly world getting the letters rather than you & I being without.

And now, at this minute stop & say Wig – & hear me say Jag – but I cant for fool that I am – je pleure – I am not always so faint hearted. It is only I think when I write to you that I feel it is unbearable and that we have been treated too badly – Oh Bogey these are tears & kisses, too. Wipe them away – & don't let anyone know I have been crying not even the little Rib. Goodbye for now – my soul – my life – my darling –

God bless us both

Wig.

MS ATL. *LJMM*, 232–4.

[1] 'Hark! from that moonlit cedar what a burst!' Matthew Arnold, 'Philomela', *Poems* (1853).
[2] William Blake, 'The Lamb', *Songs of Innocence* (1789).
[3] A howitzer shell.

To J. M. Murry, [29 March 1918]

[Paris]

CIVILIAN TRAFFIC SUSPENDED ASK KAY SEND APRIL ALLOWANCE COOKS ALL WELL LOVE BOWDEN

Telegram ATL.

To J. M. Murry, [30 March 1918]

[Select Hôtel, 1 Place de la Sorbonne, Paris]
Saturday.

My darling Heart

I *should* have been home nearly a week by now – and Im still far away. But yes, this is better than that far distant South – for as soon as a train or a boat can go – I will be on it. I have been to the M[ilitary] P[ermit] O[ffice] this morning. They have not yet received our permission from Bedford Square. The whole office was in a vague state of unquiet and the official to whom I spoke seemed to think that, while this battle raged, civilians would be held up – i.e. that eight days was all too hopeful an idea. L. M. is going off to the consul this afternoon to try and get work.

I suppose the blockade has started for no post has come today here or at Cooks. It is raining fast and the bombardment is – frankly *intensely* severe. The firing takes place every 18 minutes as far as I can make out. I wont try & tell you where the bombs fall – It is a very loud ominous sound – this super Kanon[1] – I am not frightened by it even though I have been extremely near the place where the explosions have taken place but I *do* feel there is a pretty big risk that one may be killed by it. You see there is no warning as to where the next shell will fall – neither is it frequent enough to make one stay in the icy cellars. Also one *must* go about to consuls etc & try & get away. If it were not for you I should not care whether I were killed or not. But as you *are* there I care passionately and will take all the precautions you would have me take & I you in the same straits. Today – people are frightened – quite otherwise to what they have been before – and the ghastly massacre in the church[2] has added very much to their feeling.

I tell you all this – I cant keep anything back from you. But I am *not at all* frightened. And so I want to add – don't worry about me, my own. But that is absurd. For I worry about you, too. No rather – *think* about me & tell me in your next letter that I shall at least be home for the 17th and I shall believe that. Ah, I cant say what store I set on that day – It seems to mean such an infinite thing to us – a sort of blessing from on high will be visited upon us when we walk out of the place into the street – hand in hand – and telling everybody by our smile that we have just come fresh from heaven. Rib must be there too – I shall carry him & he shall have 1 grain of rice in one hand shut up tight and one piece of pink confetti in the other. Now you are smiling – are you – my own love? I want to put my arms round your neck & pillow your head on my bosom. I just want to hold you and kiss you & *never* let you go – After all, I have fallen into this old war – I felt that one of us would – but Bogey – oh – God – I thank Thee that it is *I* and

not my beloved who am here – That – from the bottom of my soul –
Goodbye my own for now –

I adore you and I am for eternity

Your own Wig.

MS ATL. *LJMM*, 234–5

[1] The long-range 8.26 inch gun the Germans were now using for the shelling of Paris.
[2] During the Good Friday Tenebrae service, a shell from the 'super Kanon' had fallen on the church of Saint-Gervaise-Saint-Protais, in the rue François-Miron in the 4th arrondissement. 80 people, mainly women and children, were killed and 90 wounded.

To J. M. Murry, [31 March 1918]

[Select Hôtel, 1 Place de la Sorbonne, Paris]
Easter Sunday.

Darling Heart

I received today your letters of Wednesday & Thursday. I am sure that no letter has gone astray. The only thing I have *not* had was a wire you sent to Cooks. In your 2 letters you are feeling like I was just at about that time. Now thank God at least I am getting letters & I pray that mine are arriving, too . . .

Yesterday the lady called 'Long Sighted Lizzie'[1] became so violent that I got a bit jumpy & decided at any rate it was no use simply sitting here & waiting for the 18 minutes to be up before another crash came. So L. M. & I went off to an underground cantine at the Gare du Nord for soldiers & refugees – & got taken on to start today – at 1.30. It seemed to me the best thing one could do – to be underground and so busy that you'd no time to think . . . I went today – but *of course* I shall never go again. I couldn't do it, Boge. It was too hard work. When I came off duty at 7 I couldn't speak for fatigue & even now (though I could tell you a lot about it.) (Oh no its not interesting) I am pretty dished – No, I must stay here & keep down low when the gunfire is violent. I am keeping notes of the kind of thing people say about it – some *terribly* good things – L. M. will continue to go to the cantine because it feeds her too. We'll have to take the risk – Its not a great one. Do you remember where we saw those little children *skating* one year? All that is destroyed utterly . . .

I dont know why. I feel for all my fatigue – *hopeful* tonight. As though at the end of eight days they may – let me through – God knows why I feel this – for as a rule a sort of deadly fatality seems to be in my heart & its all just oh – a chance – a chance – But Bogey – I feel

I *must* come. If they go on keeping us apart what will become of us? I suppose *Brett* has no influence?[2] I thought she might have helped – but again I suppose not –

Queer thing: I am for the moment *dead* off my family – the result I think of a gay 'cheerio' card from Chaddie – which came so damned inappropriately last night. On the other hand Jack, darling, I *love* your mother. Don't you think, after the 17th she might adopt me as her daughter & I might find some name for her that wasn't Mrs Murry?

If I get back I want us to make her very happy & Arthur of course. I long for us to keep him very near.

Oh God – as I write – this all seems like a tremendous – impossible nightmare – I look round this room & think of all that divides us – see the copy of the Paris Midi, read again L[loyd] G[eorge]'s ominous message[3] – & my heart goes dead with fright. If you can convey to me what is happening in England I beg you to. My Bogey darling – oh, my love please try – for my sake to *eat* to sleep – not to get too lonely. I am thank God nearer than I was in the South – If God is kind in less than eight days I shall see you. At any rate I'll try & believe that & so live in faith. But in reality – I live in nothing but your love. Thats all – I am all yours for ever & ever

Wig.

MS ATL. *LJMM*, 235–6.

[1] Another name for 'Big Bertha' or 'Die dicke Bertha' as the German troops called the gun mentioned in the last letter.

[2] Dorothy Brett's father, second Viscount Esher (1852–1930), was an eminent civil servant, then living in Paris as Chairman of the Imperial Defence Committee. KM's passing idea of enlisting his influence, if ever put to Brett, would have been rendered unlikely by her friend's uneasy relations with her father.

[3] KM may be referring to the Cabinet message signed by Lloyd George which was published in *The Times* on 26 March. Its conclusion promised that 'still further reinforcements of men and guns are ready to be thrown into the battle'. Or she may mean the Prime Minister's telegram that was read in New York by the British Ambassador on 27 March, calling on the Americans to send reinforcements for a battle which 'is only just beginning'.

To J. M. Murry, [1 April 1918]

[Select Hôtel, 1 Place de la Sorbonne, Paris]
Easter Monday.

My darling Heart

I wonder if your holiday has begun today – and if the weather is fine. Here is April – our longed for April – the month in which we mean to get married – I felt this year that April was simply made for us – and that it would be such a glory – such a spring as never never had been known before. And now – all I think is – when will the boats start again? When shall I be able to get through? It is idle to tell you again (yet I must tell you again) how simply boundless my longing for you is. I feel I *must* see you soon with my own eyes & hold you & be held. What perils we have gone through and are going through – & to think that those fruit trees are in flower in the Heron orchard and all the flowers are open to the sun and our children walk about with handfuls of tired little violets . . .

There is no post today – I suppose that means there was no Good Friday post in England. Cooks is shut & the Consuls, so nothing can be done. Ill visit both tomorrow. I am thank God alone – as L. M. has gone to the cantine – and won't be back till late night. It has just struck 3 – so beautifully and calmly – with a kind of sunny langour – and my silly childish heart said – "Darling, shall we go for a small walk?" And away we went, going slowly, me on your arm, & talking very quietly, just for ourselves, you know. And occasionally you gave my hand a squeeze and said '*Wig*'. But no, these dreams are too sweet: I *cant* dream them while I am so far away. Shall I be home next Sunday? What do *you* think? Oh, Bogey I *must* be on my way home at least. The boats must start again and they cant keep all people away from their own country. If only we had influence. I asked for Sydneys man at the M.P.O. but was met with the coolest stare "Dont know him. Major Knight is the head of this office". So *that* was *not much good*!

At that moment a knock came at my door & the maid opened it pushing in front of her a tiny little boy in a white pinafore and white socks with red shoes. *Very* small just two years old. He was eating his goûter – a bit of bread and he staggered in & when he saw me turned his back – She said might she leave him a moment & when she had gone I remembered I had a little piece of chocolate in my despatch case. When I mentioned it he was so moved that he sort of – waded 100 miles over to me and about 200 more to the cupboard & there he stood – beating time with his toes as fast as possible while I got the chocolate out. He was so very nice. I held him up to the glass and he gave the other little baby first a crumb of bread & then a taste of the other. When the maid came for him – being anxious to kiss his hand, he kissed the bread instead & waved it at me. How fine and lovely little children can be. When he sat on my lap I felt a moment of almost *peace* as though the Sodom & Gomorrah world had stopped just for an instant. But now he's gone again – –

Every taxi that stops at this hotel stops at my heart, too. I know how utterly absurd that is. But I feel by some miracle – – – And I wonder – would they phone me from downstairs or should I just hear steps along the passage? – – – So far there has only been one shot

today – but few people are out in the streets & it is not gay.
Goodbye my own darling – God keep us both.

Your own Wig

MS ATL. *LJMM*, 236–8.

To J. M. Murry, [2 April 1918]

[? Café Mathieu, 27–29 Boulevard Ménilmontant, Paris]
Tuesday.

My darling Heart

No letter again today but I hardly expected one – I mean by that I knew that the English post would be disorganised for Easter – Tomorrow, perhaps I shall have 2 at least – Thats what I look for today.

Since yesterday the 'lutte' as they say has continued – Gunfire last evening – and at 3.15 this morning one woke to hear the air *screaming*. Thats the effect of these sirens; they have a most diabolical sound. I dressed and went down to the Caves – Everybody else was there – the place was packed with hideous humanity. *So* hideous indeed that one felt a bomb on them wouldn't perhaps be as cruel after all. I don't think I can go to the caves again – The cold and agony of those stone dusty steps & these filthy people *smoking* in that air – I crept back to bed & to sleep & woke to a perfect deafening roar of gunfire. It was followed by the sound of people running in the streets. I got up again & went to look. Very ugly, very horrible. The whole top of a house as it were bitten out – all the windows broken – and the road of course, covered with ruin. There were trees on both sides of the street & these had just come into their new green. A great many branches were broken but on the others strange bits of clothes and paper hung. A nightdress – a chemise – a tie – they looked extraordinarily pitiful dangling in the sunny light. One thing which confirms me again in my dreadful feeling that I live wherever I am in another Sodom & Gomorrah – – This. Two workmen arrived to clear away the debris. One found, under the dust, a woman's silk petticoat. He put it on & danced a step or two for the laughing crowd – – – That filled me with such horror that Ill never never get out of my mind the fling of his feet & his grin and the broken trees and the broken house.

I have just posted you a book – because of the pages about Dostoievsky. The woman, Sonia Kovalevsky, is awfully nice; her friend Anna is a b—ch,[1] I think. But perhaps that is because I can't stand women, Bogey – who 'pretend' to friendship.

I am writing to you in the Cafe Mahieu. It is a divine, warm day. I keep thinking & thinking only of you – my darling – & wishing & wishing – you know what. I went to Cooks this morning. The man seemed to think the boats would start again at the end of this week – but no, I dont dare to hope until I have been to the M.P.O. tomorrow.

On my way here I fell in with an accident. A man on the pavement said he had broken his ankle. A large crowd collected, but nobody believed him. Two policemen nearly *swore* him away – but as he groaned & sweated a great deal they decided to take off his boot & sock & see. After *pulling off* the boot I said – 'cut the sock, dont drag it' – & really it is just a fluke I wasn't arrested. You should have heard the 'taisez-vous' that was flung at me & the rest. So they pulled it off, and the ankle was all broken. His whole foot was at right angles, pale green in colour with black nails. 'When did you do it' they asked him & the fool said 'pas aujourd'hui'. At that the whole crowd began to laugh, looked at the foot & laughed – He had evidently been going about for days with this foot & I should think it will have to be amputated – But God what a joke it was for these parisians!

Bogey, the dreadful beauty of this spring terrifies me – and Bogey darling Heart I keep wondering if your holiday is begun. Where are you? Have you seen any flowers or bees? What can I say? Nothing except that I am far from my own & all else doesn't matter – Perhaps tomorrow – that is my only cry – Tomorrow – tomorrow –

Oh please dont give me up – & don't shut your heart to me. Keep it very warm & ready won't you – *My heart* is such a frail one now. It beats so fast if I look at the letter rack & hardly beats at all when I look away –

God help us.

Your own
Wig.
who loves you *terribly*.

MS ATL. *LJMM*, 238–9.

[1] The book was *Sonya Kovalevsky, A Biography by Anna Carlotta Leffler, Duchess of Cajanello*, together with *The Sisters Rajevsky, Being an Account of her Life by Sonya Kovalevksy*, trans. A. de Furujelm and A. M. Clive Bayley (1895).

To J. M. Murry, [3 April 1918]

[Select Hôtel, 1 Place de la Sorbonne, Paris]
WEDNESDAY

My darling Bogey

I had a note from you written on Sunday – That is the first sign I have had from you since a letter written on *Tuesday* – so the other letters of the other days (for you *must* knowing my trouble and anxiety have written) have all been lost. However I am thankful for this note after the long and painful silence again. If you knew the *fever* I live in – the constant strain & agony of mind – & trying to arrange my affairs *and* L. M.'s affairs here – – –

I went to the M.P.O. today. They have heard from Bedford Square saying we can go back. But of course it rests now with the question of a boat. At present there are none – So in the meantime & while most of my life is spent in trying to get home – Oh please write fully to me about anything – only <u>write</u> or my heart will really break!

I go to Cooks, to the M.P.O., to the Consul – then to a café – I make up sums, I walk about – I read the awful papers & it seems such a risk as to whether I ever get back that I feel half frozen with fright – & I <u>look</u> for letters – nearly always in vain – Risk losing them, Bogey, but for God's sake don't leave me without them. If you knew with what a fever I tore this one open & found the 2 middle pages empty! My life, I assure you, is very painful here, & I am so helpless. I can do nothing but wait for the broom to sweep me home or sweep me away –

Thats all.

Goodnight, my dearest – My little boat feels awfully knocked about tonight – & Ive had to creep into the cabin & hide my head – for Im tired & I weep – Please please don't leave me in silence.

Wig.

MS ATL. *LJMM*, 240.

To J. M. Murry, [5 April 1918]

[Select Hôtel, 1 Place de la Sorbonne, Paris]
Friday.

Darling Bogey

As usual – I might say – there is no letter from you either here or at Cooks. I have been to Cooks and the M.P.O. this morning but as yet they have no news at all about a boat sailing, so I must go on & somehow bear + all my other appaling anxieties this silence – You know I hardly sleep at all – I am so *restless*. Work is absurdly out of the question. I simply seem to spend my days asking if there is a letter or a boat – & there is neither. I have got the police permit & the Consul permit. As soon as a boat *does* sail I am ready – But when will that be? This is, you can understand – cant you – almost a maddening question if one is *alone* in a *foreign* country with absolutely *nobody* to talk to – *no* influence – a woman dependent on you who can't speak the tongue –

If the whole affair has tired you out & you feel you have nothing more to say then you MUST wire me on receipt of this letter – *cant write just now.* You must not leave me without letters unless your heart has quite absolutely changed to me – for I cannot bear it. If I know *not* to expect – then Ill arrange otherwise, but without a sign from you & when I know that english mails *do* arrive *are* delivered, my days are intolerable.

Cant you imagine them darling? You, at least, are in England. And you have a person or two to speak to & you are *chez vous* but I feel I may be swept away any minute & I need you as never before. And yet no letters come. Jack – do give a sign or you will kill your Wig.

MS ATL. *LJMM*, 240–1.

To J. M. Murry, [5 April 1918]

Let's hope on it's all the best

Telegram. Text from Murry letter 9 April 1918 (ATL).

To J. M. Murry, [5 April 1918]

[Select Hôtel, 1 Place de la Sorbonne, Paris]
To Ribni   Friday Night.
My Tiny

When I came in tonight a Miracle waited for me in the pigeon hole where key 30 hangs. Your little father had managed to send me another paper boat – and only launched on Tuesday night and for a sail oh! such a lovely poem by you both . . .[1] Such a lovely poem that I don't know how to live another moment without you both. There is the poem you see rocking in my bosom but its not an awfully calm sea, my little man –

Ah, my Ribni, our small doorkeeper. Watch him when he goes out in the morning – and wait for him when he comes home at night. Be ready to wave to him. Walk all over him and kiss him for me. Tell him every way you know that I am coming as fast as the Uglies will let me come. When he sleeps walk up and down by his pillow and keep guard. And see that the Lions and Tigers do not tear up our letters but that the doves carry them swiftly – guarded by eagles . . . I languish – I languish away from you both. I have no little laughs, no one calls me a worm – no one is my size. You are both my size. But Rib, old fellow, I trust you. I can trust you utterly, cant I? To look after him? You know – don't you that hes all I want. He's mine – and I am his and I shall never be happy again until all of us are sitting together looking at each other – holding each other tight. Dont give me up. Please keep on sweeping the doorstep with a feather and putting out the tiny lantern at night. For I am tired, my little tiny doll and I want to be home with him and with you. Its dreadful – being here. But all youve got to do is to keep him for me – *see*? Oh, Ribni, curl up in his heart & kiss him for every beat. My hearts nearly broken with longing.

[no signature]

MS ATL. *LJMM*, 241–2.

---

¹ In his letter on 2 Apr Murry enclosed his poem 'Ribni Speaks', which begins:

> I think that she has been away too long
>   And you did wrong
> Who let her go; you would not see my eyes
> Frowning my signal to you to be wise
> And understand that all you said was lies,
>   Foolish, headstrong,
> Self-cheating children who have loved too long
> To look elsewhere save in each other's eyes.

The poem was included in *Poems: 1917–18*, The Heron Press (1919), 12–14.

To J. M. Murry, 6 April [1918]

[Select Hôtel, 1 Place de la Sorbonne, Paris]
Saturday April 6th.

A boat is supposed to go next Wednesday.
My darling precious Bogey
     Thank God! A registered letter came from you today – it was written on Good Friday and Saturday – so it is a very old man – but still – oh – how I clasped it – I jumped out of bed & gave the postman 6 sous. I felt inclined to kiss his hand – & then I jumped into bed again & though the letter was very short and a sad one – it was *news news* of you – thats all and that is everything.
     They say today that a boat sails for England next Wednesday. But it is not quite definite. The consul advised me not to wire. I have been everywhere twice – morning & afternoon, I mean, to Cooks, the M.P.O., the consul at Rue Montolivet and the G[reat] W[estern] R[ailway] office where you left the 20 francs a hundred years ago. I *do* hope and yet I am too afraid to. No, the game has now been played so often that it don't take me in any more. Ill wait. Ill even wait to hope. For every edition of the papers that comes out may make ones return

absolutely impossible – and Wednesday with this second attack just beginning[1] might simply not exist – It might be blown away by the obus or swept over by the German troops – I have carried your last letter in my bag all day – as a sort of mascot. When I waited for the Consul this afternoon two such exceedingly nice people came out of the office – arm in arm – and nearly bursting with happiness (especially him) & then the doorkeeper stuck up on the wall a card to say that the Consul had just married them – His second name was Longweight and her name was Lily and she was a music hall artist . . .

This almost broke through my blind numbed anxiety – Otherwise I am half dead. Although I write like this about Wednesday of course in my heart all my faith is pinned to it already, & already I see my Rib dimpling – But oh, my treasure – if ever I do get back and into your arms again – I dont think Ill even talk or laugh or cry – Ill just *breathe* – thats all.

I want desperately to know how you are – if you eat – if you sleep. But I have such a perpetual crying need to know everything about you that its no good. No questions will do –

Kays money came today. I wired its arrival to him – that makes me alright whatever happens –

But what does it all matter? What does anything matter? There is only you and my jealous, furious passionate longing love for you. There is nothing else on earth. Give him to me & me to him & let us be – Never disturb us again – Shut the door on us – & let us sit in our lamp circle of light & rest.

For in you alone I live.

Wig.

MS ATL. *LJMM*, 242–3.

---

[1] After some days of comparatively light fighting, on 4 April the Germans resumed their attempt to force the roads to Amiens, south of the Somme, and renewed attacks on other positions in France.

To J. M. Murry, [6 April 1918]

[Select Hôtel, 1 Place de la Sorbonne, Paris]
Saturday Night.

Precious, dearest, darling Heart

I am so hopeful tonight. Two letters have come from you today – one written on Tuesday evening & one on Wednesday afternoon – & they bring you so . . . tremblingly near. I had a phone message from Sydneys[1] man at the Embassy today, too, went to see him & he said that I would *definitely* get across on Wednesday – He gave me a card to the M.P.O. telling them that it was *urgent* I should go (he was a great ponce). And the M.P.O. still say that a boat will go on Wednesday – though Cooks say it is most uncertain. I think it is absurd *not* to regard it as uncertain – for it is a race between Wednesday & this second battle – and those vile germans are still marching on. But everybody & every tree & every person & every breath seems now to *incline* towards Wednesday – If that again is just a big black hole & again there comes the uncertainty – and the waiting I don't know what I *shall do*. I am glad [Alexander] Kay was decent. Kiss your darling little Mummy for me – I am so glad that I am going to be her real daughter-in-law. & oh how I want to see the little brother again – the dear lad. But all these things come after.

First of all there is just YOU. L. M. has just lifted 150 off me: she cant help it & its alright of course – Ive plenty & shell pay me back but I wish she was not dead drunk as a result of one dubonnet. She is – & can only (as she says) "giggle" . . . If you knew – – –

The bombardment has gone on again today & its 8.30. Ive had news. Id better get back as soon as possible – But there is still a good quarter of an hour. I havent had any *bread* since this new rule came in. I do want a crust – As to butter it dont exist.

Do you know IF I ever do get back it will be just a week before our wedding – & your mother must ask us to tea (we'll say its the anniversary for she must *never* know)[2] & we'll take her flowers – lovely ones – & be very gay children – Shall we? – Shall we? Is it all before us? Not all swept away?

I spend my nights now playing Demon patience. I sit up in bed & play & play. This morning at 3 oclock a mouse jumped into my waste paper basket & began to squeak –

But I can hardly tell you these things. Wednesday begins to more than loom – Again I think – I must take him back a peppermill – & another of those red & green cups & saucers. God! If ever I do get back then I feel our trial will be over for ever.

But the German army & the big gun & the raids and all this vast horror still rolls between.

Bogey – hope *for* me – Ive been so tortured that I must have someone to *help* me *hope*. Your letters are my salvation – but that – you know.

Your own Wig.

MS ATL. *LJMM*, 243–4.

[1] KM's cousin Sydney Waterlow had resigned from the Foreign Office, but returned during the War. He would officially attend the Peace Conference in Paris following the Armistice.

[2] Murry's mother presumably believed they were already married. Although KM declared her affection for his mother to Murry, other feelings can be found in an unpublished notebook

entry five months later: 'I don't like Jack's family. I could never *bear* to have them live with us . . .
We'll come to blows about them one day. The young brother – so witty – that J. choked over his
tea – The father who found half a sovereign in his hip pocket. The mother – jam or marmal*ade*.'
(ATL.)

To J. M. Murry, [7 April 1918]

[Select Hôtel, 1 Place de la Sorbonne, Paris]
Sunday April 6th 8.30 p.m.

Darling Heart

This has been a perishing cold *dead* day & I have not been very
great shucks. Im in bed now. Ive been playing demon nearly all day –
Tomorrow I have to be at the M.P.O. at 10 – so I wanted to rest a bit
today. Im awfully exhausted by all this. All day – all day – I have
thought of you – & so often of your darling little Mother. You can't
think how I love her just now – I feel as though she *must* love me too &
take me for one of her children. Will she? During the afternoon I
looked down & saw your ring – such a Bogey/Wig ring on my finger &
I *kissed* it. When I went out for lunch, dearest I saw something. A
poilu's funeral – A very grey day with big clouds in the sky – the plain
hearse covered with the solemn flag, the cheap flowers & walking
behind it a tiny boy in a black fur coat carrying his fathers rifle. He
twinkled along with a handful of soldiers – and it was very hard for
him to keep up. It made me cry

Tomorrow my week of *hope* begins – in four hours it begins – Oh –
child – playmate – help me – wave to me, you & Rib & this time –
please God I will come –

When I read your letter how you had walked down the Tottenham
Court Road *without me* I felt as though they had tortured me so Id
never recover. But I know at sight of you I would recover in an
instant. Only I must have that sight. Goodnight my precious own –
and God help us –

Your own
Wig.

MS ATL. *LJMM*, 244–5.

To J. M. Murry, [8 April 1918]

[Select Hôtel, 1 Place de la Sorbonne, Paris]
Monday.

Darling Heart

As far as one can tell from the aspecks there is a fair chance for that

Wednesday boat. That means Id be home on Thursday. I have spent the whole day from 9.30 to 6.30 rushing from office to photographer to police station to Commissaire & Consul, Cooks & the M.P.O. It is plus that a vile icy day & pouring – the streets full of melted snow. The M.P.O. (even after my embassy card) met me triumphant. "You can't get across this week. All the boats are full." "But", I said "I have booked seats." This was a bitter blow to them. True enough I was among the First Two Hundred. But since that British visa I have had to get three more – & five photographs are required. I only had four so I had to get ½ a dozen done.[1] 2.50. Not badsome – but the background was such an *awful storm* that it rather frightens me. No letter from you today & Chaddie said she was sending me £5 but it has never come – It may turn up tomorrow. I have another *today* tomorrow. Also I am moving to a hotel at Gare St Lazare as one must be *on* the platform at *six* & with the Cannon & the raids one dont dare risk a journey across Paris.

Oh God! All this sounds as though it really were going to come true. Is it – Bogey? – I don't know. I don't even know yet. I sit up in bed during the night playing demon on a pillow & never dare to play & see if the boat is going.

I must put on record that all the authority english that Ive met here are without exception the most indifferently bred men imaginable. They behave – talk walk as though they were *stockbrokers on a golf course* – I was also a little surprised today when the Commissaire asked me if N.Z. were a part of England – & when I said it was near Australie if it were a part of Australie & when I said it was an island – 'mais tout petit enfin!' said he.

You do understand why I write in this strain? Its because darling I am really dying of anxiety. All these preparations are so advanced. Can it mean that I am coming – really coming after all. And I am still frightened to hope and frightened to believe. I know that if I do get across it will be the end of our 'night' for ever & we shall begin such happiness that everything round us will ring pure gold – But God – is this to be?

And so I go on preparing – standing in queues – filling forms – having all these papers examined & saying par le bateau de Mercredi soir – Its as though I were in a dark dark garden & I knew there was a flowery tree somewhere – but I cant even smell it much less see it & yet I am beating up the garden & – – –

Oh Bogey –

I do nearly hope.

Wig.

MS ATL.

[1] The photograph is printed in Alpers 1980.

To J. M. Murry, [9 April 1918]

Bar Monaco. Tuesday. [Paris]

Dearest Love

I am simply *desperate*. I had your two wires today – one at the hotel & one at Cooks[1] – but you can never have got a wire I sent immediately after my Friday letter saying *lets hope on its all the best*. No you cant have got it. And there is a letter from you today referring to things I know nothing of – that you have already written about. This letter was written on Friday: its the one about the letter press.[2] Oh Bogey, will it never end? I have spent the day *rushing* from the police to the police – Now it all seems nearly finished & Ive only to pack & try & get back tomorrow. I keep on writing – you know why – & now of course its in case the boat is submarined. I think I should keep on writing even under the sea . . . Yes, of course I should. I have bought 2 quarts of butter – and am going to try to bring them – but thats all I can afford cette fois . . . We leave at 7 tomorrow. You know that, though. I am speechless with anxiety & hope. I will write to you in Havre tomorrow, darling, more leisurely.

Oh God this Friday letter has something of you in it which carries me straight into your heart – Its a letter so like you – Oh my darling heart I do love you so – & I too am terribly timidly just beginning to think of a bud of hope. Ever so tiny a one.

I have simply everything to tell you – everything & I cant help today – telephoning – endlessly – "Put me through to Mr Middleton Murry. Is that you Boge?" And then I cant say any more – Can you think what I feel like – my treasure? My courage is just about mouse high – & I am nobody but your tiny timid loving

Mouse –

Give the worm a kiss & show him my new passport photograph.

MS ATL. *LJMM*, 245–6.

---

[1] Neither of these telegrams from Murry survives.

[2] Murry's letter of 22 Mar was considerably delayed. He had told her 'I've just done one of those stupid things which only I seem to do. I've just bought a letter press – one of those things wh. they used to use before typewriters came in for copying letters. Why I bought it is because it is very useful for bookbinding.' (ATL.)

II

ENGLAND –
LONDON AND CORNWALL:
1918

After the ordeal of trying to leave Paris, KM moved in with Murry at 47 Redcliffe Road. They were married on 3 May. Her continuing poor health convinced Murry that she should not stay on in his Fulham flat, but recuperate in Cornwall. By the time he joined her at Looe late in June, he had negotiated for the house in Hampstead to which they would move at the end of August. During the summer her relationship with Garsington felt the strain that followed Murry's unfavourable review of Siegfried Sassoon's war poems, and her friendship with Koteliansky was still suspended. *Prelude* was published by the Hogarth Press early in July, but the book went unreviewed, and was not admired by many of her acquaintances. Soon afterwards 'Bliss', the first of her stories to be accepted by a reputable literary journal, appeared in the *English Review*.

In August Annie Beauchamp died in Wellington, shortly before doctors accurately put a limit of four years on her daughter's life should she refuse the sanatorium regimen they recommended.

To J. M. Murry, [11 April 1918]

[Southampton]

ARRIVE WATERLOO ABOUT 11.30 THIS MORNING. TIG.

Telegram ATL.

To Ida Baker, [12 April 1918]

[47 Redcliffe Road, Fulham]
Friday.

Dearest Jones[1]

The little Messenger at the door sent me back years & years . . . Thank you dearie for the 'goods'. I am glad the box has turned up. What is the next step to take & which of us takes it? I am also glad that Stella[2] was there as well. I'd like to know what the fights are – I have been wondering about you so – – –

'Home' looked lovely, & feels so lovely – I never want to go out again. I had to spend a long time casting up my eyes at all the 'surprises' and improvements. They really *were* many. Ribni was sitting in the window on the lookout on a little box which held my letters. When he saw the taxi you can imagine how he began to wave & tap his toes on the glass – & then when I *did* come there said he was only looking to see if the milkman was coming. He has got rather out of hand & bosses me up – if I so much as move a thing out of its place –

Johnny came in last night – God! – He gave me such a welcome. Before I knew where I was we had hugged & kissed each other & Johnny kept saying 'this is a great success'. It really was! And you can imagine all the enjoyment he got out of a *fig* or two. We are dining with him tonight.

I feel horribly weak & rocky now that the strain is over – *blissfully* happy – incredibly happy – but really ill. I phoned Ainger. He is away until next week – I'll wait if I can. I weighed myself. Curse it. 7 stone 6. Ive just lost a stone, alors. Isn't that annoying. But ever since I came HOME I have done nothing but eat. I am hungry all the time so perhaps my last state will be worse than my first & I will put on stones like I've thrown them off.

But Jones – ones OWN fire – and lighting the gas & making tea, and oh! the hot bath which really was hot – & Jack & Jack and Jack.

Does it gleam to you, too – like a little jewel beyond price – those hours on the boat when you sat on the floor in a draught & I sat on the longue & we put the red on the black & wanted a seven? I was so happy – – – Were you? Try & forget that sad sick Katie whose back ached in her brain or whose brain ached in her back – Its such a lovely afternoon & very warm. I would like to turn to you & say 'Oh Jones we are quite all right, you know' –

About Saturday – Jack has got the afternoon off & we have to go & see his Mother – youll understand. Try & find a minute to write to me in – Do you want money?

Yours, dearie.

Katie

MS BL. *MLM*, 111–12.

[1] A note in *MLM*, 111, explains 'The name KM and LM both called each other when all was well between them. KM's mother and a friend, whose name also began with B, called each other "B". Katherine proposed that she and LM should call each other by the same name too – and chose Jones.'

[2] Stella Drummond – later Lady Eustace Percy – worked with Ida Baker at the Chiswick factory.

To Ida Baker, [14 April 1918]

[47 Redcliffe Road, Fulham]
Sunday.

Dearest Jones

I am wondering how you are spending your first Sunday – It is – isn't it? a rather idle day – Last Sunday was our *dead day* – we had only to wait – – – Ive been thinking about it sitting over the fire – (what a joy these Maryland cigarettes are after the camel droppings!)

Vile cold yesterday I spent looking for a medicine man who would reassure Jack until Ainger returns that I was *not* going to fold my tent like the Arab. Ainger had left 3 'locums' but they were all on military duty. A fourth who was also 'on his slate' I did see eventually. And he was 'quite decent' as you would say – Gave me an order for cream & milk provisionally & told me to repose & not get excited & eat the food of a child of 8 & not go out in the evenings – etc. etc. etc. My *back* aint as serious as I thought. I mean by that it is *not* spinal disease – I shant have to go about with my own umbrella as a substitute for the spinal column (which I had expected). Its due to my condition & must be rubbed & so on & rested – My left lung is pretty bad, he thinks, but that we knew. However Ive got all sorts of instructions till Ainger returns & thats all that matters. Jack looks after me as though I had broken through my shell yesterday & wont even let me carry a cup – and I just lie down & sip the air & eat & *look*. *All* seems so lovely because all is home – Oh God! how I loathe strange things & strange people! I feel so like a *cat* returned –

And you – Jones? Have you seen Dolly? What about clothes? What about the work? Are you going to be interested in it again? Tell me all this –

London feels to me solemn and quiet and strangely safe after Paris – The charming people persist. Kind looks and smiles seem everywhere – but its the quietness which is such a rest – Of course I only see ever such a tiny corner. I hope you are having a happy Sunday – Goodbye dearie.

Katie.

MS BL.

To Ida Baker, [18 April 1918]

[47 Redcliffe Road, Fulham]
Thursday.

Dearest Jones

I am so glad of your little notes. Please keep on sending them when you can. I am *not* remarried yet as the court has not sat on the decree nisi but all the same, dearie, will you please address me as Mrs J. M. M? If you hadn't asked me which you should do I should have asked you to, but you know how devilishly contrarywise Katie is!

I saw Ainger yesterday & discovered he was a New Zealand boy. That explains my feeling of confidence. But hes called away to France on Saturday – till the end of the war. What a bother! HE said: Yes there is no doubt I have definitely got consumption. He appreciated that a sanatorium would kill me *much* faster than cure me (Its a 2nd lunatic asylum to me) ∴ I am to try a 'cure' at home – Home is to be either Hampstead or Highgate or further afield. Must live in a summer house (*find* the summer) eat & drink milk and not get excited or run or leap or worry about anything – you know all the old wise saws. In fact 'repeat fortissimo with a good strong accent on the second note: 'she *must* lead the *life* of a *child* of *8*'. Cant you *now* hear the oboe taking it up & making it oh so plaintive with little shakes and twirls and half sobs? I must not borrow a handkerchief (this is serious, Betsy, for you know how they fly from me) or drink out of loving cups or eat the little bear's porridge with his spoon. And so on. But you see I am ever so gay – with long beams coming from my fingers & sparks flying from my toes as I walk.

(As to money – well – I keep on taking taxis for the moment – I can't help it but I will draw in my horns the moment my wings put forth). Tell me all about the coat & skirt dearest – *Most* important. In fact tell me all you can about everything. Belle & Chaddie called last night in a private kerridge & brought me some oranges & dead roses. Fergusson came to dinner & we talked strangely enough about 'this Art business' & 'what is honesty'. But however often I wander in *that* orchard I always find fresh fruits and bigger boughs & loftier trees. So its an adventure.

Goodbye darling.

Katie.

MS BL. *MLM*, 113–14.

To Ida Baker, [19 April 1918]

[47 Redcliffe Road, Fulham]
Friday.

Dearest Jones

I shall be alone here in the early part of tomorrow (Saturday) afternoon. If you 'get off' at 12 would you come over & help me? I stand forlorn in front of the chest of drawers & cant find a thing or put a thing away. *Do* come & put me in order and lay your kind hands on a very tangled, knotty disgraceful

Katie.

If you cant come early of course come later, dear, but early as you can *if* you can.

MS BL. Alpers 1953, 253.

To Dorothy Brett, [30 April 1918]

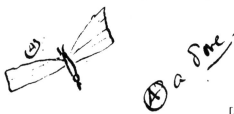

[47 Redcliffe Road, Fulham]

Darling Brett.

If you would Call for Murry on *Thursday at One Oclock* at his House of Business he would convey you on the Wings of Love to the Appointed Spot,[1] and Lunch will follow. It will be Great Fun, Larks and Jollifications. I am wearing, of course, a Simple Robe of White Crepe de Chine and Pearl Butterfly presented by *our dear Queen*. Murry, naturally, top hat and carnation buttonhole.

Blessings on thee – I hope thou wilt be Godmother to my First Half Dozen –

Katherine.

P.S. We have decided (owing to the great war) to have a string band without brasses.

MS Newberry.

[1] KM and Murry were eventually married at the Kensington Register Office on Friday 3 May. The witnesses were Dorothy Brett and J. D. Fergusson.

To Dorothy Brett, [1 May 1918.]

[47 Redcliffe Road, Fulham]

My dearest Brett,

This morning, chasing the law up and down and round about Somerset House for an Order of the Court declaring the Decree Nisi to have been made Absolute I was rapped over the knuckles by a

Legal Gent who refused, utterly and finally, to supply me with same until FRIDAY at one o'clock. So tomorrow is 'off' until Friday and alas! I am afraid that means you will not be able to come for you'll be at Pangbourne. This is very disappointing, but Authority was adamant to all my pleading. No, he cant and wont give me such an order until Friday.

Even when I told him that you were leaving for the Front tomorrow, that I was great with child and expected to be delivered tomorrow night, that Murry had symptoms of Botulism and would be shut-eyed, at least, on Friday – nought availed.

So, dearest girl, as I quite understand you can't put your journey off – we'll have to postpone the delight of your presence until Murry & I marry again. Damnation take the Law!

Your loving
Katherine.

MS Newberry.

To Ottoline Morrell, [12 May 1918]

[47 Redcliffe Road, Fulham]
Sunday.

Dearest Ottoline

It never was a secret; and certainly not from you. It is true – what you so perfectly say – I am always renewing a marriage with Murry. This last and really 'funny' one was – more than Id tell anyone – because I loathed and abominated my other legal name. Whenever it smote up at me from a passport or a police paper I hated it again. Now it's gone. But perhaps the chief reason was my hatred of the Human Snigger – and in fact, of human beings generally – of the 'Bloomsbury element' in life – enfin. I do feel now more hidden from it somehow – though perhaps that sounds far-fetched and absurd. But we were a funny party. Brett, like some delightful bird who had flown in, laughing through the bright anemone flowers –

I am so sorry – we cannot come down to Garsington. I am leaving London again on Friday for – I don't know in the least how long – and Murry is tied by every leg to his office stool. The country must be divine. I am going to *Looe* which is full of pigs and bluebells, cabbages & butterflies and fishermen's orange shirts flung out to dry on pink apricot trees. It sounds un printemps bien solide!

Life feels to me so full at present – simply *charged* with marvellous exciting things. Is it the Spring that won't be denied even at my age?

Yes, I know that God is a monster and there are moments when one *realises* the war but there *are* other moments when one rebels in spite of oneself and then – the floodgates are open and one is swept away on this heavenly tide. Do you feel that – or do you think Im *too* heartless? But what is to be done? How can one remain *calm* when even the barrel organ seems to put forth new leaves and buds and laburnum is in full flower in the Redcliffe Road. It is all – as M. would say – *too difficult*.

Yours ever with Love
Katherine

MS Texas. *LKM* I. 163.

To Dorothy Brett, [12 May 1918]

[47 Redcliffe Road, Fulham]
Sunday.

Dearest Brett,

If you are passing through on your way to Scotland don't forget to let me know. I am not going to Looe until the end of this week.

There is a show at the Burlington Galleries – a few doors away from the Leicester Galleries, Leicester Square, which has one or two very interesting "pieces" in it. Some Still Lives by Peploe and Anne Rice[1] and some early Fergussons – but no late ones – and its the late Fergusson who really is IT. There's not much at this show but it *is* worth a visit. Then Fergusson's show[2] is on Thursday. I would love love love to go there with you. But I suppose it can't be managed. (Brett you are awfully nice to go about with.)

Hurrah! Its begun to hail. Vive le joli Printemps! Murry is lying down upon the shell shaped 1840 sofa reading in a book. He is wearing a mauve shirt and pinkish socks, and above his head on the black marbil mantlepiece there is a bowl of dying lilac.
Spring Picture (2)
I saw Virginia on Thursday.[3] She was very nice. She's the only one of them that I shall ever see but she *does* take the writing business seriously and she *is* honest about it and thrilled by it. One cant ask more. My poor dear Prelude is still piping away in their little cage and not out yet. I read some pages of it & scarcely knew it again. It all seems so once upon a time. But I am having some notices printed and they say it will be ready by June. And won't the "Intellectuals" just hate it. They'll think its a New Primer for Infant Readers. Let 'em.

Curse this letter writing. If only we were together. Ive such a deal to say & this fool of a pen won't say it. *Will* it keep?

Each time I dip into the honey pot a very exquisite little bee with a message under its wing flies out & off in the direction of Garsington. Don't frighten it away. It is a guaranteed non-stingless or anti-stinging bee.

Now God in His Infinite Wisdom hath made the sky blue again. Oh dear oh dear – people are vile but Life *is* thrilling. There is a man who plays the flute in this street on these faint evenings . . . Well – well –

Addio mia bella,
Katherine.

MS Newberry. *LKM* I. 164.

[1] KM's friend, the painter, Anne Estelle Drey (née Rice), see *CLKM* I, 204, n. 1.

[2] At James Connell and Sons Galleries, 47 Old Bond Street.

[3] Virginia Woolf recorded of their lunch together (*DVW*, I, 150), 'Katherine was marmoreal, as usual.'

To Virginia Woolf, [14 May 1918]

[47 Redcliffe Road, Fulham]
Tuesday.

Dear Virginia

I have been 'kept in' ever since the summer I spent with you last week. And I thought you were leaving for Asheham sooner – that was why, missing one day, I did not send the drawings the next. I gave Murry the notices to have printed for me & I thought, as they were going to adorn picture galleries it would be a good idea to have the pictures on 'em. They ought to be ready by tomorrow. He will send you some, together with the blocks.[1] *Your* notice looks awfully nice. I hope to go away tomorrow. Curse! I feel damned ill in body these last few days. "My wings are cut I *can*-not fly I *can*-not fly I *can* not fly."

But Virginia dear – how I enjoyed my day with you; its such a lovely memory. I shall think of you a great deal while I am away – & then I must look out for your Tchekhov article.[2] But I wish you'd write your Protest Against the Exclusion of the W. C.

Well I was going to end off at the end of this page – but before I do I want to tell you that I reread The Mark on the Wall[3] yesterday and liked it tre-*men*dously. So there. I hope Asheham is lovely.

Katherine.

MS Berg. *LKM* I. 162–3.

[1] The Fergusson designs for the cover of *Prelude*, which depicted a woman's head in front of an aloe bush, were disliked by the Woolfs and used on only a few copies of the edition.

[2] A review of *The Wife and Other Stories*, and *The Witch and Other Stories*, both translated by Constance Garnett, in *The Times Literary Supplement*, 16 May 1918.

³ *Two Stories*, the first publication from the Hogarth Press in 1917, included Virginia Woolf's 'The Mark on the Wall'; Leonard Woolf's 'Three Jews' was the second story.

To J. M. Murry, [17 May 1918]

[Looe]

SUPERB ARRIVAL EVERYTHING SIMPLY SPLENDID HEADLAND HOTEL LOOE
FONDEST LOVE WIG

Telegram ATL.

To J. M. Murry, 17 May 1918

Headland Hotel | Looe | Cornwall
17.v.18.

For dinner there was:

soup
fish cutlets
mutton chops
greens
pancakes with cherry jam
cheese & biscuits
coffee
butter
½ pint milk

My dear husband

I have been sitting in a big armchair by the *three* open windows of my room wondering how I shall group or arrange events so that I may present them to you more or less coherently. But I cant. They *wont* group or arrange themselves. I am like a photographer in front of ever such a funny crowd whom Ive orders to photograph but who wont be still to be photographed – but get up, change their position – slink away at the back – pop up in front – take their hats off and on – Who *is* the most Important One – Who *is* Front Middle Seated? The morning with you was quite unreal – another dream nightmare. When I kissed you did we wake? No. When you kissed my hand I did feel a kind of thrill of anguish. (Will you understand that?) But it was all a part of this racing vile dream. Let us try & shut our eyes to it and go on as though it had not been – at least for the present, at least until the – the plaster is off your finger and the place healed again – – –

I had a very comfortable journey – The country, in the bright swooning light was simply bowed down with beauty, heavy, weighed down with treasure – Shelleys moonlight may[1] glittered everywhere, the wild flowers are in such a profusion that its almost an agony to see them and know that they are there – I have never seen anything more solemn and splendid than England in May – and I have never seen a spring with less of the *jeune fille* in it. – God! Why are you caged up there – why is our youth passing while the world renews itself in its glory!

I must confess, of course that, standing in the middle of the goldy fields, hanging from every tree, floating in every little river and perched on top of every hill there was a Thermos flask filled with boiling coffee – I have so often seen people in trains, armed with these affairs, *appearing* to uncork them and pretending that real steam and real heat flows out – but Ive never believed them – until today – At Plymouth I got out and bought two wheatmeal bigglechicks from the scrupulously clean refreshment room (fresh hot meat & potato pasties still for sale) and made an excellent tea. But indeed I had such constant recourse to the bottil that some soldiers in the carriage could not quite believe my exquisite signs of satisfaction were tout à fait sober! But twas nectar darling – & of course we shall never never be without one again – Only think for a moment. One need never want again for a cup of tea at one of those 'odd' moments which always come on journeys to us.

Anne[2] & Drey were at Liskeard – Anne – just as I had imagined – *bronze* coloured with light periwinkle eyes – carrying a huge white bag bulging with *her* thermos flask & a vest of Dreys (I didn't find where *it* came from or how) & a box of paints and a handful of hedge flowers – and the "most beautiful lemon". Drey was awfully kind. He did everything – We featherstitched off to Looe – It was very hot – all glowing & quiet with loud birds singing & the bluebells smelled like honey. The approach to Looe is amazing. Its not 'english', certainly not french or german – I must wait to describe it. The hotel buggy met us driven by a white haired very independent boy who drove the horse as though it were a terribly fierce ramping white dragon – just to impress us – you know – We drove through lanes like great flowery loops with the sea below and huge gulls sailing over – or preening themselves upon the roof tiles until we came to this hotel which stands in its garden facing the open sea. It could not be a more enchanting position. The hotel is large, "utterly first class" – *dreadfully expensive* – It has a glassed in winter garden for bad weather with long chairs – a verandah – the garden hung between the sun and the sea. Anne had taken for me a really vast room with three windows all south – the sun comes in first thing in the morning until 3 in the afternoon. It is clean as a pin – gay – with a deep armchair – a bed with two mattresses – Just across the corridor is a 1st class bathroom with constant hot water & a lavatory so superb that it & the salle de bains might be part of a sanatorium. For everything (except the cream), for four meals a day served in my room – breakfast in bed – the extra meat & so on it is 4½ guineas. There! I know its dreadful – I cant possibly live here under £5 a week alors – & Ive only just four. But I think I ought to stay here at least until I am strong enough to look for another room because for a 'cure' it could not be better. The old servant unpacked for me, gave me hot water – took away my water bottil just now on her own & filled it – In fact, Bogey it *is* a sanatorium without being one – as it were. The manageress gets the butter – so I am sending mine back to you. You see its included here – And will you please send my *sugar card*? Shell get me that, too. I think its easiest. She says she'll give me butter at each meal & ½ pint milk at each meal – ¼ of butter every two days!! Dont you think I ought to stay here – just at first & get a stronger girl? I know its hugely dear but I feel it is right – that I will get well quicker here than elsewhere. All is so clean and attended to. Anne had arranged everything, of course, & filled the room with flowers – She has just walked across to say 'goodnight'. She really *is* wonderful down here – like part of the spring – radiant with life. Its ten oclock – I am going to bed. My room has all the sea spread before it – Now with the blinds down there floats in the old old sound – which really makes me very very sad – It makes me feel what a blind, dreadful – losing & finding affair our life has been – just lately – with how few golden moments – how little little rest. But I am not across the water & you are coming down for your holiday – *next month*. It is agony to be away from you but what must be – must be – Forgive me if I have been – what was it? Ive forgotten. I find it *so* hard to be ill – But ah! if you knew how I loved you and am for ever your loving

wife

MS ATL. *LKM* I. 164–7; *LJMM*, 246–9.

[1] A phrase from Shelley's poem 'The Question', which she had quoted to Murry in a letter on 18 Feb.

[2] Anne Estelle Drey was staying near by and had arranged KM's hotel booking.

To J. M. Murry, [18 May 1918]

[Headland Hotel, Looe, Cornwall]
10.30 Saturday morning. In bed.
Having 'slept in it' I am convinced that this place is what the South of

France should have been – so still and warm and bright. The early sun woke me pouring into the room – & I looked out & there were the little fishing boats with red sails and rowboats in which the rower *stood* – in the familiar way. Rib was wide awake. He looks such a grub down here – poor darling – after his long dip in filthy London –

The old woman who looks after me is about 106, nimble and small, with the loveliest *skin* – pink rubbed over cream – & she has blue eyes & white hair and *one tooth*, a sort of family monument to all the 31 departed ones – Her soft Cornish cream voice is a delight and when she told me "there do be a *handsome* hot bath for ee" – I felt that I *had* given a little bit of myself to Cornwall after all, and that little bit was a traveller returned – I had the hot bath & nipped back into bed for breakfast. (I should have brought Charles [Lamb] rather than Dorothy [Wordsworth].) Breakfast was – porridge – a grilled mackerel – most excellent – four bits of toast, butter, homemade wintercrack jam – cream *ad lib* & coffee with ½ pint hot milk – all on a winking bright tray – So there!

I shant get up till 12 any day & then I shall just sit in the sun and read – The Three Windows are wide open now – one is almost *on* the sea –

This is only a note darling. Do you know what guelder roses are? Big sumptuous white clusters with a green light upon them – We must grow them –

Yes, as far as *I* am concerned & except for the expense – all is as well as it could possibly be – But there is a great dull ache in my heart at the thought of you – a prisoner in that vile city. I see you – so pale – always half dead with fatigue – exhausted. But you *will* rest more now the infernal worry of me is gone – won't you? If only I could feel you were a little bit *easier* – Why aren't *you* here! *You* want this just as much as I. You *will* tell me the truth about yourself & *not* spare me because I am 'ill'. That, Boge, I couldn't forgive – And *do* darling heart – try and rest a little – read a little poetry – lie down on the stickleback [sofa] and think about the Heron – And give me any books to review – I can do them well here – Thank God I am not across the water – Goodbye for now my precious.

[*no signature*]

MS ATL. *LKM* I. 167–8; *LJMM*, 249–50.

To J. M. Murry, [19 May 1918]

[Headland Hotel, Looe, Cornwall]
Sunday morning

Dear Love

Your wire came yesterday between two and three and made you feel near. Now I want a letter – of course – for I am un enfant trop gaté – yes always –

When I got up yesterday I sat in my long chair in a kind of pleasant daze – never moved – *slept* and really did not wake until tea when I opened Dorothy Wordsworth and read on steadily for a long time. The air is heavenly – but don't imagine I walk or lift anything or even move more than I need. I cant even if I would – for the least effort makes me cough & coughing is such a fiendish devilish pain that Id lie like a mummy to avoid it. However – the divine sea is here, the haze & brightness mingled. I stare at that & wonder about the gulls – and wonder why I must be ill. All the people who pass are so well – so ruddy – They walk or run if they have a mind – or row past in little boats. Perhaps the curse will lift one day –

This place is very good for *just now*. You see I am going to stay in bed all day – not going to move – and all is done for me – so pleasantly by the old 'un. She came in early & threw open my windows at the bottom – and said the air was better than medicine – which it is – and yesterday she patted my cushion & said I must try and gather up a little *harn*ful of strength. I am always *astonished amazed* that people should be kind. It makes me want to weep – you know – Its dreadfully upsetting, Bogey – What! can it be they have a *heart*! They are not playing a trick on me – not 'having me on' & ready to burst their sides at my innocence?

Anne & Drey came in last evening with an armful of those yellow irises that grew in the Marsh near Hockings Farm. They had been picnicking in the woods all day among the bluebells & were very burnt and happy – Anne must be doing *some* kind of good work, for I can feel her state of mind – a sort of *still* radiant joy which sits in her bosom –

There pipes a blackbird – & the waves chime. Would that you were here – yet, perhaps – better not. I try you too much – This is God's final joke – that even I should weigh you down – fall on you – like a dreadfully incredibly heavy sparrow – my darling, & take still more of your precious life & energy –

Try & take care of yourself & see Johnny now & then. He, I know, loves you –

Yours for ever.
[*no signature*]

MS ATL. *LKM* I. 168–9; *LJMM*, 250–1.

To J. M. Murry, [20 May 1918]

[Headland Hotel, Looe, Cornwall]
You know the last three days I was in London I had pleurisy. This doctor says I have got over the worst of the attack & have only to lie still today & tomorrow & I shall feel *much better* again. I believe that.
Monday. A gorgeous day – I really might be *on* the sea.
Dear Love

Certainly yesterday had a Big Black Cap on it, but here is dawning another blue day & I feel better – really better. Yesterday this *pain* was very dreadful and then I had the most trying fits of weeping – I was simply swept away by them – I think it was the fever – made me so feeble & wretched. Just as I had written you another *farewell* letter Anne came in, with a picture for me. And she thereupon took charge – & soon the whole hotel seemed to be off. My bed was made, boiling bottles appeared, hot milk, a shade out of an orange bag she put on the gas – & sent for the doctor – all in the most ideal cheerful manner – The doctor came at 11 p.m. the whole place shut up, of course – He is – or appeared to be about 19 – but I am sure 19 times as intelligent as Longhurst.[1] A wild Irish boy with curly hair & eyes which still remember what the world looked like at 9. He spent about an hour walking over the worn old battlefield with his stethescope – & saying – like Gordon [Campbell][2] "*wait now*". Finally decided my left lung is *pleuritic* again for the present and that is what gives it the pain – I must stay in bed – but I could not be in a better place – A man came down here in precisely my condition & in a month he had gained a *stone* and was a changed creature in every way – Anne, poor darling, was waiting downstairs to hear the verdict – It was midnight before she left & the manageress left me the Thermos flask half full of boiling milk for the night. In fact they are one and all amazingly kind. So here I am, in my bed again, but breathing the sea and the sun & *Anne*. The baby doctor is coming again today – He made me feel like an old writing woman – a sort of old Georges Sand tossed up by the tide last night. Once I can get over this attack of pleurisy I know I shall get really well. I feel it – & I keep hearing about all the wonders in the woods & fields – – –

This is an appalingly *dull* little note, my treasure – But you know what one feels like. My skull and crossbones effusion of yesterday I have destroyed – But my head is a pillowcase until I have heard from you – As soon as I am well enough I am going out sailing with these fishermen that I see from the window – So different from France – Here one longs to be *on* the *sea*.

Yours for ever. Wig.

I have still got the feeling that this place is absolutely marvellous even though I havent seen it.

MS ATL. *LKM* I. 169–70; *LJMM*, 251–2.

¹ Sidney Herbert Longhurst, who had been treating her in London.
² Husband of KM's friend, Beatrice.

To J. M. Murry, [20 May 1918]

[Headland Hotel, Looe, Cornwall]
Monday

Darling little husband

Drey has brought me your Friday letter – & it is a sad one – Yes, you feel – oh – like I do – and what – of all other things – seems so hard is how we swore *not* to let each other go again – & then how soon – – – we were gone –¹ Yesterday, thinking of all this in the afternoon I wept so – I could not bear it. I thought I must come back & *die* there rather than always this living apart. But now that I am stronger today I feel that all may *yet* be well – & the Heron – now I am away from London is so clear & perfect. Try & look after yourself for my sake: try & *eat* and try & *be happy* – I opened this letter to say Anne & Drey have both been here – & the doctor, too. He says I am getting on all right. I must stay in bed for the present – & I must take cod liver oil & iron mixed!! He is just like a student in a Tchekhov book – But he promises me that as soon as my left lung calms down I can go out & drive – and sit on the beach. Oh – such glorious prospecks! Anne is being perfect – I am *eating* all I see & milk 4 times a day & butter & cream. Bacon for breakfast, newlaid egg-wegs – The food is excellent.

Your own wife.

But you know, Bogey, *I shall always be homesick.*

Wig.

MS ATL. *LKM* I. 170; *LJMM*, 252–3.

¹ Murry had written on 17 May: 'When I got home this evening, I was very depressed. Somehow I couldn't reconcile myself to being alone again . . . .
But the depression didn't last long. I just thought how miserable I should have been if you had still been here in these rooms without a breath of air.' (Murry, 148.)

To Ida Baker, [20 May 1918]

Headland Hotel, | Looe. [Cornwall]

Dearest Jones

The maid who *do* be terrible sorry has let fall & broken my Thermos Flask. It was an awful blow to me, too, knowing what store my darling Jack set on it & was so proud of having thought of it & filled it and so. He *mustn't* know. Will you go to the Stores[1] & buy me another. This cost 8/- – it had a black cover. I suppose there is not more than one of its kind. The number is *109570*. Also I had arranged with the people here to give me ½ pint of boiling milk in mine for the night & that I must go without until the new one comes. It held a pint.

I cannot write about anything else my dear. I feel desperately ill, & in fiendish constant pain from my left lung. But the conditions here are perfect in every way & I am exquisitely cared for – But oh! the old saying: "There is no place like Home if you feel ill!" And I – I always find myself – *more* ill in *another* strange hotel. No wonder that awful room at Havre depressed me so! Write to me *please* & forget that we are not always what we sometimes so beautifully are & do keep an eye on Jack's wellbeing. It is appaling to be torn in half again – so soon –

Your Katie.

MS BL. Alpers 1953, 255.

[1] The Army and Navy Stores, Victoria Street, London.

To J. M. Murry, [20 and 21 May 1918]

[Headland Hotel, Looe, Cornwall]
Tuesday morning.

Dearest Love

I am to get up today – & I feel there is going to be a letter from you. (How dangerous these glad feelings are). Yesterday I found, in a copy of the Western Morning News that there had been a raid.[1] It made me dreadfully uneasy – it does still. I shall never conquer this *panic* I feel if you are near danger. How can I? I can only implore you to take every care – that's all. You *must* – you know. I am incredibly better really – for all this complete rest and food & sleep. I must have slept more than Ive been awake by a long chalk – Tomorrow the little young larned gentleman as the old 'un calls the doctor says I may go for a drive with Anne – & see all the butterflies and the hedges – Oh, she brings me bright bouquets that take the breath! We must have our Heron soon – Darling – you have no idea of all the treasure that still lies in Englands bosom – But even while I admire it its an effort not to *pitch* it out of the window because you are not here. Its just the same about everything. What you cant share I dont want – I keep looking out at the sea and thinking: thank God that don't separate us – There is not that to cross – One just gets into the train *this* end & tumbles out into the others arms – I am not taken in by this silky, smiling, purring monster outspread below my windows –

Darling Heart I am giving Drey the bit of butter you sent me down with (I cant write English today.) Souse it well in cold water & salt. Leave it in a pan of cold water & salt overnight & twill be as good as new – *Then* eat it! I eat everything – so you must not fail me –

Queer – I cant write letters any more – No, I cant. We have written *too* many – you know – Oh Bogey, I think it is *infernal* that we should be apart and yet I bring you nothing but anxiety and sorrow – so we *must* not be together. What an impasse! Sometimes I am so bewildered – utterly bewildered – as though I were caught in a cloud of rushing birds.

But I understand Wordsworth & his sister and Coleridge. They're fixed – they're true – they're calm –

And there you live – wearing yourself out in that bloody office – wearing yourself out in your rooms – spent – exhausted – No, its *unbearable* – Don't send me any money until I ask will you – precious? That is our compact. I can only beg you to try & keep well – & to get your holiday as soon as you can & to let me know the moment it is fixed –

Your true love Wig.

I have opened this to say the post has just been – I am *intensely* worried and surprised to receive nothing but that milk chit – Not a *word* even on the envelope – not a line! What can it mean? I had a letter from L. M. written on <u>Sunday</u> – so that means you have been silent 2 days. I must telegraph – You can imagine opening that envelope & finding not a word – not even love from Boge. Yes, if you *could* help it – it was cruel. But I am sure you couldn't. No, Bogey, Ill have faith till tomorrow and school my unquiet heart.

MS ATL. *LKM* I. 171; *LJMM*, 253–4.

[1] In the most severe air raid on London since the end of January, 37 persons were killed and 133 injured on the night of 19 May.

To J. M. Murry, [21 May 1918]

[Looe]

HOW IS YOUR COLD WORRIED NOT HAVING HEARD MURRY

Telegram ATL.

To J. M. Murry, [21 May 1918]

[Headland Hotel, Looe, Cornwall]
Tuesday afternoon.
(See that 'T'. It means it is dancing.)

My dearest Own

I sent that wire after seeing how awful the raid had been & then this afternoon came your two letters – your gay ones – & I am in touch with you again. My pen – is as though the ink flows through its veins again – just that. I will stay here then for the present. It is truly ideal – perfect room, bed, food and all arranged for me & served so decently & punctually – perfect attendance. Also I think my young doctor is about the best I could possibly get anywhere – Hes absolutely *our* generation you see, tremendously keen on this business and takes my case so intensely that Anne now feels hes the only man who *could* have such a grasp of it. She wont let me move or open a window without just running around to the surgery & asking . . .

I confess I feel better today than I have for MONTHS and I can breathe more easily. I have been up & out in the sun for half an hour – As soon as I am well enough the doctor is going to take me driving – on his rounds – but he wont let me drive at all yet – or do anything but sit in the sun – "Wait now!" he says "I can see the kind of woman you are. There's nothing but a pain like a knife that will put a stop to you" –

This place out in the sun today was a miracle of beauty – The sea & the coast line remind me curiously of New Zealand & my old servant is like an old woman down the Pelorus Sounds[1] – (my dream NZ & dream old woman, of course).

Anne has just brought me oranges & caramels & smiles and such a lovely flower picture – "My dear" she said "the idea just came to me – *sharp*, like a bite in a plate, you see – this is the place for Mansfield!" Can't you hear her? I have given Drey the butter. Now I am going to answer your numbers. (1) No, my precious. Dont send me the money now. I'll ask when I want it. I hope I shan't need so much. Its just *like you* to give like this – – – –

(2) It will be quite alright about the sugar.

(3) Dont send Lamb – but if I could have any anthology of English poetry – p. ex. a Pageant of English Poetry[2] – *or* any other – *at your leisure – No hurry –*

(4) I burn to review books. I shall do them well & promptly here & post the books back to you –

(5) Ill write every day of course & tell you more when I see more – I have only really opened my eyes wide after reading these two letters of yours.

(6) I wont climb a hill without a permit.

(7) Rib sends a kiss & if you can find him some orange & white striped bathing drawers he'll be obliged.

(8) Would you take cod liver oil & iron if I sent it you? Twice a day – after breakfast & dinner? It is better than malt. Its superb for the nerves – & is just what you need. Don't forget to answer this. Did you send Anne a prospectus?[3] I so want her to see one – I suppose Harrison[4] won't take my story. Wish he would –

As to the Armenian cushion – I shall be known by it. I feel Ill never go out without it – Its so dark & bright & perfect – I can see people at the Heron taking cushions into the garden and our children saying "no you can't take that one – its *hers*. He gave it to her."

There is a haze on the sea today from the heat – & a slow rocking swell – The fishing boats have hung out the fine tarred nets between the two masts of their boats. They look very exquisite.

You see I am just like a plant revived by your letters. I have just had *tea*. Thin bread & butter – gooseberry jam – cream & two fresh buns with SUGAR on the top – I must ask these people where they got the teapot: its very beautiful –

Yours for ever – your wife.

Wig.

MS ATL. *LKM* I. 171–3; *LJMM*, 254–6.

[1] At the north-eastern tip of the South Island, one passes through Pelorus Sound to reach Picton, where KM's Beauchamp grandparents had lived. As a child she had spent holidays at nearby Anakiwa.

[2] *A Pageant of English Poetry*, ed. Robert M. Leonard (1909).

[3] The Hogarth Press prospectus advertising *Prelude*.

[4] Austin Harrison (1873–1928) was the editor of the *English Review*. He published 'Bliss' in August 1918.

To Ida Baker, [21 May 1918]

Headland Hotel, | Looe | Cornwall

Dear Jones

Very many thanks for your letter. Do please go & see Jack as soon as you can and find out about his cold also how he looks and seems. It is *anguish* to be away from him, but as my presence seems to positively torture him – I suppose its the better of two horrors.

I feel a great deal better – & my pain is infinitely less – scarcely there. Of course mentally (here I am telling the truth again) I feel just like a fuchsia bud – cold, sealed up – hard – My hatred and contempt for Life and its ways overwhelms me – & all this beauty – *far* richer than the South – means – less than nothing – Id as soon – sooner in fact, hear the rag and bone man – Im being exquisitely cared for in every way. It is for all the world (& here I can see a grin on the face of life) a perfect sanatorium. But SO EXPENSIVE. So that is *that* – I wish I could say anything else, but I cant – and be sincere. You know the mood. I implore you *dont* spare me about Jacks condition. That would be *too* cruel.

Yours as ever Katie.

MS BL. *MLM*, 116.

To J. M. Murry, [22 May 1918]

[Headland Hotel, Looe, Cornwall]
Wednesday

Dearest

I think your Saturday letter came today – because yesterdays seemed later & yet you don't say a word about the Awful Raid. *This* one contained perfect letters to Papa & Janey[1] & the account of the Bush Fire[2] – which I hadn't seen – Pretty powerful! I am extremely glad to have this paper.

Yes, the letters to NZ are quite perfect – I am sending them back to you this morning. Another tropical morning – all the fishing boats out – I feel *extraordinarily* better – grace à cod liver oil & iron. (Youve got to take it, you know, or I shall stop.) I had a nightmare about L.M. last night. You know she *does* terrify me. I have got a 'complex' about her regard for me – I suppose I shall get over it – She isn't a werewolf – is it? Are *you* sure? The people here – the 'management' are really awfully decent to me, Bogey – I mean far more than they need be. I give a lot of trouble – (well its true I pay for it) but still – that dont account for their thoughtfulness – coming in every morning at about 7 to open my windows wide – & heating my last glass of milk at night – & always leaving me biscuits – The old 'un made me feel about *four* last night when she said, as she put my hot water down & I was going to bed – "come here while I unbutton ee" –

Anne & I have been sitting outside – she talking about the spring – She cant mention the flowers without her eyes just *cry over* as she says –

She brought me masses of pink lupins – terrifying flowers – but beautiful. This garden is so gay with real purple columbines and gillyflowers and marigolds – and early roses – At night a procession passes along the coast road of fine old sailors each with an enormous cabbage under his arm – it looks to be a *sea* cabbage – grown on their new allotments. They are beautiful, hale old men –

(She has just come outside my window – I wish I could draw her – She's a little beauty – See that queer kite shaped sail – Oh God! how I love boats!)

Darling this is just a note, sent with the letters – Eat all that extra ration of meat – eat *all* you can – as I do – God! this darling boat – swinging lazy with the tide – Give Fergusson my love – We *must* have a boat one day – Tell me as soon as you know about your holiday & try & eat fruit while the warm weather lasts – & remember what you are to me – Its no joke – My love seems all to be expressed in terms of food –

Everybody has a boat here. Little babies leap out of their mothers arms into sail boats instead of perambulators –

Goodbye for now my darling Boge

Wig.[3]

MS ATL. *LKM* I. 173–4; *LJMM*, 256–7.

[1] KM's nickname for her mother. Murry had sent on his letters to her parents for her approval.
[2] Murry had enclosed a clipping from the *New Zealand Times*. On 19 and 20 March a huge bushfire devastated the area around Raetihi, in the centre of the North Island. The smoke was so extensive that in Wellington, 150 miles to the south, the afternoon skies were blackened, and schools were closed.
[3] Immediately following this letter in *LKM*, 174, Murry included as a separate letter what was in fact a long note KM had made on a conversation with Mrs Honey.

To Dorothy Brett, [22 May 1918]

Headland Hotel, | Looe, | Cornwall.
Wednesday.

Dearest Brett

First there came a divine letter from you and then enough cowslips to make a chain from Garsington to London – with bluebells between. It is very lovely of you to do such things.

I wish I could have seen you again before you went to Scotland. BE SURE you see J.D.F[ergusson]'s show if you can. I popped in at the Private View and I thought it *wonderful* – I seem to spend nine-tenths of my life arriving at strange hotels, asking if I may go to bed, saying – "Would you mind filling my hot water bottle?" "Thanks very much; that is delicious" – and then lying still growing gradually familiar, as the light fades, with the Ugliest Wallpaper of All . . . This has been my programme since I arrived here last Friday with the tail-ends of another attack of pleurisy. However – its over again and I am up, sitting at *three* windows which positively hang over the sea, the sky and an infinite number of little ships – The sea is *real* sea – it rises and falls, makes a loud noise – has a long silky roll on it as though it purred – seems sometimes to climb half up into the sky – and you see the sail boats perched upon clouds like flying cherubs – and sometimes it is the colour of a greengage – and today it looks as though all the floor of it were covered with violets – If it weren't for the boats which are a distraction for the *drunken eye* I should become quite bedazzled and never turn my head from this 'vast expanse' as they say, again – I havent seen anything more of this place yet – Anne Rice, who is staying up in the village, says it is extremely beautiful – and "full of the most lovely drawing" – As soon as my knees do not melt backwards I shall go forth again – But tell Ottoline – will you – I have at last found – he whom we have all looked for so long and so ardently – THE doctor. He appeared at 11.30 p.m. on Saturday night – I felt they had gone up into the hills to fetch him away from his flocks and herds – He is – or looks about 18 – and is an irish peasant lad – very ardent – with curling hair – but, I suspect, a sort of natural genius. No nonsense about whispering '99' – or shouting '99' – He went over the old battlefield with his stethoscope – and said "I can see whats wrong with ye and the kind of woman ye are" – and immediately began to cure me – You can imagine he made me feel like a very old worn Georges Sand, washed up by the tide, with a pen behind each ear – But after the London quack – quacks – its a great relief –

Our time with Ottoline was a failure. We were both so ready for her – spiritually, you know what I mean? – But then she brought Philip. And Philip was not only as she said '*grim*' he lay back and yawned so loudly that each gasp took a little more of ones real self away – It was awfully silly – a waste of time. He & Murry played politics and O. and I played *books* – That was what I felt. After she had gone I lay down in dismay and heard myself saying "How awful! How awful!" Perhaps it wasn't as bad as that but I felt it was – I feel it was another ghastly failure between us – And yet I *still* feel there is that between us – which if it were only *allowed* to flower – but it isn't – at present – Curse Life!

I have been reading Dorothy Wordsworth's journals[1] – She & 'William' & Coleridge had no end of a good time – but we could have a better. If we went jaunting off in a little painted cart or if we lay in the orchard & ate cherries – we should laugh more – we should have far more *fun. Should* – indeed. I mean *shall.*

Hallo! Here come two lovers, walking by the sea – she with a pinched in waist – a hat like a saucer turned upside down and 4/11¾d. velvet shoes, he with a sham panama & hat guard – cane – etc – his arm enfolding. Hideous – hideous beyond words. Walking between the sea and the sky – and his voice floats up to me: "Of course *occasional* tinned meat does not matter but a *perpetual* diet of tinned meat is bound to produce . . ." I am sure that the Lord loves them and that their seed will prosper & multiply for ever –

Send me darling Brett – if youve a mind a skirl of the bagpipes frae bonnie Scotland – I presume you will call in on Murry on your return in kilt, sporran, wee velvet jacket & tartan bow & be discovered by him dancing the sword dance in the waiting room –

I hereupon rise, and according to the Act of Parliament declare that – I love thee –

Tig.

MS Newberry.

---

[1] Dorothy Wordsworth (1771–1855), whose *Journals* (first published 1896) KM was reading in the two volumes edited by William Knight (1910).

To J. M. Murry, [23 May 1918]

[Headland Hotel, Looe, Cornwall]
Thursday – In bed. 11 am.

The old un has just brought your Monday night letter 'right up' – Your letters all arrive perfectly now. My wire was sent really – in a panic, because of that *cursed* raid – which you evidently in the 13th Corinth. manner 'winked at'[1] – the raid, I mean –

I dont worry. But for God's sake *dont* keep anything from me so that I shant worry – That is so appaling to think of.

Today I am going for a walk – down to the Surgery to be weighed. The weather has changed. It rained in the night & this morning the light is so uncertain – so exquisite – running silver over the sea.

An idea – – – –

Are you really only happy when I am not there? Can you conceive of yourself buying crimson roses and smiling at the flower woman if I were within 50 miles?[2] Isn't it true that, now, even though you are a prisoner, your time is your own. Even if you are 'lonely' you are not being 'driven distracted' – Do you remember when you put your handkerchief to your lips and turned away from me? And when you asked me if I still believed in the Heron? Is is true that if I were flourishing you would flourish ever so much more easily & abundantly without the strain & wear of my actual presence – We could write each other letters & send each other work & you would quite forget that I was 29 & brown – People would ask is she fair or dark & you'd answer in a kind of daze – 'oh I think her hair's yellow.'

Well – well – its not quite a perfect scheme. For I should have to hack off my parent stem *such* a branch – oh, such a branch that spreads over you and delights to shade you & to see you in dappled light & to refresh you & to carry you a (quite unremarked) sweet perfume – But it is NOT the same for you. You are always pale, exhausted, in a kind of anguish of set fatigue when I am by. Now I feel in your letters, this is lifting and you are breathing again – "She's away and she is famously 'alright' – Now I can get on."

Of course L. M. would keep us one remove from each other – She'd be a help that way – Did you reckon on that when you were so anxious to keep her. For of course, as you realised, Id have given her the chuck for ever after the Gwynne affair[3] if it hadn't been for your eagerness –

You are simply, incredibly perfect to me – You are always 'in advance' of ones most cherished hopes – dreams – of what a lover might be –

But whether I am not really *a curse* . . . I wonder –

Mrs Maufe's[4] letter was most lovely –

Goodbye for now, dearest Bogey.

Wig.[5]

MS ATL. *BTW*, 482–3; *LJMM*, 257–8.

---

[1] Not Corinthians, but Acts 17: 30: 'And the time of this ignorance God winked at; but now commandeth all men everywhere to repent.'

[2] Murry had written on 20 May: 'How can I tell you of the joy with which your letters have filled me? I feel gay, light-hearted, full of sun and air, utterly confident – everything that you would have me . . . .

. . . . I *could* not be happier than I am. And yet, strangely enough, when your train went out and I left the old station and plunged into the sunlight, I knew the good thing was going to happen . . . . Everything I did was a good thing, I made my Aunt better; I lifted my father out of his depression; I made the flower-woman laugh.' (Murry, 149.)

³ See letter to Ida Baker, of 8 June 1918 below, which may partly explain the 'affair' that had upset KM.

⁴ Gladys Maufe, her neighbour in Church Street. See *CLKM* I, 340, n. 1.

⁵ A slightly different draft of much of this letter is in one of KM's notebooks, and was published in the *Journal* 1954, 134–5:

(Draft)

Are you really, only happy when I am not there? Can you conceive of yourself buying crimson roses & smiling at the flower woman if I were within 50 miles of you? Isn't it true that then, even if you are a prisoner – your time is your own. Even if you are lonely you are not being 'driven distracted' – Do you remember when you put your handkerchief to your lips & turned away from me. In that instant you were utterly, utterly apart from me – and I have never felt quite the same since. Also – there was the evening when you asked me if I still believd in the Heron – Isn't it perhaps true that if I were 'flourishing' you would flourish – ever so much more easily and abundantly without the strain and wear of my presence – And we should send each other divine letters and divine 'work' – & you would quite forget that I was 29 & brown-eyed. People would ask – is she fair or dark & you'd say in a kind of daze – Oh I think her hair's pale yellow – Well – well its not quite a perfect scheme. For I should have to hack off my parent stem *such* a branch – oh such a branch that spreads over you & delights to shade you & to see you in dappled light and to refresh you and carry you a sweet (though quite unrecognised) perfume.

But it is *not* the same for you – you are always pale, exhausted, in an anguish of *set* anxiety as soon as I am near. Now, I feel in your letters, this is going – and you are breathing again. How sad it is! Yes, Ive a *shrewd* suspicion . . . . . .

Of course L. M. will keep us one remove from each other; she'll be a 'help' that way – Did you realise that when you were so anxious to keep her – For of course, as you know, Id have chucked her finally, after the Gwynne night if it hadn't been for your eagerness –

Notebook 12. ATL.

To J. M. Murry, [23 and 24 May 1918]

[Headland Hotel, Looe, Cornwall]
Thursday afternoon.

Dearest Bogey

This is just a note on my tomorrow's letter – while I remember. Please don't send me any money at all until I ask – this is of course including the £8 for June. IF I want that £8 I will ask¹ But don't send it otherwise. Stick it in your Bank. But the £1 for the belated Times Review² please send that to my Bank when you get it & tell me when it has been sent so that I can reckon on it being there. Also, in writing for cash – how do I *address* the Bank – inside & outside the envelope – & do I cross a cheque I send them – '*pay self*' do I cross that? I haven't got the Times book yet: Id be very glad to do it. I have just had, by the afternoon post your Wednesday letter. Thats good going – isn't it? I note that the elephant³ is still on the carpet though still couchant – You won't finally fix up without a last word to me – will you? And you talk as though I intend staying here until the *late autumn*. But I don't – dear – I *never* had such an intention. For one thing I couldn't bear this coast in summer – far too enervating – However that dont matter yet a while as Anne would say –

Its a windy *fluid* day – I cant walk in it but I have started working – another member of the Je ne Parle pas family, I fondly dream – Its a devastating idea.[4] However I am only, so to say, at the Heads, at Pencarrow Light House[5] with it – yet – not even *in* Cooks Straits & they look par-tic-u-larly rough & choppy.

Goodbye till my letter tomorrow. I have just had a note from L. M. I feel profoundly antagonistic to her – & how shes *waiting her hour*!! Its in every line – but "dont you be too sure, my lady" is what I want to say.

Friday morning in bed – Drey & Anne came last evening and we sat up late talking of Anne's life. She has had a great deal of rich variety & change in her life – far more than I'd known – You know she is an exceptional woman – so gay, so abundant, in full flower just now and really beautiful to watch. She is so healthy and you know when she is happy and working she has great personal 'allure' – physical 'allure' – I love watching her – Of course she is not in the least important. Its such strange weather – not warm – with big sighing puffs of wind – and the sea a steely glitter – At four oclock I got up and looked out of window. It was not dark – oh – so wonderful – I had forgotten such things – The old 'un has just brought the morning post – letters from Marie & Mack and Will Derry.[6] I expect yours will come this afternoon – I didn't expect it this morning. God! I do feel so hardhearted – I don't care a button for Chaddie's letter & yet – it was so charming – In fact I only want to *drop* all those people and *disappear* from their lives – utterly disappear –

I am so keen Bogey that you don't send me any money. You see I do want to live absolutely on my own money if I can, and even (ha ha! chorus of ravens) earn a bit rather than have it from you – As it is my illness has cost you an incredible number of armchairs and stair carpets and corner cupboards – almost, I should think – a hot water supply – Well, work as much as you like without overtiring your darling self, but work for the Heron but *not* for the poupée malade –

I must get up – I am afraid there are no flowers in this letter, dearest – I haven't any – Im shorn of them today – When I 'see' again Ill show you, too. I feel extraordinarily better and stronger with no pain at all, but I cant write you the letters I should like to because my 'vagrant self' is uppermost – & you dont really know her or want to know her.

I wonder what *is* going to happen. If the war will end in our lives – but even if it does end human beings will still be as vile as ever – I think there is something in the idea that children are born in sin, judging from the hateful little wretches who 'play' under my window somehow – horrible little toads – just as evil as slum children – just as mean as french children – I believe if they were left to themselves the strong ones would kill the weak 'uns – torture them – and jump on them until they were flat! Well, that's excusable in grownup people – but in children . . . ! Oh, people are ugly – I have such a contempt for them – How hideous they are – and what a mess they have made of everything. It can never be cleared up & I haven't the least desire to take even a feather duster to it. Let it be – & let it kill them – which it wont do – But oh (without conceit) where are ones playfellows? Who's going to call out and say I *want* you. Come and see what Ive made? No, one must have an iron shutter over ones heart. Now I *will* get up.

A toi.
Wig.

MS ATL. *LKM* I. 175–6; *LJMM*, 258–60.

[1] Murry had told her on 20 May that he was now paid an additional £8 monthly, and that he would send her this at the beginning of each month.

[2] KM's only identified review in *The Times Literary Supplement* is her notice of Paul Margueritte's *Pour Toi, Patrie* on 4 July 1918.

[3] The Elephant was the name KM and Murry gave to the tall grey house they later rented at 2 Portland Villas, East Heath Road, Hampstead.

[4] This is probably 'the first little chapter of my big story' which she sent to Murry on 2 June. He wrote back on 4 June saying he had received 'the first bit of "To the Last Moment" ' (ATL). KM did not complete the story, and Murry renamed this 'chapter' as 'The Scholarship' when he included it in *The Scrapbook of Katherine Mansfield* (1939), 93–100.

[5] A lighthouse on the eastern side of the entrance to Wellington Harbour.

[6] Her first cousin, the son of her maternal aunt Edith.

To J. M. Murry, [24 May 1918]

Don't sign anything till you get my registered letter

Telegram. Text from Murry letter 27 May 1918 (ATL).

To J. M. Murry, [24 May 1918]

[Headland Hotel, Looe, Cornwall]

Dearest Bogey

This is a final fling from me before we land the monster – –
Would it perhaps be better to cry off?[1] To tell the agents I have

been sent to a sanatorium – "suddenly worse" – &, until we have the Heron – to live like this – I to take "provisionally" furnished rooms in Hampstead where you could come for the week-ends. Such things are not too difficult to find – I should take them with attendance, of course – Then, when I wish to go to the country or the sea – je suis *absolument* libre. Moving, all we must buy, will completely exhaust our Heron money – of that there is NO doubt, and we cannot be in the least certain of getting it back. It will & it must be an infernal strain – L. M. will certainly cost £2 a week, but apart from that I really am frightened to take her for better and for worse –[2] My love for her is so divided by my extreme *hate* for her that I really think the latter has it. I feel shell stand between us – that you & she will be against me – That will be at its worst my feeling – I dont mean "simply" against me. I mean, of course, absurdly nonsensically abnormally subtly –

The other arrangement leaves you at 47 for the week but then you only sleep there – & it is quiet in the evenings for your work – The weekends we could always share. Then we are really saving for the Heron – not touching Heron money – I feel the elephant will be '47 in the kitchen' over again – in some degree – *with* L. M. J'ai peur – Don't you think perhaps it is the Heron or nothing? You see, your QUITE INDEPENDENT idea that we should be separate until the late autumn 'frees' me in thought. I think it is the right idea. Ill wander away this summer – & when I do go back Ill establish myself in rooms in Hampstead –

Please reply to this fully darling & *dont* hate me for it.

Wig.

[*Across top of letter*]
But of course I am ready to be persuaded – I write this because I must be honest – I *feel* it at the time – very strongly – Do you be dead honest too – then we'll understand.

MS ATL. *LJMM*, 262–3.

---

[1] Negotiations for 2 Portland Villas became complicated with KM and Murry each confused about the other's views, and to what extent renting the house would affect their long-term plans for the Heron. On 22 May Murry had written of 'The zest of accumulating money for the Heron, of showing your father that we are determined to be as independent as we can be', and that the agent for the house in Hampstead said 'that as far as he knows it's a certainty for us'. (Murry, 151, 152.)

[2] Part of the plan for taking the house was that Ida Baker should live there as companion–housekeeper. KM's attitude to her friend fluctuated considerably over the next ten days.

To Ida Baker, [24 May 1918]

[Headland Hotel, Looe, Cornwall]

D.J.   Ticket number 109570

Received letter, parcel and flask today. Have not opened flask & as soon as can get to P.O. will post it back – Thanks for the idea. But what I wanted was one from the Civil Service Supply Association Bedford Street Strand – a black one – holding 1 pint – cost 8/-. If these directions are not sufficient I will send *the* flask (my old one) to them & get them to do it for me. Please tell me. I wont until I hear from you. But I don't want your sisters. I can pay you as soon as can get to post office.

Yours
KMM.

MS (postcard) BL.

To Ottoline Morrell, [24 May 1918]

Headland House, | Looe, | Cornwall.

Dearest Ottoline

Yes, its you I want to write to – yes – you. For you alone will not only 'keep my secret' – oh, I feel you will so beautifully, so fully understand and respond – – –

I have been walking up and down this huge, bright, bare hotel bedroom, really, if one had looked through the 'spiritual' keyhole – wringing my hands – quite overcome, for the nth time by the *horror of life* – the sense that something is almost hopelessly wrong. What might be so divine is out of tune – or the instruments are all silent and nobody is going to play again. There *is* no concert for us. Isn't there? Is it all over? Is our desire and longing and eagerness – quite all that's left? Shall we sit here for ever in this immense wretched hall – waiting for the lights to go up – which will never go up?

Heavens! the hysterical joy with which Id greet the first faint squeakings of a tuning up – the lovely relief with which one would lean back and give oneself up and up to it. But no – I don't hear a sound – Its all very well to say like Koteliansky: "I am dead" but what the devil is the good of that with all this *fury* of living burning away in my bosom – with God knows nothing to feed it or fan it – just burning away –

But the ugliness – the ugliness of life – the intolerable corruption of it all – Ottoline. How is it to be borne? Today for the first time since I arrived, I went for a walk – Anne Rice has been telling me of the beauty of the spring – all the hedges one great flower, of the beauty of these little 'solid' white houses set in their blazing gardens – and the lovely hale old fishermen. But – the sea stank – great grey crabs scuttled over the rocks – all the little private paths and nooks had been fouled by human cattle – there were rags of newspaper in the hedges – the village is paved with *concrete* and as you passed the 'tiny solid white houses' a female voice yells: "you stop it or Ill lay a rope end across eë."

And then – *hotels*, you know, strange hotels! The horror of them – the grimace for service rendered – the perpetual "would you please bring up my letters as soon as the post arrives?" – another *strange bed* – and the mysterious people whom one always passes going to or coming from the lavatory . . .

Oh – how I *loathe* hotels. I know I shall die in one. I shall stand in front of a *crochet dressingtable cover*, pick up a long invisible hairpin left by the last 'lady' and die with disgust. Its almost funny – loving as I do, loving passionately, beautiful rooms, the shapes of furniture, colours, quiet, I find myself wandering eternally in rooms papered with birds, chrysanthemums in urns & bunches of ribbons, and furnished with fumed oak and lace curtains – and that *glare* from the windows – that dreadful gape which reaches to every corner – that sense of nowhere to hide! But all that is only part of the other, greater curse which is upon life – the curse of *loneliness* – I am quite certain that it is all wrong to live isolated and shut away as we do – never exchanging and renewing and giving AND receiving – There ought to be something fine and *gay* that we tossed about among us – and kept ever so thrillingly in the air, as it were, and never let fall – a *spirit* – But where is it, Ottoline, and who wants it? . . . I am in despair. In such despair that sometimes I begin weeping like a green girl – but that is no use, either. My tiny world tinkles: "Of course with all that sea and air outside and all that butter, milk and cream *in* you'll be as fit as a fiddle in no time." Which is altogether too simple.

Write to me – will you? I shall be here another week at any rate. Then I must wander somewhere else I think. This place is grotesquely expensive, too – But *write* to me – if you can –

I am always your very loving

Katherine –

MS Texas. *LKM* I. 176–7.

To J. M. Murry, [25 May 1918]

[Headland Hotel, Looe, Cornwall]
Saturday morning.

Dearest Bogey

When I got into bed last night & the wallpaper, the lace curtains & double washstand were all covered up by the dark the iron shutter went up and oh, my darling I began to think of you so tenderly – and to sehne nach dir – Were you awake & perhaps thinking about us? It was about half past eleven – I felt towards you as I often feel when we are in bed together – when we are curled up together, close & warm, and one of us says (its always me) "what do you see behind your eyes?" . . . You know?

Yesterday on my way to the post I met Pagello¹ & went off with him to the surgery. Such a queer place – so absolutely 'russian' – I mean as Tchekhov has described. It will walk into a story one day. It was warm windy weather – I made a 'tour' of the town – I pretend to Anne I like it and I do in so far that it satisfies my literary sense. It is very compact – ugly – the side streets are concreted over – There is a sense of black railings – & out of that *dear* little white house with the flowers comes a female voice – you stop thaat or I lay a rope across eë. Which is just what I expect of Cornwall. But Ill stay – I am determined to stay here for the present – until the end of June at any rate – And then I shall only go off to some other country place – perhaps – *certainly* not to London. I do hope you agree about the Elephant. Oh, I DONT want it or L. M. in it, melting bits of butter in glasses of milk & following you out on to the doorstep – "Oh Jack – you do still believe me – don't you?" I can see it – hear it –

I shant stay at this hotel after my fortnight is up, dearest. Anne & I are going to look for 2 rooms. For many reasons. This place is perfect when you are ill but its frightfully *bald* when you're not – Its too ladylike for me, too, and I am not a lady – & I want a sittingroom – I cant work, cant concentrate in this bedroom – Its too big and too glaring. Also that great blue gape at the windows dont mean anything to me – Perhaps it would if I looked at it from my cottage door. But Anne says (she agrees with me) there are excellent rooms to be had – with women who cook extremely well etc – I shall go looking this next week. This place has been perfect for its purpose but j'en ai assez. I want to WORK & its too hard, here. Each time I light a cigarette I feel a refined shudder come over this hotel – I will find something first chop, sunny with a view over the snug little town as well as the sea – It could be worth staring at – this little town. Now, you see why I dont want your £8. I must do this & its right & my *diet* goes on just the same – so theres no 'break' but if I were taking money from you I'd not feel quite free. Id feel you had given it to me for this place & no other etc. etc. True, I shant need it in any other. Which is all to the good – But that is not my primary reason for leaving here – je vous assure. And as youve no faith in me, dearest, Ill agree to take no place that Anne doesn't approve of. She, being American is "up to everything". Here comes the post. A blue envelope – you – enfin.

Yes, your Thursday letter. (Where HAS this idea come from that I am to be here *4* months.) I cannot grasp it. That funny sentence was me laying down your letter & simply shouting that in my amazement!! But our ideas have 'crossed' as usual – & I am thankful – oh more than thankful that there is a chance of getting out of the Elephant. Dont lets have the monster – I hate the idea – I DON'T WANT IT AT ALL.[2] Dont lets ever have a house in London. I am sure the whole idea is wrong. I will wire you again this morning. No, what is best for us both is for us to stay as we are – I shall as I said before, stay here till the end of June or July, then go to some more bracing place – wander about enfin & when I do come back to London I take a furnished place in Hampstead. It is idiotic I think for us to be together when I am in the least ill. Waste of energy. I realise that. And really – you are like a new being already – But for God's sake WORRY me if there is anything worrying. I am not a cow – I can't be a cow and worry *kept* from me makes me feel just like a mental. Don't "*hate* to worry me" – Its awful to read that –

Now for this last piece of paper Ill let all the rest go hang & to blazes and tell you I love you – that you are the most adorable darling boy who ever walked or rather rolled over the earth. There is no other creature in the desert of darkest Africa like you – And I adore you. Your poem with the decoration of lifebelts of love is perfect. *Youre* perfect.[3] Consider yourself kissed and hugged – & held and squeezed and half killed by Wig. In *this* world there are no houses – no wings – no war – only Wigs & Boges & other cherubim – Goodbye precious one.

Wig

MS ATL. *LKM* I. 178; cited *BTW*, 486; *LJMM*, 260–2.

---

[1] Considering the doctor's boyishness and nationality, which KM remarked on to Murry on 20 May, and her *penchant* for altering names, it is at least possible that Christopher Costello, a graduate of the National University, Dublin, in 1916, was practising as a locum in Looe.

[2] Murry's letter on 23 May gave details of the expenses they would meet if they took the house in Hampstead, but left the final decision to KM: 'if you think that you would do better to leave London for good, we'll somehow manage to drop the whole scheme for the present.' (ATL.)

[3] Murry concluded his letter on 23 May with a verse that ended:

'Oil of the cod and cream of the cow
Quiet and sunshine: this is how
Wig grows strong and makes her Bogē
A boy again instead of a fogē.'

To J. M. Murry, [26 May 1918]

[Headland Hotel, Looe, Cornwall]
Sunday

Dearest Bogey

I had a wire from you yesterday – Funny french it was by the time it reached here too – But it was awfully sweet of you to send it & you are *not* to feel your coeur declinéd. Now how can I prevent that? Prevent it I must. Look here! Ill go on writing truthfully to you because I can't 'pretend' (you *do*, a bit) but if my truth is melancholy & you feel gay just pretend it is all my I and pay it no serious attention – But I can't dance s'il ne joue pas – and you wouldn't have me just keep silent. Or would you? Tell me, darling –

Its true – the melancholy fit is on me, at present. But as I told you when I was in the S. of F. (seemed to be always telling poor you) that to be alone (i.e. without you) and to be utterly homeless, just uprooted as it were and tossed about on any old strange tide, is utterly horrible to me and always will be – even though I were 12 stone & a prize fighter – though I own my horror would be a bit ridiculous, then. However – I fully freely acknowledge that *its got to be* for the present and my only salvation lies in drowning my melancholy fit in a flood of work. Which aint impossible. But what about Anne? you ask. Oh, yes, of course I see Anne occasionally – as much as both of us want to – for an hour at a time, perhaps, but you know its all on the *awfully jolly* surface – I cant really talk to Anne, at all. Still its nice to have her here and shes a distraction and "too kind for words" . . . Passons outre.

Its Sunday. Cornwall in black with black thread gloves promenades on the edge of the sea – little tin bells ring & the Midday Joint is in the air. Pas de soleil. Low tide & the sea sounds to have got up very late & not found its voice yet. Damned queer thing. I have dreamed for two nights in succession of the name of a street *Rue Maidoc*. 'Not Rue Medoc' says Chummie, but *Rue Maidoc*. There is an exhibition of pictures there and Chummie is showing 3 – two landscapes & a portrait by Leslie H. Beauchamp. We idled down the street afterwards – arm in arm. It was very hot – He fanned himself with the catalogue. And he kept saying: 'Look, dear', and then we stopped, as one person, & looked for about 100 years and then went on again. I woke & heard the sea sounding in the dark – and my little watch raced round & round, & the watch was like a symbol of imbecile existence . . .

There is a Circulating Library here. Not quite bare. Its got In a German Pension and Eve's Ransom by Gissing.[1] I took out the second yesterday – Although, like all poor Gissings books its written with cold wet feet under a wet umbrella – I do feel that if his feet had been dry & the umbrella furled it would have been extremely good. As it is, the woman of the book is quite a little creation. The whole is badly put together, & there is so much which is entirely irrelevant – Hes very clumsy – very stiff and alas! poor wretch! almost all his 'richness' is eaten up by fogs, catarrh, Gower street, landladies with a suspicious eye, wet doorsteps, Euston Station. He must have had an infernal time. Ill send you back D[orothy] W[ordsworth]'s journal in a day or two, just in case you have a moment to glance into them – to refresh yourself with the sight of W. sticking peas & D. lying in the orchard with the linnets fluttering round her. Oh, they *did* have a good life.

Well, I am going to work down till lunch. Goodbye, dearest.

Toujours
Wig.

[Across top of letter]
Boge. Please dont forget to tell the moment Harrison sends my story back. Back it will come of course. But I want to know AT ONCE.

MS ATL. *LKM* I. 178–80; cited *BTW*, 486; *LJMM*, 263–4.

---

¹ The fiction of George Gissing (1857–1903) often drew on the poverty he had experienced himself. *Eve's Ransom* was published in 1895.

To J. M. Murry, [27 May 1918]

[Looe]

THREE LETTERS RECEIVED NOT LEAVING HEADLANDS IF YOU CAN MAKE YOUR TERMS TAKE ELEPHANT AND LESLEY WRITING FULLY BY LATER POST DONT WORRY DARLING FEELING SPLENDID SEVEN ELEVEN¹ FONDEST LOVE WIRE REPLY TIG

Telegram ATL.

---

¹ KM's weight, seven stone eleven pounds. She had put on two and a half pounds in her first week in Looe.

To J. M. Murry, [27 May 1918]

[Headland Hotel, Looe, Cornwall]

While you read this feel that my arms are round you & your head is hidden – & Im telling you it all – with every part of me.

Monday.

My dearest own

I think, reading your three letters this morning I suffered every atom that you suffered.¹ Nay, more, because it was I who inflicted it on you

– you who came crying to me & saying 'this is what you have done to me! This!' Even now I cant get calm & I am all torn to pieces by love and hideous remorse & regret. I must try & explain all this away & it is so difficult – so difficult – with these great clumsy words. I could do it were I to see you – in a moment – in a breath. Only *one thing*. Never never have I ever said to myself – "shut up shop take your love away". If you ever feel that dont tell me until you <u>do</u> take it away. It really nearly killed me. The sky – the whole world fell. Before I begin to speak – you must know that youre all life to me. God – havent all my letters said just that. Hasn't all my suffering & misery been just because of that, because of my terrible – exhausting – utterly INTENSE love. But you must have understood that? That was the whole why & wherefore –

You see, I was in the S. of F. from December till April. What was it like on the whole – just HELL. As you know it nearly killed me. Then I came back to rest with you. All my longings, all my desires, all my dreams & hopes had been just to be with you amen – to come back to my home. Bien! I came. Heard how ill I was, scarcely seem to have seen you – except through a mist of anxious – felt that ALL your idea was for me to get away into the country again – Well I understood that – although please try & realise the appaling blow it was to me to uproot again – & so soon – with hardly a word spoken – Please do try & realise that. Plus the knowledge that I was more ill than Id thought & that all my precious 'privacy', my love of 'self contained' life – doing all for myself in my own way – doing all – enfin for <u>you</u> was to be taken away from me – was 'bad' for me – enfin.

However it was only for a month or six weeks that I was to be alone. Then you came down for your holiday & we went back together – I arrived – & found I was to be here (without a word explaining why this change had been) at LEAST 4 months – until the *late* autumn – No word of your coming – no word of anything else. It was the sort of ultimate comble. It knocked me back onto my own lonely self. I was in despair as you know, and I saw Life quite differently. I felt that if all I had oh so passionately pleaded & protested without shame or fear about my love – my longing for married life – as soon as possible – was to be just delayed – not understood – I could endure no more – & I fell into the dark hollow which waits for me always – the old one – & I wrote from there – I felt he has not this same great devouring need of me that I have of him – He *can* exist apart from me. I have been in the S. of F. nearly four months & here is another four – He will never realise that I am only WELL when we are 'together' – All else is a mockery of health. I depend on him as a woman depends on a man & a child on its little playfellow, but he, as long as he knows I am alright, he can play 'apart' –

Now do you see a little bit? Is it a little bit clearer? But there is more to say.

Our marriage – You cannot imagine what that was to have meant to me. Its fantastic – I suppose. It was to have shone – apart from all else in my life – And it really was only part of the nightmare, after all. You never once held me in your arms & called me your wife. In fact the whole affair was like my silly birthday. I had to keep on making you remember it – – – –

And then – all the L. M. complex is – taking the reins out of my hands. I am to sit quiet & look at the country – I cant – I cant. Dont you know that LIFE – married Life with you – co-equal – *partners* – jealously alone – jealous of every other creature near – is what I want – I am jealous – jealous of our privacy – just like an eagle. If I felt that you & she discussed me even for my own good – Id have to fly out of the nest & dash myself on the rocks below.

My little Boge-husband, you dont know me even yet. I adore you & you only – I shall not take my love away ever – not even long after I am dead. Silly little button flowers will grow on my very grave with Bogey written on the petals . . . Do you understand now? (Maintenant, c'est moi qui pleure.)
There is my answer for ever to you.

Now about the Elephant.[2] Get it if you can & we will make it a Singing Elephant with all our hearts –

As I wired you this morning I am not going to leave this hotel after all. I cannot explain to another landlady that my lungs is weak – Also the fag of wondering what I shall order to eat would mean Id order nothing. Here it comes – one eats it – & its over. And they know me here, now, & are more than kind to me. The old 'un, Mrs Honey is 'pure Heron' – Bless her – I can always hear her & my Gran'ma talking as they put the linen away. So here I shall remain & I will take your money, please. Unless it leaves you short. I will take it from you – You must try & come here, as we did once arrange – even for a week & well have a sail boat and go 'whiffing for pollocks'.[3] I am working hard & Pagello says I have made remarkable great strides.

So now, please God let us be calm again. *I will not be sad.* Let us be calm. Let our love keep us quiet & safe – like two children in a great big quiet field – sitting there hidden in the flowers & grasses.
Oh, thou who hast all of my heart. Accept me –
I am simply for ever & ever your own little

Wig.

I have told the manageress I am staying for the whole of June – *at least.*

The books came & the cigarettes – thank you, love. Tell me all the practical things. Dont spare me – Tell me all the worries. They are my

RIGHT. I must have them & discuss them. You are NOT to have any worry *un*shared.

MS ATL. Cited *BTW*, 479; *LKM* I, 180–1; *LJMM*, 265–7.

¹ Murry's response to KM's letter of 23 May was amazement and hurt. He replied on 24 May, 'It's comic how with one letter I am left shivering & naked. This time I do feel lonely. You say it all so beautifully that you must have meant it as it was written . . . . Shut up shop, Boge Murry, take your love away. Good God, what a child. Crying, crying, crying. Are you really only happy when she's not there?' (Murry, 152–3.)

That same evening, in another letter, he wrote 'You see, worm, it's true that I *was* happy when you went away. I was so confident that the sun & food and Anne and the "absolutely ideal" place would make you well. I wanted you to go, because I could see that London was knocking you up absolutely . . . . I'm not a cow or a were-wolf, after all. I'm your lover.' (Murry, 153–4.)

² Murry told her that he had accepted the Hampstead house on certain conditions concerning renovations, but it was not too late to pull out. 'A new complication' was that the agent had said Murry's own flat was now re-let, although the agreement had yet to be signed.

³ Pollocks are a fish allied to the cod; to fish for them with a handline is called whiffing.

To J. M. Murry, [28 May 1918]

[Headland Hotel, Looe, Cornwall]
Tuesday

Dearest Bogey

I dont expect a letter today – or at any rate not before this afternoon & its very difficult to write before youve had my yesterday's letter explaining . . .

Its windy this morning & sunny & theres such a loud noise of gunfire: it sounds like a bombardment:¹ the house is shaking.

I wrote a great deal yesterday. Im fairly out at sea with my new story² – the same difficulties plague me as they did before – but it certainly 'goes'. Darling will you please ask Johnny for Je ne parle pas & put it with my other MSS. He don't want to read it. Why should he?

I had a TREMENDOUS letter from Ottoline yesterday, begging me to go down there & stay in the top flat of the bailiffs house, to have the woman to 'do' for me & to be absolutely 'free' – only if I did feel I must talk there was Brett and she – If you chose to come for every weekend it was entendu that you did not have to 'even see them' – This completely took me in & I longed to do it. I feel I *could* ignore them – the food problem was solved – wed have all our weekends together. But no – Ill stay here for June & accept no bounty from them. But she can write the most *brilliant convincing* letter. If you hadn't known her – after reading it – you'd burn to know her – to be her friend, her champion against everybody – For five minutes I am completely overcome – but not for more than five.

God! I do want to know so much that I cant know yet. About the Elephant, about your flat – How soon is it to be taken over? What will happen to our things? How can I wait to hear all this? If you are not too tired, try & tell me all – wont you, but don't tire yourself, my precious Boy. GO SLOW.

I sat up in bed last night writing until after one oclock – This new story has taken possession & now of course I cant go out without my notebook & I lean against rocks & stones making notes. I expect I shall be arrested in the course of a day or two. I think these people have an idea that darling Anne & I are spies – & you should have heard the postmistress yesterday asking if the word were *elephant*. Attendez! Bogey, I love you this morning with absolute rapture. Its a good thing you are not here – I'd be a perfect plague – But are these feelings the result of a hot bath, a big pink rose I'm wearing – a grenade (the strongest cigarette – heavyweight Spanish champion – Ive ever smoked) and a sunny wind? For in the course of this letter Ive got up & now I am wearing Feltie & just off to the post.

Ah, je t'aime. Je t'embrasse *bien bien* fort.

Wig.

MS ATL. *LKM* I. 181–2; *LJMM*, 267–8.

---

[1] On 27 May the Germans broke the Franco–British lines and took Chemins des Dames near Saissons, and the Allied positions from Flanders to the Somme came under intense shelling. On the morning of 28 May the French counter-attacked and partly regained their positions, while the Germans took several towns on the Aisne front.

[2] She is again referring to 'To the Last Moment'.

To Virginia Woolf, [29 May 1918]

Headland House, | Looe | Cornwall

Dear Virginia

Its of course for you and Leonard to use em or not, and as you don't like them[1] – why theres an end on't. But the blue paper with just the title on it would be nice: I hope you use that. Six or seven orders – what extreme minginess! I blush at the idea. I shall have to come back & persuade you & L. to let me sell it on a barrow – customers to bring their own wrappings. I thought of you at Asheham: I am glad it was so lovely. Don't forget that you have asked us for later – will you – I want you to know Murry – I want to say to M. confidential, after retiring – "don't you think they are extraordinarily nice?" This is rather generous of me, Virginia, realising as I jolly well do, how much L. dislikes me.[2] I really don't know anything about this place. While the Lord continues allowing his sun to shine in this superb fashion its heavenly – heavenly – To my drunk eyes it seems all Cornwall – not at all Devonshire – *far* better than the South of France – *the* place for great artists like ourselves to wander in – and so on – But Im frankly not sober. The tide comes in very big and brimming, goes out leaving heavy, weedy rocks and pools & little creeks and long sands & winkles. There are tiny islands covered with thick forest, valleys dipping down to the sea with marshes yellow with kingcups & irises. Then there is the little town, built on both banks of a deep river & joined by an extremely 'paintable' bridge. And seagulls – and flowers – and *so on*. (I wish I didn't keep saying and *so* on. I loathe the phrase.)

Well – Virginia if you would ask the Belgians to post me 4 packets of those Blue cigarettes cut my throat I will send you a postal order by return.

I wish I could send you something in this letter. There's that tiny little horseshoe I found yesterday – it would go into an envelope – No, you'd think it absurd – No, Ive nothing. Oh, did I say before how very greatly we enjoyed your Tchekov review?[3]

                                                                    KMM

MS Berg. *LKM* I. 183–4.

[1] Fergusson's woodcuts.
[2] Leonard Woolf later wrote in *Beginning Again* (1964), 204: 'I liked her, though I think she disliked me. She had a masklike face and she, more than Murry, seemed to be perpetually on her guard against a world which she assumed to be hostile .... By nature, I think, she was gay, cynical, amoral, ribald, witty. When we first knew her, she was extraordinarily amusing. I don't think anyone has ever made me laugh more than she did in those days.'
[3] Anticipated in her letter of 14 May.

To J. M. Murry, [29 May 1918]

[Headland Hotel, Looe, Cornwall]
Wednesday

Dearest of All

Your Tuesday letter written at the office is here – I have just exchanged my breakfast tray with a poor little sole's bone on it with the old un for it. (Here's pretty writing!) i dont know what to say about it.

> "If you read it once you must read it twice
> It will make *your* heart smell sweet & ni-ice."

as the lavender gypsies just dont sing. *Re* health (as Papa would say) I am really bonzer. I went for a walk yesterday – really a walk & today I feel better than ever & am going out in a boat. Are you coming down here at all? For a week? The manageress would board us bed us light us & clean our little shoes for £6½ the two of us. That is a monster room with a balcony. Well – just say. And you have not told me how to write to my bank so as I am extremely short I shall have to ask you for the June £8 by wire. You see Ive had a chemists bill as well as all these old extras.

I *want* that Elephant now. If it falls through we must try for a flat but there are no flats are there – And yes, if we could get another person clean & honest they'd be better than L. M. I feel – Because you see we can't treat her just as a housekeeper – & I *have* I must say this horror still even though I know its 'wrong' – I have to tear a delicate veil from my heart before I can speak to her – & I feel I oughtn't to tear it. Is that nonsense?

Darling love this is absolute Heronian weather – and I think our Heron must be somewhere near here – because it is so amazingly open – and healthy – And now that the black monkeys have folded up their little tents (I see *and* hear them) I am beginning to feel like Anne does about this place – Also now that I *can* walk & look over the walls —

Forty-nine sailing boats sailed 'into the roads' yesterday. I counted them for you – There they all were, skimming about – – – This place is 4 miles from Polperro – 10 from Fowey. You can go across country to Fowey in a Jingle. Anne & I mean to do it one day. But now – before I finish this letter I talk to you seriously and at length about 'our plans'. (See next page)

Grand Sérieux!

If we do not have L. M. one bother will be the moving. We shall absolutely need HER for that. Shes the only person to be trusted to pack all that is at 47 & to understand *where* that all shall go at the other place – Also, tied as you are, there must be a second person who can see to ALL sorts of various things, like measuring for curtains – buying the 'odd' things, ringing up the builders and so on. The *so on* is really very important. It is absolutely impossible for you to attend to this & your work. No strange woman could. She's the only one. But if we took her at all like that it would have to be for ever. We could not say – leave your factory. Do all this. Then find us a housekeeper & decamp. So what I think is this: now you & I know just *how* we want to live – just *how* we think about all of L. M. and you know what a jealous woman I am. I think that if we can overlook "all the other things" we ought to regard her as God-given & take her & if she don't like her position as a 'housekeeper & friend' – well – she can chuck it. But we shall find no-one like her for the first months. Phone her. See her. Tell her my letter to her is cancelled – & explain.[1] Will you?

She will understand. The devilish thing is that now I have told you *all* I feel about her – I feel that nothing would be simpler than for the three of us to live together in Harmony.

Tck! Now how long will you be at 47? What do you intend to do? And try, precious, in your *rushing* life (I know how few minutes you have) not to be done by the agents. They generally leave us roasted oh such a brown!

I have heard from Virginia who dislikes the [Fergusson] drawings very much. So does Leonard. Well, they would – wouldn't they? Its their press. I suppose they'd better not use them. Just a plain blue cover with Prelude on it. To Hell with other people's presses! Ill send you her letter, however – & Ill write to her & ask her to send you a proof of the cover – I don't want Roger Fly on it, at any rate. (That 'Fly' seems to me awfully funny. It must be the sun on my brain.) Dont bother to type Carnation. Let it be. Youve enough to do. I am of course in heaven that you liked it cos I did, too. And you 'understood' – I meant it to be 'delicate' – just that. Has a parcel from Lewis[2] with two little pantalons of mine turned up. Oh will you please send them to me?

Oh, my Boge, my precious own darling – Anne is painting me[3] & old Rib – Rib of course – is violently flattered & keeps flattening down his fringe at the thought. He is getting very brown. He is going to bring a tame shrimp HOME, please, he says. All my letter is just one thing – I love you – in every way – always – for ever –

I am yours eternally.
Tig.

Give Johnny a big hug from me.

MS ATL. *LKM* I. 182–3; *LJMM*, 268–70.

[1] Ida Baker destroyed this presumably unpleasant letter, as instructed by KM on 31 May.
[2] John Lewis and Son, tailors in Victoria Grove, Kensington.
[3] This painting, a different work from the one mentioned on 17 June, has not survived.

To J. M. Murry, [30 May 1918]

[Headland Hotel, Looe, Cornwall]
Thursday

Darling

This weather cant go on. It will stop just before you come. That's my awful fear. Ive *never* never known anything like it. And then I feel so well – eat, walk – went out to sea yesterday with an aged boy in a blue jersey & a straw hat with some sea pinks round the crown. His name was Pearrrrrn. Rib, of course when I got home, started walking on his hands & bursting with laughter. "Whats the matter Ribni?" "Your nose is peeling now" said he – Its true. I am as brown as a halfcaste. I do wish the Elephant would take our bun that we're offering so awfully anxiously[1] – don't you. Why does it go on waving its trunk in the air (I LOVE you). Blessings on thee, my beast – do let us go for a ride on you – Bogey & I, I with what the old 'un calls my red silk *parachute* hiding us both from the world.

I had a letter from L. M. today. Extremely sensible – and just carrying out exactly what I wrote *you* yesterday.

If you do come down here[2] & I do meet you at the station I think the Heavens will open. I don't dare to think about it. No, I hide the thought away – & just occasionally open the door a tiny bit, just enough to let a beam of light out – but oh, even *that's* so blinding. You see well go for picnics – Yesterday, I saw you, suddenly – lying on the grass & basking. And then I saw us sitting together on the rocks here with our feet in a pool – or perhaps two pools.

Ill do Gus Bofa[3] & Paul Margueritte on Sunday & post them on Monday. I cant go out on Sundays because I havent a Prayer book & Hymn Book to carry. The people would stone me.

Did I tell you they are building a lugger here? To the side of the bridge? To be launched in July – The carpenter and the carpenters boy think I am so funny that now when they see 'tis herr again' they become comedians & pretend to pour tar on each others heads or to swallow immense long nails & then take them out of their ears – you know the sort of thing. But this boat building is always a sort of *profession d'amour* for me. Its your boat – *our* boat they are building – & I am just keeping an eye on the workmen until the King comes down in a jersey & he & the Queen & Ribni the Infanta – sail away & away with a silk carpet for a sail – There is a sawmill here, too, which maketh a pleasant noise.

I hope I see Anne today for last night, after I came in I wrote 4 of those 'Poems' for our book. Ive discovered the form & the style, I think. They are not in verse nor vers libre – I cant do those things – They are in Prose –
(1) To a Butterfly
(2) Foils
(3) Le Regard
(4) Paddlers
You would like them. They are very light – like Heron feathers, so to say.[4]

God! God! This sun and air and Love. What is one to do with it? The walls of the Heron are so warm – But the pantry is very cool – &

the milk stands in a shallow pan – I went in there just now – How *can* there be a War Office and MI7d. I *must* get up & go out.

Ive found a little tiny horse shoe which I am going to nail on one of our doors. Shall I send it to you? No.

Sugar please.

I love you FAR more than ever.

Toujours
Wig.

Space left for LOVE

MS ATL. *LJMM*, 270–2.

---

¹ Murry explained on 27 May that he told the landlord they would take 2 Portland Villas, but 'I wanted £90 for decorations and . . . they must put a geyser in the bathroom.' (ATL.)

² He had wired on 28 May 'Wonderful Monday letter received moment Elephant decided whichever way by landlord coming. Boge.' (ATL.)

³ Murry reported on 27 May that the editor of the *Nation* wanted a review of Gus Bofa's recently published *Chez les Taubibs Croquis d'Hôpital*. KM's review did not appear, although Murry discussed the same book in *The Times Literary Supplement*, 8 August 1918.

⁴ The proposed book, with illustrations by Anne Estelle Drey, came to nothing. One of the poems mentioned here, 'To a Butterfly', appears in the *Journal* (1954), 151–2.

To J. M. Murry, [31 May 1918]

[Headland Hotel, Looe, Cornwall]
Friday

this is a rocket

these are stars & kisses

YES. see later

Dear Darling

No post. Bin and gone – I understand why there's none alright – I got your Wednesday letter yesterday, see – but all the same – – Oh, it is so *hot* too. Why aren't you here! Why didn't you arrive last night – so that we could have a pignig today. These are not real complaints, you understand – only laments for the impossible. Anne & I are going off for the day – she with her sketchbook & I with my writing book – & our *flasks* & sangwiches. She is going to bathe. The people here even are bouleversé by the weather & lovely day.

That is one immense wave which lifted me right up into the sun & down again. Mrs Honey brought me a letter after all! And the moment when I got it & saw your black writing on the blue – oh dear – does anyone know the meaning of rapture but me?

My adorable Bogey, Ill send the first long chapitre of my story[1] this week. Your letter has so FIRED me that I know Ill write like billyo today. Its just for you for you – (but I seem to have said that before).

I must answer your 'news'. I sigh still for a Definite Elephant. They ought to let you know this week. Do please send me Frankie-boy's letter.[2] I like him for that. But then I dont *hate* him at all. Now that I see all round him he astonishes and I like & pity him – & he does enormously feed one's literary appetite. How he beats that man in Raw Youth,[3] par exemple, & yet what a man he'd be in that espèce de livre.

Bechover[4] is terribly conceited – When he was *not* – before he was spoiled he was very nice – I mean as a boy. Youll have to see Landon,[5] of course (another subscriber to the H[ogarth] P[ress]) I am glad he wrote you. Oh, they'll find out, you know – all of them –

Ill be delighted to have Duhamel –[6]

Now Ive answered all – You know what I think about L. M. I am *for* her – definitely, in her defined capacity.

The £8 are extremely welcome – I just take them, like that, but you know my feelings about them & like the Reaper in Longfellows poem I mean to "give them all back again"[7] –

I met Palliser père[8] yesterday, & had a long talk. He says theres no place like this for my complaint – Its absolutely *the* spot. And he knows. He is a very very fine chap – what one would call – and sincerely, a 'glorious fellow' – I think. Anne don't see it at all. She doesn't even admire his appearance – But of course the fact that he & the Pa man were boys together does influence me. Queer when he called the Pa man *Hal* yesterday. He has three terrific gardens here – one on the cliff cultivated in the S. of F. manner. It is a most wonderful sight. I hope *I* see a great deal of this man. He can teach me a lot for the Heron – He says the climate about this region is superb in winter, even, too. It is cold – but it is bracing – & if there is sun – the sun is here – I wouldnt be surprised if Looe was our nearest town! Yes, you & Johnny & Palliser would hit it off, sitting idle & talking about boats & flowers –

Its such weather for Love – – – And my room has a balcony looking over the sea – I simply LONG for you – Precious darling boy – try not to overwork. I am getting so dreadfully young – a sort of Pelorus Sound[9] Wig – Rib & I seem about the same age again – He is wearing my coral necklace today –

There is my bath running. Mrs Honey says I must get up –

Ah, que je t'aime – do feel my love all about you – on hundreds of little fanning wings.

Ta femme
Wig.

MS ATL. *LKM* I. 184; *LJMM*, 272–3.

[1] The never completed 'To the Last Moment', referred to in her letter on 23–4 May, and again on 28 May.

[2] Murry had received a letter from Frank Harris about his recent poem in the *Nation*.

[3] KM is comparing Harris with Versilov in Dostoevsky's *Raw Youth* (1875), a character of rapid fluctuations between his pursuit of women and his high ideals.

[4] C. E. Bechofer-Roberts (1894–1949) was Murry's secretary at the War Office. He contributed to the *New Age*, and wrote a satirical novel, *Let's Begin Again* (1940).

[5] Philip Landon, a friend of Murry's from their Oxford days when they met through the Pater Society. Landon had written suggesting that they see each other again.

[6] Murry had recommended that she read 'Les Amours de Ponceau', one of the stories in Georges Duhamel's new collection *Civilisation 1914–17*.

[7] The second stanza of 'The Reaper and the Flowers' by Henry Wadsworth Longfellow:

> 'Shall I have naught that is fair?' saith he,
> 'Have naught but the bearded grain?
> Though the breath of these flowers is sweet to me,
> I will give them all back again.'

[8] Charles Palliser, a banking friend of her father's from New Zealand, who had retired in Cornwall.

[9] See letter 21 May 1918, n. 1.

To Ida Baker, [31 May 1918]

[Headland Hotel, Looe, Cornwall]

Dear Jones

Broken & unbroken Thermos flasks seem to be flying in the air between us. So its come to this – has it!

You sent me an Extraordinarily Fine letter today. Now *burn* my last & lets have the Elephant if we can & try & live in Har-mon-y.

I *cant* write letters just now, but I am not horrible either – simply I get *stuck* & cannot cannot write. So dont hate me if Im quiet – Its not because Im horrid, really not.

Yours for ever
Jo.[1]

MS BL.

¹ An echo from the music hall song by Bennett Scott and A. J. Mills, 1896:

> Darling Mabel
> Now I'm able
> To buy the happy home.
> Since they've raised my screw love
> I've enough for two love
> Will you marry?
> Do not tarry
> Answer yes or no,
> I remain with love and kisses
> Yours for ever Joe.

To J. M. Murry, [1 June 1918]

[Looe]

AGENTS LETTER HIGHEST DEGREE UNREASONABLE COMPLETELY DENIES FIRST OFFER¹ DONT CLOSE PREFER GO GARSINGTON END JUNE YOU TO COME WEEKENDS GIVE US TIME TO CONSIDER WIRE REPLY FONDEST LOVE TIG

Telegram ATL.

¹ The agents had rejected Murry's proposal on the amount the landlord should contribute to renovations. Murry wrote on 31 May that he was prepared to 'pay £50 towards the cost . . . and deduct it from the first two years rent. They must pay £40 . . . . I shall tell them at the same time that I must hear from you before I can confirm it.' (ATL.) KM was also concerned about the apparent duplicity she speaks of in her next letter.

Murry wired back when he received this telegram 'Plenty of time to consider will do nothing more till Monday fondest love Boge.' (ATL.)

To J. M. Murry, [1 June 1918]

[Headland Hotel, Looe, Cornwall]
Saturday

Bogey darling

It is another day the spit of yesterday – I think it is the end of the world – but not a Sullivan end.¹ No, the planet will fry rather than grow cold . . . Nine oclock. The room is bathed in sun. Ive just had bregglechick & I am *so hot* that I pine for a *cold shower*. Is it hot like this in London? Yesterday Anne & I took our lunch & tea and went off for the day – We found an ideal beach – really ideal – and the flowers on the way. Every blade – every twig has come into flower – Right down by the sea there are the foxgloves, sea pinks, dog daisies – I even found violets – and yellow irises everywhere – It was really almost too hot, exhausting. I crawled into a cavern & lived there a long time.

Then I went among the deep sea pools & watched the anemones and the frilled seaweed, and a limpet family on the march! By lunch time our sangwiches were frizzling – & Anne kept wishing her thermos flask had a great platter of ice cream in it, *my dear*. We had intended to work & we tried to but it wasn't possible. All day like a refrain my heart said – 'Oh if *he* were here!' This is the most astounding place. Where we were was absolutely deserted – It might have been an island & just behind us there were great woods & fields & may hedges – I got fearfully burned and tired too. I simply had to lie down with a stone for a pillow at one period but in the cool of the evening when we came home I felt refreshed again. Only I wanted to come back to a cottage & to say Bogey – would you cut a lettuce for supper? instead of a big hotel – It was still light – pale – wonderful – at ten o'clock last night & *very* warm –

This heat – in this place – you see – the water and country – is absolutely the ideal weather, I think. And as Anne says that terrible dust you get down south isn't here – All is *intensely* clean – dazzling – the seagulls glitter even when you are close to them down at the ferry – and all the old men are clean & fine as sailors are –

Old John Lewis' pants came in their fair box, thank you, darling & the Duhamel. I read the book last night. I thought it would 'help' me with Gus Bofa – And it has. He (Duhamel) is the most sympathetic frenchman I've ever read – I think he is really *great*[2] – Well, thats not a very illuminating remark. Its his *dignity* of *soul* which is so strange to find in a frenchman – You know what I mean? (Why don't the post come? I am sure those were his steps ten good minutes ago but there is no Mrs Honey with what I call my second breakfast. I wont write more until she comes.)

Later. I have just been to the post with a wire for you to catch you definite this morning – my own – First – your adorable letter!! 'Theres nothing to say.' Second – I hope you go to the country – just to fill your reine claude eyes with the himmlische grün. Third – *Elephanitis.* Bogey – there is a snag somewhere. Why did they [the agents] so *absolutely* definitely tell us that *all* would be done – Why did they tell me it took a few DAYS to reach the other Trustee who was abroad – & now – parait-il he's in India? Why did they say the house had just been sold & the new owners were prepared to do anything – they owned a great deal of property in Hampstead & money was really no object! they wanted a good tenant? This was told me definitely. Nobody nowadays is prepared to pay £90 for decorations & *then* be tied by a long lease – or even £50. Its absurd – Its ridiculous – in the highest degree – Its a pure case of bringing pressure to bear upon you because they see you are keen.

I am sure with every ounce of Father's brain that this is a *swin*. And further – I am extremely anxious that you shouldnt take cash out of the bank. We never know in these days when we may really dreadfully need it – & you cannot grind yourself to powder, you know, darling, darling boy – P.E. suppose Hampstead gets dished by air raids & we cant sublet when we want to – we should still be liable etc. etc. This whole affair is disgraceful, I consider – I propose –

That I accept Ottoline's offer of those top rooms in the Bailiffs cottage[3] – for July or longer, & you come down for weekends – We talk it all out – I am close at hand – We discuss it at leisure. Clive & Co. go hang.[4] We can afford to ignore them. They wouldn't touch me – I dont care a whistle for them all. I feel I would get into the very middle of a Bloomsbury tangi[5] and remain untouched – The great thing for these two children to do is to go slow – keep their tiny little heads – hold hands – not walk into spiders webs, & always have a small sit down before they decide to walk into parlours – see? Well, thats what I think.

Anne has just been to ask me to go whiffing all day – But I cant stand another of those days just yet – I am sitting on my balcony all day now under my parachute – feeling tree mendously well and fit & eating away & getting browner & browner – & I want to 'work' today – She – of course, says 'if youve got your health & you feel good – to H. with Art.' But elle est plus simple et rude pour moi. What a *deadly* bore poor old Drey is & what a *chump*. She gave me an article of his on Johnny's show & another on Gaudier. They were really disgracieux – Simply not only too silly – but they sinned against our idea – you know. I felt very – the french say it better – j'avais *honte*.

What about this Billingsgate trial? Is it going to topsy-turvy England into the sea – What Ultimate Cinema is this. It is very nauseating – I feel a great sympathy for Maud Allen[6] – but I have not seen much of the trial – only Daily News without tears.

I am eating all my rations here – & beginning to sleep even alone well – which is a triumph for me – Mais tout de même c'est pas l'même chose, tu sais – Goodbye for this moment dearest of all – Just before I go – embrasse-moi encore – I feel like nothing – nothing but a force of love – I feel the air round me quivers with love as the air outside quivers in the light –

Du *reste* je t'adore.

Ta Wigwife.

P S This letter is badly written & expressed: its the dancey light. Forgive it.

P P S I wont post it until I have an answer to my wire. 4.30. No answer yet, so I must let this go, dearest. Ive not moved from my balcony all day – If you could see the water – half green half a tender violet – & just moving – It is unbelievably exquisite. But it has changed my *morning* love into a sort of late afternoon love – something more thrilling and tender and – – –

MS ATL. *LKM* I. 185–6; *LJMM*, 273–6.

[1] Their friend J. W. N. Sullivan was knowledgeable about astronomy and physics, and theories of the end of the universe.

[2] See n. 6, 31 May.

[3] During KM's visit to Garsington in July 1917, Lady Ottoline offered her the use of a cottage on the estate. The offer had now been repeated, by letter on 25 May, as KM had told Murry (28 May above).

[4] Clive Bell, a conscientious objector, was employed by Philip Morrell as a farm labourer. KM disliked Bell after hearing from Virginia Woolf reports of his gossiping about her. See *CLKM* I. 372, n. 1.

[5] A Maori mourning ceremony.

[6] The *danseuse* Maud Allen, whom KM had admired for many years, brought a case of libel against Noel Pemberton Billing, Independent MP for East Herts. In a paper called the *Vigilante*, under an article titled 'The Cult of the Clitoris', Billing claimed that the audience at Maud Allen's private performance of Oscar Wilde's *Salome* was made up of individuals mentioned in the 'First 47,000'. This was a list which the Germans were said to possess, naming sexual perverts whose proclivities might be exploited by German agents. Billing conducted his own defence in front of Mr Justice Darling, and was found Not Guilty.

To J. M. Murry, 2 June [1918]

[Headland Hotel, Looe, Cornwall]
Sunday June the second

My Precious Boge

Voilà – encore un! Il fait plus chaud que jamais – et je suis décidée de ne pas sortir – Je reste alors sur le balcon ayant pour amie intime ma vieille tante Marthe (première visite depuis le mois de Janvier. Grande enthousiasme – de la part d'elle *seulement*.)[1] Si je savais mon chéri que vous etiez à la campagne – même à Garsington. Ce n'est pas de tout le jour pour chauffer la casserole – et je sais comme vous détestez Redcliffe Road – Bogey avez-vous l'idée de venir ici? Dites-moi. Parceque, depuis votre télégramme,[2] vaguement, chaque soir je vous attends – et quoique je peux attendre pour toujours tout de même c'est inquiétant de ne pas savoir vos projets.[3]

I don't know why I am writing pidgin french: perhaps because the english in the dining room sounds so *remote* from any tongue of mine. Its a cursed nuisance. Since this hotel has filled a bit they cannot serve my repasts (except breakfast) in my room & I have to descend to the common feeding ground – Dead serious – theres not a single person there under 65 & the oldest & most garrulous is 84. A more revolting, loathsome set of old guzzlers I cant imagine. Not only with their blown-out old bellies & clicking false teeth have they the appetites of proud fierce lions – but oh – and oh – and oh! Id better not talk about them. I sit at a table pushed up against the window – & try not to look or to HEAR. Theyll make a good story one of these days but thats grim comfort. I can *smell* them all up & down the passages now – But they are just as bad as the frenchies were – in the room next to mine at Bandol. In fact they are just exactly the same – & in the same state of pourriture.

Ive reviewed *Pour Toi Patrie* & copied out the first little chapter of my big story. Ill send it you tomorrow – *both* in fact in the big envelope – registered – Oh these old *horrors* downstairs. I know what they are like. They are exactly like blowflies – but exactly – in every way – They have unsettled me so. It is so infinitely hard for me to go among them – don't you know – & of course, being the particular kind of silly that I am I cannot help but listen and look – instead of splendidly ignoring them. I simply quiver with horror.

Late last evening I went off to the village to look for (vain quest) an orange – or an apple – or any kind of fruit. Neither were there any cigarettes except 2/1 for 25. Darling will you send me a few cigarettes or (better) ask L. M. to get another box of those grenades. They are very good really –

I *hate* Sundays. One thing I always miss you twenty times worse – & I feel the need of a *home* more & I hate being tossed from hotel to hotel worse – if possible on Sundays. *But do please let me know if you can whether you are coming here.* That is très important. I am still in favour of Garsington if the Elephant turns away . . . *Dont* lets be apart. It *is* such torture really. What is fine weather & what are columbines without you.

No, I am not what you call a good girl today – But please dont let it make you unhappy. Im an awfully loving one – only I am sad – I have seen another *horror* this feed time and I cant quite *fly* after it, but have to hang on a flower & try & forget it before my wings will spread again.

God knows how I adore you – & am for ever thine

Wig.

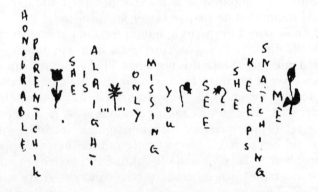

PC ATL. *LKM* I. 188–9; *LJMM*, 276–8.

[1] See letter of 23 Mar, n. 1.

[2] Murry's telegram of 28 May, telling her that he would come to Looe the moment a decision had been arrived at on the house.

[3] Translation of KM's 'pidgin french': 'Here you are – another! Its hotter than ever – and Ive decided not to go out – So Im staying on the balcony with my old aunt Martha for intimate company (first visit since January. Great enthusiasm – on her part *only*). If only I knew you were in the country – *mon chéri* – even at Garsington. It isnt at all the sort of day to be pot-boiling – and I know how you hate Redcliffe Road – Bogey are you thinking about coming here? Tell me. Because, ever since your telegram Ive been half expecting you every evening – and even though I could wait for ever, all the same its restless-making not to know what your plans are.'

To J. M. Murry, [2 June 1918]

[Headland Hotel, Looe, Cornwall]
Sunday afternoon

Are you writing to me today? You are in my mind so – in fact Im so filled to the brim with you – with the extraordinary (mild, silly word) thing that is happening to us that I cant write. No my pen refuses – Have you been living through what *Ive* been living through these last few weeks? I know you have. There is everything here – heavenly weather, birds shaped like the ocean, slow clouds, tufty flowers, but youre not – You are never to enjoy anything without me *never*. In fact when I go away from you I shall tie Ribni's sash over your eyes –

I am yours,
Tig.

MS ATL. *LJMM*, 278–9.

To J. M. Murry, [3 June 1918]

[Headland Hotel, Looe, Cornwall]
Monday

⎰ Ive two great big letters
⎱ 1 lb sugar
⎰ Frankies & Virginias.

Ill answer first – No, Before that even I shall just tell you that your letters are quite enough to turn any woman into an angel – They are the most celestial, glorious, inspiring, adorable letters that ever were penned. Rib says hes going to make a raft of one & punt off to London to fetch you – no paddle off – with an old toothbrush for a paddle "only see where the hairs have been nicely *finished off*" (I suppose he gets that from his father.) So if you *should* look out of window & see your darling winky one bobbing down below – haul him up, please – I *note* that you intend coming on the 21st. This note is such a bright joyful one that it keeps on echoing & sounding among the hills of Love . . . "Youll be glad to have him in your bed again" said Mrs Honey. I think the telegraph clerk here thinks I am a 'booky' with elephants for 'starters' (is that right?) I hope we shan't find Sir Andrew Fripp saying (see Billingsgate case) that interest in the large animals is a sign that one ought to be put away.[1] This case is a pretty exhibition – According to it Dostoevsky should be burned publicly in Trafalgar Square.

Oh – I must not *run on*.

Your calculations were so superb, so convincing that I had to send a wire in case my letter of Saturday in the slightest degree shook your enthusiasm – If we can take it on those terms & more or less live within that margin nothing can stop us[2] – And we shall have Bretts fowls & Rib will have a little cart with 2 chickens harnessed in it & go & meet you at the station & perhaps be allowed to drive your fountain pen home with him – or perhaps a 1d bunch of flowers for me. In that case of course the cart would be so full hed have to sit on the shafts (I am very silly – I can *not* be sensible today – Its your fault, too: its these letters – Bogey.)

I am sorry to say I dont care about Dillon. She dont interest me, somehow – I even feel her refusal was a kind of vanity.[3] Praps this is wrong of me – but there is something wrong with her face, a kind of *set pride* which is not the right kind of pride – But she's very young & I should not be intolerant – Ive noticed the same fault in her dancing too – the wrong kind of arrogance – Do you feel that?

Anne keeps asking me to do things I cant do. That picnic was a mistake – deadly tiring: Ill never go another till you come – She is as insensitive – as *brick red* as her neck. Here again I sound d—— cruel &

wicked – but its a fact – & of course her idea of literature is something like a lyrical bunch of bananas – This is very tiresome, you know – Elle est trop forte pour moi. Of course I *am* fond of her & so on – *not* changed – but – enfin – Ill never do a book to please her, because shes still at the *Blood & Guts* idea[4] – & how far away are we –

Frankie's letter (save the p.s. which was really very stupid and wrong of him to write) won me. Yes, it really did. He *does* know good poetry – & if someone says "that beautiful poem of Middleton Murry" I cannot help but lay down my sword & clasp his hand & ask him to come in & eat with me & is there anything I can do for him – I know, too – curious it is – that Frankie did appreciate that poem in the *right* way –

Oh, about Prelude – I really think they had better print both kinds – would it be an insult to Johnnie?[5] I dont want *not* to have the designs at all – after the prospectuses – but please decide this for me – I shall abide by what *you* think. I don't want to hurt Fergusson – but perhaps he wouldn't care.

Re CAT. Please buy a *wire* cover at the stores big enough to go over the milk jug and the meat & butter. Its a most useful thing for all times – & get Johnny to explain his butter cooler – will you? Oh, we *must* have a home. You cant go on like this. Think of standing at the foot of the stairs & calling Tig & me saying Hullo – & then me running down & you running up & us meeting like two comets – Why comets? They are positively the only things I can think of that meet.

Thats all for today – I am going to trust this non registré because its too hot & I am too fatiguée to walk to the Post – So if it does not arrive it will be a Tragedy – a black one – If you have not sent the cigarettes dont bother – dearest. Virginia sent me some today –

And now all my love again – ever so many more branches & flowers & leaves of it – without end –

From your own Wig.

MS ATL. *LJMM*, 279–80.

---

[1] On 31 May Sir Andrew Fripp, personal surgeon to King George V, appeared as a witness for Pemberton Billing in the celebrated trial.

[2] Murry's letter of 2 June (Murry 164–6) set out the details of his own and KM's financial positions, as well as presenting his argument for taking on the Elephant.

[3] Murry had passed on J. D. Fergusson's message that Kathleen Dillon, a gifted dance pupil of his mistress the choreographer Margaret Morris, turned down a job because she refused ' "to moderate her style". He said he wanted you particularly to know this because you had said it would make a difference if you knew that someone somewhere was sticking to this art business.' (Murry, 167.)

[4] KM is objecting that her friend's view of art has not changed since the days of *Rhythm*, when Murry issued his editorial call for 'guts and bloodiness'. See *CLKM* I, xiii.

[5] Her acceptance of the Woolfs' decision to use the Fergusson designs on only a few copies.

To J. M. Murry, [3 June 1918]

[Looe]

CALCULATIONS FIFTY POUND BASIS ENTIRELY CONVINCING[1] DO JUST WHAT
YOU THINK FIT ENTIRELY AGREE ABOUT DESIRABILITY SEVEN TWELVE[2]
FONDEST LOVE TIG

Telegram ATL.

[1] That is, for renovations to 2 Portland Villas.
[2] KM's weight.

To J. M. Murry, [3 and 4 June 1918]

[Headland Hotel, Looe, Cornwall]
Monday Evening.

Dearest of All

This is just a line because I feel lonely & want to talk. It is 'close on
dinner' as Mrs H. says so Ill soon have to sit among the fuzzies again.
Ive solved the tea problem – which I really could *not* stick (tea en
famille one big pot). I give my flask to the cook & she pours mine in &
then leaves it for me to descend for. I feel awfully like a spider going
down for a fly & bearing it off to eat in solitude. But it is a great idea. I
could not see those awful old claws among the bread and butter again.
Why do I *mind* uglies so? Mrs H funnily enough seems quite to
understand that I do – & talks as though she 'tended' them in their
cages – Well, I wish she did. My bregglechick in bed has become a
kind of gay feast – without em. I saw Anne today who wanted me to
go out but no – Ive spent the day up here – resting in my chair &
looking at the sea which has got quite rough. Now you can hear the
boats *creaking* in the roads & the waves sound eager –

Oh God! Suddenly it sweeps over me again. We are writers! You
are a great poet & I write stories – But how this knowledge makes me
ache for us to be together – –

I wonder what it meant – your telling me the story of Strawberry
Heart. For me it was something like this. We lay down together and it
grew dark & while we were there we wandered away to that country
you told me about – But curiously, there were moments when this
wandering was almost intolerably painful to me. I wanted to implore
you to stop. I felt Id *faint* if you went on & you went on and on. I lost –
absolutely – all sense of time & place – until it was like dying – like the
years one must go through before one dies – & then quite suddenly the
front door came back & there stood an old sniggering crone with long

long grey curls – curls past her waist – fumbling at the keyhole with a
bunch of keys & come to *spy* on us.[1]
GONG.

Well, thats over & I waylaid the waitress & took my coffee up here.
Praps they think Ive got a deserter sewed up in the mattress. And now
its cloudy & almost cold & all the ships have gone. No, Ill write no
more tonight. *I want you* & I want to pull up the tent pegs – I don't
like this ground any more. *Something smells.*

Tuesday (A New Nib.) If you could have known what an
inspiration your little 'chit' was. The post was late – I 'agreed' that I
couldn't hear from you this morning, & then down this fluttered – I
had been awake nearly all night, too. It was all so noisy & at 2 oclock
my french windows burst open – out popped the candle – the blinds
flapped like sails. As I rushed to the rescue I thought of that Appaling
moment when Kirillov rushed at Pyotr Stepanovitch.[2]Theres a big
Gale blowing this morning but its sunny –

But please don't say even in jest, my darling that you are *not* coming
down. Im only staying here because you are – Otherwise Id leave next
Monday morning & if you threaten again I certainly will. For some
curious reason (I cant explain) this is 'over' for me – I mean, my being
here by myself – Its finished – done with – It dont interest me a pin. Its
a marvellous place really – an incredible place – but Ive got cold to it
again – And this continual uncertainty about the Elephant! Not that I
want it hurried – good God no – but I do wish they would say yea or
nay – I want to put myself in it – & Im afraid to – in case they throw
me out – By myself its understood that I mean US, with every single
one of our possessions.

Note. (a) Need we *rush* into stair carpets? Foreigners dont – Champ
Connals[3] stairs were delightfully in their bones. (b) Why buy a geyser.
A big sort of stock pot with a tap on a gas ring (like those things in
Lyons) would surely cost a deal less & do the job. (c) Youre not to buy
things without ME – and please oh please dont let L. M. choose
ANYTHING. Her idea of me is so utterly absurd: its always
humiliating.

Jag: Wig. Are you disagreeable today?
Wig: No, Jag. But I feel that I am shut behind so many doors that you
cant hear me – And Im sad & exasperated – & the wind throws
everything about. Everything is flapping – even my thoughts & ideas.

But if we get into a quiet corner – a rabbit burrow – or creep under
a giant rhubarb leaf Ill lie still & look at you and you will find I am
really warm & loving – only tired of being away from the sight and
touch & look & sound & breath and ways of you –

Ich *sehne* nach dir.
Wig.

Has Harrison returned Bliss? I bet £100 Massingham wont print Carnation:[4] thats just 'by the way.' I <u>know</u> he would hate my mind.

MS ATL. *LKM* I. 189–91; *LJMM*, 281–3.

---

[1] Murry's review of a new edition of *Monsieur du Paur, Homme Public. Comme une Fantaisie*, by Paul-Jean Toulet (1867–1920), was to appear in *The Times Literary Supplement* on 18 July. He must have told KM the story of 'L'Etrange Royaume', one of the three tales in *Comme une Fantaisie*, before she left for Looe. It is an intricate *symboliste* story of Prince Coeur de Fraise and his love for his sister Maya, who frequently disappears for weeks at a time, and whom he once rescued from a hag who tried to abduct her. During one of her absences, he imagines that he sees her in a stream, and is borne down to an underworld kingdom where a series of adventures concludes in his marrying a princess. When Prince Strawberry Heart returns with her to the world of light, she dies. Her body disappears, and where she had lain, his sister now stands. With its similarities to Keats's *Endymion*, as well as its common fairy-tale motifs, KM seems to be unconsciously interpreting the tale as an allegory of separation and threat that has its affinities with her own life.

[2] Part III, Ch. 6, 2, in Dostoevsky's *The Possessed* (1872).

[3] An unidentified friend.

[4] Henry William Massingham (1860–1924), was editor of the *Nation* 1907–23. He published 'Carnation' on 7 September 1918.

To Ida Baker, [3 June 1918]

[Headland Hotel, Looe, Cornwall]

Dear Jones

I cant remember whether I wrote or intended to, to say that 'after all' I am in favour of the Elephant & of us three being there. It can I am sure not only be arranged but be a great joy. Yes, really –

And did I thank you for tea. It was a comfort – My bill for the week with my extra cream etc. was £5.13.8. Pretty staggering – Jones – I don't want any cigarettes – thanks dear – Virginia has sent me 6 packets of those Belgian ones from Richmond.

I feel ever so much better – <u>Hate</u> life more than ever – see MORE

CORRUPTION every day – & everybody seems to be evil & vile. Nearly everybody –

Still, one mustn't think – at least not aloud – But Life is a sorry disappointment, you know.

Yours
Katie.

[*Across top of letter*]
If the Nation publishes a story of mine called *Carnation* get Jack to let you read it. Its about College: Ive even put you in as Connie Baker! (Ruth Herrick[1] is coming down here –)

MS BL. *MLM*, 116–17.

¹ Ruth Herrick (1890–1983), a New Zealander who had been a fellow student at Queen's College, where as Ida Baker recalled, she 'became devoted to Katherine, perhaps too devoted' (*MLM*, 26). She later had a distinguished career with the Girl Guide Movement, and with the New Zealand Women's Armed Services during World War II.

To J. M. Murry, [5 June 1918]

[Headland Hotel, Looe, Cornwall]
Mittwoch. Die Hitze ist zurückgekommen.

Dearest. Your Monday night letter & ½ oz from Tuesday afternoon, & the Immensely Good Chinese poems¹ – (We ought to have that chap's book, you know. I think its notwendig to the Heron.)

The oranges will be positively thrilling. It is very lovely of you to send them: I do only hope they are not shudderingly dear. One really sighs for fruit here & its not to be had. Strawbugs are on the market – but teuer and they're no fun without sugar & cream –

Im much less depressed today, Bogey. Oh God I DO get black. I simply go dark as though I were a sort of landscape & the sun did not send one beam to me – only immense dark rolling clouds above that I am SURE will never lift. It is terrible – terrible. *How* terrible I could only 'put into writing' – & never say in a letter. This afternoon I am going to drive to Polperro with Anne – & we shall "boire du thé sur l'herbe fraiche". She came up to see me last night. She has quite the right idea about the country & living in it – I explained to her last night what I meant by *religion*. I feel awfully like a preacher sometimes – I really have a *gospel* – this seemed rather to startle her. Last night (this letter is like kalter Aufschnitt – please forgive it), I read The Well Beloved by Thomas Hardy.² It really is *appalingly bad simply rotten* – withered, boring and pretentious. This is very distressing. I thought it was going to be such a find & hugged it home from the library as though I were a girl of fifteen. Of course I wouldnt say this about it to another human being but you – c'est entendu – The style is so PREPOSTEROUS too. Ive noticed that before in Hardy occasionally – a pretentious, snobbish, schoolmaster vein (Lawrence echoes it) an "all about Berkley Square-ishness", too, and then to think as he does that it is the study of a temperament – I hope to God hes ashamed of it now at any rate. You wont like me writing like this about him – but dont you know the feeling. If a man is 'wonderful' – you want to fling up your arms & cry 'oh do *go on* being wonderful – don't be less wonderful.' (Which is unreasonable, of course.)

This happened yesterday.

Wig: (gets up from table & is followed by old white bearded monkey with bruised eyes & false teeth) Excuse me Modom, is thaat a New Zealand stone you are wearing.

W. yes.

O. M. Do you come from N.Z. may I ask.

W. Yes, I do.

O. M. Reely! From what part, may I enquire?

W. Wellington.

O. M. I know Wellington. (Shows false teeth) Do you know a Mr Charles William Smith a cousin of mine who was residing there in 1869.

W. – – –

O. M. But perhaps you were not born then.

W. (very faintly) No, I don't think I was.

Voilà for my grey hairs.

Oh how lovely these Chinese poems are. I shall carry them about with me as a sort of wavy branch all day – to hide behind – a fan –

I hope Ottoline turns up trumps.³ I feel *fond* of her just now. Go down if you can – do, my precious & refresh yourself. Dear Brett will keep the bad things away –

Its good, I think that I didn't meet Massingham who I am sure will not print Carnation – And please dont forget to tell me when Bliss comes back. I feel it is come. Thats why –

Goodbye for today my dear love – If you go to Garsington don't forget to let the Woolves know – + try & catch the Sunday post (if its not a bother) for then Ill get the letter on Monday – But if youd rather rest – I understand, my precious & will be happy to know it.

Your
Wig.

Was the review alright?

MS ATL. *LKM* I. 191–3; *LJMM*, 283–4.

---

¹ The *New Statesman*, 18 May 1918, published ten translations from the Chinese by Arthur Waley. His collection *A Hundred and Seventy Chinese Poems* came out the same year.

² Thomas Hardy, *The Well Beloved* (1897).

³ When Sullivan, his friend and colleague at the War Office, suffered a minor breakdown, Murry asked Lady Ottoline if he might take the cottage at Garsington she had offered to KM.

To Virginia Woolf, [6 June 1918]

Headland House, | Looe. | Cornwall.
Thursday.

Dear Virginia,

It was extraordinarily kind in you to have heard my prayer. Here (if its not stolen) is the P.O. That is right – isn't it? And now I have their address for next time: Admirable cigarettes.

I am very sorry to hear about your throat. What a very great bore for you – + not being able to smoke *or* talk. Oh dear – what's left in this lovely languorous weather – Do you sit at the window & sip cups of wine all day? I hope you'll "get better soon" –

How jolly about the Bluepaper[1] & Tristyan Edwards, too. Perhaps he will sail up the river to get his copy in a three masted brigantine with eleven sails.[2] But I am afraid not.

This place is still exquisite: I wish I felt more of a little lion than I do. However, its nice to sit on one's balcony under a campion-pink sun shade and stare at the sea and think what a wonderful business this writing business is. Ive been keeping a note book, too. Thats fun – but its rather lonely fun and it makes one feel a bit spinsterish, too. Its a form of Patience – almost.

Truth is – I miss Murry terribly – but he is coming down on the 20th for ten days and then I shall come back to London with him, *and* come & see you, if I may. (But please don't think I am a "sad old creature". I'm not.) Wish you were here. We'd have strawberries for tea. They come from Polperro, from little gardens overhanging the sea.

Goodbye for now
Katherine.

MS Berg. *LKM* I. 195–6.

[1] Virginia Woolf, whose letter does not survive, must have told KM of the blue covers the Hogarth Press intended for *Prelude*.
[2] One of the few advance subscribers for *Prelude* was a sailor.

To J. M. Murry, [6 June 1918]

[Headland Hotel, Looe, Cornwall]
Thursday

Dearest and Best of All

(As I write that the 'worm' who hears everything my pen says takes a sort of little pinging guitar out of his sleeve & begins to play – striking an attitude, you know, and rolling his eyes at me. He is a ribald wanton Worm and badly wants a beating *by* you.) I have just eaten a juicy, meaty orange – an orange that *hasn't* riped among soup squares and blotting paper like the ones down here. And theyre not only food for the body – they positively *flash* in my room – a pyramid of them, with, on either side, attending, a jar of the brightest, biggest vividest marigolds Ive ever seen. (Yesterday on m'a fait un cadeau from Mr Pallisers cliff garden – of spanish irises and marigolds – a boatload full) Its *very* warm. I have a letter from you saying the Elephant seems to want us – as did your telegram. (God how I love telegrams – I could live on them supplementé par oranges and eggs.) But I have so much to say that I *cant* begin. Let me dance my way through the flowery mazes of your letter again – until I get to (what's the place called in the middle of a maze where you stand on a little platform & look round?) Well, Im there now & standing on the top.

(1) They say there are superb *sales* here. We might jingle bells off to one when you're here – chairs, par exemple. Eh?

(2) I saw Pagello yesterday who gave me more cod and iron. He's satisfied with me & he says Ill always be a Light Weight Champion so don't expect me, darling Boge, to be a Heavy One. Jimmy Wilde is more my size than Jack Johnson.[1]

(3) Rib is glad you liked his letter. He was very incommoded by a pen – He writes with a brush made of mouse's whiskers as a rule – but you cant get them while the war's on.

(4) Nice lookout for Art when Billing is pelted with flowers and Lord A.D.[2] our conquering Hero. I feel very very sorry for poor Maud Allen –

(5) → Which is a very nice age. I LOVE you more than ever –

I am sending you some of my notebook today. Please let me know what you think of it. Ive been keeping it since I was here. Do you think the New Witness[3] might – – – ? Or am I getting a little 'fresh'. Heres a letter I got from Virginia, too, which is nice. We must try & find out who that man Edwards is. Useful.

Well, yesterday Anne & I went to Polperro. Its all my I, you know to go to places like Etaples & so on while these spots are here. Polperro is *amazing* – a bit spoiled by artists who have pitched garden suburb tents in and out among the lovely little black & white & gray houses – houses that might have been built *by* seagulls *for* seagulls. But you must see this yourself. Youll NOT believe it. I didn't & cant even now – It was a divine afternoon – foxgloves out everywhere. *AND* we found the most SUPERB fresh strawberries. Anne was a darling yesterday. You can imagine both of us at finding these – our excitement. We each bought a basket & had a basket put by for us to bring home AND arranged for the carrier (for 2d) to bring us fresh berries 3 times a week.

Wig: (feverishly) Will they last till 20th of this month.

Strawberry woman: "Why bless eë they be just a coming on."

They are grown there in gardens overhanging the sea. Anne & I took ours & ate them on the cliffs – ate a basket each (½ lb. 8d) & then each ate & drank our propre thé – and became 'quite hysterical' as she says – We could hardly move & stayed much longer than we had meant to – The whole afternoon in my memory is hung with swags of strawberries. We carried home our second baskets (just having 'one more occasionally') & talked about raspberries and cherries and plums – & tried not to say too often "when Murry comes". Looe is much more beautiful than Polperro. Polperro smells – like those Italian places do – & the people (families who have been there since the time of the Armada – that's true) are dark swarthy, rather sloven creatures. Looe is brilliantly clean – But dearest – it really is – you know – a place to have in one's inward eye. I saw Hugh W's cottage[4] but went no furder.

As I wrote that I have kept up a running fire with Mrs Honey. *She* says I ought to have children. 'It might make eë a deal stronger and they do be such taking little souls.' I agreed & asked her to order me half a dozen – The other night her husband 'waited' for her outside & she asked me to come & look at him – on the bal-*cony*. A fine, neat old man, walking a bit shaky – She said: 'He's dont look his age – do eë. He war a rare *haandsome* lad.' There is still love between these two: thats what attracts me to Mrs Honey.

Oh, dont forget to bring a bathing suit. The beach here – the beaches in fact are perfect for bathing or you can take Pengellys boat & bathe from that. At any rate you've got to bathe – I must ask Pagello if I can, too – otherwise I will sit on your cricket shirt under my parachute & wave a lily hand at your darling sleek head –

I wonder if you *feel* how I love you just *here now* – I wonder if you feel the *quality* of my love for you. I am carrying you with me wherever I go – especially as I lean over & look at the new boat – or read the names of the other boats. (There is one, pray tell Johnnie, which is called *The Right Idea*. But they have such lovely names: Harvest Home: A Ring of Bells.)

Tomorrow fortnight. It will be a real holiday – won't it?

(Dont tell L. M.) I eat marmalade puddings here – all kinds of boiled puddings. They are delicious – and these people give one *plenty* of sugar.

I ADORE YOU.

Oh what *can* I do – how *can* I tell you – Well here is your

Wigwife.

MS ATL. *LKM* I. 193–5; *LJMM*, 284–7.

[1] The American Jack Johnson was world heavyweight boxing champion 1910–15; Jimmy Wilde, an Englishman, was current world flyweight champion.

[2] After the conclusion to the trial on 4 June, when the jury acquitted Billing, both he and Lord Alfred Douglas, who had given evidence against the production of *Salome*, were cheered by a crowd of several thousand outside the Old Bailey.

[3] G. K. Chesterton (1874–1936) had taken over from his brother Cecil as editor of the *New*

Witness, a weekly which he described as 'passionately patriotic and pro-Ally, but emphatically opposed to the Jingoism of the *Daily Mail*' (*Autobiography*, 1936, 256).
    ⁴ The Cobbles, Polperro. The novelist Hugh Walpole in fact was in London attending the Maud Allen case.

To J. M. Murry, [7 June 1918]

[Headland Hotel, Looe, Cornwall]
Friday.

Darling Heart.

All the morning a thin fine mist-rain came spinning down – and the only people on the plage were the seagulls. I saw them (when I got out of bed for my cigarettes) standing on the wet lovely sand in rows waiting for the waves that came in heavy and reluctant and soft like *cream* waves – I never had such a bird's eye view of voluptuousness . . . Then Anne came, with some berries for me & sat on the bed & smoked and talked about hospitals in New York & the helpless feeling of the patient & the triumphant sensation of the nurses being a question of ANGLES. The patient being horizontal etc. etc. *Then* I had a hot bath and dressed and went across to East Looe & bought a shady chapeau (feltie is too hot.) The little hand glass had an emerald bow on it; it looked exactly like a cat. When I heard myself explaining to the girl – "the hat must appear to be painted on the head – *one* with the head an ensemble – not a projection, as it were" and saw her Cornish eyes gazing at me – *horrified*, I walked out – feeling very humbled. Everything smells so good – oh so good – & two men are lying on their backs painting the belly of 'The Good Fairy' – They are wearing green overalls & they are painting her bright red – The ferryman says we're in for another three months spell of fine weather – You will like him. His boat is called the *Annie*. He is particularly handsome & fine – though he has only one eye – and only one 'good' arm & that one ends in a thumbless hand – (He was blown up in that explosion – oh *yess*!) All the same he don't look in the least mutilated –

It is very warm now – 'soft' you know – Cornish weather, and the sea is half green half violet. I had a very large, commodious, tough old mutton chop for lunch while everybody else had a teeny little veau cutlet. This caused horrible bad blood –

Ladies: I wish I had thought to apply for *extra* rations. I could have – quaite easily with may health.

I pretended of course that it was divinely tender – melted in the mouth, & I tried to waft the choppishness of it in their direction.

No post today – not a sign – Mrs Honey promises there shall be one this afternoon. She has confided in the manageress: 'its in my heart and I must out with it. I *dearly love* my little fine leddy' – – Oh, if only she could be at the Heron with her 'little maidy' to help her – Shes only got one tooth and she's small with these rose cheeks & big soft blue eyes & white hair but how fond I am of her –

Now the tide is nearly high. Ive just been on the balcony. I heard a boat *hooting*. Its a queer little lugger with one orange sail and a tiny funnel. A man has put off from it in a boat – not rowing – standing up and – sort of deep sea punting along. The lugger is called the Eliza Mary & she comes from FY.

People have such funny names here – theres a man called Mutton and another called Crab. You must please take me into the Jolly Sailorman when you come down – Its so lovely I *must* see inside.

The post has come. Theres only this. 'Tis a book. Oh dear – it had a letter in it. This was simply *heavenly* – But why hasn't my letter come? I have been infinitely careful about the 1½d. Its just delayed, my darling love. But I know what it means to start the day without one. I am a sort of hollow cave until the letter comes – All day Ive waited for this – I shall talk over the elephant on a separate page & you must say yea yea and nay nay as you will – Its just suggestions – Talk them over with me wont you – You know – oh well Ill talk of that on the separate page.

One of my suggestions.

Shall I come up today (Friday) week for a week & discuss Elephant in all its bearings with you going as I know now how to go – *dead slow* & then shall we go to the Bailiffs Cottage [at Garsington] for your holiday? & I stay on there? We save a lot of money & a lot of mental energy this way. But on the other hand you don't see Looe. And I dont know which would be more of a holiday for you. But this is well considered before its written so dont FAIL to answer it.

Goodbye for today my Bogey
Wig.

[*Across top*]
If you agree to my 'suggestion' wire, will you love?

Suggestions for the Trappings of the Elephant.

I think front door, windy frames & gate a bright green. A house must be handsome to support blue – & green seems more in its period. But not a cooked spinach green – an 'emerald' green –

Kitchen and garden room & basement generally WHITE with all the woodwork & dresser a bright light BLUE – what they call *hyacinth* blue, I think. China and glass & food & fruit look so lovely with these 2 colours – Praps its Wedgewood blue. Do you know what I mean?

All the rest of the woodwork in the house is best WHITE – don't you feel? One can always paint a fireplace with flat ripolin if one wants to, later, but I think, coloured woodwork, unless one is going in for an immensely intensive colour scheme looks patchy. We'd better, I think then, put, as it were, a *white frame to the house* inside. This applies to the staircase, too.

For the hall & staircase – walls I suggest a good *grey*. Yellow ties one in the matter of a carpet & altogether grey with a purple carpet and *brass stair rods* which give the grey the 'gilt' it wants and drawings with a gilt frame or two – *or* one could have a blue staircarpet (lovely with grey). Grey is so kind to you as you come in – don't you think?

With all our furniture in my eye I really am inclined to say *grey* again for the huge big two in one studio. I don't know exactly why – but I am a bit 'off' yellow walls. I feel yellow wants introducing in curtains etc – but one can use purples, blues, reds, & greens with grey – & especially as youre so fond of *chintz*. Its the best background for it. However if you incline to yellow for the studio – c'est entendu. Again books are good against grey & inclined to go a bit muddy against yellow. Does that seem nonsense?

Id like my two rooms to be WHITE – quite white. Both of them.

I suggest for L. M. who of course must choose for herself GREEN – the green of my spongebag. All her bits of Rhodesian fur and everything would be lovely with green – all *tawny* colours, and the washstand set, par exemple. She ought not to have white I am *sure*. No – stop it – the room faces North – a really *deep* yellow? Its not a big room – But thats for her to say. Id STILL say green.

Why not have a little delicate flowery paper for your bedroom? If not Id have *pink* with white paint like we had at Acacia road. Oh that would be lovely wouldn't it? With coloured much patterned 'fruity' curtains – & your workroom Id have a deep cream – (with engravings of the poets against it.)

I hope this dont sound dull. But I have and so have you a horror of *patchiness*. People are so *patchy*, and I think one must most carefully avoid smacks in the eye. A cushion, or a bowl or a curtain are pleasant little flips but a door skirting board & mantelpiece are positive *blows*. I feel that the body of the house enfin ought to be *spring* – real spring & well put all the other seasons in it, in their time. But this absolutely nothing but 'suggestions'. You tell me, dearest, what you feel – and say if you think me a very dull little puppy –

Dont forget the kitchen range is broken.

To J. M. Murry, [8 June 1918]

[Headland Hotel, Looe, Cornwall]
Saturday

My precious Bogey

I have had a divine letter from you this morning writ on Thursday night.

No, dear love – God knows my 'blackness' does not come from anything in your letters. Truthfully, I think it comes from my health – – Its a part of my illness – just that. I feel 'ill' and I feel a longing longing for you: for our home our life and for a little baby. A very dark obscure frightening thing seems to rise up in my soul & *threaten* these desires – – – That is all. I know this will recur & when it is there I cannot put it away or even say this is *temporary* this is just because of so and so – – – No, again I am enveloped, and powerless to withstand it. So please try & understand when it comes. Its a queer affair – rather horrible – –

You will not always be a 'failure' even where the world is concerned, because we'll change the world. Fancy believing that & feeling as I do – all this hatred and contempt for human beings – all this desire to cut absolutely off from them. And of course I dont mean that well change the Daily Mirror world – but A world – OUR world and the world of Duhamel¹ is there and waits for us to give a sign. I believe that, profoundly. When we are in the Heron and of it there will come such a brightness and such a sweet light from it that all sorts of little travellers (young ones) will draw near. You see we have not shown ourselves yet – thats why we're unrecognised – shown ourselves in our completeness I mean and in our *strength*. Thats it. In our *strength* – thats what I mean. We have shown them our suffering (you have at any rate) but that is too hard for them yet. We have to show them our strength and our joy . . .

Bogey, my whole soul waits for the time when you and I shall be withdrawn from everybody – when we shall go into our own undiscovered darling country and dwell therein. That is the whole meaning & desire of life for me – I want nothing but you – and by you. I mean our home our child our trees and fruit our flowers our books – all our works for they are all contained in you & when I embrace you – all this treasure is in my arms – Oh God – that is so profoundly true – As I write my happiness brims up – Do you feel it? You are everything everything – and you are mine & I am yours.

After I had read Duhamel yesterday I went for a walk along the beach. My only thought was "what can I *send* him for his little child!" I must send him something. And then I picked up a tiny, exquisite shell – glittering with water & that seemed the perfect thing. Then as

I dreamed along Duhamel & his wife (she is *very* cloudy: I left her out – with her faults) and his boy came to stay with us at the Heron. And we three sat smoking and talking on the terrace while the little Duhamel walked about the garden with Dickie Murry & pointed to things & said 'Ils sont beaux' & Dickie said – a bit offhand – because they were all his '*I* like them.' This vision made me feel quite faint. I sat down on the shore – looking over the water – & I saw it all so plainly – & my heart trembled for our child. And I saw him a tiny baby – *very* serious – just awake and you leaned over him and after a good look at you he gave a funny little smile and waved his feet at you by mistake instead of his hands.

All this is true – true – as true as our love – as *infallible*. It will come to pass just as the Heron will come to pass – That I do *utterly* believe.

Later. I have just been to the post & sent you a "quite unnecessary" telegram.[2] I *had* to – otherwise my heart would have flown away. My room feels awfully quiet but the worm has gone off for the weekend with Anne. She fetched him this morning. She is doing a *Still Life* of him surrounded with marigolds. It *ought* to be lovely. She thinks he is "too perfect for worlds, *my dear*" & we are to have a sketch – Of course Rib was so flattered that he left me without a pang. Hes coming back on Monday – Anne is *more* than good to me Bogey, brings me fruit, flowers, & this morning a bottle of cider – & last evening some very superior chocolates – that Drey had sent her – She is infinitely generous, too, in looking after me.

Just remembered. It is her birthday on the *11th on Tuesday.* Do you think you could send her a wire? She'd appreciate it tremendously – if it wouldn't be a trouble for you, my darling. Tie a gnot in your handkerchief to remind you – Oh, I wish we were together this Saturday afternoon – I wish it DESPERATELY. I am so tired of not having you – Oh, its awful to want anyone as I do you – As of old, in France, I feel I *pine* for you today. Its a divine day, too. But you must be here to share it.

My darling Heart

I am your
Wigwife.

MS ATL. *LKM* I. 196–7; *BTW*, 486–7; *LJMM*, 290–2.

    [1] After reading *Civilisation 1914–17*, Murry was convinced that Georges Duhamel, the French doctor and novelist, was a kindred spirit. On 6 June he sent KM a copy of that week's *Mercure de France*, saying 'I want you to read the thing by Duhamel in it: "La Recherche de la Grâce." It seems to me very remarkable indeed that there should be another man not merely feeling what we feel, but using our words to express what he feels.' (ATL.)
    [2] This telegram does not survive, but its message can be gathered from Murry's writing that same evening 'From the words of your telegram "could I *conveniently* come?" and you'd quite understand if it were "undiplomatic" I have so far assumed that it isn't that you want me urgently. But now I come to think it over it seems to me quite likely that you do.' (Murry, 171.)

To Ida Baker, [8 June 1918]

[Headland Hotel, Looe, Cornwall]

Stricly Private. For you alone.

Jones dear

Do you know some good iron pills for anaemia? I have been taking cod liver oil & iron ever since I was here but it hasn't done me a scrap of good – and as I have had an awful bout of Aunt Martha I feel quite bloodless. (Excuse this frankness. *Don't* shudder.) Also *dead private* Ive lost 2 pounds weight – I suppose that [is] one up to you & Gwynne & your system – but it is not really. On the contrary. I know quite well why it is. I could cure myself absolutely – Its because I *am* in an institution – *not* in my own house, NOT at home – among strangers (of course not the strangers that you & Mr Gwynne would have chucked me among) but bad enough –

I do feel ghastly depressed at having lost weight – – & still to be in a Beau Rivage. After all my hatred of it. What a mockery! But IRON PILLS – if you know any – please Jones.

Katie.

Oh, arent you thankful you are not going to have dinner with 'me in this mood'!

It is not your duty, even in my "abnormal condition" to tell Jack – really not, dear.

MS BL. Alpers 1953, 258.

To J. M. Murry, [9 June 1918][1]

[Headland Hotel, Looe, Cornwall]
Sunday.

Precious darling

I have just been writing about Gus Bofa. Now I want to write to you. It all feels so different today; its been raining and 'tis loövely air as Mrs Honey says. No sun – rather cold – the curtains blowing – very very desolate & far away from everybody – 11500 miles away at least . . . Oh dear! I wish I were in London (but you'd be angry). I wish I could have some tea (but you wouldn't let me go into the kitchen). In the middle of *last* night I decided I couldn't stand – not another day – not another hour – but I have decided that so often. In France *and* in Looe. And have stood it. "So *that* proves", as they would say "it was a false alarm." It doesnt. Each time I have decided that I've died again – Talk about a pussy's nine lives: I must have 900. Nearly every night at 11 o'clock I begin wishing it were 11 a m. I walk up & down – look at the bed – look at the writing table – look in the glass & am frightened of that girl with burning eyes – think 'will my candle last until its light?'[2] & then sit for a long time *staring* at the carpet – *so* long that its only a fluke that one ever looks up again. And oh God! this terrifying idea that one must *die* & maybe *going* to die . . . The Clovelly Mansions, S[outh] of F[rance] writing 'a few last words' business . . . This will sound like exaggeration but it isn't. If you knew with what feelings I watch the last gleam of light fade! . . . If I could just stroll into your room – even if you were asleep & BE with you a moment – "all would be well." But I really have suffered such AGONIES from loneliness and illness combined that Ill never be quite whole again. I don't think Ill ever believe that they wont recur – that some grinning Fate wont suggest that I go away by myself to get well of something!! Of course externally & during the day one smiles and chats & says one has had a pretty rotten time, perhaps – but God! God! Tchekhov would understand: Dostoevsky wouldn't. Because he's never been in the same situation. Hes been poor and ill & worried but enfin – the wife *has* been there to sell her petticoat – or there has been a neighbour. He wouldn't be alone. But Tchekhov has known just EXACTLY this that I know. I discover it in his work – often.

I have discovered the ONLY TREATMENT for consumption It is NOT to cut the malade off from life: neither in a sanatorium nor in a land with milk rivers, butter mountains & cream valleys. One is just as bad as the other. Johnny Keats anchovy[3] has more nourishment than both together. <u>DONT YOU AGREE</u>???

However Ill cling to the rope & bob up & down until Friday week but not a day later. Look here! dear. Do please give me every bit of your attention just to hear this. I MUST NOT BE LEFT ALONE. Its not a case of L. M. or a trained nurse you know. Its different. But that really IS a cry for help. So do remember.

Your Wigwife.

This letter is not to make you sad. I expect my tomorrow's will appear to absolutely deny it. But it will not really. This *does* stand for all time & I *must* let you know.

MS ATL. *BTW*, 487–8; *LJMM*, 292–3.

---

[1] Murry found this letter – surely the 'interesting evidence' KM mentions on 10 June – sealed but unposted among her papers.

[2] Edna St Vincent Millay's 'First Fig' was published in *Poetry*, June 1918: 'My candle burns at both ends; | It will not last the night; | But ah, my foes, and oh, my friends, | It gives a lovely light.'

[3] A month before he died in Rome on 23 February 1821, Keats's diet was limited to a single anchovy a day, and a morsel of bread.

To Ida Baker, [9 June 1918]

[Headland Hotel, Looe, Cornwall]
Would you send me another box of those *Grenade* cigarettes if you can, as soon as you can. Failing them the Belgian Cigarette Co, 17 Hill street Richmond – if that is near you & possible to get at – their blue packets at 11d are so good. But the Grenades, dear, were delicious. Its a *rainy Sunday*. Id love to come to tea in your armoire . . . if you'd have

Katie.

Je reviens pour quelques jours le fin de Juin.

MS (postcard) BL.

To J. M. Murry, [10 June 1918]

[Headland Hotel, Looe, Cornwall]
Monday

Dearest Bogey

Heres my *third* letter. Ive torn up one attempt, kept another as 'interesting evidence' & this one Ill send. Its a process of clarifying . . . you know.

Truth is – it is one of my très mauvais jours – as bad as can be – Im filthy black – But whats the use of saying so? No use at all – It only 'confirms' me though in my determination not to spend another day here after you are gone – I could NOT stand it. Thats as much as Ill stay. Ill try & stick it until Friday week & no doubt I shall – but not a day more!! Tak por tak!

I think a letter of yours is lost. Here is your Friday letter (postmark Sat. 5.30 pm. W.C.) and a 'note' from Sunday. But you "pass over" my wire and my notebooks and the p.cs. or are all these things delayed at your end – or hadn't you time – you were too tired? Oh there are a thousand reasons. And enfin – the notebook wasn't grand' chose – postcards are a waste of money & the telegram was quite unnecessary – and out of the air – Still I would just "like to know" – Also would you try & remember to tell me if my review was alright?[1]

Thats very superb about the £13. Especially the recovery of last years[2] –

No, darling I shant buy anything on my own. No energy – I shall buy a bottle of Beaune however – because I feel I must take some stimulant regular – plus – the milk – cod liver oil iron etc – Wine that maketh glad the heart of man[3] – What heavenly words – Are they true – do you think? Then I shall be a drunkard – But they are not true.

Addio. Im in despair you see. Laissez moi. Let me wave my jade white hand & go. I love you *un*speakably – with a strong stress on the first syllable today.

Tig.

MS ATL. *LKM* I. 197; *LJMM*, 293–4.

[1] Her review of *Pour Toi, Patrie*.
[2] Murry had received a tax refund of £13 for the previous year, as well as hearing that the same amount would not be deducted in 1918 as he was entitled to £120 tax free on a salary of £400.
[3] Psalms. 104: 15.

To J. M. Murry, [11 June 1918]

[Headland Hotel, Looe, Cornwall]
See page 5 first – All this is stale now the 2nd post has come.

Tuesday.

Dear Bogey darling

It is quite obvious, upon this mornings showing that *several* of my letters have been lost in the post. And especially (1) the one with the tour of the Elephant interior in it. (2) My (Ill confess) rather precious 'Note Book' – of which I don't possess anything like another copy –

What has happened, at its very brightest and best is – that the post has been – that these treasures have been perhaps 'overweight' – there's been ∴ a 1d to pay and – naturally – no-one to pay it. So the postman has chucked them away. On the other hand one person in the house, either tops or bottoms, may have stolen 'em. Thats just as possible – in fact, very much more so.

This 'sort of thing', familiar oh – ever so familiar as one *is* with it is still devilishly wearing. So if they *do* turn up WILL YOU PLEASE LET ME KNOW. I mourn the Notebook – yes I *do* mourn that.

Perhaps you will understand *if if if* you get my letter this morning why I sent my so unreasonable wire.[1] That was the only explanation – Impatience. A profound dismay at the idea of holding out so long – a feeling that Id get cramp – or the waves would go over my head too often – or the rope would break – So, though I *know* & do absolutely realise youre hurrying as fast as your boat will sail you – I yet, simply couldnt help – lifting up my cowardly little voice & saying 'oh please do try to come faster'. You see a *fortnight* in London is so broken up into little bits, so shaken & scattered that it can be gathered up & held tight in the smallest little bag – (Bolo: What Monsieur is a million. A little pile like that . . .)[2] But a fortnight in MY world – (into which dearest dear you never will enter – even loving each other as we do) is a thing quite without beginning or end – You see 14 nights or 12 nights or 2 nights *can* be up the gathered meadow of Eternity & down again – There are hours, moments, glimpses when one cant face it, when one wants to stand with ones face in ones sleeves and just WAIL.

But. However. Having received your dear wire[3] and your darling letter Ill make the effort & succeed and on Friday week nous nous rencontrons à la gare.

I note, cher (how much more real Stepan Trofimovitch[4] is than – Johnny, for instance) I note cher that you "dined with the Woolves".[5] Do forgive my dreadfully persistent question – was there any sign of a blue cover?[6] I hate to ask you – for your tiredness comes in a great sigh of weariness through this letter, my own precious, and I do – oh – God! I do hate to add a jot to your present worry. So lay down your pen & *don't* answer captious Wig.

I fully, completely, absolutely understand about your holiday – consider my wire *un*sent. *Dont* – oh, my perfect one – *dont* try and come faster – come as you have arranged & we will be quiet together and look at (you at the boats) and I at you.

Mrs Honey: Theres another telegram come. Oh, how I wish I had delayed this mornings wire until I had your Monday night letter which wont arrive until tomorrow – might if a cherub was about be wafted me by the afternoons post – but *im*probably. I am so afraid youll take this – my morning wire as an answer to your Monday night letter. Will you understand that your Monday night letter cant have travelled so fast. One of your chiefest charms is one never knows *what* you are going to understand.

Doesnt Johnny know a woman who would tidy you while Mrs H. is ill? Make L. M. come across, too. She ought to be keeping an eye on you for me. She is behaving ROTTENLY. (What a brilliant success I am to be married to!! Curse me.)

Now I am going to read the Nation & finish this after the 2nd post – *just in case* theres something I must answer (there is, of course – your wire says youre waiting for an answer.)

1.30. Ive just had lunch *and* a glass of wine 'to it' and I have read the Nation. Your Civilisation review is excellent.[7] I, personally think your article on Gaudier[8] exceedingly, extremely good – very valuable, too – very well written – *discovered* thats the word I want. But – *warning*. You have mentioned his poverty & that he did the housework for his sister: that will perhaps infuriate some people – beginning with the sister. She is in London. By all accounts she is a very dangerous horrible woman of the Banks type[9] – and she may feel, you see, in her jealous almost insanely jealous way that youd no right to open that particular door to the public eye – THEY are not to know that he did the housework. See? So don't be surprised if she hits out. But *dont* answer her and *dont* see her. This is important, I am sure.

I have torn up & chucked into the waste paper basket all the work I have done these last few days . . . It was *hectic*. Mrs Honey brings me the afternoon post. Hides it behind her apron & says "I thought youd be wanting a caändle" & then suddenly just like a girl – shows me the letter. "Theres naught so good for eë". Well, I agree with you & my wire of this morning will 'stand' will 'fit' –

Your letter has brought you near – and lifted me up from under [the] appaling umbrella. Now Ill just turn to Friday week – & live for it & believe in it – & you are NOT to hurry, NOT to rush – NOT to worry – Take your precious time.

I cant write today. I am going off to the plage to watch the waves. (Thats your letter, again).

Im glad you got the Note Book & glad you saw the Woolves – Would the Nation print the Note Book.[10] *Much* more likely than Carnation (which they *wont* print). But you *cant* offer another. Let it all be.

Oh, yes, at this moment, youre wonderfully near – I feel 'better' today physically – much. No, we'll sit tight & on Friday week you will come. The Colonel helps the Heron too, at present[11] –

Goodbye my own love.
Wig.

MS ATL. *LKM* I. 197–9; *LJMM*, 294–6.

---

[1] See 8 June, n. 2.

[2] At the end of September 1917 the 'Bolo Affair' began with the arrest of Paul Bolo, a prominent figure in French society, also known as Bolo Pasha because of a title from the deposed Khedive of Egypt. He had received large payments from the Deutsche Bank to purchase French newspapers which would put forward German views, and taken eleven million francs in various transactions. He was executed on 17 April 1918.

[3] Murry wired on 10 June 'Dont think can manage will try my hardest Love Boge.' (ATL.)

[4] Stepan Trofimovich Verkhovensky, character in Dostoevsky's *The Possessed*, who addresses everyone as 'cher'.

[5] Virginia Woolf (*DVW*, I, 156) recorded of his visit on Sunday 9 June: 'Murry was pale as death, with gleaming eyes and a crouching way at table that seemed to proclaim extreme hunger or despair . . . . At Christmas, said Murry, I was near suicide; but I worried out a formula which seems to keep me going. It's the conception of indifferentism. I have hope no longer.'

[6] Murry told KM on 10 June, in a letter that crossed with her query: 'The Woolves have just finished the actual printing of the text of your story. The covers are left to be done.' (Murry, 171.) The 10th in fact was the publication date of *Prelude*.

[7] A review of Georges Duhamel's short stories in the *Nation*, 8 June.

[8] Another of Murry's pieces in that week's *Nation* was on Henri Gaudier-Brzeska's retrospective exhibition at the Leicester Galleries.

[9] The reference is to his companion Sophie Brzeska, with whom he had lived purportedly as brother and sister. Georges Banks was the woman who had come with Gaudier-Brzeska to attack Murry in his office in 1912. See *CLKM* I, 123, n. 2.

[10] There is no evidence that Murry approached the *Nation*. On 10 June he had written 'I haven't said anything about K. M.'s Notebook. Shall I be forgiven? You see it's appallingly

difficult for me to write about it. It grips altogether too near my heart. *I can't be objective* about Holes, or Pulmonary Tuberculosis. If something is absolutely clawing your heart, you can't say: That's beautiful, can you?' (Murry, 172.) This 'Notebook' must have been more extensive than the fragments that survive from Looe in KM's manuscript papers, and that Murry included in the *Journal* 1954, 133–41.

[11] Murry also explained on 10 June that he had to have his monthly report ready by the end of that week – 'I promised the Colonel I would; and it would look awfully bad if I cleared off and left it to some-one else to do' (Murry, 171). KM means that while Murry is in London rather than Looe, they are saving more for the future.

To J. M. Murry, [11 June 1918]

[Looe]

Fully understand about holidays Friday week alas[1]

Telegram. Text from Murry letter, 11 June 1918 (Murry, 173).

[1] KM sent this after reading Murry's letter of 8 June, and his reply to her wire on that same day.

To J. M. Murry, [12 June 1918]

[Headland Hotel, Looe, Cornwall]

Dear Darling

No letter by this morning's post so the day sets in very quiet – Its rather like waiting for a clock to strike. Is it going to strike – is it *not* going to strike. No: its well past the hour now. Still 'thanks be to Fortune' Ive the afternoon to look forward to – two chances a day: that beats France.

Re jam. Mrs Honey has got a nice little lot of gooseberries coming so – they are called 'golden drops' and do make handsome jam. She's keeping them for us. BUT do you like gooseberry jam? I do, awfully, if its homemade – & yet its not (which really *is* a point in these days) *too* alluring. I am become, since I arrived here a Gluttonous Fiend sur le sujet de marmalade d'orange. It really does seem to me one of the superb discoveries – eaten early in the morning and so prettie withal.

Yesterday afternoon, on the rocks, among the babies & family parties (*too* near me for my taste) each of us with our tea and trimmings & cigarettes Anne & I sat. And SHE talked and I added:
'Anne.'
'Really.'
'How extraordinary.'
'Yes, I can imagine it.'
Ringing the changes upon this little chime – which somehow

wonderfully was enough to bring *all* her thoughts positively rushing to me in a little urgent troop until I really (if you will please conceive of me now as a kind of little warm dim temple) couldn't have held another – – But oh – they *really* were – some of them – no end "interesting" Bogey. You were there, par example, sitting next to a "rather big girl with round eyes & a cream complexion" while Johnny & Anne (who were to meet you next night) looked on – – That was at the d'Harcourt.[1] And then there was Anne's meeting with Johnny and her first visit to his studio – worth hearing that – – – – –

Passons. I am going to spend £1 before I leave here on pottery – blue pottery – which seems to me exquisitely lovely – We shall choose the shapes together – a high fruit dish   🍷   a bowl – some flower jars – £1 will cover them all – There is *such* a shop here. I keep placing these things in the elephant – the clean, pale delightful elephant.

Why didn't I have a letter!

All the same I am a nice little thing this morning. If you were here I think you'd like my ways – I fell fast in love with you last night at about 12.30. I was going to bed – dropping my velvet coat and velvet shoes on the bank before I took a header in what I prayed was going to be a dark little pool – & suddenly I saw you in the 'garden room' – making something with a packing case, a hammer a plane – nails – "Wiggie. Hold this for me". I held it – and you banged away – 'Half a minute Jag. Ill just put a paper down to catch the sawdust." And later – you put a little pot of glue in a saucepan of boiling water where it *bumped* away while it melted.

This was so Ineffably Heavenly that I tied a love word to the leg of my very best & fastest pigeon & sent it off to you to perch on the end of the grey bed & give the top of your precious head the gentlest possible peck so that you'd wake & get the message . . . Did you?

I must go out out out in the world –

Goodbye dearest Love.

Your own little
Wig.

[*On the back of the last page, enclosed by arrowed hearts, are opening and closing messages*]

Mittwoch. Guten Tag mein Schwartz Köpfchen!

Bon soir Tete Noire.

MS ATL. *LKM* I. 199–200; *LJMM*, 297–8.

---

[1] Anne Estelle Drey was remembering the same occasion from 1910 that J. D. Fergusson recalled in his 'Chapter from an Autobiography', (Morris, 63) when in the Café d'Harcourt on the Boulevard St Michel, they 'sat beside a very good-looking lad with a nice girl', whom they later found out to be Murry and his friend 'Marguéritte'. (See *BTW*, Chapter 10.)

To Ida Baker, [12 June 1918]

Headland Hotel | Looe | Cornwall.
Wednesday.

Dear Jones

I have waited until this afternoons post has come and as there is still *no sign* from you I am very worried. You must be ill. You equally *must* let me know at *once*. Get Miss Oldfield[1] or one of your friends to write if you cannot, dear. But do, please, let me know the full truth about what is happening – as *soon* as *possible*.

I know you wouldn't have kept silence for any other reason.

Yours ever
Katie.

MS BL. *MLM*, 117.

[1] One of Ida Baker's fellow workers at the Chiswick factory, who also lived with her at Eyot Villa, a YWCA hostel on the Embankment.

To J. M. Murry, [13 June 1918]

[Headland Hotel, Looe, Cornwall]
Thursday

My own Darling Heart

I shall not write much today, I am too worried about you.[1] You *cant* go on. I am going out to wire you to see Croft Hill[2] – This you really must do. He will I hope order you immediate leave and you must come here *as soon as possible* & rest absolutely.

I had no letters at all yesterday though I waited ever so. Now this morning your Tuesday & Wednesday letters are here and I feel that the case is immensely urgent. You can obviously stand no more. If you don't do this you may break down very seriously. I implore you to take all the care you can of yourself. (Of course the main cause is my INFERNAL coldness, heartlessness & lack of imagination in having written as I have lately. No more of that, though or the pain will be too great & Ill cry out.)

Try & forgive me – that's all.

Re Elephant. Are you 'legally' free to sign the agreement in view of the fact that youre an undischarged bankrupt?[3] I saw some man was fined yesterday for some offence or other & it made me think. Hadn't I better sign? As your wife with independent means? Don't risk anything. But above all – for God's sake take care of yourself.

Your own Wigwife.

MS ATL. *LJMM*, 298–9.

[1] Murry was working extremely hard at the War Office. He wrote on 11 June that he was 'done up absolutely . . . . It's terribly hard for me to attend to anything – hard to form words into sentences.' (Murry, 173.)

[2] Arthur Croft-Hill, a medical friend of both KM's and Murry's.

[3] For the details of Murry's bankruptcy over *Rhythm*, see *CLKM* I. 130–7.

To J. M. Murry, [14 June 1918]

[Headland Hotel, Looe, Cornwall]

King of the Turnip Heads[1]

I hasten to throw this letter into the wall to tell you (in case you do 'see *your* way' (*and* my D[aily] N[ews] says there is a 'glut' of them au moment présent dans *notre* Londres) my way to make Strawbug Jam. As far as I remember its like this. ¾ lb of sugar to each 1 lb. of fruit.

Put the fruit and the sugar in a pan overnight. Turn, before leaving it, ever so gently with a wooden spoon. (Turn the fruit, I mean – Dont *waltz* round it.) By the next day the berries will have 'sweated'. Boil, without adding any water (gently again) for ¾ of an hour – And then apply the Saucer Test. (During the ¾ of an hour, Christian you must NOT seek repose.) God! as I write I freeze I burn I desire with a passion that is peign to be there all in my little bib and tucker.

"Yes Rib, dear you should have a taste on your own little dish! . . ." But I think this receipt is right, love.

Queen of the Wigglechiks.

The time for boiling here given is for a lot. Perhaps it needs less for a little. Thats a point Ive never yet decided –

If you feel there ought to be water added – well – you know our high courage on former occasions. And its always been triumphant.

MS ATL. *LKM* I. 200–1; *LJMM*, 299.

[1] Murry wrote on 10 June, 'I have a head like a turnip – a sleepy turnip.' (ATL.)

To J. M. Murry, [14 June 1918]

[Headland Hotel, Looe, Cornwall]
Friday. A Week Today.

My Precious Bogey

Wednesday evening when L. M. came & brushed you[1] & Thursday morning note are come.

ALSO just as I had tied two lovely purple bows on the shoulders of my chemise came Mrs Honey with such a sort of sweet piece from the comb that I am still tasting it – your telegram despatched this very morning as ever was – saying you are 'chirpy'. (When you use that particular word my heart always overflows. Its such an exquisitely *brave* word from you – and my 'hurray' in return has a little catch in its voice.)

You shall have strawberries, love in this happy land three times a day – & I dont see why we shouldn't take back a great basketful for jam, too – & do the government in its cruel blind eye – Oh – the Picnics! We shall have almost perpetual picnics – whole or half day ones – There is a river here, you know which Ive never yet been up. Waiting to explore it with you. Then we shall even if we don't buy a pin or a curtain ring to it – adorn the Elephant here & plan it & plot it and mark it with E & put it in the oven for Bogey and me.

Rib: "Shes in one of her worse moods. Look out, parentchik!" But its all your fault as Wilkie's girl says[2] – you ought *not* to be so enchanting.

Oh, darling Boge, wings or no wings, even if I become a sort of baby pelican with a bright eye i must be the one who looks after you – until the Heavens open and we behold the Lord with the Heron upon his right hand. Its not fair – hopelessly not fair that you should have to drag me in a little cart after you to the office and then drag me home again & that I should fall over every time I'm 'propped'. No – I refuse – for ever & ever – amen. (We are to have a couponless poulet to take back.)

Now I am going to talk to you about what you ought to bring here – If it means the large suitcase – and its not too great a nuisance – bring it for an odd corner would be most welcome on my return journey. This hotel is a . . . 1st class english Pension – *Awful* if you had to fraternise but as I have established a squirrel reputation (only descending to seize my nut or two when the gong goes & then simply flying back into the branches again) its quite alright. But what I mean is – one *changes* in the evening – & though I dont expect you to join the boiled ones you'd be happier if you had your – say blue serge – I think to get into after you have been out all day – Youll need of course your slippers, too, and some cricket shirts if you have same. Socks, ties,

hanks and spunk bag. Also a belt for wearing when we row away &
you throw your coat at me – for not even oriental embroidered braces
will do – – Corduroys of course would have you in the lock-up in
½ an hour & a jersey would have the fishing boats after you – Spose
you'd better wear a straw hat – hadn't you? And don't forget
pigglejams. You will of course be met with a jingle – Rib driving.

I thought youd wear your white silk shirt in the evening with a bow
tie. Is that a possible combination – or do I rave? These are just hints.
If you want to throw them away & arrive with your rucksack – well –
you will, of course!

Pagello – galan[t]uomo – was here last night & made a tour of the
battlefield. There is no sign of an *advance* by the enemy – they are still
more or less there in force on our left wing – but the moral of the
Commander in Chief is excellentissimo today –

This long letter is because Sunday comes in between – a dull old
day – no post.

But you must understand it has Love Love Love enough to fill all
the letterboxes in the world – It will, my own, if only youll hold it to
your warm heart a minute keep alight until Monday –

Oh God. How she does *love* him – Is it possible? What can she do to
express it. Go to the town & buy the ferryman some tobacco – yes,
thats what I'll do. Give the old boy a hug from his sister –

As to what I give YOU – & Rib throws up his arms – Yours for ever.

Wig.

Do *please* send me 'Colour'. Cigarettes are excellent, thank you.

MS ATL. *LJMM*, 299–301.

[1] Ida Baker had advertised as a 'specialist' hair-brusher in *Rhythm*, and an unkind portrait of
her in that role survives in Nan in *The Aloe*.

[2] A phrase from *The Night Watchman*, a sketch by the impersonator and comedian Wilkie Bard
(1870–1944).

To Ida Baker, [14 June 1918]

[Headland Hotel, Looe, Cornwall]
Friday.

Dear Jones

I was very glad to get your letter this morning – very sorry to hear
youve been ill. I should think it was caused by heat & rushing & bad
diet. Anyhow I rather gather you've seen a doctor & as youre 'out'
again perhaps the worst is over. I suppose if I *hadn't* sent the letter
registrée I should not have heard at all – Youre not just an agency to
which I apply for pills and cigarettes, free of charge – though your

whole letter was concerned with trying to make me believe that's what Ive brought our 'relationship' to. However if it pleases you to feel it, my dear, you must feel it. Lord knows I deserve it enough, according to the WORLD. I thought you were the person I flew to with bad tempers, worries, depressions, money troubles, wants, rages, silences, *every*thing, enfin – but the little bottles, boxes & postal orders – though God knows welcome, seemed to me to be only the trimmings – and not the feast. However you think otherwise – which is humiliating to us both –

Take care of your wicked self

Katie.

MS BL. Alpers 1953, 259.

To Ida Baker, [16 June 1918]

[Headland Hotel, Looe, Cornwall]
Sunday.

Dear Jones

Thank you for the B.P.s[1] & for the cigarettes. I am 'taking' both.

Jack writes that you have been looking after him most beautifully. He has been I know dreadfully needing a kind hand, poor boy, and yours, according to him, was quite of the kindest.

I sit writing to you in an armchair in front of the windows. The dreaming vacant sea dreaming by, and castles and mountains in the sky – I am wrapped up in my pink quilt & hot water bottle – for Ive an awful attack of that spinal rheumatiz, the worst Ive known so far. It has swept me completely off my feet this time. Oh, its horribly painful! Outside a crowd of children, accompanied by a fiddle & a 'cello have been singing songs for the Devon Hospital or something. Not hymns proper, but tunes like enough to hymns to fill one with Sunday sentiments – One wants to weep; one thinks of death; the seagulls fly into the infinite – and one wonders why on earth one should be so cursed with this perpetual ill health! It seems a mockery to be 29 and as Mrs Honey says "naught but a frame" when there is so much one longs to DO and BE and HAVE. (I wish I didn't hear you say in a small voice: but Katie you might be paralysed or pockmarked or an amputee). For it dont console me at all. I want to run; I want to jump; I want to scramble and rush and laugh.

Ah well – there you are. I dont know why I write to you so intimately. For you have quite given me up & thrown me over – in such a way, too. Walking out of the house without a word – But perhaps there was someone waiting for you at the gate – Stella –

Wenna – Hersey of the Eyebrow – little Mrs.[2] And So On. I don't know and I am sure I dont care. Its only when you are *in* the house that I love you – I never – as it were recognise you when youre dressed & ready to depart. You seem so awfully like everybody else in your hat and jacket. Yes, I only love you when youre blind to everybody but US. Thats the truth. I simply hate the person who "met Fergusson & HE recognised me. I was surprised that he recognised me. For after all hes not seen me except in the dark when hes had his back to me – has he? But Im glad he recognised me. I should like him to like me – I didn't think he even realised who I was – I never thought he'd have known me again. I wish I could see something more of Fergusson" (ad. lib. Take all the repeats).

Horrid horrid Katie.

MS BL. Alpers 1953, 260–1.

---

[1] Bipalatinoids, an iron pill sent in answer to KM's letter of 8 June.
[2] Her friend Stella Drummond, and other passing acquaintances at the hostel.

To J. M. Murry, [16 June 1918]

[Headland Hotel, Looe, Cornwall]
Sunday 11.30 A M

My Dear Love

I feel I have such a great deal to write to you today – Perhaps it wont all (it certainly will not) get written: some will have to "bide over till eë come." *Firstly*. The brown paper note came yesterday morning & I thought paid me almost *too* well for my own wisp. But then Mrs Honey brought the telegram on a silver charger. Tomorrow I shall know all that Crofty [Croft-Hill] said, but the fact that he has ordered you injections + a half holiday a week proves, darling, that I was right – Doesn't it? You must grant me that. Im awfully anxious to know just what he said – and whether he was 'intelligent' – It seems that he must have been. Thank Heaven your tiny holiday is before you & the Elephant, too. You must NEVER be left in such an impossible situation again. No wonder *you* loathe the Redcliffe Road (I confess I have 'turned' against Sullivan & couldn't greet him. Hes a coward and utterly abominably selfish.[1] Feel inclined to write to him: 'you do your share of the work, my lad, & don't worry about the planet getting cold.'

You do everything that Crofty tells you – or Rib will beat you terrifically – see? I think Ill put Pagello on to you, too, as soon as you get down here – *He* Pagello is leaving Looe – going back to Dublin in a months time. But before he goes hes going to give me a sort of programme to live by which will be very useful. I have not told you my weight this week because I am not going to the Clinic until next Wednesday to ascertain it. Ive been trying a special diet & Wednesday will "give it a chance." What a curse! The weather has changed. Its really more lovely than ever – but showery – immense clapping showers of rain – castles & mountains in the sky & reflected in the purple sea – the air smelling of elder flower and seaweed – But alas! for my bones. Its brought on a devilish fit of spinal rheumatism & I walk like little Nell's grandfather[2] – & spent until four oclock this morning – literally – wondering whether people my age could have paralysis – if not how account for being cold-stone to the knees & so on and so on. The pain is devilish devilish devilish – but I am *not* downhearted so don't you be.

Yesterday morning I went into Looe & met Mr Palliser & had a talk about chickens, tulips and boats. He is a *huge* man – a positive Titan. I came home to find another huge bouquet from his garden – mixed sweet williams – superb great velvet flowers – white & pink and red. My room looks *full* of them & Ribni's dark head shines out of velvet bows. Anne has made such an exquisite painting of mon fils chéri – <u>&</u> given it to me.

She came yesterday afternoon – strangely happy & *stout* looking – & said – standing by the bed & smiling: 'Je *crois*, je ne suis pas certain, mais il y a, enfin un retard d'une semaine – je crois que je suis enceinte!' But of course it is a *deadly* secret. As I watched her I 'recognised' her expression: women, saying that, have always looked 'just so' – its extremely beautiful to behold.

And *then* Mrs Honey brought me another letter from you – I am glad L. M. has been decent. Make her *pack* for you & look after you all this next week. Use her, dearest.

After today Friday will feel ever so much nearer. I am not going to meet you at Liskeard.[3] It means such a waiting about & though God knows Id wait about for ever for you – I feel that it is défendu until I am a bit more of a lion.

This morning when I woke up Mrs Honey was particularly honeycomb. Dear old soul – in her black Sunday dress – She said "youve not slept – thaats bad. Ill see to it that you haave your coffee right hot" – And she brought me boiling coffee and a "fried egg with bacon fried for a relish". When I had done up all my buttons & was having a small sit down she said, looking at me with her kind old eyes: 'Shall I recite you some verses I learned when I was a girl. Will eë haave The Death of Moses or A Mothers Memories.' I said Id have both. Down she sat. Each had, I should think about 40 verses to it.

She never hesitated for a word. She folded her hands and on & on went her soft old voice, telling of the "crested waves" – telling of the "lion the King of Beasts who sat under the mountain where Moses was buried and "forgot to roar".

> 'Yea from the monsters golden eyes
> The golden tears dropped down' –

I listened & suddenly I thought of Wordsworth & his 'faith' in these people – and again, Bogey, in spite of everything I believed in England – Not only in England – in mankind. You will understand me when I tell you – that I wanted to weep to cry Father forgive them – they know not what they do. O – Love – the Beauty of the human soul – the Beauty of it – the Beauty of it. Dont let us *ever* forget – You & I know it – Duhamel knows it – There will be others – we will build an altar –

No Ive not written half that I meant to, and I *cant*. My back has got the upper hand. Im off back to bed with a hot water bottil – Its no good, Betsy – But don't worry – Ill be better tomorrow. Its only *body*, *not* heart – *not* head.

Those are all Ive got intact & all yours for ever – Dearest of all – & best of all – you are coming *this week* & by Friday Ill try & be dancey – Make L. M. look after you – thats all – Phone her –

Goodbye for now – my precious – What a silly I am to be so stiff – oh so stiff – Always always your own

Wig.

MS ATL. *LKM* I. 201–2; *LJMM*, 301–3.

[1] Murry wrote on 14 June, 'I had a note from Sullivan at Garsington this morning. He seems comfortable enough and writes of everybody being "extraordinarily kind", so that's all right. I can't help feeling a bit jealous of his holiday though, because I think I'm suffering from exactly the same "brain-fag" as he, and have to do his work into the bargain. It's horribly mean of me I know; that's why I have to confess to somebody, not somebody but to you.' (Murry, 175.)

[2] A memory of the 'spare and slender form' of the feeble old man in Dickens' *The Old Curiosity Shop* (1841).

[3] The nearest railway station for Looe.

To J. M. Murry, [17 June 1918]

[Headland Hotel, Looe, Cornwall]
Monday

Dearest Love

Your telegram, which arrived at break of day found me toute émue.[1] It just stopped me from being in the least disappointed when the old post did come – & – gave me you to eat with my frügglestück.

J'ai bien mangé. I do feel today that Friday – is oh so near. I keep making preparations . . . and speculations. Will my flowers last till then? Shall Rib wear his new dress or the old one his father loves?

I feel ever so greatly better today (cant write or spell tho'.) I had a good night. Oh, a GOOD one! Anne came early & began the great painting – me in that red brick red frock with flowers everywhere.[2] Its awfully interesting even now. I must tell you the things she has told me about Johnny – They are revealing. I painted her in my fashion as she painted me in hers. Her eyes . . . "little blue flowers plucked this morning" – – –

The second post has just been with your Sunday afternoon letter on its horn. I am delighted at Crofty's news – but whats all this about 5 guineas?[3] *Dont* shame me so. Think what you have spent on me – precious. It made me blush to read that. But praps you were only making fun of me. Crofty is the right man for you evidement – Stick to him & let him fortify you with iron bars against the time – –

The reason why I have been so quiet about my weight is I was only 7.10 when I weighed last – so I didn't tell you. For I had lost a couple of lbs. I know when & why. It was when I had one of my blackest moods – I felt very dreadful – But by next Wednesday – I ought to have found them again & I will wire you the good tidings . . . Bother – wasnt it! No, precious love, dont bother about pumps. Crabshells will do – one for each foot – slippers will be high perfection. I wish you would whisper Chaddie to send me ½ lb of good chocolates – I *pine* for that sweet toothful & there is nothing here just now but chewing gum. Everbody in this hotel has told me how much better I am today than I was yesterday. Which is very naice of them.

I say – what about *Thursdays*.[4] I told Rib who became a shocking boy on the spot – absolutely too much for any woman to deal with – I threatened him finally with the Childrens Court & said I'd tell the Magistrate he was incorrigible – But he pays no attention only asks the empty air: "well why does she keep on kissing me while she says all this."

Youre not to think Ive bullied you about this large suitcase (you do.) Really & truly I have only gone into the affair in such detail to make you feel comfortably disguised – camouflaged in the presence of the chimpanzees. For tho' they don't bite their chatter is a hell of a bore – don't you think? You must not bring anything but a coloured handkerchief & a tommyhawk if you dont want to. Now take care of your darling self.

Your letter has brought Friday – rainbows nearer.

Your
Wig.

MS ATL. *LKM* I. 202–3; *LJMM*, 304–5.

¹ Murry's telegram does not survive, but his letter of 17 June says 'I sent you a wire to say I missed the late fee post yesterday.' (ATL.)

² The oil portrait now in the National Gallery, Wellington.

³ Dr Croft-Hill recommended a course of arsenic and iron injections for Murry, which would cost about five guineas.

⁴ He insisted as well that Murry take off one half-day each week.

To Ida Baker, [17 June 1918]

[Headland Hotel, Looe, Cornwall]

If you see J. before he comes down would you see that he brings my VELVET waistcoat (which 'goes' with my velvet skirt) – dear? Id also give my eyes for that crêpe de chine 'jumper' made of Chaddie's evening coat & the black satin pinny dress to wear with it. These will only make a tiny parcil. If he hasn't room could you post them me? Sending small 'factory-useful' parcil today.

Katie

MS (postcard) BL. Alpers 1953, 261.

To J. M. Murry, [18 June 1918]

[Headland Hotel, Looe, Cornwall]
Tuesday

My own Bogey

It is cold as Winter, gray with white horses, solemn boats – a pale light on everything – a feeling of great 'uneasiness' in the air. I think I may have a letter from you by this afternoon's post – none came this morning. 'Colour' came – I shook it – held it up [by] its hair & its heels but it hadn't a message – The reproductions are very beautiful – I have had a good look at them – You know Poise is extraordinarily fine, but having gone so tremendously far as Fergusson *has* gone I don't think the *mouth* is quite in the picture – It is – it is more "in the picture" than most of his other mouths are – but I think it might be more *sensitive* . . . more "finely felt." Of course I can hear his "to Hell with rosebuds" but I won't be put off by it: its too easy & begs the question anyway. To exaggerate awfully (as I always do) he really seems sometimes to fit women with mouths as a dentist might fit them with teeth – & the same thing happens in both cases: the beautiful *individual* movement (mobility) of the face is gone – Looking at *Poise* again this mouth seems more nearly right than any other – Perhaps thats what sets up the irritation in me. I must say as a picture it properly fascinates me¹ – – –

The magazine as a whole is VILE. Nothing less will do. The article on J.D.F. is such pigwash that I cannot imagine how he allowed it – There is not a hint of even low ability in one word of all the writing from cover to cover – It makes me want to start a paper of course, frightfully, but not a soul would buy our paper. We'd have to make our cow subscribe and all our little newborn chickens & ducks would be presented with life subscriptions – The birds that sang about the Heron I am sure would gladly pay a feather a copy, too, but then in the case of swallows for instance it would [be] such a *job* posting theirs on to funny strange addresses in Africa & Italy – No, no paper. Books.

Bogey, the north wind doth blow – It has found out my bones again & is playing a fine old tune in them. I should like to come into your room, light a big fire, put a kettle on – & then both of us – curl up in two big chairs – the doors & windows are shut – tight – there are books & Ill make coffee & we'll talk or be quiet. This aint a day for hotel bedrooms – If I hadnt FRIDAY nailed to the mast – but I have – I have – thank God!

I think youd better bring down your wooly weskit, darling – to be ready for weather like this. But the Lord may turn his face to Looe again by then. He just must.

I am a silly, dull girl today – I had a nuit *blanche* & my brain is still, as it were, empty with it. But Friday is in this week & thank God! you have not to cross the water – Let us make a solemn vow – never – never to let the seas divide us – Be careful not to lean out of the train window. Have tea at Plymouth – but dont miss the train while you are blowing on it. Cut yourself a large huge sangwich for your lunch. Its better to have too much food when you are travelling. I didn't have half enough on my way down here & had to keep on buying snippets. Above all – keep *warm* & remember youre looking after yourself for me as I do for you.

Your own
Wig.

P.S. Look here! I have just taken a room for you. Does that sound awful? Its next to mine. It wont cost any more than if you were in this room with me – but it will give you *platz*. You neednt sleep in it if you don't want to – we are 'side by side' – & as I have bregglechik in bed I thought you would perhaps prefer to dress & so on in your own room – It will cost just the same as this room – I feel we'll both *rest* better like that – Its a nice room – tiny, though.

Wiggie.

MS ATL. *LJMM*, 305–6.

[1] In the June issue of the art magazine *Colour* there was an article signed 'Tis' on 'J. D. Fergusson: His Place in Art'. Several paintings were reproduced, including 'Poise', a portrait of a woman.

To J. M. Murry, [19 June 1918]

[Headland Hotel, Looe, Cornwall]
Wednesday morning. Before I gets up.

My own Boge

Your Monday evening & Tuesday morning letter have come, after a jour maigre yesterday – What should I do if Friday wasn't Friday. It would *have* to be. Vous êtes horriblement fatigué. You must just be taken care of & we'll get an old sea salt to pull us up the river while you sit tight & just dabble your fingers.

I had a really bad old day yesterday. They made me a fire & brought my food into my cage & I wrapped up in my pink quiltie but it was snow use. My rheumatism was so ghastly that I could *not* write. I tried – time after time but oh dear me – my bones played such Variations Symphoniques that I had to give over. So, having no book, I watched the hands go round my watch, & wondered why the Lord has cursed me with this *vile* ill health. I who love & long so to be well. Its queer.

Evening – Anne came. Very welcome. She stayed & we talked. I showed her Colour, & on her own she remarked that Fs 'mouths' always troubled her – in fact she entirely agreed with me about them. This, from her, was a relief to me. Drey told her that "everybody" is talking of your wonderful article on Gaudier – tak por tak –

Its sunny today, but very uncertain. The clouds are pulling over again – a plague on them. When you come it *must* be fine for you – As for me, personally, I would not care if it snowed as long as I had you to look at & to listen to but I care for you. You have to turn a lovely brown and you have to paddle & swim & eat your tea *out* as they say.

Dearest *what* is the page of accounts you refer to? I never made one out & certainly did not send you one intentionally. It must have been an odd sheet which got into your letter by mistake. I dont want any money at all, thank you Mr Millionaire. My finances are quite satisfactory – and you sent me £8 for this month you know!

I am so glad you are taking the old boy to see Charlie Chaplin.[1] I wish you were taking me, too, and Rib – who would give us imitations afterwards to the life.

"One more letter – one more letter to Jordan".[2] That Ill send tomorrow & then – – Well – look out for me on the station for I shall be there –

Yours yours yours
Wig.

Later. Ive just come home from the Clinic where I was weighed. *7.11 very good* & also heard that another of 'our leading townsmen' tried to cut his throat from ear to ear last night – after (he being over 40) he had received his 'call up' notice – The doctor of course couldn't help *thrilling* rather: I think it must be his first affair of the kind. But there's a pretty state of affairs *here* – about this Tribunal business.[3] Ill not write it.

My glass was bedeckt with your telegram – darling Boge. Thank you for sending it me. Do you mean no letter from the Agents or none from me? I gave *mine* to you to a maid to post yesterday and she says oh *yes* she did but if the stupid wench caught the post or not (she'd only an hour & a half to catch it in – & the box is ½ a minute from the kitchen door) that I don't know. I dont depend on people or believe in em – but I couldnt get out yesterday. I had to trust to them. The day has now got very lovely – & the ferryman (with whom I would be very much in love if I had any to spare) has just been particularly attractive – and Friday is still coming nearer.

Wig.

MS ATL. *LJMM*, 306–8.

[1] Murry was taking his brother to see Chaplin's film *A Dog's Life*.

[2]   'One more river, and that's the river of Jordan,
             One more river, and that's the river to cross.'

The refrain of a traditional marching song.

[3] An episode, unrecorded in local papers, presumably to do with the Military and Appeal Tribunal which made decisions on eligibility for service.

To J. M. Murry, [20 June 1918]

[Headland Hotel, Looe, Cornwall]
Thursday.

Bogey darling

This will catch you before you leave.[1] Don't forget to leave our addresses – for 'Mansfield' as well. And provide yourself with food. Suggestion: Travel in your little grey felt & pack your straw with the spunk bag inside it. The weather is so funny –

Tomorrow tomorrow tomorrow – that is at full gallop.

The wardrobe "thrills me through & through" (to be sung con amore.)

Dont fall out of the train. Perhaps you had better tie a label on your top button. I don't trust you AT ALL.

Rib says: Parentchik I shall be there to meet, on the stopping of the chariot, the August Emergence.[2] He says he is going "to write a book now called Fan Tales."

Now – Oh *please* hurry, but *dont* rush. And dont forget that I shall be, once with you – simply – – – *too* excited.

Your Wig.

MS ATL. *LJMM*, 308.

---

¹ Murry joined KM at the Headland Hotel on 22 June. On the day following this letter, she wrote in a notebook of 'John's letter telling of all his immense difficulties – all the impossible things he *must* do before he could start his holiday left me lukewarm. It had somehow a *flat* taste – and I felt rather as tho' Id read it curiously apart, not united' (*Journal* 1954, 138).

² These are phrases KM must recently have read, for while in Looe she jotted in a notebook 'to meet, on the stopping of the chariot, the august emergence' (*Journal* 1954, 135).

To Ida Baker, [25 June 1918]

[Headland Hotel, Looe, Cornwall]
Tuesday.

Jones dear

Have you any tea¹ to spare? It is like this. I have borrowed £8 from Jack this month & I don't dare to ask for any more – Yet it is not enough to see me through. You see leaving here I must tip these people & get my ticket & the whole affair has been HORRIBLY EXPENSIVE. If you haven't, darling, its all right. I will borrow some more. You understand – don't you?

I have thought of you so much these last few days. I was wondering, in bed this morning, if you think of me – often – I mean. Well – do. I am a little nicer.

Yours ever
Katie.

We're leaving Saturday.

We arrive 5.20 on *Saturday afternoon*. Do come to 47 and be there at *six* oclock if you can. Praps youd help me – would you?

Katie.

Tell me if you can.

MS BL. Alpers 1953, 261–2.

---

¹ Their code word for money.

To Ida Baker, [26 June 1918]

[Headland Hotel, Looe, Cornwall]
Wednesday.

Jones love

Our letters crossed – and yours with the T arrived today. Thank you ever so. Don't forget, mignonette, to tear yourself away from your admirers on Saturday & come to '47' – will you?

You sent such an *astonishingly* lovely letter – I am thrilled about the seeds & about your coat & skirt – equally thrilled. The seed that is coming up standing on its head is particularly engaging – I am so glad that you are seeing your people – and that they are 'good' – I wish you would marry Webb or Gibson[1] & have some children. We do seem so *very* short of children – don't we? I simply pine for some but they dont want me (small wonder). Now I feel you would be superbly successful. Lay it to heart – Jones –

Jack has cried blessings on you ever since he came. You know, in him – whatever you may in your black moments think – you have a most loyal, utterly sincere friend. Hes *for* you – *for* you & he believes in you – really enough to satisfy even you – I thought Id tell you. These are the things which are so lovely to know. My back's pretty fairish – not more than that. It all depends on the day – & my wings – well they are *there* – The left one is groggy – and the right one I dont know about. But I have got used to them now & take them in my *stride* as they are no good for my *flight*.

I have had such a nice letter from Margaret Wishart that was.[2] She heard of me through a notice for Prelude. I am going to see her when I come home – She has two almost grown up sons. Ruth Herrick has not come – She always 'cries off' at the last hour, so Eileen[3] says. Her address is 53 Manchester Street. She has been ill again – & she wears her hair short – & Mrs H. is still a very great tartar – Men don't like Ruth at all – that has made her very bitter. (This is the news I gleaned for you). But the reason for it is that she is "always in love with some woman" – She becomes desperately infatuated with women just as she used to with Robin & Poppy Robinson[4] – devotes herself to them – slaves for them – just as she did when she was a 'little girl' – She sounds to me rather a tragic figure – Won't you try & see her?

My writing is vile today – but my hand shakes so – I am still filling myself with shot in the shape of these BiPalats, & if you held me by my heels I am sure I would rattle – They are good, I think.

I don't care a button for this place, Jones – though I suppose to the unjaundiced eye it is wonderfully beautiful. I dont care. No place is to me – Id just as soon be on the Mile End Road – sooner really. There are rocks & beaches & shells & pools and flowers and so on – but –

dont you know – Id just as soon let them all fall out of my lap. In fact I dont care about the sea – or the country – *or* the town for the matter of that. Oh, she is *very* hard to please. No, dearie – I like books & fires and cigarettes & flowers & fruits still – and at this moment I awfully like *you*.

I have had a long letter from Mack today on his way to Peking to be crowned Emperor of China – inviting Jack & me to go to Canada & on to N. Z. with Vera & the boys – *So* kind –

Then Ill see you on Saturday, & until then don't forget that you have for a friend in spite of everything

qui s'appelle
Katie.

MS BL. Alpers 1953, 262–3.

[1] Webb was a fellow factory worker who seemed interested in Ida Baker, Robert Gibson an officer with a South African regiment whom she had met on her voyage back from Rhodesia in 1916. Ida Baker wrote (*MLM*, 136) a painful account of how KM, and Murry particularly, later drove Gibson away. 'In a different situation, I might have married him and gone to Africa with him. But I was really leading a double life, my own and Katherine's, and I should not have dreamed of leaving her.'

[2] KM's close friend during her stay at Beauchamp Lodge in 1908–9.

[3] Eileen Palliser, another schoolgirl friend, the daughter of Charles Palliser.

[4] 'Robin' was the nickname of Miss Robinson, the assistant Matron when KM boarded at 41 Baker Street during her Queen's College years.

To Ida Baker, [15 July 1918]

[47 Redcliffe Road, Fulham]

Jones dear

I did not thank you half prettily enough for the lovely 'basket of flowers' but then I didn't see all their beauty until this morning: they are simply exquisite – especially the wild ones. Jack cannot 'get over' the roses & sees himself growing a great bush in the little glass place at the elephant. Your new coat & skirt looks exceedingly well – The shoulders & sleeves have a deal of drawing in them. I am so glad to think you have it & can be a pretty girl when Gibson takes you out . . . or any of your other charmers that I am so horrid about. I don't mean to be. *I* bought a teapot today – a big blue & white one & a little blue & white one, too – both I think very very nice. The mother was only 2/3 – the child 1/- at Liberty's[1] sale. Libertys sale made me positively swoon with covetousness – & all so cheap. I bought a duck of a perfume jar for your mantelpiece, too – a *lamb*.

This afternoon I have been to see the builders. Oh, they are a swindling lot. Now that we have cut down the price – of course he says he cant *do* any of the colours. Couldn't use cream paint at the money – nor nothing – But I beat him because I did not want what the poor middle class want – and I have had *grey* nearly everywhere. All the doors are to be grey & the skirting boards etc – & shutters – with black stair bannisters & black treads – In the kitchen white distemper with turquoise blue paint. On the top floor your room – lemon yellow with grey cupboards – The bathroom real *canary* yellow – & the 'external' paint for the railings gate & door – grey again. I think it will be lovely. He says it will look *un*finished. I wondered afterwards if the elephant name had given me the passion for the elephant colour.

Funny, odd people write to me & say how much they like my book.[2] Oh, how lovely praise is – not praise exactly – but friendly waves – & did I tell you the English Review has taken that story I wrote in the South & is going to pay me £6.6 for it?[3] I've had the proofs already – All this being so I ought to be nicer than I am. Ill try –

Mally Alexandra,[4] Jones, is living next door but one. This makes going out a great bore – I have to take such swerves.

I must go & put the kettle on. I am so longing for some *music*. Arent you? Take care of yourself darling.

Your
Katie.

Do buy some book will you Jones? Ill be so hurt if you dont.

MS BL. Cited Alpers 1953, 265.

[1] The store in Regent Street.
[2] The recently published *Prelude*.
[3] 'Bliss' appeared in the August issue.
[4] A student at Queen's College with KM and Ida Baker.

To Ottoline Morrell, [16 July 1918]

47 Redcliffe Road [Fulham] S.W.10.
Tuesday.

Dearest Ottoline,

It was with infinite pleasure that I read your letter this morning. I had thought that my stupid cry from Cornwall[1] had really disgusted you and I was to be banished, but then I heard from Brett how ill you were and I realised only too well why you had not written to me.

It is simply dreadful that you should suffer so much & that doctors should be such useless fools. What can one say? I know so devilishly well the agony of feeling perpetually ill and the longing – the immense longing – just to have what everybody else takes so easily as their portion – health – a body that isn't an enemy – a body that isn't fiendishly engaged in the old, old 'necessary' torture of – breaking ones spirit – – – "Why *wont* you consent to having your spirit broken?" it wonderingly asks. "Everybody else yields without a murmur. And if you'd only realise the comfortable, boundless numbness that you would enjoy for ever after – – –" I wonder sometimes how it will end. One will never give in and so – – All the same, it would be more tolerable if only people understood – ever so little – but *subtly* – not with a sort of bread jelly sympathy – but with exquisite, rare friendship. (Oh, dear, I *still* believe in such a thing and *still* long for it.) You see, I cannot help it – My secret belief – the innermost 'credo' by which I live is that *although* Life is loathesomely ugly and people are terribly often vile and cruel and base, nevertheless there is something at the back of it all – which if only I were great enough to understand would make *everything* everything indescribably beautiful. One just has glimpses, divine warnings – signs – Do you remember the day we cut the lavender? And do you remember when the russian music sounded in that half empty hall?[2] Oh, those memories compensate for more than I can say – –

This is all vaguely, stupidly written, but I want to be in touch with you somehow: I would so have loved seeing you today. I imagine we might have talked. There is always so much to say – Dearest Ottoline, you are so real to me – always. And now Ill confess. I was hurt a little bit that you didn't answer my letter. But only for a moment. After all – I had written and I have enough faith in you for ever to know that you do – respond – There is my feeling for you – whatever you may think of me – grown into my heart, as it were – and never to be uprooted – – – But this you know.

Thank you dearest friend, for all that you so beautifully say about my tiny book.[3]

And *do please* let me know when you are in town again.

With my love
Katherine.

MS Texas. *LKM* I. 204–5.

[1] Her letter to Lady Ottoline on 24 May.

[2] Lady Ottoline's memoir 'K.M.' recalls their attending 'at a time when the War was a black unhappy cloud over life . . . a Russian "Balaika" (*sic*) concert at the Grafton Gallery' in Piccadilly. (*Exhibition*, 12.)

[3] Lady Ottoline sent on her copy of *Prelude* to Bertrand Russell in Brixton Prison. He found the story distasteful.

To Dorothy Brett, [19 July 1918]

47 Redcliffe Road [Fulham] S.W.10.
Friday

The Artist at work with a dove behind her
head bearing a crown of laurels.

Dearest Brett

When are you coming to London again? And if you *do* come do not forget to let us know. Our last interview was so hung with drops of rain and cups of tea – I should love a longer, dryer one.

And what are you 'doing'? And how are you feeling? And are you painting? Or do you feel like I feel just at present – – another slice of *this* loaf I cannot & will not eat. I want to change the baker – the bread – everything – everything – I want to sit at an entirely new table in fact with new hands to pour out strange wines – and unfamiliar music playing – – – No, that aint enough either. Change the country – the climate, too. Lets all put on velvet masks and have our fortunes told by Chinese wizards.

Murry is exhausted again. He comes out of Watergate House, shakes himself, only to dive into another weedy little tank, trying to catch french fish for the Times.[1] And just occasionally he swims into Hamptons sale,[2] buys stair carpet as grey as a moth, sees himself awalking down it to welcome Brett and bear her aloft up above the world so high to his little study which looks over tree tops on to a kind of flashing eternity . . . There he *is* happy. Once we are 'settled' there will always be a bed and trimmings for you in the elephant (I have said that so often.)

I went to see the Naval Photographs today[3] – They are wonderful. And all the middle of the gallery is occupied by a Naval *Band* which, at the first blast carries you far far out into the open sea, my dear, so that you positively bob up and down in an open boat upon huge immense waves of sound gasping, breathless, holding on to ropes and trying to bail out your mind with the catalogue before you are swept on again. When I reached the final room I really *did* give way & was floated down the stairs & into the kind air by two Waacs & a Wren who seemed to despise me very much (but couldn't have as much as I did myself.) They asked me when I had drunk a glass of the most dispassionate water whether I had *lost* anybody in the Navy – as though it were nothing but a kind of gigantic salt water laundry –

(There's the postman – nothing for me. I do think Brett might send

me a line . . .) I was so happy today to hear that Ottoline *did* write to
me in Cornwall – and it was only the Post, my ultimate enemy, which
withheld her letter –

Addio, mia bella.

Your loving
Tig

MS Newberry. *LKM* I. 206–7.

¹ Murry continued to review French books regularly for *The Times Literary Supplement*.
² Hampton and Sons Ltd, decorators and furnishers at 8–11 Pall Mall East.
³ An exhibition of Naval photographs at Princes Galleries, Piccadilly.

To Dorothy Brett, [22 July 1918]

47 Redcliffe Road [Fulham] | S.W.10
Monday

Dearest Brett

I *tore* open your letter this morning thinking I should find therein all
your views of the case *Murry V Morrell*¹. But you neither mention nor
ignore it – you take, if I read you aright, a kind of *wang* at both parties
& that's all. Is that how you feel? Does the affair seem to you *another*
proof (if a proof were needed) of the cruelty and corruptness of
mankind? I can understand that. Of course I am not referring to
Ottoline's letter to M. Well – I couldn't be; even though I *do* think she
misunderstood – misjudged him completely & what is so much sadder
suspected him of all kinds of vile intentions. I dont care a damn for her
misjudgement or rage. I care *awfully* for her ugly suspicions. But the
flower of the affair is Philips abusive attack on Murry in the Nation –
– To have professed friendship for Murry – to have clasped his hand
and then, without a word of warning – without even a commonly
courteous note saying "Dear M. I heartily disapprove of your review
& mean to say so in print" – just to come out with this great Full Blare
of Pomposity . . . !! If I didn't feel so contemptuous – the spectacle of
Philip, rising from the sea like a lighthouse & turning his Awful Beam
upon dear Murry in the "professional armchair" would be very very
comic – But it is too ugly to laugh over really – When I think of M's
passionate honesty, his scrupulous fairness & sincerity – and then of
how he has aired himself at Garsington, I cannot understand how, at
a jump, in one moment Philip was ready to believe *anything* of him . . .

Its true, he is extreme. And there have been times when I have
cried: Oh *do* give way a little. Must you make of everything an affair of
Life & Death? Must everything be judged from one stern standpoint?
But now I appreciate that in him and wouldn't have it otherwise. I

agree with him absolutely about his review and the point that he makes that experience *as* experience is not YET Art seems to me profoundly true – and that self-BETRAYAL is NOT self-expression – that needs saying a million times –

But the curse – the plague is – Brett that I am so afraid it will change my relation with Ottoline. It *should* not but I fear it will. She wrote me asking me to come to Garsington but of course I cant ever come there again – for I wouldn't for *worlds* be under the roof tile of a man I so wholeheartedly dislike – Couldn't – for pride's sake.

I am glad that this has happened – For one thing it shows what unfriendly country Murry had been repoging in – & it forces him to show his hand – to publicly draw apart from those who dont share his beliefs.

Hurrah! I am with him. We sit together and alone, an arrogant, hateful pair – with cannonballs for eyes –

Ever your loving

Tig

MS Newberry.

¹ In the *Nation*, 13 July 1918, Murry had written on Siegfried Sassoon's *Counter-attack, and other poems*. He judged the volume to be not poetry so much as an 'incoherent' cry which 'has neither weight nor meaning of its own'. Murry felt that although the poems were moving, they did not touch the imagination, but only the sense – 'Their effect is exhausted when the immediate impression dies away.' The review distressed Lady Ottoline, who was infatuated with Sassoon, and upset others of his Garsington acquaintances. Philip Morrell's letter to the editor of the *Nation* on 20 July objected to Murry's 'detraction of a gallant and distinguished author'.

To Virginia Woolf, [23 July 1918]

47 Redcliffe Road [Fulham] | S.W.10.
Tuesday

Dear Virginia

I am sorry I shall not see you this week and her laship informs me that you are to be served hot-and-hot between two plates this week*end* at Garsington. She asked me to be there, too, but really after the great San Philip's arunning down of the little Revenge in this weeks Nation I don't think I *can* break 'crumb' in their house again. I should lose control of myself – I should do something dreadful – sin against very Decency – commit some hideous crime – eat the clove out of a stuffed orange or – or – God knows!

But it is only too plain from all this that Johnny Murry and I are arrogant outcasts with cannon balls for eyes. Do not be surprised, dear Virginia to see us arrive at Asheham, Murry en avance, with a knolled stick, fur cap, black eye, blue chin, me following with unbraided hair & a quilty shawl over my nonexisting bosom – a kind of Bill Sykes and Nancy,[1] with the bulldog tagging behind gripping a copy of Massingham's paper in his slobbering jaws. However, I 'note' as Dostoievsky is so fond of saying that Enid Bagnold[2] has all too beautifully come to Sassoon's rescue this week as well as Philip . . . Generous creature! To have told us, too, so expressly that she hears with her ear! Now how could one have known a thing like that otherwise? I defy anyone to have guessed such a thing.

'And I hear
With my Ear'

Great stuff!! as Frank Harris used to say – 'Oh Miss this is an Ewent at which Evings itself looks down'. But I wish to God she would sit up occasionally in her uncomfortably twanging bed and read her verses aloud to that intelligent organ at a moment when it is – as one might say en rapport . . . Passons.

I love to hear of Lyttons success.[3] It seems quite measureless to man. I put my head out of window at night and expect to find his name pricked upon the heavens in real stars. I feel he is become already, a sort of myth, a kind of legend. Modern princelings are hushed to sleep with tales of him and grave young duchesses disguise themselves at their Fairs and Pageants with – – the delicate beard, the moonlit hat, the shy, reluctant umbrella . . .

Yes, I am very sorry that we shall not see each other this week. Your Pearl of a Letter made me realise what an infinite deal I want to talk about with'you. But it will keep. I have spent the last two days lying on the sommier with a temperature for doux ami. But writing seems a great labour and every book I want – out of reach – the topmost leaf of the tallest tree – But I like to listen to this street. There is a piano in it, a parrot, and a man who cries feather brooms – all excellent in their way –

Yours ever
Katherine.

MS Berg. *LKM* I. 205.

[1] The criminal and his mistress in Dickens' *Oliver Twist* (1838).
[2] Enid Bagnold, later Lady Jones (1889–1981), playwright and novelist, whose memoir of the War years, *A Diary without Dates*, was published in 1918. Her poem 'The Guns of Kent', addressed to Siegfried Sassoon, appeared in the *Nation*, 20 July, and included the stanza

For there comes very faint, very far,
    As such voices are,
A sound I can hear. That I hear
    Every night with my ear.

[3] Lytton Strachey's *Eminent Victorians*, published in May 1918, was then being greatly praised.

To Dorothy Brett, [26 July 1918]

'47' [Redcliffe Road, Fulham]
Friday

Dearest Brett,

Your long absorbingly interesting letter came yesterday. You are as Kot[eliansky] would say a 'wonderful being' – and if ever in a dark hour you feel that nobody loves you – deny the feeling on the spot. For I do. I love you dearly. So does Johnny [Murry]. You seem to me to have the most *exquisite* virtues. I only hope that one day you will become a part of our life for a time and we'll share a gorgeous existence somewhere painting and writing and looking out of the window on to the sea perhaps – with painted ships sailing on it & sailors playing ball with oranges and little black niggers sitting in the bows playing twing-twang-twing on guitars made of coconuts! This I fondly dream while the rain pours down & the old lady in the basement tells 'er friend across the way that 'er legs 'urt er somethink 'orrible . . .

I am delighted to think you will be in London in September and for a long time – long enough to really *talk* and *really* laugh without the backs of our minds flying off to railway trains. If you dont think our particular Elephant a King of Beasts I shall be *very* disappointed. And now that I have fairly started and we are sitting before a fire of friendship with our skirts turned back comfortable & something hot with a nutmeg in it at our elbows Ill really answer all your letter. But again – how the dickens *can* I? The whole affair is so complicated and there is poor young Sassoon tucked up in bed with a wound in the head – given him by Murry, perhaps, in a paper cap with a carrot stuck in it . . .[1] I have read Johnny's review "time and time again" as they say. I think it is severe – terribly straight but to say that Sassoon would let himself be shot because of it, or that if someone had said it about Prelude Murry would have "stabbed them" is simply *fantastic* to me. I tried to talk it out with O. the first afternoon she came here, but it was a failure. In the first place I think she was astounded that I didn't agree with her as against Johnny. In the second I simply couldn't get on ground with her that didnt, after one minute, *rock* so that I was off again. I do wish shed say – bang out – that she hated Johnny. The picture she draws of him absolutely revolts me; and though she said one moment she utterly believed in his honesty & that he wouldn't attack S. S. personally, at the next she wondered whether he didnt wish to seize the opportunity of showing how much he disliked her – by wounding her through the body of S's book. Well Brett, the second monster is greater than the first. If that cad were Johnny Life would be a very different affair to me. It made me blush deeply to hear her say this. I could only murmur: "Oh, no, he wouldn't do that kind of thing". And then the idea that Johnny is solely a black, morbid, depressed, ill, melancholy object, like a crêpe knocker on the handle of a house, closed for the duration of the war – that isn't the case either. If you get past the knocker & open the door you'd find an extraordinarily simple eager passionate boy, very sensitive, *desperately* loyal, full of tweaks and twirls of fun – and more shy and more modest than even I, who know him pretty well, can remember. The great brick is that hes only this self when he feels safe – when he is with people whom he feels are after the same thing as he is. What is that? It is "profoundly speaking" – to be honest – That sounds so bald when I say it but perhaps you'll understand what I mean . . .

(All my letter seems to be a defence of Johnny & I feel rather like the poster of the young girl in Her Love Against the World.)

And Oh – Oh! – *don't* lets quarrel! It isn't really "like that" – As Bill Noble[2] says – "Jesus Christ! You folks just float around with razors in your socks *all* the time!" I don't want to hate people: I want to love them. If I *do* lose my faith in people I want to run to them and to cry: "Oh, please Ive lost my faith in you: have you seen it about anywhere. Do give it back to me: I wouldn't be without it for anything!" But perhaps that sounds childish to you . . .

Now it has stopped raining; the air feels lovely – I wish you were here. (I have a teeny little study in the Nation[3] this week or next – Its just a sort of glimpse of adolescent emotion: I am full of work again.)

Write again, Brett, when you have a mind to –

Your loving
Tig.

MS Newberry.

[1] Lady Ottoline wrote to Murry telling him that Sassoon had suffered a head wound, and that the review could cause his death. Murry quoted this in his reply to her on 16 July (Texas).

[2] An acquaintance of both J. D. Fergusson and Dorothy Brett.

[3] 'Carnation' which did not appear until 7 September.

To Ottoline Morrell, [30 July 1918]

47 Redcliffe Road [Fulham] | S.W.10
Tuesday.

Dearest Ottoline

Its a divine morning, quiet and hot. The water cart has just gone down the road and now the piano opposite is braiding its hair in swift, intricate braids. I cannot help feeling, today, that the world, at any rate, is the 'friend of man' and longs for us to walk upon lawns and idle in gardens and wear shady hats & dabble our feet in pools, and lie in grass and lose ourselves in forests and watch the light and the air shaking tall trees . . . Oh – these misunderstandings! Great ones & little ones – do let us drive them all into the sea. Why do we allow them to rush at us and snap and hurt us all so *horribly*. God knows we have all of us had reason enough to suspect and to mistrust . . . but "is it too late?"

Thank you for letting me see this letter. I am awfully glad that he has written a new poem. I don't know if Murry sent his letter to him or not – I hope he did. For I should hate S. S. to think ill of Murry.[1]

Sullivan came in on Saturday: he was positively merry – and we sat, four of us, *laughing*. Cant we *all* laugh one day? I do hope your headaches are better – It is vile that they should plague you so.

With love from
Katherine.

MS Stanford. *LKM* I. 205–6.

[1] Lady Ottoline sent on to KM a letter Sassoon had written on 27 July from the American Red Cross Hospital for Officers, Lancaster Gate, London, where he was recovering from the wound received in France on 13 July. He had said 'I wish I could do something to make Murry happier. My poem is finished and I'm satisfied'. (Texas.) The poem he wrote while in hospital was 'Letter to Robert Graves', *The War Poems of Siegfried Sassoon*, ed. Rupert Hart-Davis (1983), 130–2.

To Ida Baker, [1 August 1918]

47 Redcliffe Road [Fulham] | S.W.10.

Dear Jones

Come in tomorrow evening if you *can* manage, for I may be able to lend you something for your weekend – or a suitcase. Would you like Jack's small suitcase for instance? I thought of getting you some handkerchiefs – but then you are so particular about quality I get a bit frightened of buying you 'on the spec': you might despise 'em.

We are very unfortunate in our meetings. I dont *want* to quarrel, though I believe you think I do. The truth is that for the time being my nature is quite changed by illness. You see I am never one single hour without pain. If its not my lungs it is (far more painful) my back. And then my legs *ache* and I never can even change my position without such a creaking of all the joints as ever was. This, plus very bad nights exasperates me and I turn into a fiend, I suppose. And when you turn to me and say "you *did* have a bag of herbs IF you remember" as though those words of yours came out of an absolute cavern of HATE I realise "the change". All the same, and knowing and realising this as I do I *still* ask you to come to Hampstead – until I am better. For the sake of all that *has* been I ask that of you. I know I shall get better there – quite well again – but see me through these next few months – will you?

I know exactly why you talk of what you are going to do after the war – "Carrie" – the "big house" – "I may be in a factory". That is because, untrue to my first talk about Hampstead I have never made you feel part of it, and every time you say "our" I give you a vile look. This is wrong in me but at present I cant control it. Ill try and explain it a bit. You see out of all my external world only the house remains just now. Its all my little world & I want to make it *mine beyond words* – to express myself all I can in the small circle remaining. And so I am plagued with a wicked childish jealousy – lest my last doll shall be taken from me – dressed as I dont want it dressed – hugged by other arms. You wont understand this in me; there is no reason why you should. But you must believe that, as we live there, things will quite change, and if only you are 'careful for me' it will all be *quite* different & we shall [call] each other over the stairs.

Oh, it is (yes it is) incredible that one should have to explain all this. I always felt that the great high privilege, relief and comfort of friendship was that one had to explain nothing. But I have sinned against friendship, that's why.

Only I do think I am the last person on earth who has undying, unbroken faith. That will really seem to you *too* contradictory altogether. Nevertheless it is true.

If I dont see you before your weekend I hope you have a happy time, dearie, and take an old *well* Katie in a corner of your heart to think about if you have a moment.

In this imperfect, present world we have failed each other, scores of times, but in the real unchanging world we never have nor come down from our high place.

                                                            Yours ever
                                                            Katie.

If you buy a book for the journey the August English Review has a story by K.M.

MS BL. Alpers 1953, 265–6.

To Virginia Woolf, [2 August 1918]

'47' [Redcliffe Road, Fulham]

Dear Virginia,

I have been hoping to get the better of a beastly attack of my rheumatism in time to come to Asheham – but its no go. I am horribly disappointed & sorry, but the sofa leg has got me & I cant move from it. My right wing is playing up, too, so that altogether the machine is a thoroughly unsound machine and wont stand a journey. Its the devil of a blow – but there you are! And your letter promised such exciting things – a kind of sober walking by the sea with sudden immense waves of conversation scattering us, or flinging us together.

Yours funereally

Katherine.

MS Sussex. *Adam* 370–375, 23.

To Ottoline Morrell, [3 August 1918]

[47 Redcliffe Road, Fulham]

Saturday afternoon

I was simply enchanted with your letter. It came, after a dreadfully bad night, an age-long night which leaves one at the mercy of first impressions next morning. You know the feeling? One lies in a kind of daze, feeling so sensitive – so unbearably sensitive to the exterior world and longing for something 'lovely' to happen. The something lovely *did* happen to me – with your letter. I longed to get up and send you a telegram to your Hotel – just to say how wonderful it had been – but could not get up all day. So, tied to the sofa leg, I thought about it and you.

I am so thankful that the raid is over and that we shan't have another.[1] Oh, don't let us! They *are* so exhausting, and so wretched, and then when outsiders come in and start boasting on their own account I want to fly into the wilderness and like the dove in that hideous anthem[2] "Bui-ild me a ne-e-est and remain there for Ever at rest." But *otherwise* I hate the idea of perpetual wilderness and the dove idea of rest don't appeal to me at all.

We are supposed to have fought our way over to Asheham today – hung with our own meat and butter, but I couldn't face it. There seemed to have been so many things to catch and so many changes to make – a sort of government controlled game of musical chairs without any music, very grim. No, I couldn't. So instead I am sitting squeezed up in a corner of this formless room while a man cuts new pinnies for the armchairs and the sommier – lemon yellow ones with dashes of palm trees on them and parrots simply clinging to the branches. The parrots have, I think, a quite extraordinary resemblance to M. The tide is very low – at the ebb – in the Redcliffe Road and the sky is the colour of weak cocoa. I wish I could simply disappear – become invisible and find myself somewhere where the light was kinder with a superb new book to read by someone I'd never heard of before. But these are dreams and I must, when this scissor man goes – take my filet to the Fulham Road and do *shopping*. Oh! Oh! Why hasn't M. £2,500 a year? It would be so lovely to bask in money for a little.

I have a story called "Bliss" in this month's *English Review*. If you should see it will you really tell me what you think? Is that terre dangereuse? No, not really.

I will send you a cardboard box. I'd adore some flowers. But I think I have several boxes, so I shall send them all – in case they are still as rare at Garsington.

MS lacking. *LKM* I. 207–8.

---

[1] That is, the quarrel between the Morrells and Murry over the *Nation* review. For all the reservations KM and Murry continued to share about Lady Ottoline and Philip, the extravagant and self-conscious 'To O.M. and P.M.', written at Garsington on Christmas Day 1917, was included in Murry's *Poems: 1917–18*, published the following year.

[2] Mendelssohn's setting of words from Psalm 55, 'Hear my prayer' with its well-known second section, 'O for the wings of a dove'.

To Ida Baker, [3 August 1918]

47 Redcliffe Road [Fulham] | S.W.10.

Dear Jones

This is just to let you know that I am better of my rheumatism again & can walk, wear a frock and sash & sit up to table to eat my egg with a spoon.

Ive never never never seen such a piece of paper as yours this morning. Didn't rolling it into that ball take as long as folding it would have? Or had you been carrying a bun in it? Or did you push it through a keyhole? I think I must keep it, all ready as it is to stop a draught with –

Katie.

A most extraordinary thing has happened. The Germans have stolen some of my work which the New Age published & are printing it in a rotten paper called The Continental Times as "studies of the English middle class mind by Katherine Mansfield" I have seen a copy – it is published in Berlin Stockholm & Constantinople & *really* to see my work taking up a whole page gave me a *huge* thrill.[1] But isn't it surprising!

MS BL.

[1] On 7 June 1917 the *New Age* published 'A Pic-Nic', a short story in the form of a dialogue, and set in Wellington. It was now reprinted in the *Continental Times*, a German English-language paper, on 22 July 1918, as 'An English Pic-Nic, A Study of the Middle Class Mind'. It was collected for the first time in *Stories*, 215–22.

To Dorothy Brett, [7 August 1918]

47 Redcliffe Road [Fulham] | S W 10
Wednesday

Dearest Brett,

If you *should* come to Town this week don't fail to let me know – will you? I so want to see you before you disappear into Scotland.

There are not going to be any Air Raids this autumn, so I̳ propose you take a studio in Hampstead and that we meet ever so often in the innards of the Elephant, & talk about work and enjoy one another (which sounds a little "arabian" but is, like ALL my remarks, innocently meant.)

It was the lad's birthday yesterday. We had what Koteliansky might have called a *simple* fête. I gave him a paper knife and there were stewed plums for supper.

I am glad the Pup is happy and good; her home sounds nice but "hot and low" makes me suspicious of earwigs. I wish the Lord would cancel all creeping things.

Oh God! There are roses in this room which drive you *distracted*. I love flowers *too* much. Then there is this writing business – worse than the roses – and then there is this house in which I do mean to express all I know about colour and form and . . . . comfort.

Fergusson is at Portsmouth;[1] I miss him greatly. Sullivan comes & talks & is particularly nice. I have forgotten all about the quarrel, and (in strict confidence) am full of love for my friends.

Yours ever
Tig

P.S. Give Ottoline a *warm warm* greeting from her

K

MS Newberry.

<hr>

¹ Where he had to report for service as a war artist.

To Ottoline Morrell, [11 August 1918]

47 Redcliffe Road [Fulham] | S.W.10.
Sunday.

We move to Hampstead on the 25th.
Dearest Ottoline
Will you pass through London on your way to the Sea? If you do –
please let me know. I long to see you. I was so glad to hear from you
yesterday. I wish I were with you now – not on the lawn but sitting
under some tree with all dazzling, silent brightness just beyond –
where we could talk & be alone.

I heard the *infinitely* sad news yesterday that my darling little
mother is dead.¹ She was the most exquisite, perfect little being –
something between a star and a flower – I simply cannot *bear* the
thought that I shall not see her again –

Always your loving
Katherine.

Murry has 'absolutely forgotten it'.

MS Newberry. *LKM* I. 208–9.

<hr>

¹ Annie Burnell Beauchamp died in Bowen Street Hospital, Wellington, on 8 August. She was
fifty-four.

To Dorothy Brett, [14 August 1918]

[47 Redcliffe Road, Fulham]
Wednesday

My dearest Brett
I was so glad of your letter today. Yes, it is an *immense* blow. She was
the most precious, lovely little being, ever so far away, you know, and
writing me these long long letters about the garden and the house and
her conversations in bed with Father, and of how she loved sudden
unexpected cups of tea – "out of the air, brought by faithful ravens in
aprons" – and letters beginning 'darling child it is the most exquisite

day' – She *lived* every moment of Life more fully and completely than anyone Ive ever known – and her gaiety wasnt any less real for being *high courage* – courage to meet anything with.

Ever since I heard of her death my memories of her come flying back into my heart – and there are moments when its unbearable to receive them. But it has made me realise more fully than ever before that I love *courage – spirit –* poise (do you know what I mean? All these words are too little) more than anything. And I feel inclined to say (not to anybody in particular) "let us love each other". Let us be *kind* and rejoice in one another and leave all squabbles and ugliness to the dull dogs who can only become articulate when they bark and growl. The world is so dreadful in many ways. Do let us be tender with each other.

I dare say that to you because I know you understand.

With much love
Tig

MS Newberry. *LKM* I. 210–11.

To Ottoline Morrell, [15 August 1918]

47 Redcliffe Road [Fulham] | S.W.10.
Thursday.

Dearest Ottoline

How am I to thank you for your letter and for these exquisite flowers? They are both so perfect – they are like *one* gift – and its strangely true – how just as your letters *are* you – so the flowers you send couldn't have been sent by anybody else – I feel I could single out this bright sweet bouquet in Eternity & say – they came from Ottoline. You have such a lovely way of gathering flowers as you talk – or of suddenly handing one a piece of verbena or scented geranium – almost, as it were, unconsciously –

Yes, my mother's death is a terrible sorrow to me – I feel – do you know what I mean – the *silence* of it so. She was more alive than anyone I have ever known.

How are you – dearest Ottoline? And are you going to the sea? Brett said you thought of it. Garsington must be divine in this weather, though. I hope that we shall see each other soon. I am longing to be in my new house – out of this *common* passage way – *common* door. I sit in front of these three windows and feel that I am sitting in a shop – with nothing whatever to sell. Murry is, as usual, working a hundred times too hard – but he cannot stop himself and I cannot stop him. I can only look on and deplore it. However, like a little forlorn Ibsen hero the 'miracle'[1] is going to happen for him when he gets into his new house. His study has lemon yellow walls and orange curtains. I have an idea that I shall hang a parrot in it . . . . as well.

Oh, I *long* for gaiety – for a high spirit – for gracious ways and kindness and happy love. Life without these is not worth living. But they *must be*. We have – the few of us – got wings – real wings – beauties – to fly with and not to always hide under –

Very much love dearest friend
Katherine.

MS Texas. *LKM* I. 210.

---

[1] It seems that KM is recalling the last scene of Ibsen's *A Doll's House* (1879) in which the husband, in the last line of the play, unrealistically hopes for the 'greatest miracle of all' to happen: that, as his wife Nora has said, 'You and I would have to change . . . So that the life we share would be a real marriage'.

To Virginia Woolf, [mid-August 1918]

[47 Redcliffe Road, Fulham]

Dear Virginia

I do not want to leave your letter unanswered. I do hope we can come later; we were awfully disappointed, too. Forgive me – Ive nothing to say. This is just a friendly wave – I love to think of you at Asheham.

My mother has died. I cant think of anything else. Ah, Virginia, she was such an exquisite little being, far too fragile and lovely to be dead for ever more.

Katherine.

MS Berg. *LKM* I. 208.

To Charlotte Beauchamp Perkins, [17 August 1918]

47 Redcliffe Road [Fulham] | S.W.10
Saturday

Dearest Marie,

Here are the letters you asked me to send back to you. I wish I had kept more of Mother's letters; they live and breathe. These last are so radiant and they give such a picture of her – don't they? Thank you for having let me see them. I had rather thought that Father would have cabled again before now – Hadn't you? I do wish he would – and yet what is there to say? But it seems so long to wait for letters . . .

I hope, dear, you have been enjoying this perfect weather which has 'turned' today. It is quite chilly this morning & my 11 oclock tea is peculiarly grateful. We are moving, definitely, on Monday week and I am already making all fair before that happens – having a rare *tidy* and *burn* up. However careful one is ones possessions seem to shed themselves in untidiness as a tree sheds leaves and the new house is so spick and span that I feel everything that goes into it must shine like a jewel.

Before the end of next week, dear, will you let me know of the train which you consider is the best and goes furthest?

I am sending you a letter from Ellie Payne.[1] Ottoline sent me, with her letter a most exquisite bouquet of bright flowers – 'Gathered for your mother' – Wasn't it a perfect thing to do?

With fondest love
Your own
Katie

MS Newberry.

---

[1] KM's cousin, and the mother of Sylvia Payne, her closest friend at Queen's College.

To Ottoline Morrell, [19 August 1918]

47 Redcliffe Road [Fulham] | S.W.10.
Monday.

Dearest Ottoline

I have been condemned to the sommier for the last few days & not able to walk at all. There is nothing I should have loved more than to walk in your garden – otherwise – Thank you, dearest friend, for asking me.

But the King of the Hanky-Pankies is coming this morning to electrify me[1] and I hope to have new legs – arms – wings – everything – in a week or two.

I can't go on like this; even a caterpillar would turn.

We leave here next Monday for:

2 Portland Villas
East Heath Road
Hampstead

Portland Villas! – it sounds like one of those houses where a "few guests are taken slightly mental not objected to. Firm home-like treatment".

But inside it is going to be a vision – a sort of spring perpetual with delicate little flowery poems in the top floor window boxes and short stories, very rich and gay on the first floor sills. In the garden 'the Mountain' dreams of african trees – violet trees covered with bunches of violets and assegai trees with leaves like spears.

But I don't believe in *them*.

And how shall I lure you there? I have thought of that several times . . .

Its such a strange morning here – puffs of silver cloud blowing over the roofs and indian gentlemen in mustard coloured turbans prancing up and down the pavement. And now heres the electric man with his little box – He has a waxed mustache & we are beginning to ask if it is *lumber* or *ribs* – Oh dear!

My warm love to you
Katherine.

MS Stanford. *LKM* I. 209.

[1] A form of medical treatment for her rheumatism.

To Dorothy Brett, [25 August 1918]

The Old Vicarage, | Tadworth | Surrey.[1]

Dearest Brett,

Send another letter into the blue when you have a mind – will you? Its so long since I heard from you. I shall be on the Elephants back tomorrow, any time after sunset, & there is a letter-box there that wants warming.

I am *stupified* – turning into a perfect fool! This constant pain is so wearing – and *never* being able to walk or to run or to be in the least mobile – and *never* sleeping a night through. Oh, dear, I shall be old very soon if this goes on –

Thats enough – Now you are to consider this a begging letter – begging for one from you:

> 2 Portland Villas
> East Heath Road
> Hampstead.

Ever your loving little
Tig.

MS Newberry.

[1] KM was staying with her mother's sister, Aunt Belle Trinder.

III
ENGLAND – HAMPSTEAD:
1918–1919

When the Murrys moved to Hampstead towards the end of August, for the first time in some years they went to a house they cared for, and that KM regarded fully as 'home'. Her marriage, her continuing poor health, the death of her mother, and the move, each contributed to her demand for a more regulated life. She now had permanent servants, and something of middle-class comfort.

As a writer, and wife of a prominent editor – Murry took over the editorship of the *Athenaeum* in February 1919 – she enjoyed the social possibilities open to her, and she renewed many literary and personal friendships. She began a weekly column of fiction reviews for the *Athenaeum*, and with Koteliansky a series of translations from Chekhov's letters.

But by summer 1919 her illness was again severe, and at the insistence of Victor Sorapure, the doctor who advised her for the next three years and became something too of a spiritual director, she decided she must go to the Italian Riviera. She wrote an informal will, and left England on 11 September.

To Ottoline Morrell, [1 September 1918]

2 Portland Villas | East Heath Road | Hampstead. N.W.3.
Sunday.

Dearest Ottoline –

They are superb jewels in its crown – Lovely lovely flowers – and the first that we have had – The Mountain is sending back the Box tomorrow – I wish you would come into the studio & see these bright bouquets. Thank you – dearest for them – It seems so long since I have heard from you – I *long* for a letter – The builders are still here up & down the staircase – more builders than stairs. If it were not for these monsters the Elephant would be a delightful creature –

But oh I am *ill* and *sad* – I want so to be well & I have to go dead slow carrying a pain that I cant send away –

My warm love,
Katherine.

MS Texas.

To Ottoline Morrell, [5 September 1918]

It is *Portland Villas* [East Heath Road, Hampstead]
Thursday.

Dearest Ottoline

I am most fortunate and infinitely happy to have you for my friend
– You *do* know how much you are in my thoughts and how I always
long to share the things I love to hear and to see – with you. Yesterday
afternoon – when the flowers came I felt quite overwhelmed – I felt as
I took them out of the box: "unless I mention every single flower to
her how can I tell her how I *saw* them" – the black poppy – the two
pale sunflowers – all the 'different' yellow ones – and then, above all
these round bright beauties. My seaside lodging is a bower and even
M. who is, at the moment, like the bathing dress perpetual hanging
out to dry after a *sad sad* wetting – gave a great gasp of delight –

Oh, but like you I sigh for happiness – for a world which isn't
always 'out of joint'. This constant living on the defensive – how tiring
it is! Why *wont* people live more freely and more wildly. But no – there
they are – *smug* – like little plants in little pots – that ought to have
been put out in a garden years ago – years ago. But they prefer their
life on a shelf – out of the "full force" of the sun and wind – each one
tight in itself and away from its companions. But Fear, Distrust,
Cowardice, Smugness – surely they are more Horrid Worms than one
would find in any garden. – But I don't give up hope – I can't – And
here is this divine, cloudless day waiting for something more to flower
– Dearest Ottoline – remember me when you lean over the tobacco
plant – I can see it & breathe it now – how exquisite it is! There must
be fields of tobacco plant in the moon –

Isn't David Copperfield adorable. I like even the Dora part – & that
friend of Dora's – Julia somebody – who was 'blighted'.[1] She is such a
joy to me. Yes – doesn't Charley D. make our little men smaller than
ever – and such *pencil sharpeners* –

I have discovered nothing to read – and do not know how the days
pass. The electric man is still filling me with sparks – every day for ¾
of an hour. It is very comforting, and I think it is going to beat the
rheumatiz. How are your headaches?

I shall send back the box today –

Goodbye for now dearest friend.

Ever your loving
Katherine.

MS Texas. *LKM* I. 211–12.

[1] In Chapter XXXIII of *David Copperfield*, Dickens writes of 'Miss Julia Mills having been
unhappy in a misplaced affection, and being understood to have retired from the world on her

awful stock of experience, but still to take a calm interest in the unblighted hopes and loves of youth'.

To J. D. Fergusson, [September 1918]

[2 Portland Villas, East Heath Road, Hampstead]

Dear Fergusson

Of course I saw the real Picasso floating between France and England & you and he meeting now & then at some little café on the pier, called, perhaps, The Laughing Parrot.

I was delighted to see Margaret the other day. She looks better for her holiday already; in fact, she looked very lovely; there was a bloom and a brightness about her that made me think of a damson. I have a very warm place in my heart for Margaret.

The weather here is good – its exciting. Its summer still, but in spite of the papers *and* the shops there is a feeling in the air that all over the round world fruit is ripening and falling. My God! These first apples – par exemple – the smell of them & when you bite into them how they bite back again sharp and sweet. I was standing outside South Kensington Station yesterday and that swindling fruiterer was holding up a bunch of grapes. His gesture seemed to cut right through the Ages – *Man with Grapes* once and for all, don't you know.

I wish we lived in a more generous country where people were not so passionately concerned with planting early spring chimneys and late autumn railway lines – but Ive no doubt their crops suit the soil best.

Fergusson, do you get moods when you fall in love all over again from the very beginning with the Art Business? Ive got one, at present. Everything that Ive written before seems more or less a false alarm; if only I can bring this off . . . and so on. But it is extraordinary how little people have done – at any rate – at my job – and how content they have been with the chance encounter or a matrimonial stodge. All that lies between is almost undiscovered and unexplored, except for an occasional picnic, so to speak. I only hope I can take off my hat to this prospect without my head coming off too.

Murry is very well – full of fire for his friends and brimstone for his enemies. He is hard at the flat ripolin job in his spare moments – and everything is being painted – Dont be surprised to see him on the top step of his Hampstead house – standing there to greet you – a beautiful lemon yellow.

We have had some very powerful talks with Sullivan who continues to be very cheerful. (The result, I believe of bacon sans ticket.)

This isn't a letter: I cant write em. Its cheero – I hope all goes well.
Sincerely
Mansfield.

MS ATL.

To S. S. Koteliansky, [September 1918]
[2 Portland Villas, East Heath Road, Hampstead]

Come tonight, Katherine.[1]

Telegram. Text from Alpers 1980, 286.

---

[1] The friendship between KM and Koteliansky had been severed for some time. He had told Virginia Woolf the previous January that KM's 'lies & poses had proved too much for him', *DVW*, I. 108. Soon after moving into Portland Villas KM sent this telegram to Koteliansky, and a similar one to Beatrice Campbell, another friend she had not seen over a long period. They came when summoned and the friendships were renewed.

To Virginia Woolf, [September 1918]
2 Portland Villas | East Heath Road | Hampstead N W 3.

We're in the telephone
1277 Hampstead

My dear Virginia
    We have not been able to go away. At the last moment I was afraid of the strange hotel and having to look after myself – and now I *couldnt* go anywhere. The weather caught me and Im not well. I do nothing but cough and rage – and Im allowed to do nothing but be still.
    So the weekend I looked forward to *more than I can say* must be a dream for this year.[1] I cannot say how sorry I am. Forgive me. I want to write you a long letter but its no go to-day. I can only think about you instead.
With my love, dear Virginia
Katherine.

Murry sends love to you both

MS Sussex. *Adam* 370–375, 22.

---

[1] The Woolfs returned from Asheham to Hogarth House, Richmond, at the beginning of October.

To Dorothy Brett, [5] October [1918]

[2 Portland Villas, East Heath Road, Hampstead]
Saturday afternoon. October.

Dearest Brett,

Your letter came by itself with a special loud great knock at the door for it. I fancied it had been carried in the bosom of some hielan' drover, *and* saw him at the door with his dirk showing in the folds of his plaid and his ram's horn of whisky. Outside all his shaggy beasts munched the wet willows . . .

I was awfully glad to hear from you. It all sounded so far away and like a novel of Turgenev – so far away from Hampstead and London. I wish you would come back soon and have a pied à terre of your own.

It must be very difficult to live in ones family when one has flown out of the nest. What can I do with my wings now I am back? There is no room for wings in the largest nest imaginable – and its no use pretending that I haven't got 'em. They have carried me ever so far up and away – That is the sort of pipe that I should make – yet, of course, *not* having that nest to fly to – I imagine it the softest loveliest place to *rest* oneself *out* in as the Germans say.

I saw a great deal of Ottoline. She came up here often – and we talked. She was *wonderful* and I think she looks a great deal better. Oh dear, I wish I lived nearer her. Its such a joy to have one's absolute largest *fling* in talk and be not only understood – but carried away by what she flings back.

Why isn't there some exquisite city where we all have our palaces and hear music – very often – and row upon the water, and walk in heavenly landscapes and look at pictures and where all the people are beauties – moving in the streets as it were to a dance. I am quite serious. I *pine* for lavishness. For the real fruits of the earth tumbling out of a brimming horn. (Perhaps it is four years of khaki.)

No, I didn't see her doctor. I saw a big Gun on my own – who was very intelligent.[1] He says I have got this disease in both my lungs, that I can [not] get better in London but must go off to some mountain peak to be cured. "Serious but recoverable" said he. I see M. & I climbing up some peak after this war & finding a tiny little house at the top with windows like spectacles & living in it – all nicely dressed in big rabbit skins – especially rabbit skin gloves – which we shall *never* take off until we have gradually eaten them off with our bread and butter – as one does –

In the meantime Murry and I are painting the Elephant and he has bought a Press and I have typed 30,000 words of my 50,000 book[2] and the Mountain makes her steam puddings for herself and Jack.

That is what M. will look like eventually, a little set of

pudding basins . . . . with a plume of steam rising out of his hair and three raisins for buttons and two currants for eyes.

I am full of new ideas for work. Rather held up as usual by my wretched machinery which creaks and groans and lets me down – But I mean to get it in good enough order to be able to ignore it & plunge into the REAL LIFE.

Gertler is coming to supper tomorrow. I hope he will sit at my fireside often this winter – and tonight Sullivan is coming for a talk –

Dont stay in Scotland[3] too long, dearest. Just draw Ma'amselle[4] and then come back – Its too far –

And take care of yourself. Don't turn into a pixie or a fairy or a gnome or a water nymph – you might you know –

Yours ever with love
Tig

MS Newberry. *LKM* I. 212–13.

[1] Murry gives an account of this consultation with an unnamed but 'famous specialist in tuberculosis', *BTW*, 490. 'He came down from Katherine's room. "There's one chance for her – and only one. If she goes into a *strict* sanatorium immediately. Switzerland is not an atom more good to her than England is. Climate means nothing. Discipline everything . . . . If not, she has two or three years to live – four at the outside." '

[2] *Bliss and Other Stories*, to be published by Constable in 1920. The book was first rejected by Heinemann.

[3] Brett was staying at her father's Scottish property, Roman Camp, Callander, Perthshire.

[4] Juliet Baillot, who had been the governess for Lady Ottoline's daughter Julian. She was presently employed by Brett's sister Sylvia, Ranee of Sarawak, to look after her children.

To Ottoline Morrell, [8 October 1918]

[2 Portland Villas, East Heath Road, Hampstead]
Tuesday.

Dearest Ottoline,

I have been thinking of you so much since you went back to Garsington, and *realising* over & over again how more than dear it was of you to have come so dreadfully far to see me & to have given me so much of your time. Oh, but I *loved* seeing you – & when ever I feel the biting cold beginning I wrap up warm in the memory of our last 'talk'.

Such strange actual things seem to have happened. Fancy Robbie Ross dying[1] – that was surely very odd in him. He must have been, poor fellow, greatly surprised himself – to be, so suddenly, *nipped* into Eternity on a Saturday night. I expect he still feels that it is a mistake, simply a mistake. He has gone behind the wrong curtain, found the Wrong Exit – is wandering down a passage for Artists Only – Death, how dreadful a thing is Death!! I have such a horror of it; it ought not to be. We should simply go from star to star——But no – even that is not good enough. Id arrive & find Frieda swooping down upon me, with meringue wings & a marzipan wand, a real German angel.

Speaking of Frieda. Gertler came to supper on Sunday night & told us that the Lawrences are coming to live in London indefinitely – They *are* come, in fact, yesterday & are staying just round the corner in Well Walk.[2] This really horrifies me. I am sure they will turn up here, & though I have armed M. with every possible weapon & warned him against L. I have a terrible idea that they will fight – and it will be hideous and lacerating. L. has come up to look for work in an office – which of course he'll *never* do for more than three days.[3] But altogether, I feel they are better as many miles away as there *are* miles. Everytime the bell goes I hear Frieda's "*Well* Katherina – *here* we are!" and I turn cold with horror.

I had such a depressed, fish-out-of-water back-to-the-nursery little letter from poor Brett. Her father won't speak, her mother treats her as though she were a vase, the children are charming with vile nurses and mademoiselle has a well developed bosom and is fat. There is very little to eat and she is always hungry & bitterly cold. It sounds *too* forlorn. Julian Huxley has been and impressed her as *throbbing* with fire, ambition and attainments.[4] In fact it read like some unfinished novel by Turgenev, with Brett for the heroine & J.H. for a sort of Bazarov-Rudin.[5]

Oh – I *wish* we could find a new country. There is a vine outside my windows & all the little grapes are purple & down below in the yard a lady is pegging a pair of gents. woven underpants . . . Gissing in Italy – it looks to me . . .[6]

This letter is *too* dull – But I feel I must just write to you.

With very much love dearest
Katherine.

Mrs Hamilton[7] is coming to tea next week. I am jingling my political threepenny bit already!

MS Dartmouth.

---

[1] Robert Ross (1869–1918), critic and *connoisseur*, died on 5 October.
[2] The Lawrences were staying at 32 Well Walk, Hampstead.
[3] Although he had been classified in 1917 as C3, the lowest class fit for non-military service,

Lawrence was again called for examination the month before in Derby. He now came to London hoping to find employment that exempted him from any kind of war service.

⁴ Julian Huxley married Juliet Baillot in 1919.

⁵ Yevgeny Bazarov is a portrait of an emerging 'modern' mind in Ivan Turgenev's *Fathers and Sons* (1862); Dmitri Rudin is the gifted, idealistic, but ineffectual protagonist in *Rudin* (1856).

⁶ KM had earlier used the novelist George Gissing as a kind of touchstone for shabbiness when writing to Murry on 26 May 1918. His *By the Ionian Sea* was published in 1900, and a historical romance of sixth-century Italy, *Veranilda*, posthumously in 1904.

⁷ Mary Agnes Hamilton (1884–1962), an Economics graduate of Newnham College, Cambridge, was a novelist, journalist, public speaker, and ardent supporter of the Labour Party, which she represented as MP for Blackburn 1929–31. She wrote two volumes of autobiography, *Remembering My Good Friends* (1944), and *Uphill All the Way* (1953).

To Anne Estelle Drey, 15 October 1918

2 Portland Villas | East Heath Road | N.W.3
15 X 1918

Anne darling

Your letter went to the cockles of my heart – bless you for it – & curiously enough I had been thinking over the Spring Book only yesterday – seeing it & hoping that we would bring it off. Shall us? Lets –

I will send you a Bud or a Leaf as they pop out & if you like em – ça ira. I have a very definite idea at this distance, at this Temperature & with the willow leaves flying in at the windows what spring felt like – to me – & its so mixed with lobsters, winkles, the smell of the sea – weedy pools, it *ought* with the help of the Lord to have enough Body[1] – I shall get down to it – bang off – especially as I am Tied to the Sofa leg until Thursday week. That means I cant come and spend the delightful day with you until after then – Hélas – But ask me again, chèrie, wont you & Ill come along with my slippers in a satin bag & my Plain Knitting. I long to see the studio. I love the Quality of your Fine Feeling for Decoration. One feels immensely *rested* & *stimulated* at the same time – a sort of fruitful Basking – if you know what I mean.

Im sending you today a snippet of home made Cake from my home – Birthday Cake (I was 30 yesterday!) I hope it arrives in good order. You are to eat every crumb yourself!

This is the sort of picture I have of you, darling – in my romantic moments.

Scene: Channel Boat. Anne on deck, carrying un paquet chéri who wears a cap with a cerise brim, white "petal" top & black pompadour on the crown – She points to the coast & says "Voilà mon loup chéri, voila la belle France." The loup chéri replies – "C'est bon à manager?" Anne replies "Furieusement Bon."

My house is rather a joy when I can forget that the tooth glass is out of proportion with the lotion bottle etc etc etc. My Papa sent a specialist[2] to see me yesterday WHO said that if I didn't go into a sanatorium I had not a Dog's Chance – Blast his eyes – je m'en fou – I feel full of Fire and Buck – I am sure Peace is coming – don't you? Oh, I have such a longing for France. Can you hear that street cry Marchand d'habits – It sounds like '*Chandabi* & is said or *sung* with a sort of jump in the middle –

Well – God bless us all – & you especially – Your "Hedge" nods & waves as I write with orange butterflies fanning their wings over the Campions[3] –

Always
Katherine.

MS ATL. *LKM* I. 214.

[1] Again, a reference to the book of poems and drawings they planned together in Cornwall.

[2] Her cousin Sydney Beauchamp (1861–1921), who visited KM on her birthday, 14 October. He was soon to be knighted for his services as physician to the Conference at Versailles. The son of Henry Herron Beauchamp, his sister Charlotte was the mother of Sydney Waterlow.

[3] A picture Anne Drey had given KM, perhaps one of the illustrations for their proposed book.

To Ottoline Morrell, [22 October 1918]

2 Portland Villas | East Heath Road | N.W.3.

Dearest Ottoline

I was so happy to hear from you today but I wish you had not a cold. Its such appaling ghastly weather to *fight*; one needs double strength and double health. I wish I were near. I wish I could tap at your door. I simply LONG for a talk – just with you – nobody else – a long talk – in which we can really *let fly*.

Oh, my dearest woman friend – how vivid you are to me – how I love the thought of you; you cannot know. And it is such a 'comfort' to feel that we are in the same world – not in this one. What has one to do with this one? I feel that winter, cruel forbidding winter is content to leave nothing unfrozen – not one heart or one bud of a soul to escape! If only one did not feel that it is all so wrong – so wrong. It would be much happier if one could feel – like Murry – mankind is born to suffer – But I do feel that is so wrong – so wrong. It is like saying: mankind is born to walk about in galoshes under an umbrella. Oh dear – I should like to put a great notice over England – *closed* during the winter months. Perhaps if everybody were shipped off to blue skies and big bright flowers they would change. But I don't know – The miracle is that one goes on hoping and believing *through it all* just as passionately as ever one did –

It is a grey grim, pavement of a day, with slow dropping rain. When the Mountain brought me my early morning tea this morning she whispered, tenderly: "Do you think it would be a good idea to change one ton of coal for two of large anthracite? I don't think we require a special permit and even if we do I think it is worth it." My bed turned into a railway truck, shuffled off to the pit head, and two tons of large anthracite were tumbled on it . . . A very lourd paquet to begin the day with . . .

Lawrence has been running in and out all this week. He is gone off to the Midlands today – still without Frieda.[1] He seems to have quite forgotten her for the time – merely saying: "she wants me to become a german and Im *not* a german" – and so dismisses her. But I wonder why he is taken in by the most impossible charlatans – I am afraid he will never be free of them. Perhaps his whole trouble is that he has not a real sense of humour – He takes himself dreadfully seriously now-a-days; I mean he sees himself as a symbolic figure – a prophet – the voice in the wilderness crying *'woe'*. And what is amusing is his opinion of Murry as a flipperty-gibbet – "play on, ye mayflower" kind of figure who never will take Life or himself seriously enough!

This is a dull letter – a rattling old withered leaf of a thing – not what I want to send you – Forgive it and me – –

Do you think – one day – we might go abroad together? That is always a dream of mine –

Forever | Your loving
Katherine.

MS Texas. *LKM* I. 224.

---

[1] Lawrence left Hampstead on 22 October for Chapel Farm Cottage, Hermitage, Berkshire.

To Dorothy Brett, [27 October 1918]

[2 Portland Villas, East Heath Road, Hampstead]

Your letters are wonderfully well worth waiting for, dearest Brett. I read this one to Murry as we drank our coffee last night and on the wings of it away we flew, up the snow mountains to some place like *this* (see drawing). The two flies on the path are M. & me; then there is *you* in the sleigh – Ottoline is just behind the tallest mountain. Pray observe that we have got a Swiss milk cow! Oh, Heavens! How nice it is. What does one ask more! This must come true after the war. There is no reason why it should not & really, in spite of all England shrieking & imploring everybody not to make Peace until they've had a rare kick at him & a rare nose-in-the-mud rubbing one does feel that Peace is in the air.

> "It is all about, my sister
> Yet it is unborn –"

(Those lines struck me suddenly & seemed suddenly mysteriously lovely.) They took my breath away. It was like listening at the door & hearing the winter steal away – leaving spring, spring, in a basket on the doorstep of the world.

Oh Brett – let there be no more War. I have been spending all my days gradually fitting into a smaller & smaller hole as my puff gets less. Now Im in bed – & here I must stay for a bit. This is very cursed: in fact its HELL but I shall get out of it & once we have lain down our

knife & fork & agreed to eat no more German Ill be well again – But
England! What! *Peace!* Its like suddenly snatching away all their meat
coupons – What did my son die for, Sir? To keep the war going or to
end it, Sir? To keep it going Sir, until everybody else's son is as dead
as he! They, the old gentlemen over 70 who write to le Times would
like to have *such* a Peace, that they could plant a camp stool in any
corner of Europe, sit down, throw their handkerchiefs over their faces
& go to sleep there without being disturbed by *one single solitary* soul.
But they won't get their way –

Ottoline came on Thursday – It was Murry's "early closing day" &
he was here, too – Heavens! The dove really seemed to settle on them.
They looked at each other & *laughed.* But she was so marvellous – Do
you know her mood when she is wonderfully *lavish* & gay – When she
says "I am like *this* & like *this* & like *this.*" There is nobody like her –

Lawrence & Frieda have been in town. Frieda was ill & in bed but I
saw a very great deal of Lawrence – For me, at least, the dove brooded
over him too. I loved him: He was just his old merry, rich self,
laughing, describing things, giving you pictures, full of enthusiasm
and joy in a future where we were all "vagabonds" – We simply did
not talk about people. We kept to things like nuts and cowslips & fires
in woods, and his black self *was* not. Oh, there is something so lovable
in him – & his eagerness, his passionate eagerness for life – that is
what one loves so.[1] Now he is gone back to the country.

Murry-who-loves-you is full of Fire. The flu has not penetrated the
puddings. He simply thrives. I shall have him photographed in his
singlet soon, lying on a mat, you know, a-goo-gooing with
          REARED FROM BIRTH ON SUET PUDDINGS
written underneath. Of course I always feel that the Mountain has got
her own head tied up in a cloth so she can pop that into a basin &
steam it if supplies run short . . . But Murry is really seriously
excessivement bobbish, & when we are alone together, just talking, or
putting a stick on the fire – or especially when we lie in bed at night,
all neat & brushed, smelling faintly of Kalodont toothpaste & reading
out of one poetry book, our happiness quite overcomes us & we feel
positively *faint* – I don't know what it is in our love – that seems to
give everything a touch of faëry – It is a different world altogether
from the world that other people live in. One's neither grown up, nor
a child, neither married or unmarried, one simply ɪs & the other being
ɪs and so – on they fare – No, I can't explain, but you know –
otherwise I shouldn't have mentioned it.

Darling Brett, I must stop this letter – The day is divine. Do not get
flu. Do not stay there too long. We think of you & *long* to see you.

I keep on writing – its such queer stuff too. I am afraid nobody will
want it – Success to the drawings. I wish Mamselle could spare me a

little tiny bit of her *front*. Mine has *gone*. I hope it doesn't appear anywhere else –

Addio dearest friend

Tig

MS Newberry. *LKM* I. 215–16.

¹ This was the last time KM and Lawrence met. A month earlier, on 20 September, she had made a notebook entry on her bad temper: 'Strangely enough these fits are Lawrence and Frieda over again. I am more like L. than anybody. We are *unthinkably* alike, in fact.' (*Journal* 1954, 146.)

To Ottoline Morrell, [? October 1918]

[2 Portland Villas, East Heath Road, Hampstead]

Dearest dearest Ottoline

This is just a note – just to say I love to think you are going to the Ballet¹ & I wɪsʜ I were with you – in that warm light place where there's music and dancing. (It sounds as though I were meaning Heaven, except that I am *sure* Heaven will be infernally chilly.)

I am lying in my basket with a spiritual flannel round my chops. Occasionally the Mountain (8000 feet high) swoops over me & says: "Shall I *steam* it & put the custard *round* or . . ." and occasionally Murry drops an Evening News on to me – as a sort of 'sign' from the great world beyond – I have read War & Peace again – and then War & Peace again – & now I feel inclined to positively sing to it:

'If You were the Only Book in the World!'²

Dearest dearest Friend. *You* I love.

Forgive this clipped cut off DULL

Katherine.

MS Texas. *LKM* I. 212.

¹ Lady Ottoline frequently attended performances of Serge Diaghilev's Russian Ballet at the Coliseum, Charing Cross.

² 'If you were the only girl in the world' was a song from the musical *The Bing Boys Are Here*. KM had earlier referred to it in writing to Lady Ottoline on 12 Sep 1916 (*CLKM* I, 280–1, n. 1).

To Virginia Woolf, 1 November 1918

2 Portland Villas | East Heath Road [Hampstead] | NW3

1.xi.1918

Dear Virginia,

I meant to answer your letter sooner but my strong right arm refused to obey me – I should *love* to see [you] one afternoon next

week. Would Wednesday suit you? I am a very dull dog, and in bed –
but I try to look as though I were there for pleasure & not from
necessity. But do come – there is a power of things to be talked over.
Murry will send you a very pretty delicate little flowery map of the
way. Its extremely easy to find & I swear to God its not more than 8
minutes from the Tube Station.

I am awfully glad that Prelude has given a little pleasure – I have
felt guilty towards you on its account, as a matter of fact, for I thought
it had been a Bad Failure & you cursed the day – – – Well, Virginia,
dear – – –

THEY have tied a bunch of beech leaves to my bedpost. What
lovely things they are – so full of life. The cold reluctant air blows in
the fire streams up the chimney & a little clock outside strikes *three* in a
way that raises your eyebrows – "My dear child – I am perfectly
prepared to believe you; there is no earthly need to insist on it." I *hate*
that clock – Now, in France, a little clock like that would strike as
though it were all astonishment & amusement at finding itself at *three*
or *four* or *five* but – however its no matter.

Yours Ever
Katherine.

MS Berg. *LKM* I. 216.

To Ottoline Morrell, 4 November 1918

2 Portland Villas | East Heath Road [Hampstead] | N W 3
4.xi. 1918

My dearest Ottoline

Thank you for your adorable letter – I simply *fell* on it – – I shall
simply love to see you this week if you have time to climb up to this
eyrie – I always hate the idea that it is so far for you. Virginia is
coming on Wednesday – If only M. & I might see you on another
Thursday – It did make me so happy before. I really felt that the Past
had blown away – We talked so much about you after you had gone –
You *were*, you know, quite dispassionately speaking so *marvellous* that
afternoon. Come again – do come again – Let us three laugh & talk
again –

I have been quite unable to write these last days – with acute
neuritis in my arm and shoulder – Another New Dish – Thats the
worst of illness – If one could only choose ones dish à la carte – eat it –
make a grimace over it & throw the plate away – But its this infernally
boring table d'hôte with all these little side dishes & kickshaws that

you're simply not allowed to refuse – It is distracting and sometimes I feel it never will end –

I have felt so cut off from the world without a pen. I lay and read *The Egoist*. It seemed to me marvellously good in its way – and I had quite forgotten how much Meredith enjoyed writing – Its delightful how this enjoyment comes through – he shares your laugh – catches your eye – sees the point just as you do. But really a very difficult book for englishmen to read without *twinging* –

But then I read Rhoda Fleming, & that seemed to me so *false* so preposterous – one could only groan for it – & its so odious. All this lingering over the idea of a lily white white as snow jeune fille in the embrace of an ugly vicious little old man made me want to cry like Lawrence that "his sex was all wrong" – But he *is* a big man – and he *can* write wonders.[1]

These strange, wild evenings shaken with wind & rain have something of spring in them. One cant help feeling that tomorrow the first green will be there, & perhaps you will meet a little child with a fist of wan daffodils – It does not matter dreadfully that it is not true – If Peace comes I really do feel that the winter will not be real winter – it cant be cold and dark & malignant. A miracle will happen –

But I wish the horrible old knitting women at Versailles would *hurry hurry* – Do you see that President Wilson is coming to attend the Conference in Person – Already – I fondly dream of – – – oh such a meeting! A sort of glorified Christina Pontifex interview between us[2] – I am afraid I am staying in bed too long.

Lawrence has sent me today a new play of his[3] – very long – just written – I must read it. I have glanced inside and it looks *black* with miners – the frenzied miners that he felt on his spine so in the Midlands – Poor dear man! I do wish he could come up up out of the Pit for ever – But he wont –

I long to see you – Oh what *shall* we do to celebrate the end of the war –

With fondest love | I am ever your
Katherine.

MS Texas. *LKM* I. 216.

[1] George Meredith (1824–1909), poet and novelist. *The Egoist* was published in 1879, *Rhoda Fleming* in 1865.

[2] Christina Pontifex, the mother of Ernest in Samuel Butler's *The Way of All Flesh* (1901), traps her son on the sofa and subjects him to 'little quiet confidential talks'.

[3] The play Lawrence sent her was *Touch and Go*, which he had written in October. There is no evidence that KM recognized in Anabel Wrath, a young woman recently returned from France after a chest illness, and the maker of 'little statuette things' (a recasting of Gudrun from *Women in Love*), Lawrence's attempted portrait of herself.

To Virginia Woolf, [7 November 1918]
[2 Portland Villas, East Heath Road, Hampstead]
Thursday

Dear Virginia,
    This P.O. was sent me by:
    Thomas Moult[1]
    Y.M.C.A.
    Peter Street
    Manchester
May he have a copy of Prelude for it? He is a very nice creature, & he
would be one of your regular subscribers.

    I keep thinking about your new book. What a curse it is that one
must wait so long before it is published.[2] But there it *is* – at any rate, a
real exciting thing to look forward to.

    I wonder why I feel an intense joy that you are a writer – that you
live for writing – I do. You are immensely important in my world,
Virginia.

    I didn't say a quarter that I wanted to yesterday[3] – but it will keep.
(This of course I am writing under an ombré tree with the parakeets
chattering.)[4]

Yours,
K.M.M.

MS Sussex. *Adam* 370–375, 21.

---

[1] Thomas Moult (b. 1895), journalist, poet, and sports-writer, who had contributed verse to
Rhythm. His review of *LKM*, 'Katherine Mansfield as I Knew Her', *TP's Weekly*, 1 December
1928, quotes fragments of her letters to him which do not otherwise survive.
   [2] Virginia Woolf did not finish her 'new book' *Night and Day* until late November. It was
published in October the next year.
   [3] Virginia Woolf visited KM on Wednesday 6 November, and wrote, *DVW*, I. 216:
'Katherine was up, but husky & feeble, crawling about the room like an old woman. How far she
is ill, one cant say. She impresses one unfavourably at first – then more favourably. I think she
has a kind of childlikeness somewhere which has been much disfigured, but still exists. Illness,
she said, breaks down one's privacy so that one can't write . . . . Murry & the Monster [LM]
watch and wait on her, till she hates them both; she trusts no one; she finds no "reality".'
   [4] The pattern on her sommier and armchairs.

To Virginia Woolf, [c. 10 November 1918]
[2 Portland Villas, East Heath Road, Hampstead]

Dear Virginia
    Thank you so much for remembering about the doctor. Miss Case[1]
has just sent me his address & I have written to him. Why *are* doctors
so preposterous? I see them in their hundreds, moving among sham

Jacobean furniture, warming their large pink hands at little gas fires & asking the poor visitor if this will come off or pull down – curse em.

Shall we see you & Leonard on Thursday? It would be delightful. Murry is free every Thursday afternoon.

You do not know, Virginia, how I treasure the thought of you. Thats quite sober & true.

Katherine

MS Sussex. *Adam* 370–375, 20.

[1] A few days after having tea with KM on 6 November, Virginia Woolf saw her old friend, the scholar and enthusiast for women's rights, Janet Case (1862–1937).

To Virginia Woolf, [c. mid-November 1918]

[2 Portland Villas, East Heath Road, Hampstead]

My dear Virginia

Do bring Desmond M[a]cCarthy – We shall be delighted.

I have just bade goodbye to Doctor Stonham[1] – who – oh dear! – says I must expect to be an invalid until I have been in Switzerland a *year* or *so* – He says both my lungs are rather badly affected – This is *very* tiresome, Virginia – but he is sending me roots and herbs, & he was awfully kind –

K.M.M.

MS Sussex. *Adam* 370–375, 20.

[1] Henry Archibald Stonham, whose practice was in West Hampstead.

To Anne Estelle Drey, [mid-November 1918]

[2 Portland Villas, East Heath Road, Hampstead]

Anne darling

I cannot tell you how good your letter made me feel. It was a Pacific coast in itself & my heart is still taking a sun bath in it! Just as soon as it can be arranged I am going off to Switzerland – Jack will come, too – & we shall leave the house to be sublet. I don't think there will be any great difficulty –

Chère – chère cette *egg* – cette *herring* – Every time I thought about them I began to laugh again. I saw people saying: "You are quite certain this *is* a controlled egg!" & the man answering: "My dear Madam. That egg has been controlled for months. A child could eat it in perfect safety."

Of course we are all mad. But isn't the news marvellous! I keep thinking what Paris must be like. Of course I don't know what is happening in the great world here, but I *feel* people have almost forgotten that there was a war – Like Uncle Toby's advice to young Tristrams mother: "Wipe it up & say no more about it!"[1]

I am out of bed sitting on my aircushion on the sofa. About *aircushions*. I hear the Chinese are never without them. They make them of rice paper, paint [them] with lovely designs, fold them up small – And then whenever you go for a walk or a picnic and want to sit down on a stone or a piece of *hard grass* you just shake out the little packet, blow it up, sit on it & there you are. A home from home! What a people they are. This last little characteristic, in my present "état de genoudefemmedechambreisme" makes me long to join their flag.

I'd just love to see Drey any time. If he'd let me have a card & say when so that I can make "des illuminations et des arcs de Triomphe."

Do take care of your darling self – Mille baisers & a Big Squeeze from

Katherine.

MS ATL. *Adam* 300, 90.

[1] At the end of Vol.VI, Ch. III, of Laurence Sterne's *Tristram Shandy* (1759–67), concluding a conversation on the prodigious learning of children in the past, the parson Yorick remarks that one even 'composed a work the day he was born; – They should have wiped it up, said my uncle Toby, and said no more about it.'

To Ottoline Morrell, [17 November 1918]

[2 Portland Villas, East Heath Road, Hampstead]
Sunday.

Dearest Ottoline

My thoughts *flew* to you immediately the guns sounded.[1] I opened the window and it really *did* seem – just in those first few moments that a wonderful change happened – not in human creatures hearts – no – but in the *air* – there seemed just for a breath of time – a silence, like the silence that comes after the last drop of rain has fallen – you know? It was so wonderful – and I saw that in our garden the lilac bush had believed in the South wind & was covered in buds – – –

I thought of my brother and of you. And I longed to embrace you both – I shall always feel that you have understood all that this war has meant to the world in a way nobody else has – just because of your wonderful 'feeling' for life – If one thinks deeply about people really one is not at all certain whether they are turned towards Life or towards Death – or they are divided – or they are afraid – But *you* – one can't hesitate for a moment. One can only CURSE people that they are not alive enough to see your lovely gesture – (Don't think I am mad. I mean what I say DEEPLY DEEPLY.)

Oh, Ottoline, why is the world so ugly – so corrupt and *stupid*. When I heard the drunks passing the house on Monday night, singing the good old pre-war drunken rubbish, I felt cold with horror. THEY are not changed – & then the loathsome press about Germany's cry for food – My baby longing for people to "kiss & be friends" – – – How horrid they are *not* to – why don't they fly at each other kiss & cry & share everything – One feels that about nations – but alas! about individuals, too. *Why* do people hide & withdraw & suspect – as they do? I don't think it is just shyness – I used to. I think it is *lack of heart*: a sort of blight on them which will not let them ever come to full flower –

And the worst of it is I can't just accept that, calmly, like Murry, for instance – & say "very well – let them go then." No, *still* I feel full of love – still I desire lovely friends – & it will always be so I think – But Life is so short – I want them *here now* AT ONCE before Next Christmas – radiant beings – bursting open my door –

I suppose its great nonsense. While I write Murry is having a Tea party downstairs – Sullivan, sa femme,[2] Arthur, and the Mountain – I keep wishing that they never need climb so high as this little bedroom. I hope the rock cakes will sit very heavy on them –

Murry has written two heavenly short poems – I would like you to see them.

I have been translating Maxim Gorki's Journal of the Revolution[3] all last week. I find Gorki wonderfully sympathetic – This Journal is dreadful. It makes you feel – *anything anything* rather than revolution.

Here comes the 'party' creaking up the stairs – Oh – where *can* I hide –

With *love love* my tenderest love dearest

Ever your
Katherine.

MS Texas. *LKM* I. 218; cited *Exhibition, 39.*

[1] Signalling the end of the War, on Monday 11 November.
[2] Sullivan had married Vere Bartrick-Baker, a friend of KM's from Queen's College.
[3] Maxim Gorky, pen-name of Aleksei Peshkov (1868–1936), Russian novelist and playwright. Two collaborations by K. Mansfield and S. S. Koteliansky were published after KM's death: *Reminiscences of Leonid Andreyev* (1931) and *Reminiscences of Tolstoy, Checkhov and Andreev* (1934). This last volume, published by the Hogarth Press, also named Leonard Woolf as one of the translators.

To J. M. Murry, [c. 20 November 1918]

[2 Portland Villas, East Heath Road, Hampstead]

My dear Jack

I confess that these last days my fight with the enemy has been so hard that I just laid down my weapons and ran away, and consented to do what has always seemed to me the final intolerable thing i.e. to go into a Sanatorium.

Today, finally thinking it over, and in view of the fact that it is not, after all, so much a question of *climate* as of *régime* (there are very successful sanatoria in Hampstead and Highgate) I am determined, by my own will, to live the sanatorium life *here*.

(1) Father shall have built for me a really good shelter in the garden where I can lie all day.

(2) He shall also give us two good anthracite stoves.

(3) I shall buy a complete jaegar outfit for the weather.

(4) I shall have a food chart and live by it.

(5) This new servant releases Ida who has consented to give her whole time to me – as a nurse.

(6) Sorapure shall still be my doctor.[1] I shall have a separate bedroom *always and live by rule*. You must have a bed in your dressing room when the servant comes.

(7) I shall NOT WORRY.

You see, Jack, for the first time today I am determined to get well as Mother would be determined for me. If we are depressed we must keep apart. But I am going through with this and I want you to help me. It CAN be done. Other people have done this in Hampstead. Why not I?

Anything else, any institutional existence would kill me – or being alone, cut off, ill with the other ill. I have really taken my courage up & Im not going to drop it. I *know* its possible.

Your own Wig.

MS ATL. *LJMM*, 310–11.

[1] Soon after the shift to Portland Villas, KM visited Victor Sorapure (1874–1933), a consultant physician at Hampstead General Hospital. Although she saw at least three other doctors during October and November, KM decided on Sorapure as her physician, and his opinions strongly influenced her for several years.

To Virginia Woolf, [27 November 1918]

[2 Portland Villas, East Heath Road, Hampstead]

Dear Virginia,

Do come tomorrow. Your brilliant brilliant letter was so captivating that Murry suggests we frame it in a revolving frame to be a joy for ever more.

His poem makes you a humble leg and will be ready to go with thee tomorrow.[1]

[*No signature*]

PC ATL

[1] Virginia Woolf visited KM the next day, and took home with her the manuscript of Murry's poem 'The Critic in Judgement or Belshazzar of Baronscourt'. It was published by the Hogarth Press in May 1919.

To Ottoline Morrell, [2 December 1918]

[2 Portland Villas, East Heath Road, Hampstead]
Monday Night.

My dearest Ottoline

I simply devoured your letter – If you know how I furiously long to talk. You are so part of my life – I am always seeing the things I want to share with you. Do, do let us one day go for a little saunter through some exquisite part of the world – all the ninnies and heavyweight champions forgotten; it would be heavenly –

I wish I could have gone to Welbeck[1] with you as your maid. That *would* have been fun – nicely disguised with black thread gloves, button boots and a veil too tightly tied. It must have been portentous – like entering another Kingdom –

God – isn't it a joy really to have a world of one's own – into which all the unreal people never can come – even if the real ones tarry dreadfully – too – At any rate – its *there* – its *ready* – there are moments even now when all its thrilling beauty is almost discovered –

– – – Is it just because it is not so terribly cold just now that I feel everything – deep down all the spiritual *bulbs* of the earth – are beginning to stir to push up towards the light. All this unfolding is so secret and mysterious and yet I feel it is going on. Is it only because a darling wind blows today – one longs to run and embrace it – to feel it on one's lips and under ones arms – If it is gone tomorrow – will one be hopeless again? I had to send you flowers today; it was so nearly spring. Oh, why cant one live passionately – fully. Why must there be so much of this half life – this life in the waiting room – turning over the old familiar pages –

These last few days I have been writing hard. Even the Mountain could not sit on me. Would it *bore* you to read a very long story?[2] It *is* long. But I would so love to know what you think of it if you have the time to read it. I shall perfectly understand if you would rather not – I want to show it to you – because it is more the way I *want* to write than anything else – and I want to know from you whether it is too obscure!

The printing press is printing away – Alas! for me the Fly in the Ointment is that I have to swallow such a very large dose of 'young Art' – in shirt sleeves, with a grubby face – eating *everything*. How horrid I am! Every time he comes I have to restrain my longing to rush to the kitchen stairs & call: "Gertie – Mr Arthur is here. Put a quantity of potatoes in the oven and hide everything else!" He and the Mountain agree beautifully about food – She asks him whether he has "ever had enough ham" & he considers – – – – –

Life is ruined for the Mountain. Nobody *wants* her. What she had built her whole life on (*me*) has failed – and now she'd rather be a spirit. "I don't *want* to be independent" says she – "I want to just live near you – in case you may need me!" My hair rises *stiff* with horror – I shall have to send her to Rhodesia in the spring. I *loathe* female, *virgin* love. Its so false – so degrading, somehow – Oh, I wish I could throw her into the sea and make her sink or swim – This perpetual hovering on the brink really revolts me!

Brett, too, really is a problem. I so understand your feeling. She is too birdlike altogether. She wants your life to be her tree – where she can sun herself and sing and hide and never have to fly. Gertler was talking about her on Sunday afternoon – He says he doesn't think she ever will change. And I agree. How sympathetic Gertler can be; he was such a dear on Sunday[3] –

Tuesday – Your letter and parcel have just come – Thank you a thousand times dearest. I shall *rejoice* in these woolies – It is too good of you to send them to me. I shall 'gird my heavenly armour on' tomorrow . . .

Yes, why did L[eonard] W[oolf] come with Desmond [MacCarthy]? L. W. is so extremely worthy, but I find him terribly flattening. When he says 'Oh *thanks*' my whole mind seems to turn into something like a penny – I felt with Desmond one *might* wander down such delightful little paths but there was L. W. with his "don't you think we had better keep in sight of the house in case it rains" attitude. I was dished.

M. and I have been for a walk on the Heath today – The gorse is in bud. I have taken such a turn that I feel inclined to turn catherine wheels at least –

It would be lovely to come to Garsington for Christmas – but I am afraid Id better not – dearest. I might be such a nuisance – infernal. My cough is such a bore.

Murry sends his love – you know you have mine.

Ever
Katherine.

MS Texas.

¹ Welbeck Abbey in Nottinghamshire, where Lady Ottoline spent a considerable part of her girlhood, was the family seat of the sixth Duke of Portland, her half-brother.

² Probably *Je ne parle pas français*, which Murry and his brother were then printing by hand on the Heron Press.

³ On 5 Dec Mark Gertler wrote to Carrington 'Sunday for tea I saw Katherine, who seemed much better and our talk was interesting – I even told her about you!' (*Mark Gertler, Selected Letters*, ed. Noel Carrington (1965), 165).

To Anne Estelle Drey, [mid-December 1918]

[2 Portland Villas, East Heath Road, Hampstead]
My dearest Anne,

Another Colonial Cake has just been washed ashore – Here's a Bite with my love – I have a fancy that my little island is made of this mixture – and the very rocks at low tide are strewn with almonds & raisins. These cakes in size & weight are exactly like small allotments.

Marigold sits on the writing table & Penny offers a bunch of her name flowers to her engaging little Posterior *"This side up – with care"* says he. I shall have the darling little drawings framed and add them to my gallery –

Let us meet before Xmas. But you are not [to] come all the way up here – its too far. I shall come to you please – One fine afternoon next week Ill phone in the morning as you suggest & then Ill take a little old cab from here to there. I will bring the Spring Onions¹ that are ready with me –

With a Big Hug and a Kiss, my precious friend

Ever your
Katherine

MS ATL. *Adam* 300, 89.

¹ Possibly pieces KM had written for the never-realized book her friend was to illustrate.

To Dorothy Brett, [17 December 1918]

[2 Portland Villas, East Heath Road, Hampstead]
Tuesday

Dearest Brett

Your letter and sketch have just come – I shall have to wait a bit before I talk about the sketch. Its difficult – – Murry shall have it tonight. *I* was under the impression that you owed *me* a letter, and then I thought you were coming to London at Xmas time any day now. That explains my silence.

Have you and Ottoline really been having a "scrap"? I have not heard from her for Ages. I sent a letter and a Token but there is no reply. I hope tongues have not been wagging the wrong way, but I expect they have – and that's it. Oh – the cold! My feet are ice – my fingers & nose – ice – too – and shiver after shiver goes down my spine – I cannot konker it with clothes. Where did your lamb come from? Is it one of the Jaegar flock? I think I shall have to buy an immense tea cosy and wear it & crawl under it as a snail does its shell –

I go to Switzerland in early April. The cows ought to be laying properly by then – Its no good before. Then my plan is to let this house furnished for a year – then Murry will come back find a tiny farm in a remote spot & put the furniture into it & live there. I shall make my general Head Quarters abroad – a little house & a big maid on some mountain top – Italy, I think. But Murry says he *could* not live abroad so he will make his G.H.Q. in England – It will be very easy to spend some months of the year together like that & I think that – health apart even – its the best way to live if two people love each other and love Art, too. When I have found a cuckoo clock you will come & stay with me – wont you dearest – & draw mountains? Brett, at present I feel with you that Life is ugly – I am hardly alive. I have not been out for months & cannot walk up & down the stairs with any success. But – apart from that – I feel in my heart as though I have died – as far as personal life goes. I don't even want to live again. All that is over – I am a writer who cares for nothing but writing – thats how I feel. When I am with people I feel like a doctor with his patients – very sympathetic – very "interested in the case" – very anxious for them to tell me all they can – but as regards myself – quite alone – quite isolated – a queer state.

What radiant stars there will be on your Xmas tree! Are any of them nice or are they all just twinklers?

I wish I knew your plans. Are you going to Garsington after Xmas? Come soon & tell me. With love and a big warm hug –

Ever your
Tig

MS Newberry. *LKM* I. 220–1.

To Anne Estelle Drey, *[19 December 1918]*

[2 Portland Villas, East Heath Road, Hampstead]
Thursday.

Dearest Anne –

No go. Not a single Peasants Cart will take me. They will neither come for me *here* nor call for me *there* – we have phoned every garage &

stable in the neighbourhood – Its a cursed disappointment, but I shall just have to "wait a bit" –

I wish we were all in France with a real Xmas party in prospect – snow, huge fire, a feast, wine, old old French tunes on a guitar, fancy dresses, a Tree, and everybody too happy for words. Instead we are wondering whether to give the postman 5 shillings *or*, since we have only been here since August will <u>3</u> be enough? Etc. Etc. Etc. This cursed country would take the spirit out of a Brandied Cherry.

Mille Baisers, chérie
Katherine.

MS ATL. *LKM* I. 221.

To Clara Palmer,[1] 30 December 1918

2 Portland Villas | East Heath Road | Hampstead | N.W.3
30.XII.1918.

My dear Clara,

This morning Chaddie sent me your letter to her: I so enjoyed reading it and hearing your news, and I felt I must send you a greeting for the New Year. I have thought of you so often, dear Clara. I have a little photograph of you sitting in your room with little pictures by Greuze[2] on the walls and lovely flowers on the table and the corner shelf. It must have been taken just before I left for England – twelve years ago – What changes the years have brought! It is so hard to believe that my precious Mother is no more. In spite of her frailty and delicate hold on Life – one really felt that she was an undying soul. She was such a part of Life – especially these last few years. She seemed to live in everything, and to be renewed with every spring. And it was so extraordinary how *close* she kept to her children. Her last letters especially were quite uncanny. We seemed to be thinking the same thoughts at just the same time. Rare, exquisite little being – I wish we had not all lived so scattered – and it is dreadful to think of poor old Father without his wife and his "Boy" –

I am so glad that Mother sent you a greeting. I always remember her great admiration and love for you – and her "Oh I do *envy* Clara!" Will you come to England now that the war is over? – If you do you will let me know – won't you? I shall be going abroad in the late Spring for a more or less indefinite time. It will be such a relief to be strong again – I cannot bear an inactive life – and though of course I can do all my writing work just as well with broken wings as with good 'uns – there are so many things besides that one longs to take part in.

Have you had a happy Xmas? We had a real old-fashioned one – stockings, a tree – the house decorated – crackers mistletoe and good cheer. "We" means Jack and I, our "faithful souls" and the cat! I could not help thinking what it would have meant to darling old Les – his first Peace Christmas! –

As I write I can hear the "Old Men's Chorus from Faust"[3] (for which you gave me a prize) and Dance Créole Chaminade[4] – and a certain Beethoven Sonata with a mineur movement which made one's knees tremble with joy – Those old days are so clear – How Id love to talk them over!

This is a disjointed scrappy letter. But do take out of it a warm warm hug and my love and Best Wishes. And don't feel that is too effusive after so long – will you?

Yours affectionately
Kass (Middleton Murry)

MS ATL. Clarke, 24.

[1] Clara Adeline Palmer (1877–1956), a close family friend who had taught the Beauchamp girls the piano in Wellington. She was then living in Rome, where her establishing a canteen for British servicemen led to her being awarded the MBE. It was to her Annie Burnell Beauchamp had written on 6 May 1918, saying that her daughter was so ill that 'Of course if it was possible I should go home to her by the next steamer, for I know she would love to see me again, for she has at last learnt to love her Mother and Father, and has written us adoring letters lately, and so sweetly and quaintly put, poor poor darling she has missed so much in life, but it was quite her own choosing'. (Alpers 1980, 279.)

[2] Jean-Baptiste Greuze (1725–1805), the French painter remembered for his domestic scenes and his portraits of young girls.

[3] The opera by Charles Gounod (1818–93), first produced in 1859.

[4] A piece by Cécile Chaminade (1857–1944), French composer and pianist.

To Dorothy Brett, [1 January 1919]

[2 Portland Villas, East Heath Road, Hampstead]

Dearest Brett

A Happy New Year. This letter is just a chance shot for I can't help feeling you are on your way here – Every knock is your knock – & you have come up the stairs so often these last few days that I cant imagine why you are not in at my door. It is open wide –

We had a superb Xmas – stockings, a tree, decorations, crackers, puddin, drink – most potent & plentiful – parcils pouring in and out. Murry seemed to wear a paper hat (a large red & yellow butterfly) from Xmas Eve until after Boxing Day – We gradually, under the influence of wine & Chinese mottoes gave a party – charades – Kot, Gertler, Campbell etc. Oh, I did *love* it so – loved everybody – They were all fluttering & twinkling like candles on the darkest, most mysterious Tree of all – I wanted to say to everybody – Let us stay forever just as we are – Dont let us ever wake up & find it is all over – –[1]

It made me realise all over again how thrilling & enchanting life can be – & that we are not old – the blood still flows in our veins. We still laugh – The red chairs became a pirate ship. Koteliansky wore a muff on his head & Campbell a doormat tied under the chin – Can't this happen more often? Ought not Life to be divided into work and PLAY – real play? We ought not to have to sit in corners when our work is over. I feel that I have a thirst for Happiness that never will be quenched again.

Brett, my treasure, my prison doors have been opened at last – I am allowed to go out – I have found a man who is going to *cure* me. But he says I must not go to Switzerland but to a tropical climate in the spring like Majorca or Corsica. So now I am surer than ever that I shall be able to tempt you to come & visit me in a little house with a fig & a date by the door – Hurrah for Life – But this isn't a letter. It is just a Hail – and a "do let us spend a part of a very New Year indeed together".

Yours with warm love
Tig

MS Newberry. *LKM* I. 221–2.

[1] Beatrice Campbell recalled how "Katherine had prepared a tiny Christmas tree with little bags of sweets for each of us which she cut off and solemnly handed round. It was a sort of Last Supper. Kot, I felt, disliked it very much, for it seemed like one of Katherine's "stunts", which in spite of his profound admiration and affection for her he strongly disapproved of. Things became more cheerful later on and we had charades.' (Glenavy, 111.)

To Dorothy Brett, [10 January 1919]

[2 Portland Villas, East Heath Road, Hampstead]

My dear Brett

I am so sorry. I had no idea I was invited to tea with you today until I received your note. I think, in future, you'd better write me a card as Jack is a little vague.

At any rate Im afraid the weather of the last few days would have done for me and tomorrow – alas! – Im engaged with my good doctor all the afternoon. May I come on Tuesday afternoon if its *fine* or *warm*?

Yours half frozen
K.M.M.

Murry is coming to you tomorrow – of course.

MS Newberry.

To Anne Estelle Drey, [13 January 1919]

[2 Portland Villas, East Heath Road, Hampstead]

My darling Anne

After my Plan
For New Year's Day fell through
I gave up hope
Of catching a rope
Which would land me down near you.
Since then Ive been
(Pulse one sixteen
Temperature one o three)
Lying in bed
With a wandering head
And a weak, weak cup of tea.
Injections, chère
In my derrière
Driven into a muscular wad
With a needle thick
As a walking stick –
How *can* one believe in God!
Plus – pleurisy
And je vous dis
A head that went off on its own
Rode a circular race
That embraced every place
I ever shall know or have known.
I landed in Spain
Went to China by train
And rounded Cape Horn in a gale
Ate an ice in New York
Caught the boat for Majourke
And went up the Nile for a sail.

Light refreshments, bouillon raw eggs and orange juice were served on the journey. Jack M. came in, fell over the screen, went out again, came back, dropped a candle, groaned, said "Oh God does my love for you matter tuppence?" and went again, & the Faithful One changed the hot water bottles so marvellously often that you never had a hot water bottle at all. It was always being taken or brought back. All this, Anne darling, is a new treatment that my new doctor has started – a treatment by injections.

Hes a wonderful man. He was a doorstep baby, left in Paris with nothing but a shawl on and a paper pinned on his poor little chest with SORAPURE written on it. That is what he calls himself. (It always sounds to me like a soap that does your washing for you while you sit in the kitchen all comfortable with your feet in the gas stove and read "Freckles".) In April he says I ought to go to a place like Corsica. Switzerland is impossible, tank de Lord. So I think I shall. I cant help wishing we were going to help you produce *Marigold et Cie*, ma chère. Anne, if there are more than two you must give me one. Ill carry it away in my heavenly bag and turn it into a Corsican baby[2] for you in a moment. I think twins would be perfect! They would be so self contained – such a pair – you could get such a good *balance* with one on either side of the fire. Also one could play the piano while the other played the violin, one could hold the basket while the other dropped the peaches into it, one could set the house on fire while the other turned the hose pipe on to it, one could always row to shore and tell you the other had fallen out of the boat, one could pull the communication cord if the other dropped out of the train, one could always hand around the coffee while the other poured. In fact, thinking it over why are children ever born singly? It seems just a waste of time. Do please have the most engaging adorable mischievous *two*. Just think of the DECORATION you could make with two? Enfin – – if one is a boy will you call him Valentine – because he is a February chile?[1]

Well, Anne dearest, Ill keep on thinking & thinking about you – and wishing you all the luck there is. I shall be no good after today until the end of this week for I have another consignment shipped in to me tomorrow. But Ill write again then. Quelle vie!

Yours with tenderest love & a big warm hug

Katherine.

MS ATL. *LKM* I. 222–3.

[1] David Drey was born in February.
[2] KM is recalling the twins in *Les Frères Corse* (1845), by Alexander Dumas *père* (1802–70).

To Virginia Woolf, [20 February 1919]

2 PORTLAND VILLAS | EAST HEATH ROAD | HAMPSTEAD N.W.3

Dear Virginia

Alas – I have just had another inoculation and by tea time tomorrow I shall be sailing on tropic seas – I am trying a new treatment which gives me a high temperature for 48 hours each time it is applied – I wonder if you could – and would come next Monday? I want *very* much to see you.[1] You know Murry has been made editor of the Athenaeum; he was wondering whether you'd write for it. I wish you would – – – Theres a deal to talk over; I wish I were more physically stable – its dreadful mizery –

Ever Katherine.

MS Berg. *LKM* I. 224.

[1] Virginia Woolf was not aware of KM's continued decline in health, and after not hearing from her for two months, she wrote on 18 Feb, *DVW*, I, 242, 'It is at this moment extremely doubtful whether I have the right to class her among my friends . . . . The question interests, amuses, & also slightly, no, very, decidedly pains me.' Three days later she added, 243, 'But all this is made rather fine drawn & exaggerated by the simple fact that I have a letter this morning from K.M. herself asking me to tea.'

To Ottoline Morrell, [21 February 1919]

[2 Portland Villas, East Heath Road, Hampstead]
Friday.

Dearest Ottoline

I am so VERY sorry to hear you have another cold. How devilish these colds are. I do hope you will not spend another winter in this infernal climate. It is unfit for human beings – unless we could simply live in beds on wheels – never get out of them at all – I have spent a week of torture just not writing farewell letters, parting my raiment and giving myself into L.M.'s *eager* hands to be laid out. I took an overdose of a sleeping drug, which first sent me into a kind of indefinite odious sleep & then left me SO depressed that to speak was to weep & my heart refused to go. But today I can *just* ask Gertie to make up the fire without what the artists call 'a fresh burst of tears'. This was roast meat and drink to the Mountain. It made me realise more than ever that she is the born *Layer Out*. If ever a Village Flower Show had a prize for the Most Beautiful Corpse L.M. would not only get it – all the other competitors would withdraw. She would become known & called for all over the countryside – And she would keep little midget models of her favourite designs in her cottage, to be inspected by motorists for 6d. "If you would care to order one now I can do this model in your favourite colouring with flowers according to season, at a very moderate figure!" – Its very horrible. But I begin to feel that every man or woman has his murderer – or perhaps more truly that the idea of 'the poisoners' in the Milan plague was a real one.[1] There are people going about who *do* desire to dab you with a touch of poison whenever they get the chance. For no real reason except that they *are* poisoners. Are there the opposite kind of people –

too? People who for equally no reason do desire to fling you a flower, an embrace, a greeting, whenever they get a chance . . . ?

I send you the story I mentioned, dearest Ottoline. I hope you will not hate it. But you will tell me.

I do not know about the new Barbusse,[2] but I will ask M. Have you seen Blackwells new Anthology 'Coloured Stars'? There are one or two poems by a Chinese born in America which I think *very* interesting,[3] but on the whole, read in England, in February by rather a small fire – conscious of being neat but not lovely in woven underclothing it makes a very rude impression. One feels, sniffing ones eucalyptus hanky that these poor black people are sadly in want of self control.

Lawrence sent me the Le Marquis de Villemer to read. "Et le duc, encore fort agile malgré un peu d'embonpoint et quelques avaries dans les articulations sortit en gambadant comme un jeune ecolier".[4] What a gulf divides us from that but Georges Sand is obviously *fascinated.*

I hope, dearest, you will soon be better. Oh, before I end I must tell you . . . M. wrote to Santayana who replied today[5] – that Murry's letter had made so lively and profound an impression on him that he had positively *rushed* into the street & *snatched* a copy of the A[thenaeum]. But having read it most carefully & thoroughly he did not feel that it & he were perhaps after the same ideals. *It* was more concerned with units *he* with unities *it* with masses *he* with individuals. The dreadful truth is, of course that for the last 2 years the A. has not been literary at all but a journal of reconstruction concerned especially with problems such as: Why should not every Working mans Cottage have its P.W.C? Oh! I can see Santayana so plainly, sitting in the 'George'[6] – white kid gloves, cigarette held in special manner and all, turning the pages with a "mais – cher – cher – mais – enfin – –" expression . . . . .

I wrote to Frieda to ask how Lawrence is.[7] She replied that She was feeling a little stronger & more able to cope with him. She had past through 100 years of agony in the past fortnight but last night she went to a cinema!

Forgive this spider scrawl.

With fondest love
Katherine.

MS Texas.

[1] A reference to the suspected murderers in Ch. 32 of Alessandro Manzoni's *I Promessi Sposi* (1827), which Lawrence had posted her with his letter on 9 February. (*LDHL*, III, 327.)

[2] Henri Barbusse (1874–1935) helped introduce a new realism to war fiction with *Le Feu: journal d'une escouade* (1916). His *Clarté* was published in 1919.

³ *Coloured Stars, Versions of Fifty Asiatic Love Poems*, by Edward Powys Mathers, 1919. The poems KM admired were by a writer identified only as 'an American born Chinese, a valet by profession'.

⁴ The final sentence from Ch. IX of George Sand's *Le Marquis de Villemer* (1860), another of the books which Lawrence had sent her.

⁵ Murry had written to George Santayana (1863–1952), the Spanish–American philosopher and critic whom he had met at Garsington, inviting him to contribute to the *Athenaeum*. Santayana wrote 'Soliloquies in England', a series of short essays, for the first six numbers under Murry's editorship.

⁶ KM is remembering Santayana in The George, a former pub in Oxford, which at the time was a centre for littérateurs.

⁷ In the middle of the month Lawrence was struck with influenza during an epidemic which accounted for 150,000 deaths in England.

To S. S. Koteliansky, [late February 1919]

2 PORTLAND VILLAS │ EAST HEATH ROAD │ HAMPSTEAD N. W. 3

My dear Koteliansky

Is not this letter a Meisterwerk of *unselfish love*. But I am thankful Lawrence is at his sister's.¹ I am anxious about him: he ought to be kept so quiet and allowed to *rest* and who will let him? I cannot bear to think of him ill.

Are you better. Please get better. Thank Heaven spring is coming. When one remembers the *light* on spring evenings, just before it grows dusky – and that warm strange breeze blowing from nowhere – – –

KM.

MS BL. Dickinson, 86.

¹ During his illness Lawrence stayed with his sister Ada Clarke at Ripley, near Derby.

To J. M. Murry, [7 March 1919]

[2 Portland Villas, East Heath Road, Hampstead]
Noon.

Darling,

This letter from L[awrence] has just come: It is *very* nice I think. And he could do the 'a bit old fashioned' style v. well.¹

The sight of you with the rucksack has unsettled me.² I want to be off with you. Fair weather, broad hats, stout little shoes. 'Let us sit down at the next fair place we come to & have lunch' – & down swings the rucksack . . . . .

There'll be time for it.

I had a heavenly letter from Pa. You must take him to Hornsey Lane³ in June. Ill come too.

Its raining – raining – with a queer pinkish sky outside and very 'significant' shadows in. I hear L. M. & Charles⁴ playing bo-peep on the stairs. Blessings on thee Charles. Thou receivest without the flick of a whisker much that might be lavished on my stubborn head.

Enjoy yourself. Forget all the Horrors. I am *glad* you are gone away, out of your vie de chien for a little bit.

Your
Tig.

MS ATL. *LJMM*, 312.

¹ On 6 March Lawrence wrote to thank Murry for inviting him to contribute to the *Athenaeum*: 'you must tell me exactly what you would like me to do, and I will try to be pleasant and a bit old-fashioned.' (*LDHL*, III, 332.)

² Murry was taking a brief holiday at Garsington.

³ KM's great-grandfather John Beauchamp, b. 1781, succeeded to the family business of goldsmith at 95 High Holborn. He invented a form of imitation silverware called 'British Plate', but his main interests were fox hunting and poetry. He lived in Hornsey Lane, Hornsey, and was related through his wife to the painter Charles Robert Leslie (1794–1859). He also knew John Constable (1776–1837). Harold Beauchamp made much of his grandfather's artistic connections.

⁴ Charles Chaplin, a cat.

To J. M. Murry, [7 March 1919]

[2 Portland Villas, East Heath Road, Hampstead]
Friday.

My Own

At about 4.30 this afternoon there sounded the smallest possible knock on the door – so faint that nobody but Ribni could hear it. He waved his fan at me, presented arms with it & said DOOR. So I went. Opened it, looked

down

down

down

to a minute young gentleman whose boots were just seen – who was, as it were, extinguished under a stained glass halo. I realised immediately that this was an angelic visitation (the darling had 2 very small *black* wings sprinkled with diamonds & stars). But when he handed me the Bouquet I nearly picked him up as well – – – – –

Jack – you never bought them. Such flowers are never seen except by lovers, and then – rarely – rarely. I have put all in the big jar & they are on the table before the mirror. You will never never know what joy they have given me – What is the good of sitting here at my writing table. All my little thoughts are turned into bees & butterflies

& tiny humming-birds and are flown off. Now & again I take up the lamp & follow them –

Were they like this when you bought them? Or did the lovely act of your buying them cause them to put on this beautiful attire – Oh me, I dont know!

But please remember that when my heart *is* opened there will be *item* one bouquet of Anemones presented by her true love March 7th 1919.

Thank you for Ever More.

Your
Wig.

MS ATL. *LKM* I. 225; *LJMM*, 311–12.

To J. M. Murry, [8 March 1919]

[2 Portland Villas, East Heath Road, Hampstead]
Saturday.

Dearest

It is a lovely day here – very 'cool and clear' – a mother of pearl day really. I want to go out for a walk on the Heath, but must wait for the Piano man. This morning when I had gone to the P.O. to wire you he turned up, asked for ME & said he would return. Alas my knees are dissolved & I fear the worst.[1] But I must see him – More of that after he's been.

Sullivanoff turned up yesterday and spent hours over the fire. We talked about (1) you (2) him. His admiration, 'deference' and interest for and in you are reinforced now by affection. 'I am grown so *fond* of Murry.' This is a subject capable of infinite variations, and the subject I enjoy – so I *did* enjoy it. I think his personal life worries him, poor old boy, but that is his affair.

The D[aily] N[ews] has sent you B.R.s new book.[2] No, I wont post it on to you.

Sorapure came yesterday. Did I tell you? He thinks I lead too sedentary and too quiet a life. 'Tubercular patients ought to enjoy themselves' This I almost wept to hear – Its true, too, but what can one do? Nothing. Il faut attendre le beau temps pour sortir. I felt most woefully that he really despised me for sitting in my quiet room – and I so despised myself I wanted to *wail*. However all can be arranged and I shall not take to horse riding or anything, dearest Love before Tuesday.

Cant you stay a little longer? Will such a tiny rest do you any good?

Arthur came last night. His face is still his active enemy, but he was very nice. He had supper & then talked to me – très content.

Charles has his box in your dressing room & has sat in it – solid all the morning. Hes a most satisfactory animal. I confide in him – L.M. confides in him – Why the mixture doesn't kill him I dont know. How it must fight!

L.M. & I are peaceful parties. She sings 'Pale Hands I love' – but I am a good child and say nuffin.

Take care of yourself dearest of all. I am going out. The pianner man cant be coming after all. Of course my idea is he has gone off to fetch a police force, handcuffs & black Maria – & have already thought 'what a good thing it was I bought a nailbrush today'. I am sure one must live on nailbrushes in Holloway[3] –

Give my love to Ottoline – Do not forget – and do not store away in some dark place – but *remember* & *count* on all my heart. Its yours.

Tig.

MS ATL. *LJMM*, 312–13.

---

[1] Murry explained (*LJMM*, 313) that 'Katherine's trepidation over the piano-man was due to the fact that she had purchased a piano under a hire-purchase agreement in 1910 and had not completed the payments.'

[2] Murry did not review either of Bertrand Russell's recent books, *Roads to Freedom* or *Mysticism and Logic*.

[3] The women's prison in London.

To Ottoline Morrell, [c. 8 March 1919]

[2 Portland Villas, East Heath Road, Hampstead]
Monday

Dearest Ottoline,

Very many thanks for sending me back the story. After I had posted it I reproached myself for having inflicted such an ill typed MSS on you when you were ill. I only hope your cold is better. If you knew (small comfort) how truly I sympathise with your ill health. It is an agony to live by oneself in that strange world that rude healthy creatures have no inkling of. The only consolation is that spring is before us – it cant be January again – though I feel with you that its difficult to 'believe'. This has been an endless eternal winter. How *can* Nature remain so remote from ugly man – so blind and deaf to all his horrid ways – and just – calmly and wonderfully – act as though for angels! Will the sun really shine from morning till night again – Will it be warm enough for "us lizards of convalescence" (as Nietzche says)[1] to really *bask* . . .

I was thinking the other day of the beauty of Garsington in summer – your flower garden, your exquisite house – the windows and doors open and the light and shadow wandering through – the 'group' on the lawn – the ilex tree – and the bathers in the pool. What an achievement – what a creation it is! It is unforgettable – the *beauty* of it and the never to be felt anywhere else – the sense that Art is the important thing there – that one does not apologise for ones passion! I shall always be haunted by the memory of Garsington. Thinking of it is like thinking of another Age – –

I have been so enjoying *my* holiday (I am a horrible woman!). I have had the *old dogs* to see me in the evenings – but they – I confess have been awfully difficult and my stock of bones, sticks and stones is very low . . . Why won't they ever bring their own bone? Why does one always find them sitting on the mat, with a mild roll of the eye & a thump or two of the tail – waiting for you to look for and find – something to fling before they'll move. And even then – oh, that one had a longer reach! – that they weren't back in two bounds – and again ready! – – But the sense of Freedom has been lovely. Oughtn't one to live alone, really? I think one ought to *but* – – –

With love, dearest Ottoline
Yours ever
Katherine.

MS Texas.

---

[1] 'They are the most grateful animals in the world, and also the most unassuming, these lizards of convalescents with their faces half-turned towards life once more', from the Preface to Nietzsche's *Human All-Too-Human* (1878–80), translated by Helen Zimmern (1909), 8.

To J. M. Murry [? early March 1919]

[2 Portland Villas, East Heath Road, Hampstead]

To Wate
Top Floor
Ring 3. (If Bell out of Order Please do not Nock.)
Sir

A highly Respecktable Party who as known the Best of Everythink in er Day and is ony come down in World threw no Fault of Same but Illness loss by Death an Marridge etc. would be greately obligded if Groun Floor dark Gent would *lend* Same for Reading only, Essays by Wal. Pater.

No children and is Agreed Book shall not leave House.

I am | Yours Faithfully
Geo. Mungrove.

MS ATL. *LKM* I. 23; *LJMM*, 314.

To S. S. Koteliansky, [7 April 1919]

[2 Portland Villas, East Heath Road, Hampstead]
Murrys telephone number is 9712 central.

Dear Kotelianski

I was as much surprised as you to find we were nameless. No reason
was given. I shall ask M. on your behalf tonight; I shall also mention
the question of a cheque. I do not know how they pay. I gave my letter
to you with several others to the new maid to post. I presume she 'lost'
the stamp money; there is really nothing that she has not lost.

I dislike IMMENSELY not going over the letters with you.[1] I dont
want you to rely on me and M. I have long ago finished all that you
gave me – But I feel Tchekov would be the first to say we must go over
them together. However, dear Kotelianski, I dont want to worry you.

And you are depressed. I am so sorry. I wish you would come in
now, this moment, & let us have tea and talk. There is no one here
except my cough. It is like a big wild dog who followed me home one
day & has taken a most unpleasant fancy to me. If only he would be
tame! But he has been this last week wilder than ever. It is raining but
its not winter rain. – – This early spring weather is almost too much to
bear. It wrings ones heart. I should like to work all day & all night.
Everything one sees is a *revelation* in the writing sense.

Have you ever owned a cat who had kittens? Or have you ever
watched them from the first moments of their life? On April 5th
Charlie was delivered of two – He was so terrified that he insisted on
my being there and ever since they have lived in my room. Their eyes
are open already. Already they smile and smack the spectator in the
face (the spectator being their mother). One is like a minute tigress,
VERY beautiful and the other is like a prehistoric lizard in very little.
Their tiny paws are pink & soft like unripe raspberries. I am keeping
a journal of their first days. It is a pity that human beings live so
remote from all animals . . .

Frieda writes me that there is a 'rumpus' between me and – them I
suppose.[2] I see this 'rumpus' – dont you? A very large prancing,
imaginary animal being led by Frieda – as Una led the Lion.[3] It is
evidently bearing down upon me with Frieda for a Lady Godiva on its
back. But I refuse to have anything to do with it. I have not the room
now-a-days for rumpuses. My garden is too small and they eat up all
ones plants – roots and all.

Goodbye.
Katherine.

MS BL. *LKM* I. 225–6; Dickinson, 86.

[1] The 4 April issue of the *Athenaeum* included 'Letters of Anton Tchehov', four letters

translated by Koteliansky and stylistically polished by KM. Unlike similar and later contributions, this appeared unsigned.

² Although over the past few months KM had written Lawrence several letters which do not survive, and he wrote back to her, their friendship continued to be an uneasy one. The 'rumpus' may have had to do with KM's telling Frieda how she had been hurt by Lawrence, for he wrote to her 27 Mar 'Frieda said you were cross with me, that I *repulsed* you. I'm sure I didn't. The complication of getting Jack and you and F. and me into a square seems great – especially Jack.' A few days later Lawrence's anger was considerable when Murry used only one of the pieces of work he had submitted to him. As he wrote to Koteliansky on 3 April: 'I heard from Murry – very editorial – he sort of "declines with thanks" the things I did for him. He will publish one essay next week – too late to ask for it back – and that is the first and last word of mine that will ever appear in the *Athenaeum*. Good-bye Jacky, I knew thee beforehand.' (*LDHL*, III, 343, 346.)

³ Edmund Spenser, *The Faerie Queene*, I, III, 9.

To Virginia Woolf, [c. 10 April 1919]

[2] Portland [Villas] | East Heath Road [Hampstead] | N.W.3.
My dear Virginia

I have burned to write to you ever since you were here last.¹ The East Wind made my journey in the train an impossibility; it set up ponds & pools in my Left Lung wherein the Germs & the Toxins – two families I detest – bathed & refreshed themselves & flourished & multiplied. But since then so many miracles have happened that I don't see how one will be able to bear real, full spring. One is almost tired already – one wants to swoon, like Charles Lamb, before the curtain rises.² Oh God! To look up again & see the sun like a great silver spangle: big bright buds on the trees, & the little bushes caught in a net of green – – But what I chiefly love, Virginia, is to watch the people. Will you laugh at me? – It wrings my heart to see the people coming into the open again, timid, airing themselves; they idle, their voices change & their gestures. A most unexpected old man passes with a paper of flowers (for whom?), a soldier lies on the grass hiding his face; a young girl *flies* down a side street on the – positive – *wing* of a boy – –

On April 5th our one daffodil came into flower & our cat, Charlie Chaplin, had a kitten.

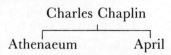

Charles Chaplin

Athenaeum　　　　April

Athenaeum is like a prehistoric lizard, in very little. He emerged very strangely – as though hurtling through space – flung by the indignant Lord. I attended the birth. Charles implored me. He behaved so strangely; he became a beautiful, tragic figure with blue-green eyes, terrified and wild. He would only lie still when I stroked his belly & said: "it's all right, old chap. Its bound to happen to a man sooner or later." And, in the middle of his pangs, his betrayer, a wretch of a cat with a face like a penny bun & the cat-equivalent of a brown bowler hat, rather rakish over one ear, began to *howl* from outside. Fool that I have been! said Charles, grinding his claws against my sleeve. The second kitten April was born during the night, a sunny compact little girl. When she sucks she looks like a small infant saying its prayers & *knowing* that Jesus loves her. She always has her choice of the strawberry, the chocolate and the pistacchio one; poor little Athenaeum has to put up with an occasional grab at the lemon one . . . They are both loves; their paws inside are very soft, very pink, just like unripe raspberries. Would a baby be more enchanting? I could get on without a baby – but Murry? I should like to give him one – but then I should like that he should be denied *nothing* . . . Love's very strange.

Virginia, I have read your article on Modern Novels.[3] You write so *damned* well, so *devilish* well. There are these little others, you know, dodging & stumbling along, taking a sniff here and a stare there – & there is your mind so accustomed to take the air in the 'grand manner' – – To tell you the truth – I am *proud* of your writing. I read & I think '*How* she beats them – – –'

But I positively must see you soon. I want to talk over so much. Your room with the two deep windows – I should love to be there now. Last time the rambler roses were nearly over & there was a sound of someone sawing wood –

I think of you often – with love

Katherine.

MS Berg. *LKM* I. 226–7.

[1] Virginia Woolf wrote after a visit of KM on 22 March, 'The inscrutable woman remains inscrutable I'm glad to say; no apologies, or sense of apologies due.' (*DVW*, I, 257.)

[2] Charles Lamb described his feelings as a child at 'My First Play', *Elia* (1823): 'Oh when shall I be such an expectant again! . . . But when we got in, and I beheld the green curtain that veiled a heaven to my imagination, which was soon to be disclosed – the breathless anticipations I endured!'

[3] Her essay on 'Modern Novels', *The Times Literary Supplement*, 10 April 1919, later collected as 'Modern Fiction' in *The Common Reader*, 1925.

To S. S. Koteliansky, [11 April 1919]

[2 Portland Villas, East Heath Road, Hampstead]

My dear Koteliansky

Would you come to tea on Wednesday? And would you go to Murry's office on Monday to see the Tchekov – & correct it to your wish.[1] His office is 5–7 Red Lion Court, Fleet Street.

I write this because we are both engaged tomorrow (Saturday) when we might have had the pleasure of seeing you.

Katherine.

MS BL.

[1] 'Letters of Anton Tchehov, II' in the *Athenaeum*, 18 April 1919.

To S. S. Koteliansky, [14 April 1919]

[2 Portland Villas, East Heath Road, Hampstead]

Koteliansky,

I forgot to arrange with you a time for us to meet that I may read you the new letters. I read them last night. They might have been written yesterday. Particularly valuable is the one on solidarity; I should almost like to publish that *every* week.[1]

Could you come on Thursday afternoon? If this suits you – do not bother to answer.

Without bouquets, Koteliansky – I must tell you how VERY excellent I think your translations.

Katherine.

MS BL. Dickinson, 86–7.

[1] Part of a letter to Shcheglov-Leontyev, written on 3 May 1888 and translated in 'Letters of Anton Tchehov, III', the *Athenaeum* 25 April 1919, reads:

'Don't you all feel suffocated by such words as "solidarity", "union of young writers", "community of interests", etc? I understand "solidarity" and such phrases on the Stock Exchange, in politics, in religious affairs and such things, but solidarity among young writers is impossible and unnecessary . . . We cannot think and feel in the same way; our aims are different, or we haven't got aims at all; we know each other too little, or we do not know each other at all. Therefore there is nothing for solidarity to catch a firm hold of . . . .'

To Ottoline Morrell, [c. 20 April 1919]

[2 Portland Villas, East Heath Road, Hampstead]

Ottoline dearest

I know I have not written for shamefully long, and my heart troubles me about it. It is always the same – if once I don't write – I fall into this dismal silence – and am nothing but a sorry wretch – the most graceless friend alive. Your exquisite letter made me feel the horror I am. And this weather – these first thrilling days of real spring always bring you before me so visibly. I know you love them as I do; I know you have the same Horror of that endless winter – – – over at last. *Will* you come & see me when you are in town again? There are so many things I long to talk over with you. So much seems to have happened and changed – I suppose it hasn't really. It is only the lifting of that appaling cold, dark wing that has hidden everything for what feels to me – an eternity – I really can hardly *remember* what happened before the winter. But I must not speak of it – The trees are trees again & one can face the light without shuddering. Garsington must be very lovely just now & your garden.

It has been a miracle to watch the roots & bulbs *buried* by M. last October burst out of their little graves and put on beauty – rather meagre London beauty – but reinforced by nine immense dandelions the garden is to a kind eye – quite gay – – –

The Mountain is still with me until I am 'suited' with a housemaid. It requires a very special kind of faith to remove Rhodesian mountains. M. and I seem to work like niggers at the Athenaeum – I wonder if you really like it. I feel rather like the pink icing butterfly on the dark sumptuous tragic cake – very unworthy. I thought the first numbers were too depressed but it is sitting up and taking more exciting nourishment now, I think. It is great fun – We both enjoy it. Its such a funny company to be sitting at Athene's tea board – But I do wish the other guests would arrive – the gay unexpected ones.

Oh this spring. It makes me *long* for happiness. That is so vague. Each year I think – this year I shall not feel it so keenly – but I feel it more – Why are human beings the only ones who do not put forth fresh buds – exquisite flowers and leaves. I cannot bear to go among them. I sit here or take small walks & there seems a blessing fallen upon the world just as long as one does not see the people or know of their ways. We have all been wintry far too long – Really – on some of these days one is tired with *bliss*. I long to tell someone – to feel it immediately shared – felt without my asking "do you feel it?" – Do you know what I mean?

No, dearest I am not Henry King.[1] I do not even know him – This is only the beginning of a letter – I could not let another day go by –

I am *always always* with love

Your
Katherine.

MS Texas. *LKM* I, 230–1.

---

[1] Two poems by Henry King appeared in the *Athenaeum* on 11 April. KM does not reveal that this was a pseudonym already used by Murry in contributing poetry to the *Nation*.

To Virginia Woolf, [late April 1919]

[2 Portland Villas, East Heath Road, Hampstead]

My dear Virginia

I enjoyed immensely your article on Defoe,[1] – and it was immensely nice to see you at Athene's tea party this week.[2] I wish you were there every week – but I am an insatiable old creature as far as your writing is concerned.

That awful fair! Never again. The time has gone by when one was young and rude enough for such things. It made me so utterly wretched. I felt there was nothing to do but sit on the stairs & lift up ones voice and – weep for Babylon. Were human beings in the mass always so shocking – or does one as one grows older shed a skin? I cant decide.[3]

I wonder what decision you are arrived at about the cottage with the tower[4] – Perhaps the house itself is very imperfect in many ways but there is a – – – something – – which makes one long for it. Immediately you get there – you are *free* free as air. You hang up your hat on a nail & the house is furnished – It is a place where you sit on the stairs & watch the lovely light inhabiting the room below. After nightfall the house has three voices – If you are in the tower & someone comes from the far cottage – he comes from far away – You go by the edge of the fields to Katie Berryman's for the bread. You walk home along the rim of the Atlantic with the big fresh loaf – & when you arrive the house is like a ship. I mustn't talk about it – It bewitched me –

Sunday afternoon. John is downstairs discussing the theory of relativity with Sullivan. I feel they are being a trifle portentous – The kittens are trying to kill their mother with love in front of my fire; the wind makes a pleasant sound but all my daffodils are fallen before it. I feel awfully happy. A husband, a home, a great many books & a passion for writing – are very nice things to possess all at once – It is pleasant to think of you & Leonard together – I often do.

Let us meet again soon and have a chat to ourselves. I wish the weather were quite summery: the cold shuts the door of my cage.

K.M.M.

MS Berg. *LKM* I. 227–8.

[1] 'The Novels of Defoe', *The Times Literary Supplement*, 22 April 1919.

[2] Virginia Woolf's essay 'The Eccentrics' in the *Athenaeum*, 25 April 1919.

[3] On Easter Monday, 21 April, Virginia and Leonard Woolf had walked with the Murrys to the fair on Hampstead Heath. 'We thought she would have enjoyed herself, from the likeness of her prose to the scene; on the contrary, she was disgusted.' (*DVW*, I, 268.)

[4] The Woolfs were interested in the cottages Lawrence had rented at Tregerthen, near St Ives, where KM and Murry stayed from April to early June 1916.

To Anne Estelle Drey, [c. 28 April 1919]

[2 Portland Villas, East Heath Road, Hampstead]
Anne darling –

Your letter gave me so much joy. I can't tell you what I feel . . . I simply died this winter; retired underground and was not. I was so continually wretched and ill that at last I gave in and turned into a kind of peculiarly horrible mole – burrowing in bed – not living.

I long to see you and to see your wonder-babe. Is is possible for you to come up to this Mountain in the first half of next week – or could we meet? The second alternative is a bother because if the day is bad I can't go out & if Ive a temperature I cant etc etc etc. This week I have not a day free but Monday Tuesday Wednesday I would with such joy keep for you – chère.

About this house – I am not going away until I have seen my Father who arrives in June & even then Murry is keeping it on for himself. Ive got a cook housekeeper who is reliable (& a char & a daily housemaid)!!! I don't think M. will leave it for the next five years –

Are you bringing your cherub to town? I imagine the drawings you will make of him this spring. I want really to stay here until September & have a Grand Exit then. The idea of travelling & strange hotels fills me with horror. It is like years since I saw you & yet such a little while – I see you as I write – Thank God that bloody winter is over.

I remember Drey meeting me one day and calling me a sale chien. Yes, I must appear so – & I shall never be able to explain. My heart is always *full* of love for you, darling and I always think of you vividly. But I have been living with a Black Monkey all this winter – voilà.

All the same I am ever

Your devoted
Katherine

MS ATL. *Adam* 300, 89–90.

To Virginia Woolf, [5 May 1919]

[2 Portland Villas, East Heath Road, Hampstead]
Monday.

I have mislaid that form. When I find it I will fill it up.
My dear Virginia

It is indeed thrilling to think that Higher Tregerthen is yours.[1] God forbid that you should find the rooms too small or some Dreadful Inconvenience that I have forgotten. But when you sit at the tower window & look out upon that amazing hill I cannot but believe you'll feel its enchantment – – – Early this morning there was a white mist here & a smell of burning. It made me think of Cornwall – of those enchanted misty days when you go just outside the door & are spirited away.

It will be great happiness if I may come & stay with you in the summer – *great* joy to look forward to – White & purple veronica would grow excellently well there – But wait until you see the yellow irises & the foxgloves over 6 foot high – red indian encampments of foxgloves burning with passion & pride in the field next to yours –

My dear Virginia, I feel quite overcome with pleasure that you should have so wonderful a place to go to. (It sounds as tho' you were just 'saved'.)

I cannot help feeling that Mrs B's book ought to be called *The Life at Charleston 1652*.[2] It is very intriguing. Murry has on several occasions lately expressed the wish that he knew Duncan Grant & your sister. He admires them extremely –

The brilliant but cynical hero[3] dined with us on Saturday. We ran over the 18th century in a very lively & high spirited fashion – a kind of small tour with a basket of wine under the front seat – in the dogcart of the period! Aldous came in later, lay upon the sofa, buried his head in a purple pillow and *groaned* over the hor-rible qual-ity of Smollett's coarseness – In the afternoon of the same day Lytton came to tea. I was excessively dull but he was charming.

Pray come to tea on Friday. I shall keep the day for you. Now I review *The Moon & Sixpence*[4] – curse it. My mind says: But the fly is dead. Why bother to spin such a web round it – – Why indeed.

Ever

K.M.

MS Berg. *LKM* I. 228–9.

   [1] The Woolfs had been in touch with the landlord, but later decided against living in Cornwall.

   [2] Virginia Woolf must have spoken to KM of her sister's house Charleston, near Firle, where she found conditions rather primitive. She frequently referred to Mrs Brereton, Charleston's long-term governess, as 'Mrs B.'.

   [3] Possibly Desmond MacCarthy.

   [4] 'Inarticulations', KM's review of W. Somerset Maugham's *The Moon and Sixpence*, the *Athenaeum*, 9 May 1919.

To Ottoline Morrell, [early May 1919]

[2 Portland Villas, East Heath Road, Hampstead]

Dearest Ottoline

I am simply overjoyed at the thought of seeing you on Wednesday. I shall keep it *free* for us. If only the day will be still and warm; then my room is so remote from all the London horrors that distract one – I am so near to you in spirit all these days.

But why is there this division between humanity & the lovely external world – With all this beauty why cant we *all* come forth radiant? Just at first – one is overcome by the beauty & the divine relief of Spring and it is enough – but *after* it makes one feel more solitary than ever. It seems so much less natural to rejoice alone rather than to grieve alone – I'd so much rather share my JOY. But nobody wants it. M. comes into my room sometimes as though the Athenaeum were edited down a coal mine – I ought not to write this. It is no use – no use expecting miracles. The only consolation is WORK. But why is one always met with the gape, the stare – or silence. Sometimes I feel one lives among automatic pianos, & I hate them so much while I am fumbling for that penny to start them going – – – Forgive me dearest – Life is particularly unpleasant today. Young Arthur is here also, eating up the loaves & jam pots & saying 'I don't know how it is I'm hungry'. His mother never ought to let him leave the house without a pudding in a basin.

People ravage one – & yet . . . one longs for them so. *What* can be done?

How I look forward to Wednesday. If you knew!

Yours ever with much love,

Katherine

MS Newberry.

To Anne Estelle Drey, [7 May 1919]

[2 Portland Villas, East Heath Road, Hampstead]

Anne, ma chere

Your letter was mislaid and I found I had not your address in my address book. When I asked Murry he was positive it was Church Street *Chelsea*.[1] I remembered the Church Street, but I would have sworn it was the other. However he at last convinced me & this

morning my letter is returned! La voila. Is it too late for us to meet?
Would you suggest a day? I just long to see you –

> Toujours – ma chere amie
> Katherine.

MS ATL.

¹ KM's letter (of *c*. 28 April) had been sent to the wrong address.

To Virginia Woolf, [c. 12 May 1919]

[2 Portland Villas, East Heath Road, Hampstead]
My dear Virginia
    It was very nice to get the two *new* books this morning; they look
enchanting.¹ I immediately re-read your story; its quality is exquisite.
I have a queer feeling about the conversations. I don't feel that I
understand in the least what is being said – any more than the snail
did – or the flowers. They are as you say just 'voices' – Even *Simon*² is
like a word Ive never heard before. I think your end pages are a little
pity.³
    Eliot – Virginia? The poems *look* delightful but I confess I think
them unspeakably dreary. How one could write so absolutely without
emotion – perhaps thats an achievement. The potamus really makes
me *groan*. I don't think he is a poet – Prufrock is, after all a short
story⁴. *I* don't know – These dark young men – so proud of their
plumes and their black and silver cloaks and ever so expensive
pompes funebres – Ive no patience.
    (The bread was delicious –)

> Your
> K.M.

MS Sussex. *Adam* 370–375, 19.

¹ On 12 May the Hogarth Press published three new titles: Virginia Woolf's *Kew Gardens*,
J. Middleton Murry's *The Critic in Judgement*, and T. S. Eliot's *Poems*.
² One of the characters in Virginia Woolf's story.
³ Roger Fry had designed the covers for *Kew Gardens*.
⁴ 'The Hippopotamus' was in Eliot's new collection; 'The Love Song of J. Alfred Prufrock' in
Prufrock and Other Observations, 1917.

To Ottoline Morrell, [c. 23 May 1919]

[2 Portland Villas, East Heath Road, Hampstead]
Dearest Ottoline
    The exquisite tulips & some sprigs of rosemary & verbena have

brought your flower garden into my room. How I love them! Each time I get up from the writing table I go over to them and take a long long look – And oh – I want to say to them: live for ever! Don't fade – dont die. If you knew how we have longed for you you would not have the heart to be one petal less perfect than you are – at any rate not for a long time – Thank you for them, dearest friend.

How very delightful it sounds – a driving tour. I look at your postcard & wonder where you wrote it – what was happening just at that time – I felt the sudden little pang of strange cold as you went into the church where the lovely windows are. God be praised – the weather is divine. I sit in my room, writing or reading: it is like being on a ship that has *at last* found a fair harbour. Even if I cant put out to sea just now or even share the pleasures of the shore – it is enough to be out of the cruel weather –

I was VERY disappointed – not to come. But my doctor would not let me.[1] There is a kind of small fire at present in my left lung which mustn't be fanned or fed. What a cursed thing – But its no use lamenting.

I wonder if you feel too, this year more than any other year, a longing for the Spring to *stay* Spring. The flowers have fallen from the pear tree outside my window – just a few little silver petals are still spinning down – & the green is darker. I grudge it so. My Lotus Land would be an eternal first spring day when everything is in full leaf and the buds just unfolded.

If only we could meet more often and for longer. When Brettie's house is finished[2] perhaps you will come and stay with her & we can sit on the Heath – uninterrupted. (There is a gramophone playing 'Wie Einst in Mai' – overpowering –)

Goodbye dearest friend. Do not forget how much I love you.

Katherine.

MS Texas.

---

[1] Lady Ottoline had invited KM to join her on holiday during the last ten days of May. A notebook entry on 22 May makes clear the state of her health: 'Temperature 100.2. Cough troublesome: signs of blood persist until noonday – severe pain in the lung & feel very cold and nauseated. Shivered all afternoon but temperature 101. Lung still very painful at each breath.' (*Journal* 1954, 155.)

[2] Brett was soon to move to a house at 28 Thurlow Road, Hampstead.

To Virginia Woolf, [c. 27 May 1919]

[2 Portland Villas, East Heath Road, Hampstead]

Dear Virginia

I am very sorry you are not coming to the Party.[1] I wanted everybody to be there & you to be there. I wanted the small private satisfaction of looking at the party *with* you. However it cant be helped. If you do come to Tea on Monday you will be very welcome. I am thankful people are buying a copy or two of Prelude; I hate to think of it loading up your ship. I dont see how your Press can be other than a Prodigious success. It must be very nice. cruising about among the islands & deciding to put in – now here – now there & seeing what the natives have to bring aboard. (Alas, my dear woman, I have no poems. I am not a poet.)

God be thanked for this divine weather! The Vicar called upon me yesterday & asked if he might come occasionally & administer a LITTLE Private Communion to me at any time . . . Just a drain of wine I suppose and a crumb of bread. Why a little? It puzzled me greatly. But I told him that while this weather continued I was nothing but a living Hymn of Praise, an incense, a harp responding – Which is more or less true. Addio

K.M.

[*Across top*]

Tchekov has a very interesting letter published in next week's A . . . what the writer does is not so much to *solve* the question but to *put* the question. There must be the question put. That seems to me a very nice dividing line between the true & the false writer[2] – Come & talk it over with me.

MS Berg. *LKM* I. 229.

[1] KM's party was on Thursday 29 May.

[2] A letter to A. S. Souverin, 27 October 1888, in 'Letters of Anton Tchehov, VI', the *Athenaeum*, 6 June 1919. Chekhov wrote: 'You are right in asking from an artist a conscious attitude to his activity, but you are mixing up two things: the solving of the question and the correct putting of the question. It is the latter only which is obligatory upon the artist. There's not a single question solved in "Anna Karenina" or "Onyegin", but they satisfy completely, because all the questions are correctly put.'

To Ottoline Morrell, [late May 1919]

[2 Portland Villas, East Heath Road, Hampstead]

Dearest Ottoline,

I am awfully sorry you will not be at our Party. Heaven knows it won't be a thrilling affair but I longed for you to come & for us to *exchange a wise glance* – About the other Party – well, I think people are mad and bad and so STUPID that ones heart grows cold.

Dearest – Murry asks me to say he would love to come on the seventh for the weekend – – – Would you have me too? Is that like Julian H., proposing myself so blandly. But if we go down together to Oxford & take a car I know I could manage it by then. I feel much better: it would be such a great joy. If you have not a corner, OF COURSE I understand. I can't tell you how I long to see Garsington – to be with you there and walk in the garden & talk – – – Whenever I think of you things to say – rush into my heart –

Oh those insufferable stupid little people –

I am idiotic from translating. I am turning into English La Jeune Fille Bien Elevée for an American publisher, and every moment one wants to say: but its so much better in french – do let me leave this little bit in french[1] –

Its an exquisite day here but my "house party" is very miserable. I meet them on the stairs, pictures of heavy woe – drear nighted decembers.[2] How can one do without them?

Ever your devoted
Katherine

MS Newberry.

[1] There is no evidence of how far KM proceeded with her translation of *La Jeune Fille bien élevée* (1909) by the novelist of small-town *mores*, René Boylesve (1867–1926).

[2] A phrase from the album verses John Keats wrote in 1817, 'In drear-nighted December'.

To Lytton Strachey, [early June 1919]

2 Portland Villas | East Heath Road [Hampstead] N.W.3

Dear Lytton

I am glad you did not come to the Party. It was a very dull dog indeed. Perhaps all parties are – Jack Hutchinson[1] came & was so immense. We seemed to revolve round him like stars round the moon (no they don't revolve – no matter.) Frank Swinnerton[2] came too with whiskers – like an Irish terrier, & Roger [Fry] sat on the sofa with Gerard Hopkins'[3] poems & Edward Dent[4] told me such a terrible long story about a cabman who drank some fairy wine – – – its not finished yet – – My far little sister [Chaddie] hung with bright Indian beads chattered ever so gaily to your brother. Poor Murry was rather like a porter who had got at last! his passengers into the railway carriage but couldn't somehow leave them until the train went – the train *would* not go. Our kitten, full of deliberate malice tried to tear off Bertie's trousers while Bertie talked of Spring in Sicily[5] – and Clive [Bell] was in Ercles vein[6] –

No I feel my part in parties now is a corner away from the door & the window, beating time with a fan & trying to keep my mittens over my elbows –

I hung my head when I thought of my silly little review of The Young Visiters.[7] It was *very* bad & the book really is – as you say – full of suggestions. I cant understand just why it is so awfully attractive. But Miss A. should have died after it instead of jazzing in a plum coloured gown. There was a charming letter of Pet Marjorie's quoted in last Sunday Observer: 'I now sit down on my botome to write to you.' That sense of settling in to her letter couldn't have been better expressed . . . She was *five*.[8]

It is very nice seeing you. I hope you will come again.

Katherine.

MS Strachey.

[1] St John Hutchinson (1884–1942), barrister and unsuccessful Liberal candidate for Parliament, wartime legal adviser to the Ministry of Reconstruction, and married since 1910 to Strachey's cousin Mary Barnes. He had refused to write a reference for KM when she was looking for a flat in early 1917, because she 'lived in sin'. (See *CLKM* I. 293.)

[2] Frank Swinnerton, essayist and novelist, at that time drama critic for the *Nation*.

[3] The poems of Gerard Manley Hopkins, ed. Robert Bridges, were first published in 1918.

[4] Edward J. Dent (1876–1957), who six years before had written for the *Blue Review*, was now music critic for the *Athenaeum*.

[5] The only book with this title was a diary of a journey through North Italy and Sicily by Henry Festing Jones (1904). But KM's capitals may be doing service for quotation marks, and Russell may simply have spoken of Italy.

[6] 'This is Ercles' vein, a tyrant's vein', *A Midsummer Night's Dream*, I. ii. 40.

[7] 'A Child and her Note-book', KM's review of Daisy Ashford's *The Young Visiters* in the *Athenaeum*, 30 May 1919.

[8] The 'At Random' column in the *Observer* on 1 June quoted the first letter written by the child prodigy Marjorie Fleming (1803–11), friend of Sir Walter Scott. By the age of eight she had written poems and journals.

To Ottoline Morrell, [4 June 1919]

[2 Portland Villas, East Heath Road, Hampstead]
Wednesday

Dearest Ottoline

The East Wind has done its worst with me & Im not allowed a journey. Was there ever so *damnable* a thing. Why should one's delights be so snatched away – But my cough is the devil again & I have to keep "still as a mouse" – I shall simply have to give up finally

my longing to come to you at Garsington – Alls against it. I am cursed
like Job. The disappointment is really *awful*: I had set my heart upon
those days – & here I am 'shaking the bottle' indeed. Added to that
(as if that weren't enough) M's printers have declared a holiday. He
will have to get an issue of the A. out over the weekend & is simply
tied to the office. Nothing can be done: he's tried everything &
Sullivan's blackbird has called him away into the country so his work
too falls on M's head. We are undone – Please try & forgive us. I feel
you would if you knew how we'd looked forward – – – –

The marvellous basket (which I hope has arrived safely) put the
party to shame. Such a wealth of beauty! I have never seen such
flowers or so many. I half expected to find the infant Moses under the
irises – – But all through the Infernal Dull Dog of a party I saw the
peonies & the delphiniums & the lilac & simply *clung* to the sight of
them. No more parties – no more people – The flowers are so much
lovelier. I am glad you were not here. It was too dull & everybody
seemed so preposterous. Clive out-Clived himself. Jack Hutch sitting
on a sofa like Humpty-Dumpty but alas! never falling – Roger whom I
cant see except as a sheep with knitting needles in his hair & the
mountain offering sweetness as though she had the head of John the
Baptist on a charger. When it was over I wanted to lie down and
groan.

Shall I see you soon? I went one day to see poor Brett. Poor little
creature! Like a flea on a ladder in her Victorian jungle.[1] She will
never be straight. What a ghastly place it is – so huge and so
portentous. I felt wretched for her. She is so *helpless*. One stepped over
old curtain fittings and old boxes and ladders – & she kept wondering
what one does to *floors* – Does one stain them? Are boards beautiful?
Someone had come & said they were – – – –

I am so désenchantée – I cannot write today – Forgive me. I am
tired of the lean years –

Ever your loving
Katherine.

MS Newberry. Cited Alpers 1980, 292.

[1] The house in Thurlow Road.

To Virginia Woolf, [4 June 1919]

[2 Portland Villas, East Heath Road, Hampstead]
Wednesday

Dear Virginia

I have not thanked you yet for the lovely columbines. I enjoyed them so much. They are favourites of mine – very early favourites – intricate delicate things –

I am glad you did not come to the Party – It was a dull dog. In fact, all parties are cursed if one cannot remain invisible at them. *Then* they must be heavenly – But to be a body revolving round other bodies is very heavy work.

I have been reviewing your story – Virginia – You must forgive the review – I cant hope to please you – tho' I wanted to – For one thing I hadn't enough space – & Id like to have quoted – almost the whole –[1]

But I wish you would come & see me one day & talk about it.

What a pleasure it is to talk to Lytton. E. M. Forster came the other evening. I *don't* care for him. Partly perhaps because he dreadfully dislikes me – But I could forgive that. What I can't get over is a certain *silliness*. Is that unfair?

Its raining. That, I suppose will put off the Lord appearing on a cloud at the Derby.[2] I thought he was going to – I wish I could take an umbrella & walk across to you.

Lovingly
Katherine

MS Sussex. *Adam* 370–375, 22–3.

[1] 'A Short Story', her review of *Kew Gardens* in the *Athenaeum*, 13 June 1919.
[2] The papers had made much of that year's race as the 'Victory' Derby, to be run before the King and Queen.

To S. S. Koteliansky, [6 June 1919]

[2 Portland Villas, East Heath Road, Hampstead]
Friday.

I do not feel that all that money should be mine. And I WISH our collaboration were closer. However, *I do my very best* always with these wonderful letters & can do no more. Wonderful they are. The last one – the one to Souverin about the duty of the artist to *put* the 'question' – not to solve it but so to put it that one is completely satisfied seems to me one of the most valuable things I have ever read. It opens – it discovers rather, a new world.

May Tchekov live for ever.

Katherine.

MS BL. Dickinson, 88.

To Dorothy Brett, [7 June 1919]

[2 Portland Villas, East Heath Road, Hampstead]

Dearest Brett

I feel Murry was very silly at the party to say that I was frightened by your new home. He acknowledged afterwards he had only said it "for fun". What I̲ told him was their size and difficulties frightened me. ALL there was to do and only you – a leaf on a ladder – to do it. It made me feel you'd such a giant's task. For they *are* difficult – so big and so assertive in their way. But I expect you will laugh at me for my timidity: I am a mouse these days. Laugh as much as you like – *do* laugh but *dont* be cross with me. And come & see me – will you? And tell me how you are getting on.

Ottoline has been here today. She looked wonderful. And I felt what silly little dull dogs they are who cry her down. She was in a radiant, radiant mood – you know that mood when she's like a tree in the light – in the sun –

Brett – I want to see you. Come to Tea soon –

As I write the willows fly streaming in the sun – & someone is playing the piano – oh! so wonderfully – seeking out, gently, tenderly, with light, whimsical fingers *something*. Wonderful – wonderful life – I wish one could be certain of living to 100. Isn't it awful to feel full of life and love and work and joy & to think one will have to turn up one's toes & be still one day –

Yours with love Brett dearest
Tig

MS Newberry.

To Ottoline Morrell, [7 June 1919]

[2 Portland Villas, East Heath Road, Hampstead]

My dearest Ottoline

Today was perfect perfect – I leaned out of the window after you had gone and watched the willows flying in the sun. Someone was playing the piano – *seeking* something, lightly, whimsically – & then suddenly there was a great plunge and oh! one was out of one's depth and breathless with it. How can I tell you what it is to be with you & to enjoy your presence – I feel as though Ive come to another country – where – even to breathe the air is thrilling. Do remember how wonderful you are – how beautiful. This hideous corrupt London has fallen away from me – (It does even mount up here, like a great muddy tide.) I love to think you are away from it.

My *incredible* good fortune to have you for a friend!

Katherine.

MS Texas.

To Ottoline Morrell, [10 June 1919]

[2 Portland Villas, East Heath Road, Hampstead]
Tuesday.

Dearest dearest Ottoline

I have to thank you for a Perfect letter. If you knew how greedy I am of these glimpses you give me of your life. Its so strange. I positively lead another life with you there – bending over the flowers, sitting under the trees, feeling the delight of the heat and the shade . . . I have written to Frank Prewitt[1] asking him to come & see us on Saturday. From his name one sees someone slender, dark, with something of the bird and the Indian in him. I hope he comes. Yes, I know JUST how you feel about Brett & when I had read your letter I felt tender towards her & sorry for her – for her incompleteness. But alas! yesterday afternoon she came to see me – It was Bank Holiday, hot & fine & in she came in that really grubby wool dress, unfastened down the front, showing the linen buttons. She carried a large bunch of ticklers and her felt hat was covered with paper feathers. The ensemble was like a dream. And I *cant* leave this unsaid. Is there no tap at Thurlow Road that she can put her toothbrush under? What a vile thing to say – but I was haunted by it all the time she was here – And then her idea to faire ménage ensemble with Gertler and Nelson[2] seems to me madness. She seems to spend her entire time with them, creeping in as she says after twelve oclock at night – and still her rooms in disorder – still paint pots – – – Only to hear of it – only to grin and watch an imitation of Chili[3] rolling drunk made me so fatigued I felt I could have *died*. And she really hadn't another word to say – not an idea. There she was, poor little creature like a jug on the doorstep of Thurlow Road waiting for Gertler *or* Nelson *or* Chili to come by with a little wagon and a rattle of cans – When she ended by saying she must get a little black frock like mine because it doesnt show the dirt, I felt, as Clive would say c'était la comble! It is vile of me to write like that – but – I DO feel it.

I have been working all the morning, trying to discover why 'Java Head' is not a good novel and trying to say it is not a bad one[4] – But one always seems to arrive at the same conclusion – nothing goes deep enough – the *risk* has not been taken – Whenever the crisis is reached they decide to wait until the sea is calmer – How tired one becomes of all these surfaces – Why do not more people live through and through. Must one spend ones life paying calls on the emotions – Why isn't the dreary fashion obsolete – – – And if it is not this superficial nothingness it is M. au grand sérieux, throwing himself bodily into the milk jug after the drowning fly! Piffle before the wind – – –

Dearest I have a plan which is so sweet to think of – – – Is it possible? When I am established in a little villa in San Remo (or near San Remo) would you come & stay a month with me – or as long as you wished? I mean to have a little villa and a good maid. Couldn't you escape a month of this winter and come – You know (but not altogether) what joy it would give me to do all I could. I feel nobody understands how you suffer from these headaches – I DO. The change might do you good. Then, at last, there would be time to talk. I am going the first week in September. But oh – if we could have a few weeks Gaierty.[5] The sun burns today and our mysterious plant the anchusa is in bloom. But I should like to see whole vast plains covered with it. But instead I must go down to the Laundry Office & ask why they have carried forward 10/8. Why – oh why – and what a mission to take one forth on a golden day. And then Bertie [Russell] says a woman is incapable of real detachment. But only to think of the things that do catch at our heels if we try to fly! I can imagine a whole rich Hell where the weekly books were always late, always more than one expected and always had unaccountable items.

How one grudges the life and energy and spirit that money steals from one. I long to spend and I have a horror of spending: money has *corrupted* me these last years.

But oh – dearest what am I doing – writing these wretched things to you. Forgive me: I will not do it again. How lovely the fields must be. I wish we were walking there – at our ease – those bright silver daisies are in flower and the sorrel is in feather – We should pause and admire and talk until suddenly I felt music come streaming down those great beams of sunlight & little trills, little shakes came from the flowers and the wind ran among the harp-like trees & the beauty of Life was almost too great to bear – I am sure if we were together we should be caught up to heaven in chariots of fire innumerable times.

Goodbye, my wonderful friend. I am your DEVOTED

Katherine.

MS Stanford. *LKM* I. 232–3.

[1] Frank 'Toronto' Prewitt (1893–1962) was a Canadian, part Sioux Indian, whom Siegfried Sassoon introduced to Garsington. His *Poems* were published by the Hogarth Press in 1921, and another short collection, *The Rural Scene*, by Heinemann in 1924.

[2] Geoffrey Nelson, (*c.* 1896–1941), a painter and close friend of Mark Gertler.

[3] Alvaro Guevara, the Chilean painter who was another of Gertler's intimate friends. KM had met him at Garsington in the summer of 1917. (See *CLKM*, I, 310.)

⁴ 'Glancing Light', a review of *Java Head* by Joseph Hergesheimer, the *Athenaeum*, 13 June 1919.
⁵ KM is adopting the erratic spelling found in Daisy Ashford's *Young Visiters*.

To Dorothy Brett, [10 June 1919]

[2 Portland Villas, East Heath Road, Hampstead]

Dearest Brett

After all Friday will not suit. For I quite forgot Virginia is coming to talk over the Centenary of George Eliot with me.¹ That puts the stopper on this week. I will try & come & see you: I should like to very much. I am afraid I was a dull dog yesterday – my back *hurt* me –

About what you said of – more or less – launching a second Ark.² It depends so awfully what effect tumpany has on your work. Perhaps it stimulates you; then I think you are ever so right to do it. It does the opposite to me. I have to keep solitary as I can – to have nobody *depending* and to *depend* as little as I can. Even if I had footballs for lungs I wouldn't go out often, for instance – couldn't. But then my particular Graces are very jealous & very shy & I have to humble myself and sit ready for their knock. Well, its no hardship – There could never be a choice between them and the present "world" – But I am no criterion, dearest girl – I want my "flings" today to be oh! such delicate flings & if a drunken Chili [Guevara] blundered in I could not bear it. I can't help it, I *do* feel so increasingly fastidious & frightened of rudeness and roughness – Life today is such an affair that I don't feel one can afford to rub shoulders with the world that goes to Parties. You will think me a sad old frump – but of course, like everybody else, I don't think I am – Gossip – tittletattle, Nina Hamnet³ & Gertler *spreading the news* – all that fills me with horror – Were I perfectly sincere I'd have to confess that I was always acting a part in my old palmy days & now Ive thrown the palm away –

Your devoted dull old inwalid

Tig.

MS Newberry. *LKM* I. 231–2.

¹ Virginia Woolf's essay 'George Eliot' appeared in *The Times Literary Supplement*, 20 November 1919.

² The name given 3 Gower Street during the months they shared the house in 1916–17.

³ Nina Hamnett (1890–1956), painter and writer, and one of Mark Gertler's circle of friends. Her reminiscences, *Laughing Torso*, were published in 1932.

To Ottoline Morrell [c. 12 June 1919]

2 Portland Villas | [East Heath Road, Hampstead]

Dearest

The flowers! I came in from posting your book and the whole house had a sweet scent. What peonies! And the roses. I am saving the petals to dry. Oh, they are all so wonderfully beautiful. When M. came home we made a solemn journey & reviewed all the gay bouquets. He has such a longing to grow flowers – and when they really *do* set him alight he glows almost enough to satisfy me . . . I *embrace* you for them. While I sit writing here I am conscious of them all the time – I wish I were a poet. I'd so much rather write about them than – the things these poets write about – pompes funèbres.

The sound of the wind is very loud in this house. The curtains fly – there are strange pointed shadows – full of meaning – and a glittering light upon the mirrors. Now it is dark – and one feels so pale – even ones hands feel pale – and now a wandering broken light is over everything. It is so exciting – so tiring, too – one is waiting for something to happen – One is not oneself at all in this weather – one is a being possessed – caught in the whirl of it – walking about very lightly – blowing about – and deeply, deeply excited . . . Do you feel that, too? I feel one might say anything – do anything – wreck one's own life – wreck anothers. What does it matter. Everything is flying fast. Everything is on the wing.

On Bank Holiday, mingling with the crowd I saw a magnificent sailor outside a public house. He was a cripple; his legs were crushed, but his head was beautiful – youthful and proud. On his bare chest two seagulls fighting were tattooed in red and blue. And he seemed to lift himself – above the crowd – above the tumbling wave of people and he sang:

"Heart of mine – summer is waning."

Oh! Heavens, I shall never forget how he looked and how he sang. I knew at the time this is one of the things one will always remember. It clutched my heart – It flies on the wind today – one of those voices, you know, crying above the talk and the laughter and the dust and the toys to sell.[1] Life is wonderful – wonderful – bitter–sweet, an anguish and a joy – and oh! I do not want to be resigned – I want to drink deeply – deeply. Shall I *ever* be able to express it. It is always ʿof *you* I think when I see & feel these things.

I have had such a tragic letter from Brett. Its made me feel a perfect wretch to have written as I did about her. I wrote to her, too, and said I really didn't like flings unless they were 'delicate' flings & drunken Chilis I could not bear. And poor little Brettie said she agreed – she didn't really enjoy her Bolshies and hated the tittletattle of Nina Hamnet. But what can one do for her? She sounded so helpless. *I do not know.*

Have seen 'Mary Olivier'? By May Sinclair. It is coming to me for review.[2] It sounds from what I have read – most extraordinary – And the new Quarterly 'The Owl' flew into the house the other day – What a forlorn old bird – what pickings for a nest![3]

My cat and kitten are fighting and loving on the couch. First the cat devours the kitten & then the kitten eats up the Mother. Lawrence would see an Unholy Meaning in them – –

Goodbye for now, dearest Ottoline

Ever your devoted
Katherine.

MS Texas. *LKM* I. 233.

[1] It may have been her recollections of this day that KM put into her sketch 'Bank Holiday', written the next year and published in the *Athenaeum* on 6 August 1920.

[2] 'The New Infancy', the *Athenaeum*, 20 June 1919.

[3] The first number of the *Owl*, a quarterly miscellany of literature and art edited by Robert Graves, included poetry by Thomas Hardy, W. H. Davies, Graves, John Masefield, Siegfried Sassoon, and J. C. Squire, as well as a story by Max Beerbohm, a play by John Galsworthy, and essays by Logan Pearsall Smith.

To Ottoline Morrell, [18 June 1919]

This is such a choppy letter, bumping over the waves. But *deep down* I am simply rejoicing & rejoicing because *we are friends* –

2 Portland Villas | [East Heath Road, Hampstead]
Wednesday.

Dearest dearest Ottoline

Your letter this morning was *Great Joy* – There is so much I want to answer. How cursed that you must go to a Nursing Home on Monday.[1] Why does one have these complicated internal arrangements when they can be disposed of. I do wish we were more lightly furnished. Its such a waste of energy keeping all these mysterious contrivances in repair – and oh! such an expense!! Murry is on the track of books for you – so am I. I shall get the Mountain to leave a parcel on Monday, dearest. Please don't *attempt* to come up here; it is so tiring. When you are well enough to see visitors – may I know. I shall hire a car and have a blessed half-hour with you – even if we don't talk.

Oh, Ottoline, surely it is possible that you may come abroad for a month or six weeks in the winter. At any rate, I shall *hug* the idea. I shall spend my play time seeing the little villa, the garden – the stone verandah, preparing your room, going to the station to meet you, waiting for years before the train is signalled – – – It MUST happen!

I cannot get five pence out of my sister. Somehow, at sight of me, her gold purse vanishes. She is far poorer than I am – I almost offer to pay her fares from Dover street to Hampstead.[2] She shows me her new shoes – 'seven guineas my dear!' and her new little frock – 'sixteen, and only foulard! Dont you know the address of some really cheap little woman who would press my tennis skirt for about one and sixpence!' She and the stockbroker aunt [Belle Trinder] come purring up to town in the new Rolls Royce – motoring through the New Forest – – – And last time, for a *great treat* "my dear, we have brought you some Harrods chocolates." Half a pound of Harrod's chocolates tasting of the Carpet Department!! I hope but don't believe I will get my own back in Heaven. But after all, one does get ones own back on earth. How dull they are – Their life is really based on food. I always see that easy, smiling approach to the fat table – the drawing in of chairs, the shaking out of napkins. They have the art of IT to their finger tips. It is their Ballet – their theatre – their book that they have a perfect right to criticise, dip into, taste and enjoy – – Did you realise, when you wrote it that *exquisite touch* about the White Peony – When I read that I saw the whole weekend, as it were. It was *perfect*. I believe dearest Ottoline, you *always* take away that ravishing white peony.

Every morning I think the rain must come – but it does not come. The adorable sun shines through the silver – I feel I should like it never to rain again.

Prewitt – we liked very much. He was extraordinarily nervous, poor boy, but his sincerity was so good. I hope Murry can help him. I felt he could. He told us in such a charming way what Garsington had 'meant' to him. That warmed my heart to him . . .

Brettie and Gertler came in on Monday. She wrung my heart again, especially as against Gertler's external competence. She had taken aspirin and was almost stone deaf. I must be more tolerant and try to help her and be 'neighbourly' – Have you seen 'Mary Olivier'. I reviewed it this week. Will you tell me if you think I am *wrong* about it? It took me hours to do.

I *love* this little picture of you . . . M. knows nothing of the new André Gide.[3] The other books he says are not up to much. Have you seen the New Decameron?[4] It is like a canvas suitcase full of travellers samples of canvas shoes – *awful*.

Dearest this letter is a scrapbook – but I had to write immediately – yours has made my day so happy.

Ever your devoted
Katherine.

MS Texas. Cited Alpers 1980, 296.

¹ Lady Ottoline's ill-health continued throughout 1919, until she entered a private hospital in Welbeck Street to have her tonsils removed on 24 June.
² KM's widowed sister Chaddie [Marie] frequently stayed at the Empress Club in Dover Street.
³ *La symphonie pastorale*, 1919.
⁴ *The New Decameron*, a collection of ten stories by ten different authors, whose setting is a group of travellers on a yacht, each telling a tale. Francis Carco's 'A Memory of Paris Days' was one of the stories.

To S. S. Koteliansky, 22 June 1919

2 Portland Villas | East Heath Road [Hampstead] N.W.3.
22.vi.1919.

Dear Koteliansky

I have received from you this morning a cheque for £2.3.0. being my share of the translation money. Thank you very much. The MS both used & unused I will forward you tomorrow evening so that you may expect to receive it on Wednesday morning.

K.M.

MS BL.

To Ottoline Morrell, [c. 25 June 1919]

[2 Portland Villas, East Heath Road, Hampstead]

My dearest Ottoline,

I am in the grip of an appalling chill, plastered with Baume Bengué,¹ safety-pinned into a wadding jacket with the Mountain over above under and around me. I have been too ill to write until this afternoon.

. . . . the cold wind caught me in the middle of a quarrel with the cook.² Their combined knives I suppose I swallowed.

[*Part of letter missing*]

Did you enjoy Virginia I wonder?³ She was coming to see me today, but I have not the puff or the brain. Roger [Fry] dined with us on Thursday; the knitting needles were *very* large. He seemed to have a kind of composite coiffure of knitting needles and cobwebs. There is something almost dreadful in a man of his age,⁴ still so naive (!!) still not at all certain what anything else means. He is like a lesser character in one of the hired carriages at a Tourgeniff⁵ pic-nic. Everything Murry says he appears to write down as a kind of prescription, in a little book – a dose or two of this – a dose or two of that *might* be helpful. Je crois que non.

A big bored blackbird is fluting away in the pear tree outside. I am sure he knows a great deal more about the secret of art than these baa-baas. He (Roger) thinks that Virginia is going to reap the world. That, I don't doubt, put on my impatience. After a very long time I nearly pinned a paper on my chest, '*I too, write a little*'. But refrained.

Oh, dearest, they don't matter. But 'artists' as Tchechov decides in this week's Athenaeum are dull dogs.[6]

At that moment I was interrupted by 'Elizabeth'[7] coming in out of the rain, hung with fringe, fur and feather. I have not seen her for ten years: it was so queer. We sat, talking across a hollow and saying very much the same things in very much the same way –

[*Incomplete*]
MSC Alpers.

[1] A French proprietary ointment.
[2] For KM's more extensive views on her cook, as well as what may be an account of this quarrel, see *Journal* 1954, 161 ff.
[3] Virginia Woolf stayed at Garsington on 21 June.
[4] Roger Fry was then fifty-three.
[5] Ivan Turgenev (1818–83), the Russian novelist whose work KM admired.
[6] Part VII of 'Letters of Anton Tchehov', the *Athenaeum*, 27 June 1919, included a letter to A. S. Souverin of November 1888, which pointed out 'If actors, artists and authors are indeed the best element in society, then we are in a bad way. Fine indeed must society be if its best element is so poor in colour, in desires, in intentions, so poor in taste, beauty, initiative.'
[7] 'Elizabeth', KM's second cousin Mary Annette Beauchamp (1866–1941), married Count Henning von Arnim in 1891, and became a celebrity on publishing *Elizabeth and Her German Garden* in 1898. She continued to write fiction under the name of Elizabeth von Arnim, and in 1916 married John Francis Stanley, 2nd Earl Russell.

To Ottoline Morrell, [27 June 1919]

[2 Portland Villas, East Heath Road, Hampstead]
Friday.

My dearest ever dearest Ottoline

I was so thankful to hear from you. Its dreadful that you should suffer. Operations are such a strange shock to one, too. They are, somehow, *mysteries* when all the surface activity of them is stripped away. It doesn't in the least matter if the operation is what they call slight or deadly serious; the effect is the same – I feel.

I understand *exactly* what you say about Virginia – beautiful brilliant creature that she is and suddenly at the last moment, turning into a bird & flying up to a topmost bough and continuing the conversation from there . . . She delights in beauty as I imagine a bird does; she has a *bird's eye* for "that angular high stepping green insect" that she writes about[1] and she is not *of* her subject – she hovers over, dips, skims, makes exquisite flights – sees the lovely reflections in water that a bird must see – but *not humanly*. She wrote to me the other day telling me that Roger was good enough to be pleased with me (!!) and also that she considered him a type of almost perfect middle age – what middle age ought to be, enfin. That *does* make me hold up my hands. I wish there was another 'Young Visiters' called 'Roger Fry's Surprise' – including a visit to Paris . . . I can imagine the fun.

This devilish cold persists. I am still in my life jacket, plastered underneath with unguents. Oh – these nights – sitting up in bed, waiting for the black trees to turn into green trees. And yet, when dawn does come, it is always so beautiful & terrible – the coming of the light such a miracle – that its almost worth waiting for. And then, as the hours strike through the night I wander through cities – in fancy – slip along unfamiliar streets, invisible – wonder who lives in these great houses with heavy doors, or, down on some quayside I watch the boats putting out in the dark & smell the night scent of the open sea – until lying awake becomes an ecstasy.

Ones own life – one's own secret private life – what a queer positive thing it is. Nobody knows where you are – nobody has the remotest idea *who* you are, even.

The Brontes – Last night in bed I was reading Emily's poems. There is one:

> I know not how it falls on me
> This summer evening, hushed and lone,
> Yet the faint wind comes soothingly
> With something of an olden tone.
>
> Forgive me if I've shunned so long
> Your gentle greeting, earth and air!
> Yet sorrow withers e'en the strong
> And who can fight against despair?[2]

The first line – why is it so moving? And then the exquisite simplicity of "Forgive me" . . . I think the Beauty of it is contained in one's certainty that it is not Emily disguised – who writes – it is Emily. Nowadays one of the chief reasons for ones dissatisfaction with modern poetry is one can't be sure that it really does belong to the man who writes it. It *is* so tiring – isnt it – never to leave the Masked Ball – never – never –

The house is full of women, today. The peevish old lying cook in the kitchen who says it is I who make all the work; L. M. bringing my lunch with a 'take, eat, this is my body' air; an old 'un sweeping the stairs away & down in the studio a little dwarf sewing buttons &

strings on to Murry's clothes and making immense pale darns in his Hebridean socks . . .

M. has moved into his new offices[3] and the burden is a trifle lighter. Tomlinson is in the same building & they occasionally have a little gaiety on the stairs – heat pennies, tie them on a string and slip them under Massingham's door[4] – or lean out of the window and angle for passing hats with a bent pin. This cheers M. greatly.

I keep thinking of Elizabeth's hands. Did you notice them. Tiny and white covered with large pointed rings. Little pale parasites, creeping towards the thin bread and butter as if it were their natural food –

Oh – how I LONG to talk with you – Dearest – are you comfortable in the Nursing Home? Do they give you a fire and enough hot water bottles. Is the pain less today? You will take very great care of yourself – won't you? It is a joy to think that you may be a great deal better now this is over –

I try and console myself with – half a lung is better than no head – but at present I don't feel Ive too much of the latter.

Ever your devoted
Katherine.

MS Texas. *LKM* I. 234–5.

[1] In *Kew Gardens*, which the Hogarth Press had published the month before and KM recently reviewed, Virginia Woolf used the phrase 'the singular high stepping angular green insect'.

[2] An untitled poem which KM would have read in *Brontë Poems, Selections from the Poetry of Charlotte, Emily, Anne and Branwell Brontë*, ed. Arthur C. Benson (1915), 65.

[3] At 10 Adelphi Terrace.

[4] Editorial staff of the *Nation* were in the same building. H.M. Tomlinson (1873–1958), a close friend of Murry's, was a novelist and journalist; H.W. Massingham, the paper's editor, was known for his political journalism.

To Ottoline Morrell, [1 July 1919]

[2 Portland Villas, East Heath Road, Hampstead]
Tuesday.

This is M. & me six? seven? years ago – when I had short hair.[1]
Dearest

You are at home again: I love to think it – I know the relief you will feel in leaving the *strange place* – It is so horrible to be uprooted, to be in nobody's bed – It makes me feel like a little child. When the tea comes I want to put the sheet over my head and wail for my *own* cup and saucer! I can feel, when the moments of arrival are over, how everything that belongs to you will unfold in the stillness and live again for you – come to life at your look and touch. Do not be angry with me if I just *flit* through . . . There is the delicious delicate perfume I remember – you have a fire; they will bring in the lamps & draw the curtains – heavy rain is falling – your gloves are put away – you are resting – you are bending over the flowers that tremble from the cold, rainy air.

Do not trouble to write to me. If I may just know – on a card – how you are. But do rest. It is a brutal day for travelling. Are they looking after you perfectly? . . . I wish I knew.

I, too, am sick and weary of the gossip-mongers. Why should one put up with them. And what have they done that they should dare puff themselves up so. Its ridiculous. I often feel you are far too tolerant of them. The absurdity – the utter absurdity. What in God's name have they ever given birth to. They are old midwives grouped round the Omega cradle,[2] Clive making the woolly bonnet & Roger the bootees and Mary [Hutchinson] all ready with the rattle – but where – tell me where is the Baby? –

I confess that at heart I hate them because I feel they are the enemies of Art – of real true Art. The snigger is a very awful thing when one is young and the sneer can nearly kill. They profess to live by feeling – but why then do they never give a sign of it – and why do they do their very best to ridicule feeling in others? It is all poisonous.

No, I have not seen the new James Joyce novel. Dearly I should like to – Is it to be had in book form? Lytton came yesterday and said that Mary H. had given a reading of a few chapters to a *picked* audience. But it might be very good.[3]

Such a strange day – a purplish sky – the rain falling – falling – as one imagines the rain falls in China – and through it the thrum thrum tinkle tinkle of a little string band. For Mrs De Maurier is giving a Garding Party. I have such a funny vision of the party – the vicar's straw hat, so wet and sticky – Mr G. de M. blowing his nose in the same charmingly intimate way *off* the stage as he does *on* – and Mrs flashing her teeth and her ten fingernails at Socierty.[4] I saw these remarkable hands (I seem to have a 'hands complex' at present) hovering over & positively shooting beams of light on to a box of plovers' eggs at the fishmongers, the other day, while she cried, for the pit, gallery, porter at the door and attendant in the Ladies toilet to hear: "Are they *ripe*, Fishmonger? Are you sure they are *raipe*." What a world – dearest – what a world!

The cook has given notice. How blessed! It is dreadful enough to be without servants but to be with them – is far more dreadful. I cannot forget the dishonest hateful old creature down in the kitchen. Now she will go & I shall throw her bits to the dustman & fumigate her room & start fair again – I feel so much *more* sensitive to everything than I used to be – to people good or bad, to ugliness or beautiful things.

Nowadays when I catch a glimpse of Beauty – I weep – yes, really weep. It is too much to be borne – and if I feel wickedness – it hurts so unbearably that I get really ill. It is dreadful to be so exposed – but what can one do?

Here is M. home from school –

Goodbye for now, dearest precious friend. My thoughts are with you.

Ever your most devoted
Katherine.

MS Texas. *LKM* I. 235–6.

[1] Probably one of the photographs taken when she and Murry lived at Baron's Court in 1913. One is reproduced in Alpers 1980.

[2] In 1913 Roger Fry had founded the Omega Workshops, 'Artist Decorators', at 33 Fitzroy Square, to encourage and employ young artists, to exhibit pictures, and to take commissioned work.

[3] *Ulysses* began to appear serially in the *Little Review*, Chicago, in March 1918, and by July 1919 ten episodes had been printed. During 1919 the *Egoist* in London published episodes II, III, VI, and X. The Woolfs had been offered *Ulysses* for the Hogarth Press in April 1918, but it must have been some time later that an event occurred which Virginia Woolf did not record until 15 January 1941: 'One day Katherine Mansfield came, & I had it out. She began to read, ridiculing: then suddenly said, But theres something in this: a scene that should figure I suppose in the history of literature.' (*DVW*, V, 353.)

[4] The actor Gerald Du Maurier, then at the height of his career, and his wife the actress Muriel Beaumont, were neighbours in Hampstead.

To Dorothy Brett, [9 July 1919]

[2 Portland Villas, East Heath Road, Hampstead]

Me running into the sun
followed by Athenaeum

Brett dear,

Can it be lunch instead, tomorrow? For this reason. You remember dear Earnest?[1] He can see me tomorrow afternoon, or rather my toes at 4.40. And his time is so precious & toes seem to be so plentiful that I don't dare miss the chance. I am going to take a car down there – get it to wait for me & spirit me home again. So, dearest Brett, come to dejeuner at 1 oclock instead if you can – will you? I so much want to see you before you go away for a long time – in fact I *must* see you for dear knows where I may be setting out for by the time you are back. I HOPE you will come; Ill expect you. No, thats bullying. Just come if you can & if you cant – it cant be helped.

Yours
Tig

Oh, this day! Summer again – and Life changed again – the other side of the sun – indeed – I can see both sides and all round it . . ————

MS Newberry.

———

[1] KM's chiropodist.

To Ottoline Morrell, [c. 13 July 1919]

[2 Portland Villas, East Heath Road, Hampstead]

My dearest Ottoline,

If I have not written before it is not my fault really not my fault – it is this confounded weather which puts me so out of tune. I hate to send such a Jangle – Here I sit, staring at the writing-table like some sea sick traveller who dares not lift his eyes to the waves outside but he will be quite undone – IF I do – there is the grey cloud chasing the black cloud and the trees in their dark ugly green tossing their branches like old crones at a weak-tea party telling how that Autumn has come back unexpected and has turned Summer into the Street and Summer has gone off dear knows where without even her flowery shawl poor lamb and Autumn has wired to winter to curtail his journey and start for home – *home* – This desperate news makes ones flesh creep again. I heard a coal man pass this morning and was half inclined to put a black cross on our door –

Do not think I am not grateful for the exquisite sweet scented basket, *dearest* of my friends – All my flowers this year have come from you – I never shall forget them – Its so strange. I feel that I have spent almost a whole summer at Garsington: each of these flowers is a remembrance. I love your garden: I often walk in it invisible. How long *is* it since we have really walked there together. Why does it seem so long? My heart aches at the thought.

I have seen nobody and have not been 'out'. Brett was my last guest. She is pitiful. I do not think she has any idea of what is to happen to her – she lifts with one wave and is thrown back upon another. I think her only salvation is the WILL to work. Do you thinks she has it? I have a horror of Nelson (whom Ive never seen.) I feel he is a type of the dog eternal – not *waiting* for the crumbs that fall from the table – but positively sitting up to them – and to those of the largest size. Does he intend to make a meal of Mrs Baker[1] who most certainly (if what Ive heard is true is no chicken among the chickens.) What upstarts these creatures are! How dare she sit on your lawn!!

These preparations for Festivity[2] are too odious. In addition to my money complex I have a food complex. When I read of the preparations that are being made in all the workhouses throughout the land – when I think of all these toothless old jaws guzzling for the day – and then of all that beautiful youth feeding the fields of France – Life is almost too ignoble to be borne. Truly one must hate humankind in the mass – hate them as passionately as one loves the few – the very few. Ticklers, squirts, portraits eight times as large as life of Lloyd George & Beatty[3] blazing against the sky – and drunkenness and brawling & destruction. I keep seeing all these horrors, bathing in them again & again (God knows I don't want to) and then my mind fills with the wretched little picture I have of my brother's grave[4] – What is the meaning of it all? One ought to harden one's heart until it is all over. But Oh – Life might be so wonderful – There's the unforgettable rub! And weve only one life and I cannot believe in immortality. I wish I could. To arrive at the gates of Heaven – to hear some grim old angel cry "Consumptives to the right – up the airy mountain, past the flower fields and the boronia trees – sufferers from gravel, stone & fatty degeneration to the left to the Eternal Restaurant smelling of Beef Eternal." How one would skip through! But I see nothing but black men, black boxes, black holes, and poor darling Murry splitting a very expensive black kid glove his Mama had made him buy . . . One must get out of this country.

Did you read about Mrs Atherton.[5] It was a strange peep through the windows. I wanted very much to write to the Earl of March & thank him for his evidence – How queer it all was. There were touches positively Shakespearean. When she said to her maid: "this is the last time you will brush my hair" and "please hold my hand a little" it was like Desdemona & Emilia[6] at 47 Curzon Street.

Oh God how Id love to talk to you now! Why cannot we just appear to each other without railway trains and hills & cold blasts –

Forgive my black mood. Don't forget me – And remember how *much* I love you – & am always your devoted

Katherine.

[1] An acquaintance of Brett's friend, the painter Geoffrey Nelson.

[2] The Peace Treaty, signed at Versailles on 28 June between the Allies and the German National Assembly, was officially celebrated throughout Britain on 19 July.

[3] The fireworks display in Hyde Park was to include portraits of Royalty, of the Prime Minister Lloyd George, and a group representation of Sir David Beatty, Admiral of the Fleet, with other military leaders.

[4] Her brother Leslie was buried at Ploegsteert Wood, near Armentières, close to where he died on 7 October 1915. See *CLKM* I, 197 ff.

[5] The forty-seven-year-old society figure Mrs Arthur Eliot, who continued to use the name of her first husband Colonel Thomas Atherton, shot herself at her home in Curzon Street on the night of 8 July. On 12 July the press reported evidence given at the inquest by her maid, as well as by the Earl of March, who had received a letter from her claiming that her husband was conducting an affair with his step-daughter. The Earl spoke warmly of Mrs Atherton's loyalty and friendship. However the charges against her husband were not sustained, and a verdict arrived at of 'Suicide while of unsound mind'.

[6] KM was reminded of *Othello*, IV..iii.

To Virginia Woolf, [c. 15 July 1919]

2 Portland Villas | East Heath Road | Hampstead

Dear Virginia

Please do. We shall be enchanted to see you both on Sunday.

How well one understands the Turkish point of view about Armenians:[1] there is something maddening about them which makes one finally want, as Kot says, 'to beat them simply to death.'

I have just had an invite from Mr. Keynes and Mr. Bell.[2] But if one hasn't a pumpkin and mice of one's own its impossible to go: I'd like a farewell glimpse, otherwise.

The roundabout is grinding out its one tune;[3] the dwarf[4] is sewing green buttons on the purple 'body' – Athenaeum is sitting on my lap purring like an aeroplane and I am trying to think about a novel called The Land they Loved[5] instead of Monks House in September.[6]

yours ever
K.M.

MS Sussex. *Adam* 370–375, 23.

[1] There were Turkish massacres in Armenia in 1915, and when Russia withdrew at the end of the War, these began again. Virginia Woolf must have written to KM of her dinner on 12 July with Ernest Altounyan, an English-speaking Armenian doctor with ambitions to be a poet, whom she found extremely trying.

[2] Maynard Keynes gave a party on 29 July.

[3] KM may be referring to the Albion press set up in the basement of Portland Villas, on which Murry's brother printed *Je ne parle pas français*.

[4] See letter to Lady Ottoline, 27 June 1919 above.

[5] 'Poser', KM's review of *The Land They Loved* by G. D. Cummins, the *Athenaeum*, 1 August 1919.

[6] The Woolfs shifted from Asheham to their newly acquired Monks House, Rodmell, Sussex, in early September.

To S. S. Koteliansky, [? July 1919]

[2 Portland Villas, East Heath Road, Hampstead]
The manuscript came today. In Heavens name why do we not prepare the book immediately & race Mrs G?[1] It is the only thing to do. If you are satisfied with my small labours I can devote some hours of EACH day to it. When you think that the english literary world is given up to sniggerers, dishonesty, sneering, DULL DULL giggling at Victorians inside whiskers and here is this treasure – at the wharf only not unloaded – – – – I feel that Art is like a sick person, left all alone in a house where they are having a jazz party downstairs and we have at least something of what that sick person needs to be well again. Cant we thieve up the back staircase & take it? If you have the time *only to do it roughly* I will *do my utmost*.

Yours K.M.

Here is the little pin on the letters, again.[2] Please let us not lose it. It is important. Perhaps it is the smallest pin in the world & will make our fortunes.

MS BL. Dickinson, 87–8.

[1] Constance Garnett's *Letters of Anton Tchehov to his Family and Friends* was published in 1920. KM's wish to anticipate her was not realized, although *The Life and Letters of Anton Tchekhov*, translated and edited by Koteliansky and Philip Tomlinson was published in 1925.

[2] A small pin which passed between them as a kind of lucky charm.

To Dorothy Brett, [18 July 1919]

[2 Portland Villas, East Heath Road, Hampstead]
Friday

My dearest Brett
I have just been doing the flowers. They look so lovely; pictures – especially these in my room which are small white roses with gay little leaves; fairy-tale roses. Downstairs the Dwarf is making me what she calls a "cotton body" – a very *useful* possession, I should think. I wonder if shed make me a fur body for the winter with a little hot piping round the waist. Further downstairs, in the tool box Charlie has just been delivered of 6 kittens. She is in a dark cupboard, among the rakes and hoes & old bulbs, twisted with yellow twine, and straw and red flower pots & bunches of twigs. I put in my head & feel I shall see a bright star in the crack above Charlie – & hear a chorus of angels – Athenaeum *hates* them. When M. went to him & told him that God had sent him six little brothers & sisters he fell off the studio window ledge right through the glass house, breaking two large panes of glass. I love his sense of the dramatic necessity – but all the same next time he must *not* be told. C'est trop cher.

I am very horrified by your account of Mrs. B.[1] Can't she be flung over the garden wall? *Must* she cling? Can't you harden your heart. And if she threatens to kill herself why should she be stopped? (Provided she didn't do it at Garsington.) I dont know a single enemy who wants to share a house & to whom I could fling a bramble. But be firm – don't have her in your room – that is the worst of brambles – there is never an end to them – They creep under the doors, they catch you whenever you want to fly & they can be more than a nuisance – they can hurt. I think she ought to join something and become a ——? or a ——? or a ——? Its no use her staying Mrs. B, evidently. I am awfully hard-hearted about *clinging* – one must just use a knife as quickly as possible. I hope you don't feel lonely at Conscience Castle & that you get a real painting mood. When the sun shines I feel that is enough to make one do anything.

This house seems to be an R34[2] today, rushing through the air. Everything is in flight. Its as much as one can do to catch anything. The windows all open – the curtains moving – a smell of cherry jam boiling from the kitchen – Gertie saying "If you please m'm the nasturtiums in the front are out" as if they were walking up to the door – advancing upon us.

Oh Life – mysterious Life – what art thou? Forster says: a game – I feel suddenly as though from all the books there came a clamour of voices – the books are speaking – especially the poets – How beautiful willows are – how beautiful – how the sun rains down upon them – the tiny leaves move like fishes. Oh sun – shine forever! I feel a little bit drunk – rather like an insect that has fallen into the cup of a magnolia.

Write again – | Love dear Brettie
from Tig.

MS Newberry. *LKM* I. 237–8.

[1] The 'Mrs Baker' of KM's letter to Lady Ottoline *c.* 13 July.
[2] The R34 was a British airship built to the pattern of the German L33. It crossed the Atlantic both ways in July 1919.

To Ottoline Morrell, [19 or 26 July 1919]

[2 Portland Villas, East Heath Road, Hampstead]
Saturday afternoon.

Dearest Ottoline

Murry is taking tea with his family – far away, remote, in Wandsworth. I am terrified by [the] thought that he may bring young Art back with him and I shall see him lounging on the sommier with his feet turned in. "Wont you come for your coffee, Arthur?" "Thanks. Parse it along" as though it were a penny ticket on a Wandsworth tram. The Mountain, twice the size, dropping myrrh, dropping honey, is attending a very difficult confinement – The cook who goes on Monday is I imagine filling a carpet bag with jam, sugar, and tea – and its raining and I feel lonely and cold and forsaken. Pray for me. How well I know that wraith-like disembodied feeling; it has been mine all last, this week. One lay in bed & felt like a shell and wept & weeping made one cough and summer was over. I asked my doctor the very question. "What would one do if one had to cope with life." & he replied "why, you'd be in an institution & paid for by the state." So there is one horror spared.

I am infinitely grateful to you for these chapters of Ulysses. Heaven send the drain that will soon receive them. I think they are loathsome & if that is Art – never shall I drink to it again. But it is not Art; it is not even a new thing. Why these young men should lean and lean over the decomposing vapours of poor Jules Laforgue[1] is inexplicable – but there they do. In Joyce there is a peculiar *male* arrogance that revolts me more than I can say – it sickens me. I dislike his method equally with his mind & *cannot* see his power of writing. Power? That beautiful quality that makes one feel a man is at ease among all these difficult and simple & intricate and moving words – and knows their perfect place and meaning – but Joyce gapes before an immensely great rubbish heap & digs in it for his swollen dogs & – – – No, I can't mention the stuff. Then I glanced at that unspeakable Ezra Pound[2] and the rest of em –

It only makes one feel how one adores English prose – how to be a writer – is *everything*. I *do* believe that the time has come for a "new word" but I imagine the new word will not be spoken easily. People have never explored the lovely medium of prose. It is a hidden country still – I feel that so profoundly.

Monday – The weather has 'got me' completely dearest; I am ill again. I have coughed so much that I feel like a living rattle – Theres nothing to be done. *Why* won't the summer come back? What has happened to it? One must drug oneself deeply deeply with work and try and forget.

You will take care of yourself this treacherous weather – Forgive me – I cant write – I feel *numb* with despair – and only want to creep away somewhere and weep and weep –

Your
Katherine.

MS Texas. *LKM* I. 236–7.

---

[1] Jules Laforgue (1860–87), was an inaugurator of *vers libre*, colloquial diction in poetry, and an ironic self-deflation.

² KM explained the origin of her strong dislike for Ezra Pound (1885–1972), when she wrote to Murry on 4 Nov 1919, 'I'll never forgive that creature a letter he wrote to Spender: it makes me utterly detest him.' (ATL.) Presumably this was J.A. Spender, the influential political journalist, friend of Murry's, and editor of the *Westminster Gazette* from 1896 to 1922.

To Dorothy Brett, 29 July 1919

[2 Portland Villas, East Heath Road, Hampstead]
July 29, 1919

Are you drawing? Have you made flower drawings? I wish you would do a whole Flower Book – Quarto size – with one page to each flower – its leaves, roots, buds, petals – all its little exquisite life in colour – very delicate with an insect or two creeping in or a blade of grass or a tiny snail. I see something wonderful. Did you ever see those books Karl Larsen made of his house and garden and children? They didn't need any words at all – They were *fascinating*¹ I wish you would make such a book; you have just the vision for it – delicate – and light, light as a flying feather. But I daresay you will rap me over the head for my imperence – But time is flying – soon or late it will be closing time – let us be divinely drunk while we may –

I wish you did not mind what they say – what anybody says. Why are you hurt by G[ertler]'s wooden airs? I think like the man in *Mr Polly*, he wants his head boiling – he wants the MIGHTY to say to him, "Oh, *boil* your head!"² Whenever I hear his absurd literary opinions I burn to make that my cry.

Now, what is the news. M.'s poems are out!³ and he is printing at lightning speed a long story of mine – We are both *slaves* to the Athene but when we do escape we are happy and talk and build sand castles. Will the treacherous tide have them – knock them flat? I don't know.

The wind set up such a song in my bones that my dear doctor is once more sticking longer, stronger needles into my behind. Although I walk like the only child of a crab and an Indian colonel I feel it is going to do the trick. Pray for me, Brett. Burn a candle for me if there is a Roman Catholic chapel in Oxford.

It is very quiet here, green and silver – the movement of the leaves is so secret, so silent, that I could watch them all day – I try to find words for how they lift and fall.

MS lacking. *LKM* I. 239.

¹ Carl Olaf Larsson (1853–1919), a Swedish artist whose book illustrations of country cottages and small children were extremely popular, especially the volume *Das Haus in der Sonne*, 1909.
² In Chapter Seven, Part 6, of H. G. Wells's *The History of Mr Polly* (1910) the title character

thinks of a neighbour 'that Rusper's head was the most egg-shaped head he had ever seen . . . when he found an argument growing warm with Rusper he would say "Boil it some more, Ol' man; boil it harder."

³ *Poems: 1917–18* was dated 1918, but a colophon read 'This book, the first of the Heron Press, was printed by Arthur Murry and John Murry, December 1918 to June 1919.'

To Lilian Trench,¹ [August 1919]

2 Portland Villas | East Heath Road | Hampstead NW3.
Dear Mrs Trench,

It is most kind of you and your husband to ask me to come & stay with you in October. I should love to: thank you most sincerely. I ought to tell you that Ive been ill for nearly three years & am only *getting better*. That means I cant walk very much or climb & have to go slow. It doesn't mean anything more – I promise you I never wear a little shawl, or whimper faintly or ask for a cup of Bengers . . .²

I am going over to France in September. Will you be in London before then? It would be very nice if we could meet.

Yours sincerely
Katherine Mansfield Murry

MS Onuma.

¹ Lilian Trench, the wife of Herbert Trench (1865–1923), minor poet and playwright. They were acquaintances of KM's since her association with *Rhythm*.
² Bengers Food, a malted mixture for invalids.

To S. S. Koteliansky, [early August 1919]

[2 Portland Villas, East Heath Road, Hampstead]
Dear Koteliansky,

Thank you for the cheque for £2.10.6. *I hate money*. Yes, thank you I did receive the Tchekhov & have already dealt with it. I hope there will be more letters published this month: it is a pity there cannot be.¹ I wonder if you have read Joyce and Eliot and these ultra-modern men? It is so strange that they should write as they do *after* Tchekhov. For Tchekhov has said the last word that has been said, so far, and more than that he has given us a sign of the way we should go. They not only ignore it: they think Tchekhov's stories are almost as good as the 'specimen cases' in Freud.

My God, if I am sitting on the back bench A.T. is *my* master!

K.M.

MS BL. Dickinson, 88.

¹ Between 4 April and 25 July there had been nine instalments of 'Letters of Anton Tchehov' in the *Athenaeum*. They were now discontinued until the beginning of September.

To Ottoline Morrell, [13 August 1919]

[2 Portland Villas, East Heath Road, Hampstead]
Wednesday.

Dearest Ottoline

Forgive me. I have been too ill to write until today. Today I am up & trying my legs again but I have had a bad time that I don't dare to look back upon Everything seemed to assail me at once and I could not beat them off.

It has determined me to go into a Sanatorium next month & to stay there until April. I am not 'up' to a villa or to anything. I cant go on 'like this' so I am waiting to hear of some more or less human institution where I can read & write & lead my private existence undisturbed. And as soon as I hear of one and am fit to travel – I shall go. There is nothing else to do. In April I hope to be fit to escape & take a small villa and enjoy another summer – But oh – this agony of ill health & worry is too much. Besides Life – darling Life is still here – waiting to be lived – not merely frowned at from a sofa. So I shall shut myself away – After all, six months hard should be an amazing opportunity for work.

I have thought of you continually. I keep *seeing* myself writing you letters – & waiting – waiting for the post to come with the unmistakeable envelope –

You have sent me flowers and Garsington lavender & Ive never said a word – for all that I have loved them. The lavender is in a big sachet. It breathes of that afternoon when we gathered it – of the cool darkened green room where the trays were spread – of the aeroplane high up, glittering above the trees – that looked so lovely – I feel that all waits to be written – its as though something magical drew a circle about that afternoon holding it for ever . . .

Has anything happened in the world while I have lain under my dark umbrella? Murry tells me nothing – except that he went to the exhibition of French pictures¹ and liked some very much – especially Derain² & L'hote.³ He (L'hote) is going to write for us in the Athenaeum on French Art. We have not yet told Clive and Roger – I hope they will look to their roses. I long to see these pictures: they *sound* so radiant. But there is always something fascinating, captivating, about the *names* of pictures: 'Woman Drying Herself; Woman in a Hammock; Lady on a Terrace.' One seems to dip into a luminous life – unlike this heavy old pudding of a London.

Now I understand your headaches – I never knew what a headache was until these last days – a real one – in which ones ears and jaws & eyes & neck & shoulders all ached together –

I must lie down again.

Ah, my dearest – I *do* think of you so often – When this curse is taken from me – we'll be happy together somewhere – for a little? My deepest tenderest love

Katherine.

MS Texas.

¹ An exhibition of contemporary French art at the Mansard Gallery, Heal and Son, Tottenham Court Road.

² André Derain (1880–1954), painter, illustrator, stage-designer, and sculptor.

³ André Lhote (1885–1962), first exhibited at the Salon des Indépendants in 1906, but became more important as a critic and champion of Cézanne. His 'Cubism and the Modern Artistic Sensibility' appeared in the *Athenaeum*, 19 September 1919. He then wrote frequently for the paper.

To Virginia Woolf, [13 August 1919]

2 Portland Villas [East Heath Road, Hampstead]
Wednesday.

Dear Virginia

This is the first day I am up again and able to write letters. I have been rather badly ill – and its left me for the moment without an idea . . . except that I must go abroad into a Sanatorium until next April. I can't take a villa or manage anything for the next six months. I must just lie in the air & try & turn into a decent creature. Do not think I am forgetful of you. You would not believe me if you knew how often you are in my *heart* & *mind*. I love thinking of you. I expect Asheham is a glory these days.

I will write again very soon. This is just really a wave –

I would I were a crocodile. According to your Sir Thomas Browne it is the only creature who does not *cough*: "Although we read much of their Tears we find nothing of that motion."¹ Thrice happy oviparous Quadruped!

Ever yours
Katherine.

Ms Berg. *LKM* 1. 240–1.

¹ From Sir Thomas Browne's *A Letter to a Friend*, published in 1690. It was addressed to a friend whose own 'intimate friend' died at the age of thirty-five from phthisis.

To Anne Estelle Drey [13 August 1919]

[2 Portland Villas, East Heath Road, Hampstead]

My darling Anne

Your letter has been waiting to be answered for nearly a week, but I have been rather badly ill and am only up for the first time today. It was a Thousand Joys to hear from me [i.e. you]. I *searched* the wee photograph for all there possibly was to see of you and David. Ah, que vous avez de la chance! He looks a perfect lamb – distinctly as though he were thinking about that blackbird, taking it seriously & making a thorough study of the bird – I hope I *shall* see him one day.

My Pa arrives tomorrow and my plans are still rather en l'air until I have seen him. Why, I don't know. But he seems to me a kind of vast symbolic chapeau out of which I shall draw the little piece of paper that will decide my Fate.[1] But that is absurd. For my plans are to go abroad in about three weeks time and there to remain. We are on the track of several different places – and not decided yet, but – c'est tout.

I shall be more thankful than I can say to be out of it all here – I hate the place and the people always more and more – and I am sure the whole of England is finie – finie. Perhaps it isn't if you have a baby to laugh things over with – but otherwise – and plus *Life on a Sofa* its just Hell. What wouldn't I give for one of our *laughs*, ma chère. As it is, things aren't funny any more. They only make me feel desperate. 'It's time for me to go' as the song says. The only thing I have got out of it all these months is pennies. I have earned quite a few. That gives one a good sense of freedom –

Forgive the dullest dog that ever lay beside a cottage door – I will write again darling woman when things is more lively. Kiss your angel for me – just behind his left ear. As I write I see you and love you so much so dearly – Id give a world to hear your Hil-*lo* –

Ever your devoted
Katherine.

MS ATL. *LKM* I. 240.

---

[1] Harold Beauchamp visited his daughter at Hampstead on 16 August, the first time they had seen each other since March 1912. Indecision in her plans seemed to depend on whether her father would assist her beyond her annual allowance, which at some stage during 1919 was raised from £208 to £300. After the unfortunate meeting with Murry described in her next letter to Ottoline on 17 August, Beauchamp clearly thought that Murry, on £800 a year, should be able to provide for his wife.

To S. S. Koteliansky, [mid-August 1919]

[2 Portland Villas, East Heath Road, Hampstead]

My dear Koteliansky

The letter arrived safely; I am copying it for this week's issue of the paper. It is an extraordinarily *illuminating* letter. But I feel that 'Ivanov' although he is a typical russian is also exactly true of many of *this* generation. The glimpse he gives of Sasha the female – how good that is.¹ And then, particularly I like the postscript. That is typical Tchekhov.²

Koteliansky. Would it not be possible to prepare a book for the American & say that you will give it to him for £50 down on delivery of manuscript? It is an unheard of bargain. If I help – I do not want to be paid. You have the £50 and let him have the book. It is quite simple. Can't you suggest this to him?

I am going away the third week in September, I think – to the Italian riviera. Then I shall have *unlimited time* to work. I do not want at present to start a new life in a new country, like Lawrence – But to be alone and to work – really that is preferable to going to Heaven.

I have just read Mrs G's last volume 'The Bishop' which includes the Steppe. She seems to take the nerve out of Tchekhov before she starts working on him, like the dentist takes the nerve from a tooth.³

My new kitten, 'Wing Lee' is lying on his back on the sofa waving his legs and arms. He runs like a rabbit. I am longing to write a story where a kitten shall play an important role.

Are you worried about money? Then do not send me my half of the translation money this month. My dear friend, simply keep it.

Katherine.

MS BL. *LKM* I. 238; Dickinson, 87.

¹ The long Chekhov letter KM refers to was not published for several months. It appeared serially in two issues of the *Athenaeum* on 24 and 30 October. In writing to A. S. Souverin, 30 December 1888, Chekhov said that the title character in his play *Ivanov* was 'a university man, with nothing remarkable about him; his is an easily excitable nature, fervent, very much disposed to infatuations . . . . Disillusionment, apathy, nervous exhaustion and lassitude are an inevitable result of excessive excitability, and such excitability is, in an extreme degree, peculiar to our younger generation.'

Chekhov also analyses his character Sasha as 'a girl of the latest "school." . . . . She is one of those females whom males conquer, not by bright plumage, or brilliance, or courage, but by their woes, lamentations, and failures. She is a woman who loves men at the hour of their downfall.'

² After a complex letter discussing his play, Chekhov concludes with three brief personal notes.

³ Constance Garnett's translation *The Bishop, and Other Stories*, 1919, which Murry reviewed in the *Athenaeum*, 22 August.

To Ottoline Morrell, [17 August 1919]

[2 Portland Villas, East Heath Road, Hampstead]

Dearest, wonderful Friend

Here's an absurd situation! My doctor strongly urges me *not* to put myself away – *not* to go into a sanatorium – he says I would be out of it in 24 hours and it would be a "highly dangerous experiment". "You see," he explained, "there is your work which I know is your Life. If they kept it from you you'd die – and they *would* keep it from you. This would sound absurd to a german specialist but I have attended you for a year and I know." After this, I with great difficulty restrained my impulse to tell the doctor what his words did for me. They were breath, life – healing, *everything*. So it is the Italian Riviera after all, a maid to travel with me and a little villa – Being ill, & bearing all the depression of those round me had I think almost made me insane. *I just gave up hope.* Now I am full of hope again – and I am 'off' the third week in September. M. is going across the first week in September to find me a villa and then I go. It is a blessed relief. And to think there will be the sun and another summer and unlimited time to write – It is next door to Heaven.

Your wonderful letter! I walked and talked with you & we were in the garden together and everything but the thrilling wonder of late summer was forgotten – Oh, how I cherish your friendship. It is there – for ever and I come to you so often – to talk – to know you understand just how *this* and *this* appears – Life is so strange – so full of extraordinary things . . . Today, this afternoon, waiting for my Father to come to tea – I felt I could have made – but only of that waiting – a whole book – I began thinking of all the time one has 'waited' for so many and strange people and things – the special quality it has – the *agony* of it and the strange sense that there is a second you who is outside yourself & does nothing – nothing but just listen – the other complicated you goes on – & then there is this keen – unsleeping creature – waiting to leap – It is like a dark beast – and he who comes is its prey – – –

Yes, my Father is here; he arrived yesterday – just as I had imagined, but even fuller of life, enthusiasm, with his power of making all he says vivid, alive, and full of humour. I find him adorable; I could listen to him for hours – But Alas! I had so longed for him and M. to meet & like each other – *longed* for it to happen and M. was in one of his moods when he laughed & looked away – never spoke *once* to him – paid him not a moments attention. It could not have been more fatal. Why wouldn't he, just for my sake, make the effort – (You know how one feels?) But no. Though he confessed afterwards how amazing he thought Father was – he treated him as if he was not here – This is dreadful mizery for me. Why *will* people behave like that? Its so unimaginative – so tactless – Oh, my efforts to get M. into the conversation – I look back on them with dismay – and M. like a fish would not be caught – swam the dark waters and refused – Good good! It was again the *spontaneity* of father which fascinated me – and it was just that which made M. go dead. How tragic this is. It really does seem to me tragic that M. is (except in his work) so covered with a dark wing. But he is – & will be. I really don't think he wants anything else; anything else feels false to him – Oh, I long, I long for merriment – joy, excitement – Even though we *do* work – because we take our work seriously we MUST <u>live</u>. Not in stupid pleasures, nor in Clives way nor in Chilis, but real warm thrilling life – with music – and light . . .

I do hope dearest I see you before you go to Ireland. I want to so tremendously. If you have sold Bedford Square does that mean you will spend the winter in the country?[1] Or does it mean you might, perhaps, *after all* – come out to me for as long as you wished?

I want to see the French pictures – M. liked some – I cant bear Roger's art criticism: this patting on the head & chucking under the chin is so tiresome.[2]

Everybody has deserted me – I don't hear from a soul –

But oh – I am tired of sorrow – The beautiful earth – your tobacco plants – the scent – dearest dearest Friend. I LOVE you

Katherine.

MS Texas. *LKM* I. 241–2; cited Alpers 1980, 296.

[1] The Morrells had owned 44 Bedford Square, Bloomsbury, since 1906, when Philip was elected Liberal MP for South Oxfordshire.
[2] Roger Fry discussed the French exhibition in a two-part article, 'Modern French Art at the Mansard Gallery', in the *Athenaeum*, 8 and 15 August.

To Ottoline Morrell, [21 August 1919]

[2 Portland Villas, East Heath Road, Hampstead]
My dearest beloved Friend

I am going to indulge myself in a letter: I have been thinking about writing it all the while I dressed – and thinking how impossible it *is* to write one thousandth part of all I want to say. Please forgive the funny writing; my eyes have now turned traitor with the rest of my belongings & until I am equipped with a pair of horn spectacles for reading and writing I dare not strain them at all & have to sit far back – I feel rather as tho' I were in a valley writing my letter on the side of a hill . . . I can just read enough to keep up my work for the

A[thenaeum]. They will get alright but I *have* given them an unmerciful dose of about 10 hours a day & so for the last few days I have been lying on my back – such a queer time. You know my insomnia trips into unknown cities – well – they assailed me whenever I lay low – cities and trees & thousands of horses at full gallop & forests – with a violent headache – Brain-fag the doctor says – and advises me when I get to Italy to paint landscape especially tender skies!! Picture me dearest darling Ottoline in the next Allied Show[1] "Now Fades the Glimmering Landscape on the Sight" by K.M. – *or* "Just a Song at Twilight" –

My beautiful velvet flowers are still full of life & the carnations and the bell-like very mysterious fäery flowers that I dont know – Thinking over it – you have sent me all the year from earliest spring – Who else living would have done such a perfect thing for a friend. I think & think over the gift I want to bring you – the best that I ever write must be yours. But oh! that won't compare with the flowers you have given me while I have not been able to see them – I nearly should have forgotten them – Id have despaired of them often – but always at the perfect moment you have said "Look, Katherine" and the Beauty of the world – the undying *splendour* of the world has been revealed again.

M. is seeing about his passport today; that seems to bring the journey nearer. I intend to stay away indefinitely; but one always does –

It is divine here today – a brilliant sky and high, brilliant shapes of clouds. M. is lunching with Father; he will *have* to talk to him then & perhaps all will go well. And Id love you to meet him one day – just for the *fun* of it.[2] He is not tall – very healthy looking – with white hair and a small clipped beard – large blue eyes – an expansive voice. In fact he looks a typical Colonial banker!! And simply *full* of Life.

I see Virginia's book is announced in todays Literary Supplement.[3] I expect it will be acclaimed a masterpiece & she will be drawn round Gordon Square in a chariot designed by Roger after a supper given by Clive.[4] Did you like Lyttons article on Voltaire? And on the Walpole Letters.[5] I thought the latter was really a tour de force – & put his imitators in the deepest shade – But this is not [at] *all* what I meant at all – – – Would I were sharing this shining day with you – Shall we meet soon again, I wonder? Will you be in town before the third week in September?

Have you been reading 'something good?' How nice a *new book* would be – Dearest – you have all my love – my friendship. It is a joy to know you are in the Same World with me.

Yours
Katherine.

MS Texas.

¹ The Allied Artists' Association was founded in 1908 to enable painters to exhibit without the intervention of judges or dealers. Its large annual exhibition was open to any artist who paid the subscription.

² Lady Ottoline did meet KM's father, but not until several years after her friend's death. Soon after he visited her in the summer of 1932, she wrote 'Sir Harold Beauchamp seemed so unimportant that I have half forgotten him – just rather a cunning old Boy, a Banker, & anxious to tell me that he really allowed KM sufficient money. "She had only to ask for more etc." ' (*Dear Lady Ginger, an exchange of letters between Lady Ottoline Morrell and D'Arcy Cresswell*, ed. Helen Shaw (1983), 50–1.)

³ *Night and Day*, published in October 1919.

⁴ After the death of their father, the Stephen children established a household at 46 Gordon Square, where Vanessa Stephen continued to live after her marriage to Clive Bell in 1907. It became both a family and intellectual home for their Cambridge friends. When Maynard Keynes took over the house in 1916, he made it the centre of what Quentin Bell, *Virginia Woolf* (1972), II, 90, called 'an enlarged and altogether more amorphous "Bloomsbury" '.

⁵ Strachey wrote a leading article, 'Voltaire', in the *Athenaeum* on 1 August, and on 15 August reviewed the two-volume *Supplement to the Letters of the Fourth Earl of Orford*, ed. Paget Toynbee.

To S. S. Koteliansky, [21 August 1919]

[2 Portland Villas, East Heath Road, Hampstead]

Dear Koteliansky,

I *hate* to think that you must give up your serene existence. If I were a wealthy woman you should not. I should find a perfectly secure way so that the money you wanted was there – and that was the end of it . . .

Will you send me the biographical notes? What shall I do with them? Tell Fox¹ to come & explain to me. Murry gave me the Five Pages yesterday. Yes, I am sure your explanation of Ivanov is right. It is like Tchekov to have done this.

I have re-read 'The Steppe'.² What can one say? It is simply one of *the* great stories of the world – a kind of Iliad or Odyssey – I think I will learn this journey by heart. One says of things: they are immortal. One feels about this story not that it *becomes* immortal – it always was. It has no beginning or end. T. just touched one point with his pen – and then another point – *enclosed* something which had, as it were, been there for ever.

I always miss you when I am away, and often there comes the illogical nonsensical certainty you will be at a station. Nevertheless I go gladly with all my heart.

Katherine.

MS BL. *LKM* I. 242; Dickinson, 88.

¹ Koteliansky's dog.
² The long story which Chekhov wrote in 1888.

To S. S. Koteliansky, [5 September 1919]

→ Disappeared on September 11th 1919.
                    2 Portland Villas | East Heath Road [Hampstead] | N.W.3.
My dear Koteliansky

I leave here for Italy next week – on Thursday morning – under a sworn promise to my doctor not to remain there a shorter time than 2 years. As soon as I am there I shall send you my address and any work you forward me will be done immediately. Do you think it will be possible in 2 years time to go to Yalta?[1]

These last days are hideous. It is not being ill that matters; it is the abuse of one's privacy – one's independence – it is having to let people serve you and fighting *every moment* against their desire to 'share'. Why are human beings so indecent? But soon it will be over, and I shall be at work.

Forgive my complaining. I love the sea. But not now. It is too cold and I cannot bear it should look angry.

Goodbye.

[*no signature*]

MS BL. Dickinson, 88–9.

----

[1] Chekhov settled in a villa of his own in Yalta in September 1898, and returned there frequently until his death in 1904.

To Frank Swinnerton,[1] [8 September 1919]

                    2 Portland Villas | East Heath Road | Hampstead N.W.3.
Dear Swinnerton

I cannot refrain from thanking you for your Jane Austen – It was extraordinary pleasure to find it in this weeks Athenaeum.[2] What an admirable, beautiful little article it is – Are you going to write more often for the paper? Will Murry persuade you? One of the great joys of being a writer (even though, God knows, I am only a beginner) is enjoying another man's work – That's what I have been feeling all this morning. I am leaving England on Wednesday for – more or less – ever more. It would be nice to think that you and Murry were seeing something of each other –

                                                        Goodbye
                                                        K.M.

MS Alpers.

¹ Frank Swinnerton (1884–1982), a prolific novelist and critic, and currently a freelance journalist and publishers' reader, had been a friend of KM's since his contributing to *Rhythm*. He records his memories of her in *The Georgian Literary Scene*, 1938.
³ Part I of 'Jane Austen', the *Athenaeum*, 5 September; Part II, 19 September.

To Ottoline Morrell, [9 September 1919]

[2 Portland Villas, East Heath Road, Hampstead]

Dearest Ottoline,

Its too horrid. Lunch is impossible for me tomorrow. I have a farewell engagement with my Papa that I cant escape, or be free from in the early afternoon. If only Belsize Park¹ were nearer Oxford Square I'd love to ask if I might see you here tomorrow morning for morning 11 o'clock tea. But these distances are so great! I am so very sorry to miss you.

> More than I can say.
> Ever
> Katherine

MS Texas.

¹ Belsize Park was the nearest Tube station to Portland Villas.

To J. M. Murry, 9 September 1919¹

[2 Portland Villas, East Heath Road, Hampstead]
September 9th 1919.

My darling Boy

I am leaving this letter with Mr Kay just in case I should pop off suddenly and not have the opportunity or the chance of talking over these things.

If I were you I'd sell off all the furniture and go off on a long sea voyage on a cargo boat, say. Don't stay in London. Cut right away to some lovely place.

Any money I have is yours, of course. I expect there will be enough to bury me. I don't want to be cremated and I dont want a tombstone or anything like that. If its possible to choose a quiet place – please do. You know how I hate noise.

Should any of my friends care for one of my books to remember me by – use your discretion.

All my MSS I simply leave to you.

I think you had better leave the disposal of all my clothes to L. M.

Give the woolly lamb to Brett, please, and also my black fox fur.

I should like Anne to have my flowery shawl; she loved it so. But that is as you think.

Jeanne must have the greenstone.

Lawrence the little golden bowl back again.

Give Pa all that remains of Chummie.

Perhaps I shall have something Chaddie would like by then; I have nothing now – except perhaps my Chinese skirt.

See that Rib has an honourable old age and don't let my brass pig[2] be lost. I should like Vera to have it.

Thats all. But don't let anybody *mourn* me. It can't be helped. I think you ought to marry again and have children. If you do give your little girl the pearl ring.

Yours for ever

Wig.

K. Mansfield Murry (for safety's sake).

MS ATL. Alpers 1980, 297–8.

[1] This letter was left with the manager of the Bank of New Zealand, Queen Victoria Street. Murry did not receive it until after KM's death.

[2] The pen-wiper her father had given her as a present before she left Wellington in 1908.

INDEX OF RECIPIENTS

GENERAL INDEX

Reference to the page and the footnote giving biographical details about individuals immediately follows their names and is printed in italics prefixed by *B*. *B*I directs the reader to fuller biography in *CLKM* vol. I.